THE DIARIES OF DAWN POWELL 1931–1965

THE DIARIES OF
DAWN POWELL
1931 – 1965

EDITED WITH AN INTRODUCTION
BY TIM PAGE

STEERFORTH PRESS
SOUTH ROYALTON, VERMONT

Library of Congress Cataloging-in-Publication Data
Powell, Dawn.
The diaries of Dawn Powell, 1931–1965 / edited
with an introduction by Tim Page.—1st ed.
p.   cm.
Includes index.
ISBN 1–883642–08–6
1. Powell, Dawn—Diaries. 2. Women authors, American—20th century—
Diaries. I. Page, Tim, 1954–   . II. Title.
PS351.O936Z47   1995
818'.5203—dc20   95–40271
Manufactured in the United States of America

Second Printing

CONTENTS

DAWN POWELL

Dawn Powell was born in Mount Gilead, Ohio, the second daughter of Roy King Powell and Hattie Sherman Powell. Although Powell usually gave her birthdate as November 28, 1897, there is some evidence that she may have been born on November 28, 1896. She ran away from home at the age of twelve and was raised by her aunt, Orpha May Sherman Steinbrueck, in Shelby, Ohio. She graduated from Lake Erie College with the class of 1918 and moved immediately to New York, where she lived and worked for the rest of her life. She was married to the advertising executive, Joseph R. Gousha, and they had one son, Joseph R. Gousha, Jr.

Powell published fifteen novels—*Whither* (1925), *She Walks In Beauty* (1928), *The Bride's House* (1929), *Dance Night* (1930), *The Tenth Moon* (1932), *The Story Of A Country Boy* (1934), *Turn, Magic Wheel* (1936), *The Happy Island* (1938), *Angels On Toast* (1940), *A Time To Be Born* (1942), *My Home Is Far Away* (1944), *The Locusts Have No King* (1948), *The Wicked Pavilion* (1954), *A Cage For Lovers* (1957), and *The Golden Spur* (1962). Her play "Jig-Saw" was published in 1936 and some of her numerous short stories were collected in *Sunday, Monday and Always* (1952).

At the time of Powell's death in 1965, virtually all of her books were out of print. An article on Powell by Gore Vidal in *The New York Review of Books* helped spark a revival of interest in her work and, since 1989, eight of her novels have been reprinted.

INTRODUCTION

What right does anyone have to publish another person's diary? And then, once the decision has been made to proceed, how does one prepare a manuscript? I do not claim to have found any definitive answers to these general questions; still, an explanation of the procedures I followed during the assembly of this book may be in order.

Four considerations led me to seek a publisher for Dawn Powell's diaries: their extraordinary value as autobiography, literature, social history, and psychological case study; the hope that their publication may spark greater interest in a neglected and misunderstood figure in American letters; the immediate and enthusiastic support of Powell's surviving friends, family, and estate; and the fact that, in her will, Powell specifically named her diaries among the "unpublished documents . . . manuscripts, papers, notations, letters, sketches and memoirs" that might be sold or printed after her death.

Indeed, I believe that Powell had one eye on posterity much of the time when she was writing in the supposedly "private" medium of the diary. To begin with, many of the entries are decidedly impersonal—playful, fascinated reporting rather than soul-searching. No clandestine love affairs are recounted (anybody looking for details of Powell's supposed *ménage à trois* with her husband and Coburn Gilman will be disappointed, although both men figure prominently in the book). The deaths of her father, her sister, and her favorite aunt are summed up in single sentences while Powell spends close to 700 words describing the sudden collapse of a stranger at a cocktail party. Nor was Powell especially interested in recording her own reactions to the major events of her time:

Pearl Harbor, Hiroshima, and the assassination of President Kennedy all go unremarked.

Powell valued the opportunity to observe human behavior (her own and that of others), then put it down on paper while it was fresh. Some of these scenes—a nighttime visit to the top of the then new Empire State Building, her husband's encounter with a drunken lawyer in a restaurant bathroom—ended up incorporated into her novels. Others are perfect vignettes on their own—flashes of long-ago reality, vivid and vital as the best photographs by Weegee. Some entries are frankly trivial; still, because yesterday's trivialities are so quickly forgotten, it is an eerie experience to eavesdrop on an ordinary conversation in a Long Island bar half-a-century ago. We tend to remember the climaxes and crises in our lives but the day-to-day flow is easily lost—and Powell wanted that flow.

It was originally my intention to provide brief chronological summaries for every year that Powell kept a detailed diary (that is, from 1931, when the substance of this book truly begins). Ultimately, it seemed the better idea to let Powell tell her story without impediment and so I have limited my commentary to footnotes and occasional connective passages. A succinct (and necessarily incomplete) biographical listing is found at the end of the book.

The diaries, currently housed at the Columbia University Rare Book and Manuscript Library, are contained in thirty-four prefabricated volumes with years and dates already stamped on their cover pages.* Powell was careless about such strictures: for example, her entry on the murder of Maxwell Bodenheim was written on the page allocated to February 3, 1954, although Bodenheim was killed on February 7. It is likely there are many more such misdatings throughout the diaries—Powell wrote when and where she felt like it.

I would estimate that three-quarters of Powell's diaries are here preserved. She wrote in many different moods and (it must be admitted) sometimes in what was clearly a state of intoxication. And so some entries are perfectly crafted, with whole phrases reworked again and again, while others are little more than quasi-legible scrawls—foggy, redundant, and broken off in mid-sentence.

Therefore, I decided editing was both prudent and necessary; I do not believe that any professional writer, particularly one who worked so hard

---

*The 1931 diary apparently no longer exists but has been reconstructed from a photocopy provided by Jacqueline Miller Rice, Powell's original literary executor.

at the craft as Powell did, would want incoherent first drafts published to the world. And so, without adding my own words to the text or changing any of Powell's meanings, I have gently—algebraically—tightened many of the entries. I say this with neither pride nor apology but as a simple statement of fact: had somebody else edited these diaries, for better or for worse, it would have been a different book.

My criterion for inclusion was simple: an entry needed some kind of lasting interest—as autobiography, as literature, as secrets of the writing trade, or simply good gossip. Some legendary people make cameo appearances in these pages—Theodore Dreiser, Franz Kline, Djuna Barnes— and we may regret that Powell tells us so little about them. On the other hand, Coburn Gilman is now likely forgotten by all except his friends and family, yet he is clearly one of the book's central attractions, enormously funny and likable throughout his travails. "I sometimes think a writer could become immortal merely as a chronicler of Gilman," Powell wrote in 1940 and, in these diaries, the pleasant, hapless Gilman does attain a kind of immortality.

In a few—*very* few—cases, I have obscured names or circumstances as a courtesy to persons still living. But it is a safe guess that readers who were close to the late Esther Andrews, Peggy Bacon, Virginia Pfeiffer, Margaret De Silver, Edmund Wilson, or Gerald and Sara Murphy will be less than thrilled by some pages in this book. Powell was very fond of these people—her letters, her devotion over the span of many years, and, in some cases, other entries in the diaries prove this conclusively—but she could be terribly caustic about her closest friends when the mood was upon her. So why preserve a passing, private irritation? My answer must be subjective: I didn't feel I had the right to cut this self-portrait of an artist and her era any more than seemed absolutely necessary. If Powell here stands revealed with all of her complications, I believe she will impress the sympathetic reader as a funny, courageous, deeply understanding, and essentially compassionate human being and—the distinction that might have meant the most to her—one hell of a writer.

Tim Page
July 15, 1995
New York City

THE EARLY DIARIES

Dawn Powell lived to write. In her case, this statement is not an empty phrase, nor is it an exaggeration. Powell was writing steadily by the time she was twelve; in the last year of her life, when she was mortally ill, her concerns were not so much with her failing health and ever-dwindling weight as with her inability to make headway on any of her writing projects.

Considering the difficulties Powell faced throughout most of her sixty-eight years—an unconventional and sometimes deeply unhappy marital life, near-constant money troubles, the demands of a mentally and emotionally impaired son, heavy drinking that was debilitating at times, recurrent (and often mysterious) health problems, and what might now be described as a "bipolar" personality—it is astonishing that she wrote so prolifically and wrote so well. Besides her fifteen published novels, Powell left at least 100 short stories, half-a-dozen plays, an enormous quantity of book reviews and occasional pieces, thousands of personal letters, and her magnificent diaries.

Exactly when Powell began keeping a diary is unknown. She ran away from home around the age of twelve, because her stepmother had burned her notebooks and stories; that notorious bonfire may well have included some early diaries. A volume filled with observations, drawings, and poems, dating from after her runaway (circa 1910) survived into the late 1960s but has now apparently disappeared. During the summer of 1915, while working as a maid and waitress at a summer resort called the Shore Club on Lake Erie, Powell kept an occasional journal in a school notebook, addressed to an imaginary friend named "Woggs":

1

Dear Woggsie, I'm melancholy again. It's too bad that I'm always confiding in you on those days I feel the bluest. This book is enough to make a stone weep and if anyone should read it they would think the writer was indeed in pathetic straits. But no one will ever read it so I think I'm really wiser to do it this way—tell my blue, weepy thoughts to you, who will never reveal them to another soul, instead of inflicting them on the people around me—and when I'm in a flip, gay mood, I take it off on other people.

This would set the pattern for Powell's diaries in general. Her abundant jollity was expressed in her novels, plays, letters, and social life; fear, pain, and despair were largely confined to her diaries.

Even as a teenager, Powell was extraordinarily self-aware, prescient, with "intimations of immortality":

I was dreamily prophesying my future the other day for the girls. "In ten years from now," Katherine said, "you'll be left. You get all the men you can on the string and make them unhappy and pretty soon when you want a man you'll be left. You are too flip altogether." "Yes, I'll be left," I said slowly and with overwhelming conviction. "Ten years from now I will still be Dawn Sherman Powell—but girls, that name will be famous then. Ten years from now, I will have arrived." And Woggs, I know it will be true. I never entertain the slightest fear of an obscure future. I'll be before the public eye in some way—and you know it, too.

I must make myself strong for the knocks that are to come, for no matter what you tell me—"You've had enough knocks, you'll have happiness the rest of your life"—something in me says that life for me holds more knocks than joys, and the blows will leave me crushed, stunned, wild-eyed and ready to die, while the joys will make me deliriously, wildly, gloriously happy. It's the way I'm made, Woggs—that Irish strain in me, perhaps. Yet better for one of my nature to have it that way than to have life a peaceful, placid flow of quiet contentment. I must have days of rushing excitement.

Much of the notebook is taken up with long, charming but fairly conventional teenage apostrophes to "Woggs"—this boy, that embarrassment, understandable irritation with her menial job—but here and there we find flashes of the mature Powell:

Well, Woggs, we are destined for a hard ride in life, with many bumps and jumps, but it will be a swift, breathless ride and we will arrive all the sooner. So we may as well pull down our hats, button up our coats, and hang on to our seats, instead of pausing to speculate.

All of which sounds suspiciously like the motto Powell adopted for herself in later life—"Allez oop!"

Powell graduated from Lake Erie College in 1918 and moved immediately to New York. By 1920, she was living in Manhattan (at 569 West End Avenue, now demolished) and deeply in love with Joseph Gousha, a poet and music critic from Pittsburgh who became a successful advertising executive. A tiny little black booklet entitled—appropriately—"The Book of Joe" has survived; one suspects that most of the entries were shared with (and possibly written for) its principal subject. The dating is inexact and most of the entries are only a sentence or two long:

> My Adorable came tonight. Our last Sunday alone . . . Joe was so adorable today. We decided tomorrow is to be his lucky day . . . I went to Joe's house for dinner and we walked to the Bay. My Adorable is so lovely . . . My Adorable. I wonder what he truly wants. I wish it was the same thing I want . . . I made a peach pie— the very first and my Adorable said it was good. I love him so much and I will be so happy when we are together for always . . . My Dearest took me to the Bretton Hall* for lunch and then we rode in a hansom lined with plum color through the park . . .

And so on. One reads through this small volume with a wistful sadness. Judged purely as writing, this is the sort of banality that Powell would later send up with acerbic brilliance. Certainly, there are no signs that the author of these lines would ever make a satirist; everything in this diary is deadly earnest, the proverbial "hearts and flowers." But if Powell was ever again so happy and contented for such an extended period of time, her diaries do not reflect it.

Powell and Gousha were married on November 20, 1920 at Manhattan's Little Church Around The Corner and they spent their honeymoon

---

*The Bretton Hall, now a residence hotel, still stands on the corner of Broadway and West 86th Street in Manhattan.

at the Pennsylvania Hotel on Seventh Avenue and 32nd Street. Powell described their first apartment together at 31 Riverside Drive as an "attic, but so lovely"; this building, too, was long ago razed.

An entry marked June 23, 1921 reads:

> I want so much for my lover. At night when our beds are drawn close together I waken and see his dear yellow head on the pillow— sometimes his arm thrown over on my bed—and I kiss his hand, very softly so that it will not waken him. He is happier now that he is writing a play. I know he will succeed with it. I think we will have a boy baby and he will be born on the 20th of August. Everyone else has a girl baby and at times I don't believe I should mind having a little Phyllis Dawn but Dearest wants a boy and I do. Besides, it must be a boy—the little golden-haired boy in the blue rompers . . .

The "Book of Joe" breaks off here. On August 22, 1921, Joseph Gousha, Jr. was born at St. Luke's Hospital and it was immediately obvious that something was seriously wrong with this much cherished "little golden-haired boy." Often labeled "retarded," Jojo—as Powell's son was known throughout his life—probably suffered from a combination of cerebral palsy and schizophrenia. He needed close medical supervision from the beginning and was confined more-or-less permanently—a ward of New York State—long before Powell's death. Powell loved her son dearly, and her joys in his small successes, anguish over setbacks, and elaborate plans for improving his condition run through all of her diaries.

In 1922, Powell began her first full novel, an autobiographical story of a young girl fresh from the country come to conquer the big city. *Whither* was published in 1925 by the Boston firm of Small, Maynard and was almost immediately disavowed by its author. She never mentioned it in lists of her works and her friend Hannah Green recalls that, some 35 years after the book's publication, Powell was less than pleased when Green found a copy in a secondhand store.

Diaries of sorts survive from 1925, 1926, 1927, and 1930 but these are little more than appointment books, with terse commentary thrown in here and there; I have retained only a few representative passages.

1925

In 1925, Powell had just moved to Greenwich Village, where she would live for the rest of her life (some early addresses were 46 West Ninth Street, 72 Perry Street, and 106 Perry Street). Her social circle included the editor Esther Andrews and Andrews' lover Canby Chambers, the poet Charles Norman, the nightclub entertainer Dwight Fiske, the poet and editor Eugene Jolas, and the writer and translator Jacques LeClercq, all of whom would become lifelong friends. She grew very close to the radical playwright John Howard Lawson and there are numerous, seemingly coded, references to him in her diaries through 1934 that suggest there may have been a love affair, after which he practically vanishes.

She spent a good amount of time in the speakeasies—"very drunk" is a recurring comment—and worked on articles for the magazine *Snappy Stories,* while finishing a novel with the title "The Dark Pool," published in 1928 (after more than two dozen rejections) as *She Walks In Beauty.* She began her association with the New York *Post,* for which she would review books (on and off, mainly in periods of financial hardship) much of her life.

February 21: Debut of *Whither.*

March 15: First reviews—Boston *Transcript, New York Times.*

April 3: Dinner at Algonquin and the Follies.

April 6: Letter about "The Marrying Kind," saying "This Dawn Powell writes so attractively I hate to return her story. But——" he did.

April 11: Joe worked on novel at office, copying it, and I worked on editing at home. Mentioned four times, including Charles Norman's review, in N.Y. *Evening Post.*

April 12: Finished "The Dark Pool" at 12:50 midnight. It's good.

April 13: Macy's, Brentano's and Womrath begin to move *Whither* as result of Charles' review. Things look brighter.

May 17: Riverside Drive Park with Jojo who rolled in grass.

August 14: Papa* comes. Went to Bernaise and then to "The Poor Nut."

August 15: Drunken party. Papa gave me $10.

August 17: Wrote "Lady of the House" at Central Park this morning.

September 22: Successful party. Check for $35 from *Snappy.*

September 28: Putnam's rejected "The Dark Pool." Started story in office, "The Good Little Egg."

October 13: Tea with Jack Lawson. New things to think about. New blue dress.

October 18: Joe and I decide to readjust our lives.

October 19: Jack L. called up. I was flip. Lunch on Thursday. Lunch at Pen and Brush Club. Jack L. called in evening and I told him about my novel.

October 21: All day with my child . . .

October 26: Jack called up for Thursday luncheon date. Louise sick.† Dinner with Cornelia [Wolfe] at Moscovitz.

October 27: Saw *Snappy.* Also Curtis Brown and saw Harper letter praising "The Dark Pool." Wrote note to Jack calling off all Thursday dates.

December 12: Working on novel. Dinner at Moscovitz with Joe and Jacques. Joe drunk.

1926

By 1926, Powell had begun a novel she alternately called "Sophie" and "The Truelove Women." (Titles were always a difficult matter for Powell: *My Home Is Far Away* was almost named "Almond Tree Shall Blossom" while *The Locusts Have No King* was plotted as "Prudentius Psychomachia.") During the year, she sold several stories to *College Humor* which paid extravagantly for the time—$150 to $200 per piece.

---

* Powell's father, Roy Powell. This was his last visit to New York.
† Louise Lee, Powell's long-time housekeeper, who worked for her for more than thirty years.

In July, her father fell ill in Oberlin, Ohio and Powell returned for the deathwatch and subsequent funeral, stopping off afterwards to see the aunt who had raised her from adolescence, Orpha May Sherman Steinbrueck, in Shelby, Ohio, and her sisters Mabel Powell Pocock and Phyllis Powell Cook. Some new acquaintances included Malcolm Cowley (who would help edit Powell's last novel, *The Golden Spur*); the biographer Paxton Hibben (who was romantically involved with one of Powell's friends, Mary Lena Wilson); Mordecai ("Max") Gorelik, the visionary stage designer; John Mosher, an early writer for *The New Yorker;* and the poet Genevieve Taggard. Most important, perhaps, Powell began her long and happy friendship with John Dos Passos.

January 4: Dwight Fiske's recital. Dwight at our house later for liquor. New cerise velvet evening coat.

January 7: Started copying "The Truelove Women." Eugene Jolas arrived. Party for him with Jacques and Dwight.

January 10: Ferry ride alone. Idea for fourth novel.*

The Bad Girl. Bad. Novel of Delphine and Mamie. Delphine's point of view. She and her girl chum on the edge of circuses, dance halls, factories (small town), telephone operators—the naive pagan excitement of the *bad girl.* The nice girl of the place and Delphine's bewildered obsession with her. Both in the end trying to go on stage. Nice girl fails. Delphine succeeds because she—the man explains to the bitter nice girl—has always romanticized herself. Bad women are always the romanticists, the sentimentalists to begin with. They are bad but tragic or beautiful to themselves and it is this quality of imagination that makes them artists.

January 22: Worked hard on Scofield party chapter in novel. Went to Esther and Canby's in evening and was drunk and garrulous. Sue and Jack Lawson.

January 23: Breakfast with Jack.

February 5: Went with Esther, Canby, Sue and Jack to Lewis Gannett party. Got drunk and amorous with Carl van Doren.

February 13: Went to "The Great Gatsby."† Check from *Evening Post* $4.

---

*This would appear to be the genesis of *Dance Night*.

†Fitzgerald's novel had been adapted for Broadway.

February 21: With Mary Lena all day. She was in trouble about Pax's wife and another mistress.

February 26: Heard possibility of Harpers taking "The Truelove Women."

March 1: News that Harpers accepts new novel if it continues in same quality. I will publish "Rooms" later.

March 3: Opening of Jack Lawson's play "Nirvana" and party later at Esther's. Disappointed in play as acted.

March 5: Took Mary Lena to dinner. Went to Earl Carroll's "Vanities" later.

March 11: Mary Lena's for dinner. Bed early. Bought tickets for Dos Passos' play at the Cherry Lane tomorrow night.

March 17: Cornelia, Jacques LeClercq, his girl, Dwight, Harry Lissfelt. I had a tantrum and fired them all out at five in the morning.

March 30: Did Sophie's house story. Wrote 61 pages or 18,000 words since March 6. This has all been consistently fine and satisfactory.

April 5: Got sick on street. Wrote review of *Firefly* and took it down to *Post*.

May 4: Worked. Have 173 pages done on novel. Had gin in office with John Mosher.

May 7: Check from *Snappy* for $15. Typed on novel. It gets better as it goes. Typed to page 111. Dinner at Roma, a place Joe knows.

May 23: Joe and Jojo and I had lovely day together. I love Joe so much—more and more.

May 25: Wine at Monte's on Macdougal and at 157 Prince Street with Captain [Paxton] Hibben and Mary Lena. Talked of his Beecher biography which is almost done.

June 3: Called on Curtis Brown and arranged to see [William] Lengel of *Smart Set* tomorrow. Lunch at Blue Ribbon with Joe. Must reduce as Yacht Club liquor enlarged me.

June 7: Wrote review of *Co-Ed*, also a chapter in my novel. It seems to move more slowly as it gets on. Collecting more and more complications and involvements.

July 3: Left for Oberlin because of wire about Papa's illness.

July 8: Papa died at 4 P.M.

July 11: Papa's funeral. North Olmstead. Went into Mabel's in Cleveland.

August 12: Joe drunk. Jack Lawson, Griffin Barry, Robert Wolf and Genevieve Taggard came in and we all went for drive in rain and I was drunk.

August 14: Sold "A Good Little Egg" to *College Humor* for $150. Bought dress and hat. Harpers said to come up Monday.

August 31: A mad day. Canby took me for cocktails; dinner with them, later calling on John Mosher and Jack Lawson. Door bell not ringing. Man in dress clothes (as tight as I was) let me in and brief conversation— he's president of Harpers and said that they would take my book. Wells.

September 7: Dinner at Prince Street. Joe went to Brooklyn and Malcolm Cowley and wife, Jack Lawson, Max Gorelik and Bob Wolf all called. Called up and found Harpers deal was all off. The biggest blow of my life, I think.

September 20: Reviewed Beresford novel. I felt rotten. People exhaust me. I should like to be just with Joe for a little while.

September 24: Ran into Mr. Wells of Harpers twice today. He said John Dos Passos had spoken highly of me. Ran into Mary Lena.

October 24: Dinner with Canby and Esther. Later Dos Passos came in. We discussed maternal instincts. Jacques LeClercq dropped in before dinner.

October 27: Dinner with Malcolm Cowley and Griffin Barry at Prince Street; later to Sammy Schwartz* with Jack Lawson, Dos Passos, Canby, Esther. Saw Conrad Aiken, Max Bodenheim, etc.—then on to Moscovitz where was Konrad Bercovici.

October 28: Saw Jack Lawson. Never want to see him again. Bores me. Tea with Malcolm Cowley. Also bored.

November 19: Worked. Had best party. Had new dress and was very drunk. Met Floyd Dell at dinner.

---

* A famous Village nightspot.

November 20: Our sixth anniversary. Lunch at Prince Street with Mary Lena and Pax. Tea with G. Taggard. Max Gorelik came in and was very stimulating.

November 25: Party at Sue Lawson's. Joe drunk. Jack brought me home.

November 26: A terrible day. Joe didn't appear at office. Jacques hunted for him. Dinner with Jacques and Griffin Barry.

December 14: Jacques Jolas's recital. Later party. Very drunk and fell down stairs.

December 15: Canby, Esther, Jack, Sue and I went to saloon and played dice. Jack took me home.

December 23: Party at Esther Andrews'. I got very drunk with Lewis Gannett. All had dinner at Prince Street.

1927

In 1927, Powell wrote a short story, "Women At Four O'Clock" that was immediately turned into a short novel called *Women At Five O'Clock* and then revised into a play called, once again, "Women At Four O'Clock." The first of her theater pieces, "Women" is highly expressionistic and has not been produced to date.

She continued to write short stories—often in the children's room of the New York Public Library, where there were chairs to accommodate her small frame—and worked on *The Bride's House.* Her social life remained active (at least once she was present in a speakeasy during a raid) and her circle of acquaintance now included E. E. Cummings, Michael Gold, and playwright Francis Faragoh, with whom she became quite close.

She attended many plays, Village and Harlem parties, and the famous Carnegie Hall premiere of George Antheil's "Ballet Mechanique." Not surprisingly, she was also in the crowd when Charles Lindbergh received a ticker-tape parade after his solo flight across the Atlantic. 1927 seems to have been the first year that the Gousha family took a summer cottage near Port Jefferson, Long Island, in the hamlet of Mt. Sinai; this would become an annual tradition.

January 3: Took care of Jojo all day and in evening wrote another story, "Spinster's Holiday."

January 4: Went to library and wrote best story I think of my life, "Women at Four O' Clock." Dinner at Prince Street. I need to be alone a great deal to know my own thoughts. I have been too crowded with people. I need more just Joe.

January 8: Lunch with Joe at Schrafft's and planned to expand "Women at Four o' Clock" into novel. Mary Lena in evening. Was sick.

January 12: Went to Sam's for dinner. Met Jacques LeClercq there. Sam's raided. Went to Esther's later. Mary Lena and Gorelik there.

January 14: Slept. Went to Esther's. John Mosher, E. E. Cummings, Jack Lawson and Sue there. Dwight Fiske came in late from party at Cosmo Hamilton's.

January 20: Saw Jack. Revamped some of novel. Dinner at Prince Street. Very drunk.

January 25: Elizabeth Arden's. Dwight's recital. Wore gold dress and new evening cloak. Lovely time. Letter from Viking Press recommending me to take book to Morrow.

February 19: Party at Jack Lawson's. Francis Faragoh, author of "Pinwheel," spoke of my story, "Saturnalia," which he read three years ago. Tonight with Faragoh and Jack made me want to write play.

February 20: Arranged "Four O'Clock Women" in play form. Went with Sue to rehearsal of Jack's play "The Loud Speaker." It was tremendous!

March 6: Dinner with Jacques and Edith. Later to Esther's where Gannetts were. Very drunk. Went to Jack Lawson's. Stumbled on Playwrights* meeting and was escorted home by Dos Passos.

March 9: To opening of "Earth" and party with the five playwrights Faragoh, Em Jo Basshe, Dos Passos, Michael Gold and Jack at beer saloon in Hell's Kitchen.

March 13: Slept late. Walked on Staten Island. Went to Sam's at dinner with Floyd Dell.

---

*The New Playwrights Theatre, a brief-lived collective group.

April 10: Antheil recital. Stood up with Jacques and Edith.

April 16: Dwight Fiske and Jacques LeClercq in for tea. Dinner with Canby at Sam's. Later with Francis Faragoh to Hall Johnson's party in Harlem.

May 27: Drove out to our cottage in Port Jefferson with Jack at 6 in the morning.

May 31: Came in from Port Jefferson with Dos. Dinner with Francis Faragoh, Dos and Mike Gold at Prince Street.

June 10: Sick all day. Louise took care of me. Joe drunk. We quarreled.

June 13: Went to see Lindbergh parade.

June 16: In Mt. Sinai. Love our little cottage. Started story "And Diamonds." Jack came down and we swam off our pier and had tea.

June 19: Supper on porch for everybody. Much gin.

June 24: Went to town again. Saw Canby off on *Majestic*. Joe and I quarreled. Black day.

June 25: 135 and 1/2 pounds.

July 2: Esther, John Mosher, Francis Faragoh, Dos Passos all out for weekend. Swimming with Jack and Francis.

August 10: Sold "Blue Sky" to *College Humor*. Drove out with Jack.

November 7: Wired Swanson at *College Humor:* "What do you think of 'Women at Four o'Clock'?" He wired back: "It is now 4 and I have no opinion of women. How about story?" Saloon with Jack Lawson.

Friday, November 11: Party at Genevieve Taggard's. Been working night and day on play. Finished Act II.

November 13: Went to Prince Street for dinner with Joe and got very drunk.

1930

No diaries survive for the years 1928 and 1929. In 1928, Powell published *She Walks In Beauty*, which, disclaiming *Whither,* she would insist was her "first" novel. In 1929, *The Bride's House,* her study of a woman with two lovers, was published. Both novels were issued by Brentano's and received respectful reviews but sold poorly.

By 1930, Powell was living at 106 Perry Street, where she finished *Dance Night* (which she later called her favorite novel) and the play "The Party" (eventually produced by the Group Theatre as "Big Night"), and began *The Tenth Moon* and *Turn, Magic Wheel.* She had begun her long relationship with Coburn "Coby" Gilman, a Denver-born magazine editor who was reportedly her lover for a time and remained one of her best friends until the end of her life. Reports to the contrary, the two never actually lived together—Gilman kept an apartment on Lafayette Street, near what is now the Public Theater—but they spent a great deal of time with one another and Gilman is a vivid (and often hilarious) figure throughout her diaries.

Another close friend was Margaret Burnham De Silver, a woman of enormous wealth who was active in a number of liberal and Left causes, and the lover of the Italian anti-Fascist leader Carlo Tresca. A loyal and supportive friend to Powell, De Silver took her traveling, helped her out financially on several desperate occasions, and set up a trust fund to support Jojo. De Silver is the dedicatee of Powell's last novel *The Golden Spur* and Powell was at her bedside when she died.

Several celebrated figures pass through the 1930 diary: Theodore Dreiser, Rex Stout, Harold Loeb, and Louise Bogan, among them. None became close friends.

January 9: Margaret De Silver's party in Brooklyn with Dwight playing.

January 25: Costume ball—"Salons of America"—with Coby. Joe came in tight and all-night session. Very upsetting.

January 26: Finished up to Jen's runaway. Decided she and Morry couldn't possibly break through town.*

January 30: Dinner with Coby. Copying up to Page 140 in novel. How slow this one goes.

February 1: Dinner at Catalan's with Dreisers.

---

*Jen St. Clair and Morry Abbott are the leading characters in *Dance Night.*

February 17: Lunch with Coby. Novel still not under control. Biggest job I ever tackled and not sure yet I can do it.

February 19: Saw Harrison Smith of Cape and Smith who wants to publish me; so does Charles Boni. Probably nobody will want me when I actually have novel all done and for sale.

February 24: Saw William Harris, Jr. to see if he wanted "Party."* Very nice and interested. This novel like tightrope walking—each step so precarious.

February 25: Harris called up, prepared to start play negotiations again. Joe said to keep eye on Elsinore in novel as key note never to be lost.

February 26: Joe tight so much and mentally blurred so it's impossible to talk with him. Makes me sick at heart and so tired emotionally to see him blah-blah drunk all the time with nights of horror that make me sorry for him yet worry so.

March 4: Offered $500 a week to go to Hollywood at once for three months. We need money but that stuff is not in my direction and life is too short to go on unpleasant byroads.

March 8: Worked. Dinner with Dwight at Jungle Club and then to his apartment. This luxury constantly before me would send me either to Hollywood at once or to the ghetto. Met Helen Carlisle (*Mother's Cry*) who writes very good novels in six weeks.

March 10: Hate novel as if it were a personal foe—it's so damned hard and moves so slow. I want to write plays that go fast. Can't conceive of having energy ever to attack a novel again. They're so damned huge and unwieldy.

March 12: Dinner at Brevoort† with Rex Stout.

March 26: Went to Bermuda with Margaret De Silver.

April 9: Signed contract with Farrar & Rinehart for three novels. $3500 advance.

---

* "The Party," a scathing comedy about the advertising business, was written in 1928 during a period when Joe had been laid off from just that business. As "Big Night," it would be Powell's first produced play.

† The Brevoort Hotel, at 5th Avenue and 8th Street, was a Village landmark for almost a century.

April 10: Sold "Eden" (rejected 13 times) to *Delineator* for $1000.

April 11: Sickish. Started semi-hemorrhages.

April 21: Dr. Holliday says I have tumor displacements.

April 22: Trying to work.

April 23: Party at Denys Wortman's. Met Frank Sullivan—very nice.

May 15: Letter that Barrett Clark likes "The Party." Reminding me of his lecture at school.

May 28: Lawsons home. Seem to be changed.

June 15: Finished novel *Dance Night* at Mt. Sinai.

June 22: Coby said novel was superb. Jack said play was terrible.

July 8: Sold "The Party" to Theatre Guild. Can't imagine they will do it.

July 21: Dinner with Max Gorelik and Mary Lena then went to Harold Loeb's apartment.

July 22: Lunch at swell Chinese place on 14th Street with Reginald Marsh. Dinner with Coby. Tight most always on very little. Wish I could work and get into it.

July 24: To Coby's. Met Louise Bogan and her husband Raymond Holden. Dull.

July 26: Very nice vacation sort of weekend. Wish I could start work— could if I had a studio now.

July 27: Jack and I straightened our argument on theater (chiefly "The Party").

July 28: Jojo came in from country to go to Mt. Sinai with Louise and Bobby.* Sick-looking. Worried about him.

August 2: Joe's 40th birthday. Beach party. He went out in canoe for hours. So worried.

August 3: Bored stiff with country and bridge-fiend people.

---

* Bobby Morrison, Louise Lee's son and Jojo's favorite playmate.

August 4: Took studio—marvelous—at 21 E. 14th. I think I can write a New York novel here on my favorite street. Asked Ann [Watkins] for loan. Hotter than hell.

August 6: Got check for $300 from Farrar & Rinehart.

August 17: Got very tight at Mario's and sick too.

August 30: Rain. Telegram from Paramount apparently wanting me for work there.

September 11: Heard Guild is to renew option on my play.

September 19: Interview with Theatre Guild who were wonderful to me. Teresa Helburn just like Miss Brownfield, Lake Erie College dean. Evening to "Symphony in Two Flats" by Novello.

October 10: Dance Night came out with dull thud. Went to country and very discouraged and weepy. Never so close to my own stuff before.

October 23: Feel like working hard, only very discouraged about way Farrar & Rinehart handling novel. No ads and all represented as "sweet tender book" to get trade. Wish I'd stayed with Brentano's where they respected my literary ability.

October 27: To John Farrar's. He heard I was dissatisfied. Very true.

October 28: Worried alternately about book and Jojo. One worry lulls and absorbs the other. In three weeks since publication only one day of ads and only four reviews. Ignored because publishers did no ballyhoo of book itself.

November 2: Took Jojo to Dr. Jamieson's at Seagirt [New Jersey] for school. Beautiful place but it was hard on the poor little darling and me too.

November 5: Pompous letter from Jojo saying he's studying French and German so I guess he's happy.

December 1: Came home sick with pleurisy all week. "Shadow on heart" enlarges. Not quite so painful as before but temperature of 102 at nights. Not much pain by Thursday and hard to remember how much it hurt. Everybody sent flowers.

THE DIARIES

1931

January 1: The tragedy of people who once were glamorous, now trying in mediocre stations to modestly refer to their pasts. Kind, stupid friends pity their "lies" until grand relic must shout and brag, "You see me in this little town—ah, but Bernhardt told me I was a great actress!" They brag only because no one believes anyone is more than he seems at this moment.

January 9: Finished "Love Among the Skyscrapers." It's the kind I despise because it's so slight and I have to make it good in my way and it isn't worth it. Nothing seems so shoddy to me as a carefully polished piece of cheese. Better slop it off in the way it deserves instead of putting it in such an elegant setting you'd think it was amber.

Lunched with Ann Watkins who wanted me to try Hollywood for at least six weeks. I said I would but second thoughts were nightmares and called her up at once to say I wouldn't.

January 13: Grippe—chills, fever again. Afraid I'm going to have it every week now until I get my tonsils out.

January 16: It's very curious but I woke up today a changed, happy person. Night after night of nightmares—volcanoes, earthquakes, and last night I dreamed I was electrocuted—until my head and body buzz permanently and my insides are dark, frantic, desperate things and the nightmares go on in the daytime. Hangovers, of course, make it worse. Then came my dream electrocution, and I am happy. I have by some curious inner process wiped out the last five or even ten years and it seems if I should look in the mirror I would be there young and charming.

It is as if suddenly I had found religion, yet it has nothing to do with willpower or reason. The catastrophes and failures of all my circle of friends has weighed on my soul and held my imagination: Jed Taggard* (whose husband went mad and tried to kill her and their child) and H. Kirk (whose father and mother died, who lost all on the stock market and now has affairs with a doctor on the iron post-mortem table of a hospital morgue) and Esther (with Canby paralyzed for life) and Mary Lena (whose lover died and left her with ten wasted years) made me afraid to live, as if there were an evil pattern to life, as if a stern, vengeful fate stood around every corner with a club.

After my dream electrocution, I threw off all my friends, my sympathies, and found my old philosophy again—all these misfortunes are not the scheme but the errors in the scheme; the plan itself is beneficent. The only thing is, I don't want to see my friends of the last few years—the ones in whose fates I have been so violently interested. Their woes have grieved me far more than they have them.

January 20: Heard much talk of what a "great writer" Ursula Parrott was and that great—really great—work *Ex-Wife*. No book is great in the eyes of newspapermen till its author has made half a million on movie rights.

January 28: Opening of Pirandello's play "As You Desire Me." Another lesser work of a great playwright who has not yet written his masterpieces.

January 30: Charming wire from Stuart Walker who wishes to dramatize *Dance Night*. How funny life's loose ends tie up. Barrett Clark, as New York lecturer, dazzling me at Lake Erie College, suddenly sells my play 12 years later. Stuart Walker, the axis of our Drama Club at L.E.C., decides to dramatize my novel 12 years later.

February 1: Saw "The Three Sisters" last night. It made me think how poor other plays were—our American plays which have no rich philosophy as their base, no sense of the drama of destiny. Our national nature is

---

* Genevieve Taggard's nickname was "Jed"; her first husband was Robert Wolf.

to drive our own Will-To-Do through all mystical supernatural forces, through philosophy.

February 4: Saw "O Promise Me"—a fine, rowdy comedy with a new type of roué. Instead of pinching the girl on the cheek sighing "You little minx," he slaps her on the fanny.

February 11: Saw Philip Barry's "Tomorrow and Tomorrow"—so highly revered by critics. It was facile and slight and trivial and silly but harmless. He has nothing to say nor the slightest notion of what people are like or how they speak. "Will you go——?" "That I cannot." "My sweet—my great!" they say to each other, and on the whole act like any other British drawing-room stock comedy of 1900.

Stayed up till 2:30 and finished Act II. I want to call it "Walking Down Broadway" now.

February 14: Jojo came in for the day. He looked fine and happy. "Got any food in this house?" he said, and proceeded to eat everything in sight. Then he went into his room and asked not to be disturbed. Worked there for hours on all of his different dictionaries—Latin, French, etc. He seemed very proud of his schoolhouse—its three baths, radio, two cars and all other suburban advantages, so we'll have to get them for him. I was relieved to see him looking so well and so serene.

February 19: Went to "Private Lives" by Noël Coward. A delightful example of how drawing-room comedy should be written and played, but I dread to see its followers. The mad lightness must be part of the playwright's own character instead of part of his observation. Philip Barry has listened to people who talk like that but missed the well from which such gay lightness springs. I think Coward is really the most important playwright of the light comic school—a perfectly dazzling thoroughbred madman.

February 20: To see Eva Le Gallienne in "Camille." The audience wept; hundreds of old ladies dabbed handkerchiefs under their glasses, gentlemen coughed and blew their noses, and Joe, always delighted with old traditions, was very happy. I was bored and unconvinced until the last act.

The thing is romantic and needs to be overplayed. Modern sophisticated acting and naturalistic reading of lines only emphasizes the highly artificial plot. It is theatrical and should be played theatrically.

February 28: Delivered play to Ann [Watkins]. Dinner at Coby's, then to a skyscraper architect sort of party at Henry Billings where people talked of the theory of the horizontal line until I was driven to reveal my own theory that the horizontal line was just the old perpendicular lying down.

March 1: Too tired to do anything about all the mess of bills we're in and so all I can do is worry and despair over any security. It seems to me I've worked so long and so desperately and for such little return. Two dollars to spend is as rare now as it ever was, only poverty more embarrassing because one's position is more public.

When I get money, it is immediately gobbled up by debts. It's like housework—do it over every minute and your house is always dirty and all you get from it is enough fatigue to make the sleep of death not fearful.

March 7: Went to Harlem with Harry Gousha and Chapmans. Ran into Franz Emmerich at one dive and Adolph Dehn at another.

Terribly sore in armpits and chiefly a special spot on my back. Should go to doctor but haven't paid last bills.

Ann didn't like my play. It takes a real theatrical eye to read plays and see them as something more than a printed page, so I have little faith in either her praise or her criticism. What she *does* have, though, that makes her remarkable, is an almost unerring nose for "It"—she senses the real thing a mile off, even without knowing what it's all about.

Statement from Farrar and Rinehart shows that, with all their adolescent ballyhoo, they didn't sell much of *Dance Night*. I get no kick in contemplating giving them my next book. Wish I'd stayed with Brentano's. I could use a rest before starting anything else but I guess my rests will have to be hospitals or change of work. I don't see much hope for anything else. Well, it's the same with Joe. He never gets a rest—nothing but a change of trouble.

March 9: My work has progressed slowly but a little. Like the writer in Maugham's *Cakes and Ale*—if not capturing a public by the charm of my work, I can at least stun them by its weight. *Dance Night*—two years work—received less attention than my other books because Farrar and Rinehart hate to mention anything but "tripe" virtues in connection with their publications. This is bad because while it sells tripe (Widdemer, Brush, etc.) it only angers a tripe-hunting reader to find he's been misled into something literary. I owe $2100 on the book.

Wish I could change publishers—not to make money but to be quietly, decently published as honest work, worthy of intelligent attention. Joe and I are always arguing. He says faith in yourself is enough reward. It is enough faith to go on writing (as God knows we all seem to do) and have fatigue as our sole reward for a year's work. To convince others of our faith in ourselves as artists is pure salesmanship and in no sense part of an honest artist's equipment.

Louise and Marie arguing all morning about wanting their money. If I make any, I'll pay them, but in another month it will be the same. Either the perpetual worry of their wages and what miracle will pay it—or tell them to go, and do my own housework and everything else, and prove that we are definite failures, not only as poor as when we got married but a million times worse off.

March 16: Horrible thing. There was a worm inside me. Nine inches long—died and came out. Doctor laughed and gave me vermifuge. I wonder if it was on my nerves for immediately my spirits rise.

Saw Barrett Clark. I wish publishers were as nice to me as theatrical people, managers, etc. They talk so much more intelligently and sensibly about things—less fear of "Art" in them.

March 17: Clark likes play "Walking Down Broadway." Ann, naturally, feels skeptical of everything I do, after the flop of *Dance Night*. I still think it was a good book and probably better than anything I could write right now. That whole artificial boom followed by the exaggerated flop crushed me utterly and I find it hard to get back any resilience.

March 23: Went to tea at hotel where Lester Cohen and Sam Ornitz have their Collaboration Factory—stenographers in one room, drinks and beds for collaborators in the other.

March 24: Tea with Bill Smith who stayed on, then Denys Wortman and Hilda came in and a banjo player. Same old business of keeping gay with crowds and dates and drinks that I had on Ninth Street, when I was in same state about futility of my career. These new publishers are all wrong for my kind of thing. It's like doing a play under contract for lousy actors—you don't have a chance with the wrong presentation.

March 25: After I finish this novel of "Shadow of the Heart" I want to do the one of the woman (or man) frustrated in the little town—crying out their greatness, their art, to jeering village multitudes.*

March 28: Went to Salons of America ball and had swell time. Auction of their stuff. Alec Brook was the auctioneer, all but falling off table. "Here is a picture you could live with," he said. "At least I could live with two of the people in it."

March 31: As soon as this new book came to life, my other one seemed too stiff. This one—Madame Benjamin—laid in the little town, is known to me. I smell the town, with its bonfires of autumn leaves, the meadows far off with wild flowers in them. Every person is familiar to me. Perhaps this is what really wanted to be done all the time; these others had to be weeded out before I could get to this.

April 6: Got $200 from Ann finally. Applying for jobs.

The only way one can be happy, I suppose, is to realize that nothing is final but one's own death. This book, this story, this one interview, always has seemed to me to be the thing by which my whole life must stand or fall. It isn't true—it's the sum total that matters. I know the single success is not final; why must I always believe so completely in the single failure?

April 8: This frenzied financial tangle is too much. It used to settle down to a worry after a while but for the last six months every day has been a crisis.

Those first years in New York I was perfectly happy—including Jojo's first two years, in spite of his sickness. I should know now that happiness

---

*The principal theme of *The Tenth Moon,* which Powell usually called "Madame Benjamin" during its creation.

for me consists of three things—1) having people I like like me, 2) being in the place I want to be (New York, usually), 3) being able to write what I want. Ability to live luxuriously, pay bills, have material things, really doesn't come into this so it's illogical for me to sacrifice my three necessities.

I wonder now which of the these two novels to write—the nurse one or the Benjamin one. Both are good. The Benjamin one, calling on my Ohio background as it does, offers an escape from modern New York desperation (too much a part of my own life for me to write about calmly) and a prison in another sense, shutting me off completely from my present life and interests.

April 9: That Ferdinand Goetel book *From Day To Day* is a great book, I believe. It is a novel and a diary concerning a novel (like this) mixed up; the sincere story that emerges from a trick technique encouraged me about that Lila book.*

April 12: What I want to do now is to get a place comfortable enough for Jojo to be home. We need each other and he is not happy where he is. Healthy and under necessary discipline, yes—but he needs humor, music, books and personal freedom just as I always needed it. This must be arranged.

April 14: Ann Watkins' tea party. Bertram Bloch was the nicest person there. A lawyer named Joseph Bickey; he could be Denny in my book. Dorothy Speare, radiantly be-gardeniaed, rushed up. "My dear, you are so perfectly fascinating—isn't she, Mr. Bloch? Isn't she too fascinating?" I said, "Well, you're quite a little witch yourself." She said she was simply too intoxicated by all the great people around her (there weren't any) to drink mere liquor. As a class, writers are only nice in their early stages. At the semi-success period they are either asses or envious sons of bitches.

April 15: Dinner at Coby's with Edmund Wilson and wife† and Jean Gorman. More female conversation about how hair was being worn, etc., than I've heard in years.

---

*The "Lila book"—sometimes called the "nurse book"—would evolve into *Turn, Magic Wheel.*
†Edmund Wilson was then married to Margaret Canby.

I started my work on (of all things) *She Walks In Beauty** play today. That New York novel sounded so strained and unnatural as I started it. I could see I was a fish out of water. Besides, I need a fresh mind to do a novel and I can't work on the worn-out dregs of two or three years hard and fairly discouraging work.

April 18: I wonder what's going to happen to these plans for novels and plays. I fly at things as frantically as a neurotic rich wife sails into each new hobby. This damn twitching going on under my skin all the time; Joe being tight so much; everything being so insecure. Fat as a fool and quite without any vestige of youth or attraction any more beyond my sterling character.

I must put more theatrical effect into this new play. Realism is all very well but only to serve the highlights of art. If the theater doesn't give you a thrill—of fate dealing the cards, of the Mounted Police coming, of suspense and second act catastrophe, of third act final rescue or magnificent defeat—then what is it?

April 22: Went to Stravinsky's "Oedipus Rex" and Prokofiev's "Pas d'Acier" last night at the Metropolitan. The music for the former seemed abstract to the point of sterility, yet I am not so sure. It may be that its very originality makes it devoid of any associated images for the listener. So, clinging to nothing familiar, it stirs no emotions. (This is sophistry and I know it.) There were passages of clear, cold perfection that were beautiful in so far as the abstract can be beautiful. But it seemed to me a structure for music rather than music itself; a gaunt steel frame, appealing for its engineering work rather than its artistic beauty; a spider web of steel; a cantilever bridge—perfect, but not really a bridge unless it fulfills its function of conveying something from one place to another.

The Prokofiev ballet was trivial, amusing in a childish way and on the whole quite silly.

May 2: Went to Lawsons in Mastic.

I'd go plugging on at the nurse novel only I dread doing another "Women at Four O'Clock"—shallow, phony, pretentious writing with tricks. Better never to write anything—take a job in the movies. I will not

---

*Powell completed the play and called it "Red Dress."

cheat myself so as to start a novel in which I do not believe. Let it be lousy when it's finished. That's different. But, to save my soul, I hope I never have to undertake a big novel with no faith in it or myself.

So tired, so many dull people, nothing in sight but struggle and pains, struggle and panic, varied by trouble over Jojo's future or over Joe's drinking. The best to be hoped is the oblivion of another heart attack.* I feel like an old soldier panting along in his last parade—lucky to be able to walk, let alone trying to stand straight or keep step.

May 4: Returned to New York. As soon as I got home, the demands began. Is it impossible for active friendship to exist after some years? The individual struggle for survival becomes too vital to permit consideration for anyone else—one's friends, anything. For the first time, I am amazed to find myself wanting the country—and I don't mean a suburban community but frankly the country, alone with Joe.

My New York novel is underway, though I don't see what I'm going to call it now that Willa Cather is calling hers "Shadows on the Rock." "Shadow on the Heart" seemed such a vital part of this theme. Titles aren't as damned important as they seem. The only title I really am crazy about is *The Bride's House.* I like *Dance Night* but suffered too much from that book to enjoy seeing its title around.

May 7: I might as well be a hypochondriac, although I'd never be a good enough one to even think up all the things the matter with me—teeth, sinus trouble, tonsils, rheumatism, tumor, ovarian cysts, and dandruff. I want to get away. I *have* to get away if any pieces are to be saved.

May 8: I want to do a story about someone like Margaret—with Esther, the Lawsons, Adolph [Dehn] all disagreeing over Margaret's charities. Since everyone is cutting off each others' noses, finally they fire her maid because she is taking home a quarter of a pound of cream every night. The fight among the buzzards.

May 12: Prospect of $40,000 from picture rights on play. Very unlikely, yet I know something of the sort is in the air. If I could get away—people are

---

*Powell was hospitalized in 1929 for what may have been a heart attack, but was more likely complications from her teritoma, which would not be explained for years.

driving me crazy—I could work on this novel. Perpetually teased by trifles of New York life.

May 13: Charting my Lila novel and hating it. It is hard to remember whether I ever started a novel before with such hate and contempt for it. I've had the feeling afterwards and in the middle of the writing but as a rule I have a fine excitement in the beginning. As a matter of fact, I've hated and despised everything I've written since *Dance Night*. The way that quart of blood was cheapened and degraded in its presentation made me forever afraid of myself, suspicious of my inspirations, and certainly I've hated New York and all the people in the world ever since.

May 14: Plays are so much easier to write than novels. They count for more, too, and don't matter so much to you, the writer. If I could go away—some hotel in Asheville, Montreal, anyplace—I could work.

May 18: Worked at library. Started Madame Benjamin novel. Did three pages. Such a relief after the Lila novel. That was so superficial—though so clear in my head it seems a pity not to do it.

Met D. H. Lawrence's widow [Frieda Lawrence] and her radiance gave me a new excitement about life. She is a blue-eyed Valkyrie who radiates strength and joy. Instead of the downcast widow, she is a triumphant one. She is no longer Lawrence's wife—death has released her from that. Now she *is* Lawrence. She can answer for him, say what he meant by this, what he thought, without argument from him. At last she has convinced him he thought *this,* he believed *that*—with no horrified denial from him. Amusing and catty and vagabondish even at 50 or thereabouts.

May 20: Insane that all through life the same things are important, the same people. Emotions pursue their same twisted course—hope, disappointment, astonishment, despair, indifference, fatigue and, finally, plans for revenge. The revenge idea varies in its strength—from desire to hurt people responsible for the failure to the mere will to live. It is always a sign of life, at least.

May 21: I understand others better than I do myself.

Silly fight with Joe at 4 A.M. I packed my bag. He dressed and left home. Ten minutes later we both were in our beds, chastened and asleep. (He was waiting out in front to carry my bag for me.)

May 23: Various quarrels with Joe about borrowing money from other men. I have to get carfare somewhere. Getting very hard-boiled about things.

May 25: Louise on vacation. Got up at 8 and revised first five pages of "Madame Benjamin." Wish I could creep up on this book but life is so exciting, with war and revolution in the air, I want to be in that instead. I never will be able to write of contemporary excitement in a novel. I may in a play, though.

June 3: 14 pages of novel done and it pleases me. I think it will be a fine book, probably better than any I ever wrote, but I doubt very much if anyone else will be attracted by it. I felt that *Dance Night* had more popular appeal in its excitement and glamour than any other book of mine but it turned out to bore people since its excitement ran contrary to theirs.

June 4: Tight at Louie's and a fairy threw glasses at me because another fairy liked me.

Jack and I devoted friends again and admiring of each other's works.

June 7: Wrote three pages on Decker.* Daren't stop to think now of whether it's worth doing or not—too much tightrope balancing. Always have a time with normal bourgeois people, trying to make would-be musicians anything but offensive. I try in vain to think of a *decent* would-be artist. Well, that's the assignment; can't get out now.

Going over my old memoranda I find that *She Walks In Beauty,* which I began sometime in October, I finished on April 10 of the next spring. Six months work. No trouble in writing it apparently, with one to three short stories and two or three book reviews a month, besides. I suppose this was because it was first year free of housekeeping. Anyway, it was my first year in the Village.

---

* Blaine Decker, the principal male character in *The Tenth Moon.*

Then *Bride's House* begun on December 1—doing 25 pages the first 11 days (1925—six years ago) and on February 11 took 75 pages up to agent and by March 30—four months—I had nearly 150 pages done, exclaiming all the way how fine it was. Slowed up after that, working against whoopee, new friends (Cornelius Burke, Dwight, etc.). Tired all the time —with weeps and parties and reviews—finally remarking with some surprise that it was getting harder to do as it went along. Drinking, etc. Then Papa died. Finished novel on July 11—about six weeks longer time than the other. More parties that fall, with Dwight's and Esther's crowd and our own. No novels—just short stories.

In July 1928 I began *Dance Night*. Stopped for ten days after Joe lost his job to write play "The Party." Then in 1929 did little but play "Wedding Ring" and one short story. In 1930 worked more on novel and finished it on June 15th—actually about 14 months work, fighting it, feeling it was too much, right to the very end. Very different from my original feeling of ease and grace about writing.

June 13: Lawsons came to cottage for supper. Jack believes Starr Faithfull committed suicide. He told of trying to get on his college paper (Williams) and with contributions and points to his credit he was repeatedly turned down till junior year because of Jewish prejudice there. He and I both have ways of not facing things we don't want to. The only way of ever surmounting obstacles is not to see how big they are.

June 15: Lawsons went to Hollywood. In the evening to Margaret's in Brooklyn. Evelyn Scott and Jack Metcalfe were there. Joe was drunker than I ever saw him. He fell all over everybody and I can't understand why but I attacked him suddenly. My nerves were so taxed by pretending it was funny—his being so blah-blah drunk before all those people he would like to respect him. Shot to pieces afterward with shame over my outburst and having been so mean to him.

June 18: Jojo came home from Sea Girt for good. He should have piano lessons and a man tutor—I don't know how to arrange this. He is very good but I don't sleep when he's home and neither does he. I hear him trotting back and forth in the bathroom, whispering to himself and repeating French or Italian. He's crazy about languages—in fact, crazy about any out-of-the-routine study.

June 19: I am in as serene a state now as I can ever expect to be. I think it's because I'm more or less a flop, I suppose. This means I'm not invited to any smart houses where I am furious at not having clothes, carfare and so on. Since I'm not asked, I don't mind a bit. Even seeing shops doesn't fill me with frustrations and envy; they're out of my life. This may mean that poverty—and we certainly are poor now—is my proper state and I'll always see things out of focus when (or rather if) we have funds.

June 22: Did three pages on novel. Tired to death but work out of sheer nervous desperation, weight of responsibility, necessity for making plans about Jojo this fall, making money for these plans. I can't see or think of anything else; Joe's concern over me, to the neglect of his child, makes me doubly responsible. What other fate need I have expected after my first 21 years training in work, worry, insecurity and frustration? One has to be born and raised fortunately in order to be forever fortunate.

Thinking it over, no great woman writers ever raised kids, did they (except Sigrid Undset)? All the "charming" lady literati have had charming children but then they write magazine trash. Women seem to me the greatest opportunists, the most unscrupulous artists in the world—they turn any genius they have into money without a pang—whereas the man artist, supporting his family by distortions of his genius, never ceases to bemoan his lost ideal.

This new novel seems to ring true but it is not anything important or unusual. It runs along easily and solely by intuition, unlike the careful solid planning of *Dance Night*. It is very slight—as thin and usual as the works of Ellen Glasgow or Isa Glenn—so easy I scarcely miss what goes out of my brain. I neither like nor dislike it. I only feel that if I were stronger and not so crippled by the disappointment of *Dance Night*, my domestic panic and responsibilities, I could do bigger stuff than this light lady-writing.

June 25: Went to party for Blair Niles late at night. The only glimpse of any outside life I've had for weeks. It's so important to receive a little flattery and attention—as if one were a normal human being instead of a thing.

Dwight Fiske came down and we're doing a story for Texas Guinan which isn't any good but all right for her.

I notice Claire Spencer's novel is being dramatized with Pauline Lord as lead. A sure hit, of course, since C. S. is financially secure, doesn't work for her success, therefore has it, along with prestige handed to her on a silver platter with warning to Gods: "Right Side Up." Mistakes in luck are seldom made in these cases. They're so padded with good fortune that nothing else will stick to them.

June 29: Looks as if "The Party" is all set for the movies and I'm to receive $10,000 unless Ann queers it by holding out for more money.

Those *Medieval Latin Lyrics* are heavenly, only I ache so for such clear, live, love songs written by such long dead lovers and the more vivid their desires, the sadder I feel that lovers should ever die—as if the mere yearning for each other were enough to keep them immortal.

Ansonius (to his wife):

> *Love, let us live as we have lived, nor lose*
> *The little names that were the first nights grace*
> *And never come the day that sees us old,*
> *I still your lad and you my little lass.*
> *Let me be older than old Nestor's years*
> *And you the Sybil, if we heed it not.*
> *What should we know, we two, of ripe old age?*
> *We'll have its richness, and the years forgot.*

What makes it ache is to read in the notes that the "little lass" died a year or two later.

July 8: An evening up on the Empire State roof*—the strangest experience. The huge tomb in steel and glass, the ride to the 84th floor and there, under the clouds, a Hawaiian string quartet, lounge, concessions and, a thousand feet below, New York—a garden of golden lights winking on and off, automobiles, trucks winding in and out, and not a sound. All as silent as a dead city—it looks *adagio* down there.

July 15: Dreadful evening with Coby and Joe. Not doing a thing in town but bite my nails and wait, so best go to country where at least I sleep well.

---

*The Empire State Building had just opened.

All most people do is complicate my responsibilities and force me to worry about them and make up their deficiencies. Selfish, ungracious thing to say—I don't know what's gotten into me, but I've certainly turned into a bitter, ill-tempered, acid, selfish, frustrated old maid.

July 20: When writing was a hobby I wrote five to seven hours a day regularly. Now that it is a profession, I find it almost impossible. Is it because I am tired, in bad condition, worried by finances or, as I suspect, because my life is so complicated it takes all my energy weaving in and out of it?

Nostalgia for the old days at *Snappy Stories*—a salary every week, nice clothes, independence, routined life. Finding myself driven more and more into the position of helpless neurotic wife who has dropped her dear little hobby for the time being. That is what I dread—being unarmed, even against one's friends and husband, so that one has no rights but the little privileges permitted a capricious little wife. I want the dignity of my own work, my own earnings and control of my own life. The only way to accomplish this is by constant production. One can't just run from the idle futility of town (not even dissipation is possible there now) to the lazy sleep-and-eat of the country forever, without accomplishing something somewhere. It's up to me.

It seems to me that ever since I finished *Dance Night* I have been marking time, waiting for something that doesn't happen. I can't buckle down seriously to big job but just do little odd pieces—marking time, really, in my mind, waiting for *Dance Night* to come out with great *éclat*. As if it had never come out—a rocket that only sizzled because it was rained on. Still wait for the blaze in the sky. It did a very funny thing to me, that dead rocket.

July 22: Even out here, I cannot escape the tension of false expectations. In New York it is unbearable—$10,000 in movie money always about to happen but never quite closing, phones ring but never bring business.

July 29: Went Sunday to Mastic to the Lawsons and yachted around till we broke the propeller. Did some work on novel—up to page 52. When Stanley [Rinehart] and John [Farrar] asked me, hopefully, if my new book was about New York, I explained a little of the plot—enough to make their faces fall in obvious consternation.

More hooey about the movie rights of "The Party" and finally Ann left for abroad. I am very concerned about my interests—no sales of anything for a year.

August 3: Wrote up to page nine on short story "Rumble Seat." I sustain the wish for that quiet spacious family apartment on East 10th Street and it helps me to rush through tripe like short stories.

August 4: Lawsons came over with Canby. He can stagger around a little on crutches now, his legs in braces.* They took me back and we opened a gallon keg of corn liquor. Sue and I had a terrible fight—she said I was a God-damned fool for not realizing that Jack patronized me. I was knocked out by the crack, went up to bed, then suddenly rushed down and told her I hated her, she was terrible and all sorts of awful things. I was quite sick afterward and of course unable to do a bit of writing all week.

August 7: Dinner with Philippe Soupault, and his wife Mary Louise. Soupault—a surrealist, I believe—is charming. He says Isaac Babel is a better writer than Pilniak and to read *Red Cavalry*. He is delicate, charming, scholarly—a little like Jacques LeClercq. Jacques is at the Hotel Victoria, Geneva. He and his wife like us and we them. He translated Joyce's "Work In Progress" into French. Philippe said Matthew Josephson told him I was the wittiest woman in New York. Impossible!

Saw "Green Pastures"—simple, charming, stained glass with sound, so simple as to be almost a new technique.

August 8: The country. The Lawsons, Esther and Canby appeared. Relations calm again. Jack very mad because I liked "Green Pastures." Joe says Jack deprecates all persons and things likely to contribute to my success. The only way he can survive through these years of no applause, no prestige as a dramatist, is by deprecating all others who are receiving any kind of recognition. In anyone else, it would be small-minded. I don't know why it isn't in Jack, except that his limitations are on such a huge scale they have almost the magnificence of virtues. You could no more call him a little, envious blowhard than you could call the tyrant Nero an old "meanie."

---

* Canby Chambers had been stricken by polio and had lost the use of his legs.

August 27: Wish I would hear from Ann's office. It wouldn't hurt to let me know what happened. If it was bad, it would save me a few days of false hopes.

August 31: Weigh 142 pounds. Dropped all but coffee for breakfast.

September 4: Heard that "Walking Down Broadway" was sold to Fox for $7500.* Dizzy with shock, though still uncertain since check is not in hand.

September 11: Got check for $6509.70—first money I've made since last October—from Ann's for motion picture of "Walking Down Broadway." Thank God something has gone through. Katherine† is broke—raising Cynthia on $25 a week—so I'm taking her to country for weekend and sending her $200. I want to send Phyllis $100 or $50 and clothes.

September 12: Coby was out. Katherine and Cynthia. Cynthia played jazz on Sunday and Jojo stuck his head in the door. "This is a sacred day," he said gravely. "Shouldn't I play the Victrola?" Cynthia asked. Jojo hesitated since he adores the Victrola. "It's sacred," he said more weakly. "Don't you like me to play them?" Cynthia persisted and Jojo's truthfulness overcame him. "Yes, I do," he said.

I swam out deep and he screamed for me to come in from the beach. "Mother, don't go out so far. I want to play anagrams with you tonight."

September 13:

Savings	$1500.00
Joe	2200.00
Debts	433.00
Clothes	1022.50
	$5155.50

Dropped all but salad for lunch.

---

*The film was released as "Hello Sister" after the original director, Erich von Stroheim, was fired.

†Katherine Chapman, Powell's friend from her earliest days in New York with the Naval Reserve.

September 16: Took lovely apartment at 9 East 10th. I hope to have more organized life for my writing. Give Louise $20 a week (or less) to run house on. Let her shop in morning and come back and dust up, keeping my suite reserved till I tell her to do it.

September 21: Poor darling Jojo had to go through two hour exam at Friends School and so disappointed when they said he wouldn't work well in a big school. To Pennsylvania Grill at night to see his "favorite artist," Rudy Vallee, in person. He was perfectly behaved and yet thrilled to pieces. I'm not sure what to do about his school. It is a terrible problem.

September 26: Sleep—that seems all I'm good for except shopping and that's got to stop. I am frightened at the enormity of moving into that sumptuous place at 9 East 10th. $183 a month. I've put $1500 in savings but Joe knows it so I suppose it will have to come out in a month or two to pay speakeasy bills or maids. His salary would swing the new apartment—with mine to furnish it—but the only way I can depend on not being put out by January is to count on earning enough for it myself. He's an excellent manager, except when he knows I've saved some out for Jojo. This he takes as an insult to his earning capabilities and a presumption on my part. I love him but I do not see how we're going to adjust finances except for me to turn over everything and blind my eyes to whatever happens. This will restore his self-confidence and that is worth much to both of us.

I must work—cut out routine friends and lock myself up to work. A new novel ought to be ready in a few months and certainly the new play. Let's forget this new place—a mere change of address, not a tremendous and precarious step—and work as if nothing were happening.

October 3: Moved to Fifth Avenue Hotel, Suite 1624, until 9 East 10th is ready. Working on play about Atlantic City convention.

October 6: Esther and Sue over for lunch. Sue and I still [indecipherable] but polite. A pleasant, comfortable woman, shallow and lazy and scatter-brained. I hold it against her that she is dulling Jack to her level, making a rather average person of a very extraordinary genius. A female advantage that keeps him from being desirable to better women than herself, of course, but a sad spectacle.

October 10: In the country, trying to rewrite "The Party" for Brock Pemberton. It needs rewriting, too, but from a staging point of view. I noticed that in Act II Myra is offstage for seven pages at a time and is not missed—that is, her importance is not sustained by the remaining characters' conversation. Trying to fix this. But I'm damned if I'll do the silly things Mrs. Antoinette Perry suggested, such as making her an ex-kindergarten teacher turned model through some misfortune.

October 12: Moved to 9 East 10th Street and love it passionately. So quiet —calm, spacious, one's soul breathes deep breaths in it and feels at rest. I am almost neurotic about it: I want it all alone—with Joe and family, of course—but outside of Port Jefferson, this is first material thing I've loved. It comes over one suddenly—like love—that this is home.

October 23: Talk of Pemberton doing my play with the Provincetown people. I believe this is an excellent idea and I think it will go through.

Raging and stewing constantly. I can't understand this unless it is that I am actually physically contented in this new place but must automatically balance content with restlessness in order to whip myself into writing.

Carol,* in overbearing way, has decided to change my publishers. I was obliged to put my foot down.

November 1: Alone and sober—a thing that has been almost impossible these last few hectic weeks. My simple nature wants to write the simple, quiet story of Connie Benjamin and Decker. Circumstances and people have forced me (or attempted to force me) into a quick, sensational flashing success that is contrary to my real nature. The resulting confusion —outer influence against inner conviction—brings about mere paralysis.

I did a little more on Connie and decided to forget for the moment Lila's novel. I could not understand why, with Lila's story so clearly and concisely mapped out, I couldn't whiz right through it. Finally it came to me that I cannot work from factual knowledge. A novel must be a rich

---

*Carol Hill, later Brandt, at that time working for Powell's agent Ann Watkins.

forest known at the start only by instinct. To have all the paths marked, the trees already labeled, is no more incentive to enter than Central Park is a temptation to explorers.

Such trips through known and classified territory might be an excellent enough challenge to creative ingenuity in someone else. But with me the basic urge to write is neither knowledge nor the desire to expound but pure curiosity, the bottom of all laboratory experimentation. I am curious about Mme. Benjamin, fascinated by Decker. The prospect of a long winter with them satisfies me utterly. But please, my publishers and friends—don't lash me into a fit of conscience over immediate production and a sensational work, for this should be a quiet, interesting study, nothing to be recommended for steamer-baskets or dull weekends.

The reason Sue and Jack together make up one such dull, amiable, soggy person is because they are happy together and two happy persons make up one dull stodgy blob. Happy people are dull—they're happy because they're dull and dull because they're happy. They have nothing to give because they give it to each other. It is pleasant to see these amiable matches but not inspiring—and the reason it is more often than not depressing is that such connubial content is based seldom on physical (let alone spiritual) attainment but on having arrived at a mutual recognition of the importance of material goods and a mutual determination to have or to hold property.

This must be because there are no group ideas. Man alone can be an idealist. A woman alone can approach idealism (though it nearly always merely signifies retaining her virginity—actually a material property). But two individuals together reduce their idealism to words and "beauty" becomes a house and "virtue" becomes a family, with attendant maternal considerations.

Did story about Otto Kahn with Dwight yesterday. Lousy. Strange how a brilliant mind can get dulled through having its second-rate stuff applauded. First rate standards are lost in the shuffle.

November 9: Francie Dewey had party. A man sang "I'm Ritzy, the Toast of Vienna, cause I landed buttered side up."

November 12: Dinner at Matthew Josephson's with Henry Billings and M. Cowley and R. Coates and Coby. I hate slightly familiar people. Strangers

I adore, and five old friends. In-betweens I resent furiously as a waste of valuable time.

November 13: Wonderful party at "The Mansion" for Bernard Sobel, Follies press agent who has written a book on burlesque. All old burlesque queens there, with new Vanities and Follies girls, too. Faulkner, Floyd Dell, Anita Loos, Thyra Winslow, Marc Connelly, Walter Wanger—what their connection was I don't know but there they were.

November 14: Saw Stanley Rinehart and told him—since they are so worried about *Dance Night* losses and large advance due on next book— I would pay back from next advance the money they lost. Their being upset makes me upset.

November 15: Took Jojo to Empire State Tower. A storm up in the clouds. The most magical spot in the world. Bizarre, theatrical—it is impossible to believe in it and people jumping off are (I'm sure) caught on rubber mattresses a few feet below their jumping off place.

November 21: Party with Vincent Sheean, Coby and Mr. Baby. I asked where was Mrs. Baby (I'd forgotten their names, only remembered they called each other Baby) and he gravely said "bust up." That's what happens to these babies.
   Tighter than I've been in years.

November 22: Slept all day. Did two pages at night.

November 24: Drew out $100 to pay Joe's dentist bill so he could get teeth fixed. Found out he was away from office all afternoon and evening, paying at least half that much for speakeasy bills. As usual, wave of feeling that money is nothing between two people was lost in resentment at men in general, though I so often have done the same thing.

December 2: Lawsons went to California for indefinite time—forever, I suddenly thought. Have been working steadily—averaging two pages per day but it gets more and more hard. The name of this novel arrived Saturday—"Come Back To Sorrento."

December 3: More depressed than I have ever been over friends leaving. I try to shake off feeling I will never see them again, but it persists.

December 9: I must get more and more work done, though I really work pretty hard—just seem to have slow results. I can't see Farrar and Rinehart even reading my new manuscript, let alone printing it. I think I will get a few people with names to read the manuscript so that a similar advance presentation can be given as it was to *She Walks In Beauty*.

December 10: Gave Jojo examination in *Alice in Wonderland* and asked who was his favorite character in it. He said "Alice, because she changed her size."

December 26: Left for Hollywood with Ann Watkins.

December 29: Arrived in Pasadena and was met by Eric and Gertie Hatch in Rolls Royce. Hotel Chateau Elysée, my perfect dream hotel (being crazy about hotels)—an elaborate suite even to a sun porch.

December 31: New Year's dinner at the Hatches in Beverly Hills. The whole place is so kindly gay (rather than melancholy gay as in New York) that it is very soothing.

1932

January 1: Hollywood. Chateau Elysée. Frances Mayer came in, still in her New Year's evening clothes. Went to dinner with the Lawsons.

I should write a novel about a boy, like Charlie Miller, who works himself up from class to class to factory head, then unable to understand the strikers, explaining he's one of them—there *are* no classes. Finally ruin of success; prepared for great deeds, he could not stand up to rich man's private life.*

January 2: Dinner at Santa Monica. Home in Rolls Royce. Jolly, futile, childish fun.

January 7: Impossible to keep track of time or anything out here—life slips pleasantly out of your control almost at once.

January 8: Shopping on Hollywood Boulevard. Dinner with the Lawsons at the Brown Derby. Now impossible to sleep. The gaiety of early morning brilliant sunshine, immense green trees and singing birds leaves me depressed and weepy by noon. This climate picks you up and throws you down in the most amazing way.

January 9: Dinner with Lawsons. Drove around Mulholland Drive with Paul Gangelin to find place he wrecked car before.

January 13: Cleveland. Dinner with Edgar and Mabel at tearoom where

---

*This would become *Story Of A Country Boy*.

Mrs. Joe Taylor, tea-owner, spread herself on my account very hand-somely and I was touched, not knowing I'd been heard of here.

January 14: Saw Phyllis in Canton then came home and Mabel had a fine party with champagne and everything. People are really much kinder to each other away from New York and much more frankly interested in everything, instead of (as in New York) dumb but too sophisticated to ask questions.

January 25: New York. Writing nights steadily till two and three o'clock, and finding that I get more done by these uninterrupted midnight hours than a day of half-interrupted work. I hope to have this done by March 15th and I rather think it is possible unless things break in. It would mean money by April 1 then—to take care of Mt. Sinai cottage and season family ticket, perhaps even a Ford.

January 26: Louise left for Boston or someplace. This always happens when I get going on a book but I am determined to rise above it and write just the same at night on the damned novel.

January 29: Faragohs in to dinner and Lester Cohen and Eden Grey and Franz Emmerich afterward. I drew a complete blank for the first time in my life and did not know anything from the moment the Faragohs spoke of leaving till the next morning. It turned out that in this period I staged a great amorous farewell with Lester but I recall none of it—rather fright-ening in a way because for the first time I see such things are possible.

February 2: Louise returned. I am tired with the strain of teaching Jojo all morning, including piano, going over "The Party" with Ed and Frances [Mayer] who say they will produce it, trying to keep a grip on this elusive, tenuous novel, too.

Start on a novel about Charlie Miller, successful man, this fall, August, say. It could be Morry grown up now, an official in Lamptown factory, and still yearning for cities, to go away and see Jen, their egos still fighting.

Went to Literary Guild tea at Hotel Chatham for James Branch Cabell. Rather awful with so many people there on the make, trying not to make a social error. Worse than any I'd seen, I thought.

February 5: Decided to do next book about Charlie Miller—shy boy who only hopes to do his work in Handlebar Factory well, who works dutifully and is pushed up and up until he is general manager of big factory. Puts money in real estate—because he doesn't know how to buy luxuries beyond fine hotels, Miami, Hollywood, San Bernadino Hills, etc. Great empty house without pictures or books, lots of dogs and cats and good automobiles and good food.

Then strike. Workers shoot at him as his car goes to work, call him lousy capitalist; he is horrified because by instinct and labor he is one of them, hurt by their lack of loyalty. They're all workers together, the reason he has a chauffeur is he's so damned nervous he can't drive, he has maids because of bad digestion caused by his wife's cooking.

They hiss, and he goes back, the factory is weakened, he is so upset by accusations of his living on fat of land that he is flattered at dawning realization that he is one of those marvelous idle rich. He starts in furiously doing all those things—women, drinking, cars, New York—but he is simple peasant stock, he can't take it in his stride, he must either work or play. Canned from job, he drinks at home all day, uses his private golf course as public one, uses house as tea-room, finally is back with old father saying "No such thing as a man being worth more than $25 a week" and happily damning the damn capitalists once again.

February 8: Lunch with John Farrar who disturbed me by saying no hurry on novel—not coming out till August. Since I was getting along fine by being in a hurry, what to do?

February 10: I read some more Proust. How thoroughly he embalms his thoughts and people—not a sentence or character escapes without wax flowers on its chest and a sickening funeral smell.

February 21: Went to Park Central and then to hear Gieseking with Coby. He played Debussy as if he had him in bed with him, all of his stuff he played with fingers in ten little bedroom slippers, tiptoeing up and down Schumann. He crouched over the piano with big hands hiding the keys; I expected a mouse to peep out of his fists. In fact he acted as if the piano was his Valentine and little white birdies with notes marked "I love you" might twitter out of it any minute. Music was so diminished under his microscope, made so tiny and perfect that it could be neatly placed in one ear.*

March 6: This damned womb of mine now under observation by Dr. Holliday seems to be affecting my whole left side, numbing my left leg so that it's always asleep.

March 20: Jojo was proposed to by Ann Lissfelt who said "I'm going to marry you." He said "Who said so?" She said "I say so." He said "Don't be silly." Later he said "These girls are full of baloney."

March 21: No matter how little or how much I do on that God-damned son of a bitch of a novel it always turns out to be no more, no less (yes, often less) than eleven pages a week, like a cow that can only give so much milk. The awful part is realizing that it isn't very good. I figure that everything I ever did is one quarter of what it could be and all that consoles is the knowledge that many worse people get better reputations on less. Perhaps if I worked every second as apparently Evelyn Scott does— or does she?—it might turn out to be more fully realized.

March 22: I am in a cross, cynical stage when I think of quiet subtle revenges on all sorts of people for being nothing more than simple and kind and straightforward—a reasonable excuse for Sicilian justice in my warped mind. The Lawsons are returning soon and I suppose Esther later and, with my regular sparring companions, I won't be so unamiable.

March 26: Dinner at Margaret's with Evelyn Scott and Carlo Tresca. It makes me so mad that I can't seem to do more than 3600 words a week— all in a lump or slow and regular. Staving off this operation a little longer but scared of it, though it isn't dangerous. I am filled with dread trying to think how to explain this book to Farrar & Rinehart and have an instinctive feeling that this—like that marriage play and the novelette *Women At Four O'Clock*†—is one of those things I have in my system and must do for vague laboratory reasons but are not particularly vital and are born dead.

---

* Portions of this would be incorporated into *Turn, Magic Wheel.*

† The surviving copy of this novellete is actually labeled *Women At Five O'Clock.*

Dos' *1919* is knocking people cold. He is no longer a promising writer but as arrived as he can ever be—like Lewis or Dreiser—and is scarcely older than I am.

March 28: I dread and in fact cannot see money for that operation but perhaps it's that difficulty in addition to my native laziness that makes me scarcely able to do a day's work per week. I think too that with this lovely contented house a certain brain fattening takes place, an emotional smugness—generally called "balance" or "control" invariably associated with comparative material security.

A great change has taken place in me. I believe Hollywood was the last mad gesture. Pride (family, professional and personal) has asserted its normal control—as it should when the on-sweeping thirties make flamboyance ridiculous. Another sad change is the calm weighing of my work and the conclusion that I haven't made as full use of my years as I should and cannot command a great novel. I am more sure of a flashy success with my particular type of play and will surely do one before the summer is over.

This business inside me is rather sapping. Typed a little today but no work as yet. Ought to do two pages or so before bed. Dread—almost sickeningly—the copying, the editing, the explaining, the defending! I feel that the next book will receive the real appreciation—I adore it already, ought to start on it, with map and chart. Call it "Farmer Boy," make it Long Island.

April 1: Dinner at Margaret's with Evelyn Scott, Josephine Herbst and John Hermann—then the *New Masses* ball.

April 5: Doctor gave me a tonic which is working almost at once. Romanoff's Drug Store (10th and University Place). It's ghastly to be so tired, so sleepy and dull-headed that I can't get work done, no party or even pleasant gesture seems worth the trouble. I'm afraid I'll have to have the operation after all.

April 21: Joe read novel and says it's fine—better, he feels, than any of my others. I have dedicated it to him because, oddly enough, it's one of those stories I would never have been able to understand nor to see any but the funny side of without him, without having absorbed part of his point of view after many years together.

April 22: Handed in my novel.

April 25: John Farrar called up (as did Ann) to say this was a "literary gem," worthy of a Willa Cather, etc., and Coby says it's by far my best book. Odd I should feel so little emotion; the whole thing was a trick to save me losing more blood as I usually do in my novels. Though I think I did a fairly excellent study of certain characters, they are my adopted children—I do not find my own dear faults coming out in them, or my own ideas.

May 7: Jack came back and Faragohs and he were over to breakfast, then we drank all day with party in evening.

May 11: Wonderful time seeing boat *Europa* off (Dwight also sailed). Best boat I ever saw. Esther came over in afternoon. I am perfectly and completely happy with these people—they are like an absorbing drug, all other things slip away. These last few days—on top of having finished my novel—have been heavenly.

May 12: Sue arrived and we celebrated with large party. Later all to dinner in the cellar of Ticino's* on Thompson Street, then to Fred Boyd's where we all threw things in the old-time manner and Sue knocked people around. I see now what's ailed me has been no physical thing but pure lack of my pals as I seem to go through ferocious bats with perfect vigor.

May 25: Went to "Ten Days That Shook the World," then at midnight Jack called up from Gannett's and I went to party there.

May 29: We are in a big jam about rent and other money—must raise $350 almost at once. As usual, my practical sense gets paralyzed and I can only think of doing some big thing. I could do that Lila New York novel but I think it's too easy to struggle over and I can't be sure whether my

---

*The Grand Ticino, opened in 1919, thrives on Thompson Street to this day.

aversion to writing a new novel so immediately is based on laziness or sound feeling. There ought to be a decent lapse between big jobs so that one gets a somewhat refreshed motor to run on.

No denying that nothing has ever taken less of me than this *Tenth Moon* novel. How I wish they would have allowed me to call it "Come Back to Sorrento"; since one gets so little else for one's work, a title that pleases the writer seems such a little boon to ask. I expect nothing at all of this book—no announcements have been made of it though dozens of announcements have come out on Katherine Brush's much later book.

The Tenth Moon—how I hate the empty, silly, pointless title!—is an excellent, lucidly written book—above the average, point for point, the only thing I've ever done completely on brain power—a correct book—a work that can be measured with all the proper rulers—therefore no margin of wonder in it, therefore not a vital living work. I can listen without much interest to what my friends think of this—they can't break my heart (as they might have in my other three books). None of my heart is in this book; I can't wear it lightly so soon after *Dance Night*.

June 5: Read a swell book—*Laugh and Lie Down*—by Robert Cantwell. He seems to me to have more than Faulkner or Hemingway.

June 6: That same feeling—alone with nature and faced with the truth, a hopeless, twisted, aching truth. I wake, as I did in Hollywood, where things are laid out in red letters against the vast emptiness of nature— with rain in my heart, things weeping steadily inside me, silently, and the way they daren't find words for themselves but these blind endless tears that exhaust me so much more than real ones but are not so nerve-wracking, I suppose, as logic or analysis.

We say so little—as if with the tacit decision not to talk about one thing, we had nothing else to talk about.

June 8: Drove in with the Lawsons and party at Esther's where Sue and I were great pals but in parting I socked her, also Jack.

June 10: Delighted to leave for Jean Gorman's at 2 A.M. to drink with her and Frances Mayer. Jean says Carl Van Doren says *Tenth Moon* is a simply marvelous book. Stayed out till 5—saw Frances home to Hotel Warwick and rode home alone in the lovely New York skyscraper daylight.

June 11: Went to "Merry Go Round" with Dos and Esther—a fresh, brutal play, combining the life-sense of a realistic play with the sharp suspense of melodrama—clipped scenes, a turn-style stage which kept the many scenes smoothly running—a compact beautiful piece of work on every count, though full of horror.

Went up to Warwick and got Frances and went down to Esther's where a thoroughly Greenwich Village party was in progress. Home at 3:30.

June 12: Slept. Mary Lena came in and I went up to T. R. Smith's for dinner with Frances. He has the manners of a pansy but is really just a raconteur. Frances went to bed and waked up sober and we had fun except that T. R. said I was a female Jim Tully and I can't think of being anything more unpleasant looking but I suppose it's a big head and square shoulders—do I really look like a thug?

June 14: Barrett Clark phoned that the Group Theatre wanted "The Party" as one of their scripts had fallen through. (This turned out to be Edmund Wilson's new play which oddly enough is a party play—all three acts being laid at the party.) I am upset—not knowing what to do. I can't let Newman down, even though I know that as usual he will let *me* down in a few weeks with a big thud. Wait to see what develops.

June 15: Saw Group Theatre people today and told them my problem about Newman. They are so damned decent—like Clark—that it is like a breath of fresh air to be able to slip off guard and be perfectly honest without the suspicion that all this will later be used against you.

June 16: Settled with Group. Ann was furious—had never heard of them, of course—and I had to give her another lesson in play-handling. I called up Newman and was bawled out as a louse and no good could come of such a dirty way of doing business—all of which I was aware of but I've been a sucker so long and been loyal up to the minute I get the kick in the pants which is always forthcoming.

Party at Esther's with Lawsons and Frances Mayer. Sue threw things around and started beating up Jack—a habit she has which always makes him look so ridiculous. But he told her this time to go to hell.

June 17: Harassing day fixing everything up with Group. Then Jack sold his play to the Group, too and we went to Sam's and drank with E. E. Cummings till five in the morning—a simply heavenly spree. Cummings' conversation (in its drunken fantastic aspects) permits no interchange—it is a dazzling, glittering spectacle, a parade of wonders and fantastic nonsense. His sarcasm is savage but I note that art and humor both vanish when pretty young girls ask him the meaning of his work—his explanations are as pompous and flattened as any Floyd Dells.

July 5: Dinner at the Brewery, later to Horace Liveright's penthouse. He's a man in a book all right—a semi-glamorous, cheap, New York novel.

July 12: Jack and Joe and I went to dinner and then to "Of Thee I Sing."

August 3: Denys Wortman in. Since I have clung so long and so futilely to a few intimates who leave every few months I have decided to build a life apart from them and enter it wholly. I can't go on in this childish way being desolate and suicidally bored for eight months of the year when Esther and Jack and Sue and Margaret are out of town. And I must get down to a more definite working plan. It would be excusable—my one novel and nothing else a year—if I had a fine time in all my wasted time, or if I didn't have many ideas. But I have so many complete ideas ahead and so many unfinished plays, stories, etc., that my confusion grows greater and greater every time I'm in the mood to work. I ought to clear up a few of these things and my mind would be a little better off.

I wonder if the reason I can't get into my play isn't that I want to do that novel instead. I want the man to be at heart a simple peasant, with an inborn passion for cattle, farmland, soil, stable smells, that is his only life. What has bothered me was doing an inarticulate type when my whole success is in emotions and sensitive grades. But he is not dumb—he is deeply moved by earth and sunsets and all the simple primitive things—alone in the woods, hunting on the marshes, etc. This needs the same elaborate charting and constructive preparation that *Dance Night* did—

unlike *Tenth Moon*. John says *Tenth Moon* won't sell and nobody wants to buy it. I doubt if I'll know whether it's out or not when it appears.

August 6: Went to Dover Furnace to see the Group.* Albert Bein, a queer, sensitive little guy with a wooden leg was up there writing a play. Cheryl [Crawford] says he's a real playwright only he doesn't know how to write a play. He was raised in a boy's reformatory, lost his leg riding freights.

Maxwell Anderson's just finished a play, "Both Your Houses," a political burlesque which he gave me to read. It was very amusing but curious in that it began like a tough fist fighting the world—an attack, you would have said—and then you saw it was not so much a fist as a ball of cotton and even at that it was not knocking at the world but at the door in a genial social call.

A rehearsal of my play proved excellent—I could not ask for a better cast—but a first reading of Jack's "Success Story" sounded confused and miserable, considering that it is a magnificent play. The actors held a meeting of great indignation afterward and all united in saying it was terrible and I was sick over it, knowing how hard he'd worked and what a tremendous play it really was but what good is that when it is only apparent to a few close friends?

But Cheryl, Lee and Harold† continued to say it was fine, fortunately, in the face of all this talk, saying actors always were mad at their vehicles. It seems they are like publishers, regarding the author and his work as nasty stumbling blocks between them and the public, and if they could only brush aside this horrid obstacle and act (or publish) freely without the barrier of writers' words, everything would be fine.

Must raise money today quick.

August 11: Anxious to reduce down to 130.

Very queer how once I get in a low state everything contributes to making me feel inferior—a curious unveiling of all sources of inferiority—as uncomfortable and almost weepily self-conscious as if they'd asked me to dance and I was stepping all over them with my drawers

---

*Dover Furnace, New York, north of Manhattan, where the Group Theatre was in residence for the summer.

†Lee Strasberg and Harold Clurman, the other two founders and directors of the Group Theatre.

falling off. I must remember not to drink again—at least until I get in a lighter frame of mind—or I will weep all over people.

I think this book will be a freak—it will scarcely be noticed for months and then someone will give it a big discourse and it will get a belated _cheer. I wish I could get underway with either my novel or a play. This summer has been a futile marking time—I hope someday to be able to finish a novel and take an immediate trip instead of always having my advance foresworn and dragging along without energy to work or to cook up new ideas or even money to have a good time. Wish I could go to Dover Furnace for this week if only to work and get new thoughts. Domesticity crowds me.

Fortunately the old painful despair of waking has left and a morbid calm takes its place. This shamed self-consciousness might go—the feeling that everyone who knows me looks on me as a failure and false alarm and everyone who doesn't know me looks on me as a fat, queer-looking person.

August 15: An unexpected sensation of hope today—a conviction that something positive has taken place and its effects will slowly make themselves known. These feelings I have from year to year I believe in utterly—whether it's a private antenna which catches the turn of the wind or whether it's a glandular or creative process I don't know—perhaps the ghostly arterial system which is the creative flow suddenly goes in one direction as far as it can and then, like a blocked river, must flow the other way.

Since sophomore college days I don't remember ever being in such a feeble nervous state, ready to weep over a blot, a lost pencil sharpener, a pound gained. I sleep a lot but it doesn't seem to refresh me and I'm almost in the state I was before my sickness in 1929—so ragged that if Joe's back wasn't in such shape I would beg him on my knees to take me away somewhere—that it's almost life and death. Oh God, why can't I be independent? I earn enough. At least Joe can manipulate his finances to take care of his private desires.

There is certainly something the matter when I am forced to confess that for the past year I am bored almost to the screaming point. Mr. and Mrs. Jones visit Mr. and Mrs. Smith, Mr. and Mrs. Smith return the call, and the doughy, numbing routine of bourgeois matrimony continues— blah!

The reason I write is because there is no one to talk to and I might as well build up a completely private life.

August 17: I begin to take an interest in life again. A slight hangover is the cause.

August 18: Very happy and easy now for no reason. Completely confident of next year. Planning novel. Can't remember being so happy in years and utterly confident—all with no basis. I think I collect friends out of the ether.

Wind is blowing all my papers. How I loathe wind! It makes one simply frenzied.

August 19: Jack came back from Dover Furnace and Sue started big fight which went every place. Very queer the way people get more jealous of a *thing*—like someone's absorption in work—than of a person. Rightly.

August 20: Drove up to Provincetown with Lawsons. It was grand—in spite of Lawsons' continued fight—to see all the people I like best together again. Everyone talks about the Group. Jack is thinking and talking so much more clearly and directly than ever before owing, he says, to Trotsky and a study of Marxian theories applied to creative work. The business of thinking straight—what do you want to prove and what type of protagonist will best prove your idea and is the idea sound to begin with?

In trying to follow what Jack pointed out for clear thinking in my new works planned, what do I want to prove in this "Farmer Boy" novel? Answer: that a simple, clear person is forced to serve a cause distasteful to him but because of his simplicity does not see where he changed from proletarian to capitalist. I wish to show that these labels and classifications are external only, but that the external label slowly forces its way inside if you are to be happy. Chris' tragedy is that he remained a barefooted farmer boy through his capitalist career—a friend of the workman, against capitalism always as he had been taught by his father and did not know the mask was on him until the laborers hooted and stoned his car in the street.

August 29: To town. Began plotting Christopher Bennett's story. Plan very different from *Tenth Moon*. Jack's system of Marxian criticism and his insistence on right ideology before work is attempted very helpful on this. For that reason I should like to dedicate it to him.* He actually has influenced me enormously in all my work since *She Walks In Beauty*. I have talked over all my plans with him and each time he knows exactly, from the most casual outline, what I must watch out for and what main direction I must stick to. That is why, as I grow older and more egotistical, more centered in my work, I would sacrifice almost anyone for a little hour with him going over these quite selfish matters.

It is impossible to talk of things so important casually with other friends. Coby believes that nice people don't get so vulgarly absorbed in their own work, that a measure of lightness and good taste should be preserved by a *real* artist—in fact that to be really a decent person socially one must be a dilettante. Losing oneself (and, incidentally, everybody else) in one's work is a little too conspicuous and a good artist surely would never be willing to appear ridiculous.

Harold Stearns reviews my book in next Sunday *Tribune*—an excellent, understanding review crediting me with a fusing of the new stream-of-consciousness school and the directly realistic. This is definitely what I set out to do—to crash down new dimensions in character work, to make and know my people so that their past, present, future, wishes, regrets, dreams, and actualities were enclosed spirally in a conch-shell sort of growth, all braided simultaneously with time into one fused portrait which was not the image but the reality.

Jack and Sue came over to cottage after supper and we swam at beach. I wonder if Jack and Sue can ever patch it up again. He is in that death-state of all love—fond indifference—and I believe it's all completely over her own stupidity, hanging in utter mental and emotional dependence on him. Nothing or nobody outside yourself should be so important. I never believed in trusting my head so sweetly in the lion's mouth. A lion's a lion, I always say.

Denys Wortman the other night had a strange little man on hand. This one told anecdotes of greats he had known and after a while it developed that he had known them through serving processes on them. Then he told of the sinister, grisly details (with great enjoyment)—how he served a process on this dentist, how foxy he had to be, as if he were a Scotland Yard man.

Story Of A Country Boy was in fact dedicated to Jacques LeClercq.

Beach party with John Herrman, Josie Herbst, the Lawsons, etc. Very insane.

September 6: Sue all day. Discusses taking her problem to psychoanalyst, for Christ's sake. A loose-brained, amiable, lazy, racketeering Southern girl, despising the type and being it with a vengeance. Not her own fault—because she's so flabby, for one thing. Not one thing she *wants* and want is what the spine is made of. She can't want even Jack or she would go to some trouble to be desirable to him.

September 8: Went to Cafe Royale on East Side with Mary Lena and Harry Lissfelt, later to funny little Gasthaus on East 10th. Mary Lena is one of few friends I have who has as good a head as mine—even better in its concentration in some ways. I looked at her in the little barroom, so like the German bar she used to go with Pax—so like, surely, so many little cafes she went with him. And all I could think of was "Her lover is dead! Her lover is dead!" as if these bleak words were printed on her forehead and behind everything she said.

September 9: The Philadelphia *Record* says *Tenth Moon* is like the sound of a flute heard across water at twilight, like a lark at sunrise . . .

One important key in this new novel: the *new* Ohio must be the keynote—the dizziness of speed through broad auto highways, hot dog stations, not the tranquil hayfields of my recollection. That was one problem with *Dance Night*—an arrested background. Backgrounds should be fluid to be alive. And Morry was not real—he was observed. Even Elsinore, who seemed more real, was observed. Chris will be a failure too, unless I can be him as well as I could be Blaine Decker.

September 15: To dinner at Sam's with Jack and later to Empire State Building. It was divinely beautiful and strange up there. Clouds, as white as if the sky were baby blue, swam beneath us and stars were below us. They glittered through the clouds and the town lay spread out in its spangles like Christmas presents waiting to be opened, its clangor sifted through space into a whispering silence. It held a secret and when suddenly letters flamed together in the sky you felt—ah, so that's it. "Sunshine Biscuits," the message of the city.*

---

*This vignette was developed into one of the finest set pieces in *Turn, Magic Wheel.*

September 16: Jack was surprised at my organization of notes in "Young Christopher"—all the result of his talk to me, though he had no idea how I would translate his words into my private needs. Unconscious advice is all I can take.

Heard that Farrar & Rinehart wish to cut contract on my next book in two. *Tenth Moon* only sold 2,200. Evelyn Scott wrote me it was a "complete work of art." Carl Van Doren says "natural perfection of proportion and execution." Farrar can never sell my sort of book and my next one shouldn't just be thrown in their wastebasket as the other two were. I would feel better with another publisher.

September 19: To Arthur Garfield Hays' where in a solemn little group these grave problems were under weighty discussion:

A) Mrs. Hays' daring and radical theory that the law should allow one to put a cancer victim out of his misery at his request.

B) Mr. Hays' theory that many writers were becoming radical-minded (in the last few hours, you would have thought).

C) What is the difference between Communism and Socialism?

Francis and I got convulsed and could scarcely believe such a brilliant assembly could be so sincerely feebleminded.

Dwight had me do story. I have no feeling for Dwight anymore—his affectionate telegrams humiliate me by their thinly-veneered desire for me to do something for him. He is unscrupulous and heartless and thoroughly materialistic.

September 25: Telephone still off. Curious about financial disabilities. They are a hard symbol to be gratefully clutched as a legitimate source of misery when the real source is some emotional or spiritual disability or disappointment.

September 26: Jack's play opened.* It was by far the best play I'd ever seen and the audience was tremendously impressed, except for those who resent a natural emotional language. I believe Jack's greatest contribution to drama is a truthful language for emotion rather than the accepted stage language for emotion.

---

* "Success Story," produced by the Group Theatre.

September 29: I wake each day with a panicky grateful feeling—"So far, so good"—because for almost five weeks I've been fairly normally sane, and I realize how long and how incredibly morbid, despondent and panicky I have been for the past four or five years, ready to scream with despair over matters which may come up any minute again. I regard myself with cautious apprehension as one looks on a wild beast under a drug—*so far* the drug is working fine. I never knew before I was afraid of myself and of the black misery I could open up to myself.

October 3: Drove to Baltimore with Sue, Margaret, and Esther to see opening of Jack's Guild show "The Pure in Heart." I could no longer struggle against the conviction that here was a tawdry, incredibly stale (even in 1890), cheap, dull show. I was ashamed of Jack for having written it but more ashamed for his stupidity in thinking he could put such crap over on even the most moronic audience. His "Success Story," which he believed over an audience's head, is getting to be a hit. I think what you yourself believe in has the best chance of getting over—an artist's own conviction is the most convincing thing in the world, and no harder to get over than a lie.

What has struck me so much in the fugitive glimpses I've had of it is the loneliness of success and how important it is to realize that success is a stronger test of one's real friends than failure—and harder to sympathize with.

October 7: Decided to do Madonna play quickly—using all the selfish mothers I know as base for it—the futile, idle women that America is so full of.

October 19: Rehearsals started.* The whole play was so cluttered by unrelated detail that you couldn't make head nor tail of it. Cheryl has the same faults that Terry Helburn has—meticulous detail, absolute verisimilitude on minor matters, with scenes lost in a welter of detail. It looked muddled to a positively inspired pitch.

November 20: The final *Times* review of *Tenth Moon* made me realize how discouraged I am about my work—rigidly classified as "accurate photog-

---

*The Group Theatre had begun preparing "Big Night" for production. Cheryl Crawford was the original director, later replaced by Harold Clurman.

raphy" when a study of feeling (as this is) could not possibly be done by photography, nor could those people be so cheerfully listed as "small town types." I do not see where I am going. Apparently with each better book my reputation shrinks—understandable in writers who simply turn out stuff for a market, but I sincerely believe each of my books is more or less unique. I don't see at all that I am a "regional writer."

Rehearsing the play is depressing, too—it shows it up as nothing much and certainly my fast dwindling name will be worse than dwindled when it opens (if). I don't see how I can bear the deathly depression of another lonely, discouraging year like last year, and already it seems begun. I feel almost too tired to take it and can think of no philosophic adjustment that would make it easier—reasoning and clear thinking make it worse.

Saw "Firebird" last night—a beautiful, deftly contrived production of nothing.

November 23: Saw Rachel Crothers' play "When Ladies Meet"—seldom seen so many fine, clear-eyed women speaking nobility in every line. A good, well-built show nonetheless. It made my new Madonna play seem plausible at last. The treatment—a study of lines only as against Group treatment—showed that comedy of manners should be a line study and allow the audience to comment and fill in. For the actor to comment and fill in ruins the comedy. I think I could do my play now very rapidly—keep Jojo in country perhaps.

Realized as I worked on novel the other day that combining responsibility for child and writing seriously was impossible. Also there is a question whether making myself indispensable to my son is of real value to him. I think the next step should be a house in country where he could attend school and I could see him weekends. Then, when I get this play finished (about December 21), hire a secretary for a week, have her type corrections in play and then make copies, also copy my various short stories. Life is too short not to make use of things which simplify work—to use creative energy to do diddling tasks.

November 25: Had cocktail party. Went on to a place on MacDougal Alley —from which some perfect stranger had just called up and said "Come over here, Miss Powell, and bring all your friends." I did but they were surprised to see so many—14. Jack and Frances Mayer and I combed the kitchen liquor supply.

November 28: Afternoon celebrating birthday with Genevieve T. I have seen a number of good motion pictures lately and have grown immensely interested in them as possibility for new technique. They are beginning to use more and more their own special facilities (particularly for comedy) and so many dramatic items are possible in them—why do they limit themselves to the limitations of a stage play? They ought to travel more—a company ought to be on the go and use real houses, real town backgrounds, real people. Photography never advanced when people and clients came to their studios, rose in hand and fixed smile—it was when they got real pictures, snaps, genuine types, real lighting effects.

On my hangover I had a magnificent motion picture idea which I outlined and am convinced beyond shadow of doubt is a knockout. Can be done and will be sold—quickly, too. I know.

December 4: Rehearsal of play for backers and movie people. All felt play was good—production bad. Stella [Adler] was poor as usual, though to me the whole thing seemed so much better than usual that I felt better about it. Jack didn't like my movie idea but I still think it's good.

December 7: Jack was in and the Dos Passos' and we went to the Workers' Theatre. Went to Louis' on 45th Street and had a swell time except I was sick on five Tom Collins. It seems to me I could be happy just with Dos and Jack as friends—the two people to be lost on a desert island with.

December 9: Although Jack and Francis say production is lousy, I do not feel discouraged since the comedy came out so much better than it ever did. It still is not played nervously enough.

December 12: Jack called up and said they weren't coming here for cocktails as planned because they wanted to save me all that trouble; I'd been so fine about things, it wasn't fair. I was touched by this nobility but in the afternoon the Passos' and Faragohs came in and gaily explained that Jack was at Berenice's. I don't see why he had to call me to make up such a big lie. We went to Ticino's and to Lewis Gannett's. I must have drawn a blank—I don't remember crying all night as Joe says I did.

December 21: Rehearsal of "Big Night." Jack came to it (with his first wife's son) because Cheryl wanted changes made in second act and thought he could do it. He thought it looked much better—personally I've passed the time when I can criticize it. If other people like it, I do—if they don't, I don't. It's up to an audience now.

In the evening Jack and I went to see the Behrman play, "Biography," with Ina Claire, who is perfect for Jack's new play "Gentlewoman" and incidentally perfect for my Madonna play. Later to Louis' where we discussed the drama of all things with Lawrence Langner and Lee Simonson.

December 22: Very queer about material things and avarice. There are people whose lives are dedicated to acquiring what they never had, then there are those who are only active in a greedy way in hanging on to what they have. Jack has a little of both, but I have the latter. I've never gotten over my surprise of owning what I do—and with each added convenience comes an accompanying passion for hanging onto it. Certainly I would be stirred to even a Hollywood job if there was acute danger of losing this apartment, these servants, the piano, etc. The one thing I will work myself to death for is the protection of my own laziness.

December 25: To a party at Cheryl's. Decided to do a rowdy modernist version of Aristophanes' "The Knights," which Cheryl was eager about—have hecklers, stooges, big placards through the house, "The Theater is Propaganda" across the curtain. Have the senate in back of house; sausages rushed through audience; passed-out Cleon and Sausage-Seller have fight of swear words across audience. Dress in stylized Greek costume, shirts, etc. Have scenes described in play actually take place either by marionettes or by movies, have music, have people sell things between acts like a burlesque show.

December 27: Group had party at 101 Seventh Avenue for Jack. As dull as if there were speeches.

December 28: Faragohs had dumb party for Lawsons farewell. More upchuck over bathroom, more broken bottles, more wild futile drunkenness than I've seen in years. Coby was drunker than anyone and curiously enough was exactly like Joe—talking about cosmic rhythms, basic ideals, integrity, etc.—the same inner innocence, pleasing when sober, but Christ-how-tiresome when glorified in alcohol. He made Joe seem like a model drinker but anyway I think drinking is getting to be a really terrifying thing so far as Joe is concerned.

December 29: Lawsons went to Hollywood for six months. Tinged with my regret is the feeling that now I can get down to work. I am too fond of them to work much when they are around.

December 31: Saw "Dinner at Eight" and enjoyed the click-click of the machinery—old, tried theater, even though there was nothing to be said. For the first time I saw that "Big Night" might seem amateur playwriting—feeble and untheatrical, and even its comedy might come out banal and amateur. I realized, too, that I have no preparation made for a flop or the stupid sort of dramatic criticism Jack got on his other plays.

1933

January 2: To the Abbey Theatre. "Far-off Hills" homely, unpretentious comedy with perfect human satire but a dowdy optimism that was as offensive as any other type of propaganda. I begin to understand that the theater is always propaganda in [entry breaks off]

January 3: Shopping for dresses for cast. The girls want "tawdry, funny clothes" such as the characters in the play would wear. Their idea of businessmen's wives is a businessman's wife's idea of an actress. I am getting crotchety at their moral, superior attitude about the play: the people seem to me to be anybody, only their high points are exaggerated beyond normal. Certainly "cheap" is not the word for the lowest human common denominator any more than "brutal" is the word for truth.

January 6: Dos dropped in. He had just finished his play "Fortune Heights," laid in garage or filling station. It sounds swell. I try not to be influenced by him or Jack too much but I cannot help feeling there is something in their praise of my strictly female writing ("Women At Four" —*She Walks*—*Tenth Moon*—*Bride's House*)—and their crying down of my bigger efforts such as *Dance Night*. In a great deal of *Dance Night*, chiefly the end, my material forced me into a limited, matter-of-fact style and angle which is not my own, is in fact cramping. I have so much more ease in dealing with emotions than factual backgrounds.

Lila's book should be full of delicate sharp outlines of New York of today—the sharp detail as seen by one who sees it seldom but then with desperate longing. The Empire State—Coney Island—the Ambassador or Waldorf—the pattern of New York. I think I could do five pages a day on Lila—and she probably wouldn't be more than 150 to 170 pages anyway.

January 13: These dress rehearsals of my play before Jewish societies or Socialists are amazing. I never realized how unrelated to reality our so-called realism is—even an apartment furnished by Macy's like their own makes them furious, except for the few people who honestly enjoy honesty. As they are held up to the mirror so the author is, too, and for the first time I see what I have written and I know what I think and what I can do.

The Group has put on a careful production with no knowledge whatever of the characters—as they might put on a picture of Siberian home life—made up bit by bit of exact details but the actual realism of the whole missing. People have one drink and therefore they are drunk. People are unconsciously selfish or cruel, therefore they are consciously selfish or cruel. People strive blindly and vaguely for something, therefore they are intelligently striving for a definite thing. This heavy-footed literalism weighted the play down but on the other hand was not distortion and was better than the sweetening that a lighter production would have given it. I wish, in fairness to the play and in vengeance to others, that the Group could have laid their chilly hands on "Private Lives" or "Once in a Lifetime," and by similar literal translation of lines made "Uncle Tom's Cabins" of them all.

This was the day hours were spent debating about the curtains—whether or not they'd ruin the play. On Saturday as the stage was being torn apart again I remembered the importance of the curtains and saw how silly they were, of how little moment details were when the essential base was wrong.

These are dreadful days—one goes about in a daze, not afraid but numb, waiting for the bell—incapable of any feeling till then.

January 17: Play opened.

January 25: The reviews were almost unanimously angry and denunciatory. At first I was dashed, then the accumulation of stupidity challenged me and even flattered me—to be attacked as a menace to the theater was the first real sign that I had a contribution to make there. It was like finding out you could hurt the elephant—the only defeat or failure is in being ignored or being told you have appeased it. In either case you are lost—just so much hay for the elephant. I was not hay; I was the barbed wire in it, and so I made far more impression.

My plays I always felt were of slight consequence—I knew they were good of their kind but not as important as my novels. After this I respect my dramatic power far more than the other. I believe that if the Group Theatre is remembered in 20 years it will be as the producer of my first play.

The theater has a harsh truth about it that appeals to my own desire for truth. It doesn't soften its blows or its cruelties for me and I need not pull my punches for it. It is a worthy foe—no false excuses or restraints—no *politesse* but back and forth honest blows. It is an open battlefield, not a discreet exchange of notes, and the old Sherman fighting blood smells raw meat—always a damn sight more exciting than the faint fragrance of the pressed rose.

The Group took it off before I knew it and this was the third shock I'd had from them—a shock to find people you'd come to believe in are yellow-livered amateurs who talk of their ideals for a new theater and their independence from the ignorant group of present critics and then are absolutely destroyed by a bad review and the chance of its not being a box-office hit. I said this about them before but later came to believe in their protestations, so I was shocked to see their natural yellow streak and the complete lie on which they are based.

The asininity of the critics—they always seemed unusually bad judges of a play but I always believed one or two of them had a grain of intelligence—amazed me. "These are not people one would care to meet. They are horrid. One comes to the theater to advance socially, and how can one if you have to associate with your equals instead of your social and mental superiors?" It was like old ladies on weekly county papers saying "The test of a good novel is 'are these people such as you would like in your own drawing room?'"—if not, then it isn't a good book.

After closing the show Saturday night, LeClercq and Mary Lena and Joe and I went up to Tony's and Heywood Broun sat with us. A big blonde came up and insisted on sitting down. "Last night I was out all night—at 8 this morning my ex-husband walked into the apartment and by 8:25 I'd laid him and laid him gorgeously," she said, clutching my hand. "And do you know why I laid him, honey? It was because I was crazy about another man and I had to have somebody." She said she was out on $1000 bail for killing a man.

I am in my usual winter state of amazed loneliness though by this time I should be adjusted to a life free of Andrews, Chambers, Lawsons, Dos Passos, etc. Certainly even when the Lawsons are here, we are in no sense on easy terms. Sue seems definitely a closed page—we scream at each other through carefully locked doors but even then can establish no external semblances of our former friendship. I vary in hating and despising Jack (for his mental and emotional cowardice in his work and in his life) to admiring him beyond reason (for his occasional flashes of heroic courage or strength). Both phases are beyond the power of most men but, as one grows older, sustained honesty compels one's respect; the balancing of extreme deceit with extreme candor seems theatrical—the two phases only cancel each other.

Dos has been so sweet and kind during this whole play mess—he is the only person aside from Joe and Coby who hasn't made things worse by manner or speech. Most people are furious at me for not lying down and screaming so they can forgive me and have a friendly pleasure in seeing the punishment sink in—the Olympian privilege of providing big-hearted consolation. Failing in this—I persist in regarding the whole thing as near a success as I've ever had—they decide to take digs.

I wish I could get this novel swinging along. Since I have no other immediate plans I don't see why I shouldn't be up to page 50 at least by the end of February—90 by March 30—140 by April 30—190 by May 30—235 by June 30—290 by July 30, finish—330—by August 30—publish December 15.

In the Brevoort at lunch a fat, petulant, pretty woman implored a sleek, foxy Jewish man of 50. "Let me be yours again for the next few years—I'll be nice—I'll change—I know you think I'm frumpy but I'm going to change. I'm going to branch out. I'm going to get a blue cape and a hat to match—you'll be sorry if you don't take me back." The Brevoort manager stood at all the tables saying "how-do-you-do?" and "how's-the-steak?" She was just saying "I'm going to change and look wonderful—I'm going to get thin—be like I used to when you liked me so much" and sailing into a huge steak when he stood there. "And how is the steak, Madame?" "Oh, fine," she said.

February 2: Louise has been away all week and answering Jojo's questions, cooking three meals, airing him, and seeing and doing no one or nothing else has played hell with my frazzled nerves. Scarcely no work done and a state of positively pathological fear of going out or seeing people for fear they'd clout me. On the other hand a horror of being alone—in fact a thoroughly bad state to be in.

I realize more and more how instinctively pessimistic I am of all human kindness—since I am always so bowled over by it—and am never surprised by injustice, malice or personal attack.

February 19: Retouched and retitled three short stories—all three to eight years old—for Claire Leonard* to type. Everyone pressing us for money and the chances of getting away not as convincing even as they were twelve years ago. Even the dentist calls and asks me to bring up a check when I come.

February 23: To Coby's. Alec Brook, Peggy Bacon, Niles Spencer and Betty Spencer were there—all slightly lit and anxious to tell dirty stories but no one could remember any. "The best one," stuttered Niles, "is the one—well, I'd better not tell it—it's pretty bad—ladies would get insulted—anyway there's a lot of French in it and so on—I really forget. It isn't so funny, anyways, it's the way it's told and in the end the fellow says 'Someday you'll go too far.' Ha ha." Coby knew one in Cockney only he'd forgotten the end and besides couldn't speak Cockney.

To a party at Brentano's. A banker named Dickinson was leaving and everyone said good-bye. And so did I. "Good-bye" he said as he shook hands. "I haven't had the pleasure." "Good-bye" I said. "You wouldn't think it was any fun anyway."

February 25: Letter from Jack.†

This *Adolphe* of Benjamin Constant's is perfect in its psychology. "People reveal themselves in their absurdities and then, uncloaked, feel that the writer has betrayed a confidence they had reposed in him." And, again, "Ellenore seems to have her unique social position take the place of a mental originality." La Rochefoucauld said of someone like Constant—

---

*Claire Leonard served as secretary to the Group Theatre.

†None of the many letters Lawson apparently wrote to Powell have turned up among her papers.

"They would never have loved at all if they had not heard love talked about." And: "We spoke of nothing but love, for fear of speaking of something else." And: "People were against her because she had not inspired her lover with more consideration for her sex."

So tired that not one bit of work done on novel this week but its contours are filling out in my mind. Madeleine and Chris* begin to approach reality of existence instead of the reality of imagination. I am amazed how poorly I have fed my so-called real characters heretofore, how meagerly I have equipped them with the life signs I myself test others' characters with. Chris and Joy need a lot of breathing on—some features from known life—before their simplicity will be plausible. I hope to combine here the objectiveness of *Dance Night* with the subjectiveness of *Tenth Moon*. I feel that I can break a little further through pages into life. I hope in this to have a new freedom, to be able to use my complete language. How stingily I preserve my own self for my own life and give nothing that I might miss to my work.

March 10: Ann called up and said that little gadget I wrote sold to *New Yorker* for $70. It would be strange if, after all these years of having my writer's reputation so different from my personal one, the two should finally merge. It has seemed obvious to me for years that I could do light writing better than many of the people now earning good monies at it but I have been consistently turned down and sweating at it spoils it, of course. There's no sense in working for comedy—it either succeeds or is *not*. But now it seems to me—having failed completely in all serious work, barely getting a reputation for average, let alone anything else—with this encouragement in the far-too-easy-for-me light touch I believe I may change—see what I have, inasmuch as it seems to be superior of its slight kind, and be opportunistic from now on.

March 19: Finished Act I of play.

What a pleasure to work on a play after being tied in knots over a novel. (It is true the knots come afterward.) I work sometimes eight or ten hours on a play and go out for the evening too. It is refreshing work that I do enjoy, as much fun as a party with amusing new people, and not half the strain.

*In *Story Of A Country Boy*.

66

March 22: A fire on Broadway and 8th with black smoke rolling over the block like black plush. Even after four hours the firemen were still working. It must have been a clothing store for in the back, amid charred rafters and wrecked furniture, two firemen in great oilskins were trying on brand new straw hats; one big man had a tiny Panama stuck on his head.

March 28: Chester Miller, the very amusing White Russian came in for tea—also Mary Lena, who was unpleasant and bitter. I think she has a sharp, shrewd brain and a thoroughly self-centered, tight, stingy spirit. She won't allow herself to like people or love them unless they first bow and make offers of devotion—five cents worth for five cents, no more, no less, because her innate gentility and small Methodist respectability won't allow her to be in the horrid position of having opened herself up and not been properly received. I understand it a little in male/female relations but not for the world at large.

Went to Tallulah Bankhead's "Forsaking All Others."

March 29: Went to "The Cherry Orchard" with Coby and saw Nazimova. A marvelous play due—as in most Chekhov—to his making a character live with a few lines. I still find more beauty and richness in old Russian literature and drama than any other country's.

April 1: Finished Act II. Went to dinner at Y. K. Smith's, a really fine, beautiful person with no faults except the faults of a precious metal made up without sufficient alloy to prove its superiority. His Russian wife, Julie, is a curious, complete person—to say you like her is nonsense she would not tolerate. She is charged with power—the sort which usually finds outlet in driving young men to do something, to be something. But instead she does things herself—embroideries, sculpture, playwriting. To be married to her would be as satisfactory as being married to a proven philosophy and would give a restless, skeptical man the same security. They are happy together in an active, constructive, stimulating way. He, probably long kept from using his honest gifts by his too high standards and fear of public ridicule (as well as by his own physical weakness—he has T. B.), finds in her an engine to carry out his own desire to do and be part of doing—he helps and criticizes as she does, so has outlet for his creative gifts as well as satisfaction of seeing things done fast and, even to his critical mind, worthily. She is a ruthless surgeon of people, throwing out everything but the bare essence of the person (and that too if it looks poor to her) and I believe she is a savage but infallible judge.

April 3: Chester Miller came in for tea with Margaret De Silver. He stayed forever. I got very tight—I don't quite see how—and found it was possible to see double really.

I want to travel very badly—England or Spain or Africa.

April 4: My feelings go on as unaccountable to me as the earth's interior movements. My resolute defenses against my own weaknesses function so well I do not know which is real person, the defense or the weakness. Apparently, I feel a distinct failure in my last public works—my entire publishing with Farrar and Rinehart and my plays. Caring less about my plays, I am able to go on with them but I can never write so good a novel as *Dance Night*. Nobody thought it was of the slightest value. *Tenth Moon* was slop—fine writing and nothing else, but its very nothingness should have recommended it to the intellectuals if not to a public.

I would like to finish this play and then be able to go away (possibly to Mt. Sinai for two weeks) and finish up Lila. She needn't be more than 150 pages long—I could do it in a month and finish off my Farrar and Rinehart obligations. Besides, it fits in with my present attitude toward my writing: continued faith in its value is dogged proof of amateur egotism (they can't *all* be wrong in ignoring me as not up to the Isa Glenns, Ellen Glasgows, Storm Jamesons and other crap writers) and so it's possible my own standards are at fault. Therefore I write now as I did at 22 years old—to find a public somewhere for something, if it's only in *Snappy Stories* or *The New Yorker*. Write *Tenth Moon* crap if that's as much reality as people can stand.

April 18: Esther came back and we went to "Design For Living" again and tonight to "Strike Me Pink." Got $60 for English rights to Bermuda story. Shopped with Esther and Margaret and they made me get red dress and hat I loathe since it can do me no good. One dress for the year, and that one red. I am so sick and depressed—money so hard to get that I weep over each penny spent for no pleasure. I make plenty—$135 to $175 a month—but all of it goes to maids or deficits and I am sick physically at this unexpected $60 (which could have at least bought me something to wear) going into that. I am sick of everything anyway—waste, futility, failure afresh with every day.

May 1: Started rewriting third act which seemed stuck on 18th page. Expect to finish it by Sunday. Then work on novel furiously for a week—do at least 6000 words so I can see where I am and get on right basis again—have 100 pages done by July 1st. Our three week June vacation ought to set me up 80 pages. Steady work. Then finished by September 15.

The novel is my normal breath—I never feel I've done anything on plays or short stories and in working on them I feel insecure, unsatisfied, hysterically delighted at best. The Novel is my lawful married mate. I miss it when I go in my study at night. I miss the loneliness of a room with only me and my novel in it at midnight—the loneliness and yet complete peace.

May 5: The shock of my life today. This little tiny constant pain in my heart, the X-ray and Dr. Witt says, is a tumor or cyst over it and between the lungs. Nothing to worry about, he says, just a question of waiting. And waiting for what? Waiting for it to grow enough to cut out and only one man can do it—one Dr. Hoya. Nothing to worry about! Just waiting for that. I walked down Madison Avenue not looking in shops for the first time because I thought it extravagant to buy or even want things for so short a while. It doesn't matter what the corpse wears.

Later I realized what he said had already been true many months—and nothing had happened. Nothing probably would.

May 9: Finished play "Jig-Saw."

May 16: Took play to Ann.

Jojo wrote a very funny play which I named for him "Fur Instance." He then played it and took all the parts himself.

May 17: Ann says people in play—those gay, charming people—are all so *sordid*.

May 21: Dos in, a little bent still with rheumatic fever but undoubtedly one of the gentlest, sweetest, finest characters the world has known—as instinctively and unpremeditatedly a fine person as Esther Andrews is.

May 22: Submitted "Jig-Saw" play to Terry Helburn and called up William Harris who was so lovely about declaring how much he wanted to read it that I was touched. In the evening Harry Gousha* drove us in his fantastically sumptuous new Cadillac up to Bear Mountain, his radio going all the way—Amos & Andy over George Washington Bridge, "You Made Me Love You" going through the Storm King country and a military band from a submarine drill 300 miles away going through Croton.

June 1: Would like to get through to Page 90 by Monday. No reason why not since I'm doing nothing else out here beyond reading a very little and cooking. Work from 4 to 9 hours a day on book which is, after all, the only way to get anything done, although I'm a little apprehensive of overspinning. I can't tell any more whether the facility with which I write means a certain deadness of talent or a more professional command of my medium. My instinct is to believe the former.

June 2: I read Georgette Carneal's book *The Great Day* and through half of it I was struck by the masterly sweep of her material, the pungent smell of New York, the prostitution of minds and bodies that success seems to demand. But, at the end of 437 pages, I believed the book was as cheap as its people, the attitude that there was no possibility of human nobility—no striving, even foolish, except for money—seemed not cynical but stupid. And the sentimentalization of prostitution—"I did it for my mother," as if the fault were in the system and not in the man or woman —seems to me always a tawdry, weak falsehood. There is no one in this book like me or the people I like—that is, people who selfishly refuse to suffer any indignity, humiliation or labor unless it helps them do their job, not win sheer money. Whoring of mind and body can be a jolly, zestful end in itself but it is cheapened by those who find sentimental, lying excuses for it.

June 4: Wrote 45 pages in the last eight or nine days—more than ever before in my life—an average six week's work for me.

June 5: Into New York to get Jojo. Found out that the Guild (Teresa Helburn) and Brock Pemberton both felt things could be done with this

---

*Harry Gousha was Joseph Gousha's brother.

new play. I was touched by their interest since so few people feel I can do anything. I wonder if a possible easy production and some success could come of it—those things *do* happen to some people and they aren't immediately afterward stricken dead.

June 6: Today I posed eating a pineapple at my typewriter for the J. Walter Thompson Agency—the funniest thing I ever heard of, so funny I couldn't help doing it even though Coby Gilman thought it was a hideous lowering of myself. People came and went all day—Edgar,* Adolph Dehn, Al Saxe the little Agit-Prop boy, etc.—and I wondered how I ever did any work when my days in New York are so cluttered with people.

June 7: Delighted to dash out to Mt. Sinai. Physically worn out by people—they leave you so little of yourself that you must hide it before the birds pick that final grain, too.

June 11: Esther and Canby drove out. Terrific storms here all the time. I have been writing poetry so I must be feeling young and energetic to have this old habit bubbling up again all unwarranted.

June 15: Sold my play "Jig-Saw" to Theatre Guild and received $500 for option—also sold short thing to *New Yorker* for $70. Went to tea for Bernard Sobel at Pierre's; Ogden Nash and I got tight and pigged all the cocktails we could find. I paid Francis $100 of the $650 I owe him, paid Louise $100, Marie $50, Dr. Hornbeck $20, Mr. Davis $20, Joe $60, Ten Eyck $39.50. Funny how little you can do with $500—barely stave off lawsuits here and there.

June 18: Came in with Joe and had dinner at 49th Street Grill.

Trying to copy my novel. It is like *Dance Night*—whenever I have perspective on it and leisure to consider it I am appalled at the ambitiousness of the theme and certain of my inability to carry it through. It should never be weighed or appraised; I should do it blindly, bit by bit, since the plans are so immense they paralyze me.

June 25: To Canton to see Phyllis. I am amazed at the change in the Midwest—it is exactly like Hollywood or Forest Hills. The radio, the war, the

---

*Edgar Pocock, the husband of Powell's sister Mabel.

automobile have leveled off the entire country—the only different place is still New York (and that the bohemia of New York since Park Avenue is so much glorified Westchester which is so much enlarged Shelby or Galion).

There is not the anxious "striving" to be like society that used to characterize the Ohio little towns. Their possessions are more truly a gauge of their financial stations than the city person's possessions, which are merely a testimony to his glibness with creditors.

The first day I was here "Oley Olson," the Swede (who is really a Dane and named Charlie Nelson) sent word he wanted to see me. 20 years ago he took me to school on a handcar down the railroad track. He came in at eight in the morning, all cleaned up, and told me of his own particular hell. 15 years in the steel mills at $20 to $30 a day until he keeled over giggling and with numb fits, his savings spent on doctors, finally submitting to a test at the Insane Asylum. Dismissed as sane but left there among the lunatics for a year because his wife never answered his or the doctor's letters or let him be taken out until finally he had to go to court about release. Now stays on farm, broken, poor, unable to go to wife because she, with her four children, is on the street and running around, fed by the town charity.

Went to Great Aunt Lib's down in Edison. She showed us pictures of relatives, said Andrew Miller (her grandfather) was one of the original 19 families to settle in Cardington. It never seemed to me there were many more than that there even 100 years later.

July 2: Returned from hot Ohio to cool New York and Mt. Sinai. Shelby seems like a dream, though like all dreams becoming more real steadily in retrospect and I am more excited by the strangeness of it than if it were Hawaii. It so chanced that the conditions at Auntie May's were so nearly like those I left—with Mr. Lahm coming on Sunday nights with a crate of berries, and Auntie May and I content as always to talk about all things all day, never bored with each other—that now it seems as if me at 15 was laid parallel to me at 36 for comparison, so nearly did the two lives graze each other.

The graves of my great-great grandfather Amasa "Shaerman" and his wife Lois "Shaerman" in Purvis Cemetery at Bethel seem clearer to me now than when we looked at them beneath the tangled weeds, and the visit to the Betts—who live in my mother's and great-grandfather Delano

Sherman's home at Bethel—is clear now. Going into the great kitchen and knowing where everything was was the only proof I had that I'd been there before (as a baby).

Those hot Ohio days—impossible to think or breathe or rest, destroying every bit of vitality you have. Now I find it hard to get back to my novel and as always when I can't work it is incredible that I ever could.

July 14: To Katherine Brush's party for Stan Rinehart. Her house is so fabulous it does not inspire either envy or pleasure but knocks one on the head and leaves one unconscious. It is hard to imagine what it must be like to live in such a world, since it is neither society nor bohemia, but as bare, bottomless, roofless as Hollywood. It has to be warmed by one's meager body and that isn't enough.

Dwight's book,* dedicated to me, is receiving tremendous acclaim. He has set his traps so well, managed himself like a shrewd businessman managing an artist—not a bit of his own value does he miss or underestimate. All this means work and he deserves his success. Of the 25 stories, I did a large part of 13, so it seems bitterly ironic that the reviewers (like Stark Young) who were so savage about my play should rave so about lines (usually mine) from this book. Book reviewers who have ignored my hard-fought novels find whole columns to rave over this work by Dwight in which I helped so considerably.

I cannot envy his success, for he worked far too hard, maneuvered, fought, and it is not as a writer but as a personality that he seeks a unique recognition. I do despise the reviewers so easily bought, as Dwight sardonically knows, by a mere smell from Society, so cringing before Money and Social Register when they should divert that reverence to a Wells or Balzac or even an O'Neill. I have almost equal contempt for myself for trying to attain any celebrity by sheer hard work and a sincere desire to tell a story that the country annals need for social history. I hope I have learned enough by this time to waste no time on attempts at absolute perfection. Life is too short and appreciation can only come if the work is sufficiently cheap to make the reviewer feel superior or socially set up.

July 17: Wrote 30 pages on novel. Feel it is flying along as it should but on a different line than I expected. The people have taken charge of it. I only hope they continue to run it themselves; after all, it's their business.

Without Music.

July 18: This is the last month of my money from Farrar and Rinehart or from anywhere—from now on, nothing—and the morbidity has set in that invariably has its base in finance. I am appalled at this secret, iron determination to make money—to win the artistic esteem its possession automatically confers. What I want is only possible after the world has seen and envied. It is the lesson I learned from Dwight—he set out for years to win something he personally despised but had a worldly significance. Now—having his smart world licked, his serious reviewers off guard—he can give them a symphony and they will listen. A sincere symphony from a serious composer is nothing—but one from a celebrity is something else again. From now on, by God, I am determined to distort every thought into the tawdry easy lines the world can applaud.

By this time next year I will have a fortune, have cut the throats of my best friends, have kicked my inferiors in the pants, have refused to be connected with any strangers except properly identified ones, and be loved and respected by all. And, if I can show enough automobiles and the proper manner, perhaps I will be considered a real artist, a positive dreamer, a genius.

September 1: Borrowed $20 from Ann and went up to Martha's Vineyard to see Margaret and Esther. A small affectionate little island, as kind to human beings as a puppy—little winding roads through cow pastures and fences up and down hill, little fishing towns and little elegant suburb towns. The people, no matter what they may be in winter, New Rochelle or Bronx or Scarsdale or Park Avenue, in summer take on the warm colors demanded by the island, are neighborly, old-fashioned, undemanding of any conventions. Not bohemian, not chic, but modern—accepting everyone's life in its exact spirit. This is a geographical effect—the smallness, cunningness of the plump little island permits people to be big.

Esther and Canby have a little tiny shack, remote-looking in the marshes; one night before I left I stayed there. We had to get up at daybreak to get the boat and I never had such a terrible sense of fate hanging over as on that dark morning. Canby on the other side of the partition muttering curses, trying to crawl over to his wash-basin, his poor dead legs—each morning waking up, seeing the sun—ah, a fine day—and then remembering his legs and pulling the shades down quickly over his mind, fastening on the little routine problems of how to get here or there with the least difficulty. Suddenly I thought, why that man, that legless man is Canby—Canby!—someone who used to dash around after the prettiest girl at the party, now figuring how few motions it takes to get a glass of water. And that gray-haired woman in the other bed, getting up now to wheelbarrow him to the toilet, waiting to wait on him, that's Esther—Esther who used to be gay and reckless and free—and in the little dark room I thought my heart would break.

I was thinking of influences—of Marinetti's *Italian Futurist Manifesto* and somewhere the words "Consider yourself not as the observer of the picture but the center of it—take your angle from that." And it seemed to me all my plays followed that line. Now I think it is the key to great satire. In Petronius, John Donne, in Aristophanes, Moliere and Restoration plays, the vitality of the satire is derived from the completeness of the picture—not one acting part or thought represents the norm, the audience, the critic or the author—there is, in a word, no *voice,* no pointer to the moral. In good satire, there is an absolute denial that there are people any different than those in this picture. The enjoyment of satire is that of nine-pins—seeing the ball strike truly and the pins go down. Audiences who can enjoy satire and at the same time recognize its imputations are limited, but there are millions who should be able to enjoy its surface entertainment. It should not be so bitter as to cancel its theatrical duty to an audience.

October 6: 24 days to raise $500 to save rent, piano and all establishment my cocksureness of future got us into. Decided to do play on Margaret and her house—the fortunate rich woman surrounded by artists, radicals, schools, dancers, etc., all telling her she's a bourgeois. Her constant expiation of sin of wealth.

October 9: It is curious that the most powerful influence in my life has been and still is Esther and her group—Lawsons, Dos, etc. Now I am disturbed by her utterly unjust, ridiculous chill toward me and devotion to the Lawsons—particularly marked, since they behaved so abominably toward me that her championship is in itself a declaration of hostility. The thing is to stay away I guess, till she is more anxious to see my good points.

October 10: Party at George O'Neil's for Aline Bernstein and her lovely family. Either I'm getting young again or slowly getting back my old enjoyment of people and parties. Anyway, I had a grand time.

I am worried about my novel—or rather not worried so much as puzzled. Coby read it and said "excellent and competent" which is a little crushing if you want impetus to finish something. By page 240, you ought to be more than "competent." Mr. Farrar says politely "oh, terribly grand" which is practically the same as competent. Do you suppose really that's all it is?

Anyway I'll have to finish it and not the tired way I wound up *Dance Night* either but slowly and steadily and as variedly as I began it. More and more I have slipped out of good writing habits into sloppy wife ones.

October 12: Dinner with Coby who seems rather gloomy and not a particularly eager host. Or am I getting stupid and garrulous and boresome myself or—worse—was I always?

October 13: Tea at Aline Bernstein's at the Gotham. Late in the evening to the Mayfair Yacht Club as Dwight's guests and I was surprised and dazzled as always at Dwight's performance and the way so many lines by me come out so peculiarly and definitely his. We decided that we had the same sour, realist angle on life—was why we were so fond of each other and worked so well together.

October 14: Came out to country. At noon Bertram Bloch called up and asked if I'd like to rewrite a play. I said no and then suddenly realized this was Opportunity and said "Is there immediate cash in it" and he said yes so I went up to his and Sydney Phillips' office and got the script to read over the weekend and lunch on Monday with him.

October 20: No further word on rewriting play for Phillips—we conferred and referred. I could not say anything definite since nothing had been asked of me and they couldn't say anything definite since they didn't have any money.

October 21: To dinner at Catalan's with Sue and Esther—down under Brooklyn Bridge. Lots of fun with some men eager to be gay. One told me he ran a column. "Where? I'll read it," I said. "Don't be silly, Baby, you never read a word in your life," he said. In fact by his comments I judged I looked more a fine lay than an intelligentsia. He said to Sue "You're a waitress, aren't you, sister?" and since anybody would rather look like a tart than a waitress Sue was secretly mad at me and later at Sam's struck me, on pretense of something else. Funny the way we always start out so jollily and end up with the same old row.

November 4: To "Ten Minute Alibi," a detective mystery play which— like bridge—required brains and wore one out to no purpose. I drank afterwards at Tony's but can't much more since it goes straight to my heart and it feels now constantly like a bruise—as if someone had socked me there.

November 5: Radio City with Jojo who is fine—a very polite, sensitive, original little boy and now taller than I am.

November 6: Did some valuable revision on "Barefoot Boy." Odd about the benefits of that complete outline and chart I made for this book. Like any other support it weakens intelligence. I faithfully and fairly easily do all the scenes and climaxes as arranged but the results of each one are blank. Scene goes to scene with no connecting link or character change or effect. I realized this in my sleep so got up and fixed a few places. Must fix a few more before John or someone tells me to and paralyzes me. After this I must not attempt anything but emotional stuff in novel—stay away from plot stuff like poison. I don't have the brain for it. Write about the only thing I know, which is feelings.

November 9: Heart hurts for first time in months so have to go easy on liquor.

November 12: This novel alarms me—or, rather, I alarm myself. I no longer enter into my work, I poke a finger into it. I write nervously and rather thoughtlessly, too full of other worries and interests to lose myself anymore in an imaginary world. It was like on the end of *Dance Night* and all through *Tenth Moon*—not once was anything really real to me— and all through this. I write with some top of my mind and I'm sure there must be great lapses. Neither people or situations are convincing in this. I expect a thorough razzing on it—enough to throw me completely out of the novel field.

November 14: I would like to have a baby now—give up the whole business and relax on being mere woman, all selfishness, laziness, meanness canceled by the great answer: "delicate condition." I don't see how I can ever get through this book or how I'll ever do anything else if I don't. It hasn't worked out at all the way I wanted—clumsily handled situations, people never convincing, and such a long row to hoe ahead, with no interest or pride in it, yet it's the best I can do.

November 20: Celebrated 13th anniversary by dinner at Leon & Eddie's and later a lousy play "Three and One."

November 24: Endless weeks of never more than a dollar at best and usually two or three nickels instead, three year old clothes, morbid fat, make me increasingly tired and depressed. Nothing ahead but dreary, unrewarded and limping work. Sustained hate and bitter envy of everyone —very unlike me but so tired and discouraged that almost everyone seems more blessed.

December 5: Went to Repeal Ball at Roosevelt with Joe Bromberg and Bobby Lewis and some girls from the Jooss Ballet since I didn't want to go anywhere with the Lawsons now that I see they are really dangerously insane so far as I am concerned.

December 12: Finished my novel, started in October of 1932 with charts made then and no more than 45 pages done up to May 27th of this year— owing to rehearsals and work on "Big Night" and also writing of "Jig-Saw." From p. 45 to p. 338—May 25 to Dec. 12.

[The following is found in the 1933 diary on the page allocated to December 19 but is marked January 1, 1934 at the beginning of the entry. No reference to whatever occurred is mentioned in the 1934 diary.]

Such a dreadful nightmare has just happened to me—like nothing ever before in my life, and with it came such a quiet realization of facts that I do not believe anything like that can ever touch me again. I am erasing the picture from my mind and half of my own heart at the same time. From now on I will be absolutely free, no affections can touch me, nothing. It is sad to learn the final lesson—that the only way to avoid such stabs is to school yourself to a denial of feeling, both pleasurable and bad. This is such a queer physical sickness and I must control it—the cause and effect must go and, by God, *will*.

1934

January 1: Went to tea yesterday at Cheryl's, then to party last night at Teresa Helburn's, then to Rosie Miller's, ending up with Veuve Clicquot at 6 A.M. at Lafayette.*

January 10: This year I want to do my Lucky Spoon comedy right away, so that come what may on "Jig-Saw" I will not be too affected by its fate. The play is to concern the merciless exploitation of the rich by communists, artists and deserving people. Before I was to have just the one rich foil—now I think others should appear: one rich, extravagant friend who has no pleasure in her luxurious clothes since they make her poor friends cry. The point is a completely Restoration rogue play—that to take is noble, to be taken from is unforgivable.

After this play I want to do my Lila novel—a thoroughly New York book with the beauty and sheer thrill of New York running through it, in contrast to the imprisoned life it is possible to live here and which Lila does. A novel of no plot but of mood, feeling, atmosphere, even glamour, seen but never attained. This should be done in shaded fleeting photographic shots with the basic reality of the book her heartache—not a neurotic ache but a real one.

I must start work soon—living too gay and expensive a life.

January 15: Dreadful evening for no definite reason except the air. Dinner at Greenbaums, with a Mary Badger and a lawyer named Alfred who said not a word till 9:30 when he said goodnight and left. As soon as he left,

---

*The Hotel Lafayette, at the corner of East Ninth Street and University Place, was one of Powell's favorite hangouts and inspired the setting of her novel *The Wicked Pavilion.*

Dotsie and Eddie began telling anecdotes about this silent departed guest, the perfectly screaming things he used to do, until a dynamic, devastating personality was created for this silent stranger. He made the party. If we were ever to see him again we would wink knowingly and remind him of what fun we'd had together. It was like a suit of clothes arriving after the guest had appeared naked.

Miss Badger badgered everyone about their zodiacal signs and used it as a means of insult, largely. Yes, you *would* be a Leo—high noon, I'd say. I was a Sagittarius but Taurus must have been around since I looked like a bull. Eddie spoke of his firm's Mr. Jennings, who did nothing but Titles and Titles Foreclosure, who seldom spoke but—"You know that Queen Anne Grant of 1687—ha ha ha—most people think it runs to Nassau Street and all the time it runs to William Street. Ha ha ha?" The dinner—in retrospect—was a dinner with Mr. Jennings and Alfred.

Later with Jacques LeClercq to the Plaza bar and then to the Madison— the papers say the Guild does the Bruckner as its 8th and final play. I was depressed but as usual these kicks straighten out my spine as nothing else does so I'm settling down to a working determination. Some short things for *The New Yorker* for publicity purposes only.

January 17: Saw jacket of *Story Of A Country Boy* which is set for March 22. Then went to that Gypsy Tea Room for lunch at Fifth Avenue and 38th. Booths with not the usual tearoom chatter of women's voices since most of the lunchers are alone. They sit with their teacups already overturned waiting for a gypsy to sit down at their table and reveal. On the walls are mottos—"Listen to the Gypsy's Warning" and "Tea Leaves, Tea Leaves, Please reveal to me, Who my future husband is going to be."

In a corner booth a sign says "Palmistry, Rajah, the White Hindu" and here a big Irish policemen (Rajah) sits with a fez on, reading palms. A cat roams about and a kettle hangs on three sticks. The gypsies are named Ramona, Juanita, etc. Ramona sat down by me, said I was to go on a sea journey; sleep soon in a strange bed; sign a contract with the letter P; that I was a dancer; said something about my foot; said I would make more money than any man but must concentrate on it as I had a highly spiritualized mind to which practicality was foreign; that end of March would be nice to me, also April and May; that a dark man born in September felt violent about me and not to argue with him; that a man with initial C.

born in September worried about me; that I should beware of any contest as no success was possible for me without complete personal liberty; beware people born in January—March best—September people attracted to me but make me unhappy. In four weeks an old friend comes back and trip is discussed; also, follow first impressions always of everything.

January 22: Ratio of income:

    1925—$ 545.25
    1926—$ 526.62
    1927—$1344.00
    1928—$2335.00
    1929—$2133.00
    1930—$5500.00 minus commission
    1931—$7500.00 minus commission
    1932—$1996.00
    1933—$1980.00

To keep out of debt ought to make $5000 a year.

Owe Mary Lena $10—Esther $250—Margaret $800—Faizgsh $550—Dr. Holliday $70—Witt $70—Hornbeck $140—Drug $6.70—Adolph—$90. Started work on "Lucky Spoon."

January 23: To dinner at Blue Ribbon and a mild, harmless, inoffensive comedy "The First Apple." The audience spoke well of it and in the entr'actes looked proud and happy as if their pleasure was based on there being nothing said or done on the stage too bright for their comprehension—no wit they couldn't have thought of themselves.

If I dared be merciless I would say that what I needed was a brutal reception for my new novel such as I had for my play. One learns nothing about one's weaknesses or one's basic firmness except through these attacks. I learned out of the attacks on my play more of what I could do, what I was prepared to fight for in my plays, and what I must improve, than in any classroom acceptance of fairly good stuff. My novel side gets more and more confused all the time and needs a tonic treatment.

January 31: Lunch with Carol Hill and turned over contracts for future, etc., to her.

Dr. Witt examined me with X-rays and fluoroscopes and said the tumor *in* my lung and *on* my heart is slowly, almost imperceptibly, growing—faintly ominous—slowly crowding the heart, filling the lung until one day I will strangle—unless it's cut out before. No maybe. It terrifies me, even though in sensible hours I see that this may move as slowly as any glacier and not fulfill its destiny for centuries.

February 1: Posed for Peggy Bacon and dinner at Coby's. Saw Peggy's little-girl paintings and drawings and thought how much better genuine primitives are than grown-up imitation-primitives, since the power of the genuine primitive is in its eager striving toward sophistication and *more,* while in the pseudo-school they know more than they allow themselves to portray. So it comes out stilted and sterile and utterly without the essence of simplicity, having only the manner and form.

February 2: Finished proof on *Country Boy.* The early part depressed me—it was so dull and awkwardly written and leaden, utterly undistinguished. Then it picked up and held even the author's interest and admiration to the last—the first of my books to do that. It isn't as good a book as *Dance Night* but is much more compelling since its people are real and living and contemporary. It will probably sell around 20,000 no matter what the reviews, since it has the basis for popularity.

February 8: Saw Peggy Bacon's pastel caricature of me which looked just like me, depressingly enough, though without any central quality, which to be good it should have. Huge body; teensy hands; gross, sensual face and curves all trying to be dainty and intellectual; each feature of itself trying to refine and deny the sensual effect of the whole ensemble. Peggy and I got tight afterward and I drew a blank.

February 9: Disappointed in the page proofs of *Country Boy.* Only 303 because of fine print, when it is 1/4 longer than anything else I've done. Dinner at the Wents' who remain more English than when they were in England, contented, tidy lives, tenderness coming in a stray visiting cat whom they name Carrots—spends his days there and his nights in some unknown home; also in collections of stuffed dogs, queen dolls and tiny bric-a-brac from England. The same words and stories and habits repeated give them pleasure and security.

February 10: Evening at Pietro Montana's—an Italian sculptor with a house on W. 70th, a beautiful, simple Italian with a Swedish, huge-busted wife and two floors of great plaster saints, harrowed pilgrims. I was surprised at the devotion to *respectability* these midtown foreign artists had—less of the vaunted artistic flare than in any Cleveland candy salesman. Pleasant, sincere good people but I derive no comfort or stimulus from these; I prefer discontents.

February 12: I want this new novel to be delicate and cutting—nothing will cut New York but a diamond. Probably should do a night job on it as on *Tenth Moon*—it should not be a daylight book but intense and brilliant and fine like night thoughts. No wandering but each detail should point to the one far-off star and be keyed by Lila's own waiting excitement and preserved youth. It should be crystal in quality, sharp as the skyline and relentlessly true. No external details beyond the swift eager glance over the shoulder.

February 13: To Dotsie Greenbaum's sculpture show—beautifully done, nothing attempted beyond her power and extra energy spent on perfecting that. No one therefore could say she attempted a Samson and couldn't do it. Instead, by doing a perfect rabbit, a perfect baby, she is credited with being able to do a Samson. Yet the shooting-beyond quality in an artist, the being unafraid to fail in a large project, is the sign of the great. With money behind her, she can cast and mount each object perfectly, yet Paul Fiene, who dares attempt heroic figures, has to show them uncast, in plaster, and no critic can see beyond this patent declaration of financial failure.

February 14: I liked the show at the Anderson galleries—same old warm, jolly Academy pictures, each telling an elaborate story. In the doorway two young colored fairies stood back to back, each guarding a room, talking. "I got to write letters tonight. Should have last night but there are some people I simply cannot write to, you know." "I wrote to George but I haven't heard a word. I'm going to leave him alone." "John called me up again." "Really? You must have some charm for him." "Don't know what it is I'm sure." "Mae West knows her charm—you ought to know yours." "Wish I did—I'd sharpen up on it."

In the hall an elderly man, well-dressed, sat on the steps and complained that when he had things to sell they were out of fashion but when he wanted to buy, they were in.

The Lawsons were in—curious how different, how devitalized they are, and as he grows older his Jesuitical logic becomes more unforgivable. They keep the coats the Faragohs put in the box for the Starving Miners because they want to save money, yet Jack's name is on all the Starving Miner committees. He talks sternly against Caldwell but never read him.

February 17: Peggy Bacon came in. We were going to her show (with my portrait in it) but she resisted so we sat listing our hates, with details. We agreed that she can stand more sheer kindness and goodness than I can but that I can forgive more unrespectability in people whose talents or person I like.

April 23: Play "Jig-Saw" opened in Washington and seemed a fair success.

April 26: Interesting to watch different comedians—their techniques. Spring Byington studies her own role with the greatest care and intelligence, reads it with every pause studied, each merry laugh, but has nothing to do with the other characters, does not listen to them, and doesn't know what they've just said, is concerned wholly with her own projection of her role. She is upset by untidiness on stage, cannot keep her eyes away from fallen bit of paper or string, misses cues even over a pillow askew.

Cora Witherspoon and Ernie Truex have the perfect comedy technique. They are primarily at ease, they listen to the other scenes and speakers with quiet poise, minimum of facial and body motion, they hold in their mind their next speech so securely that they are in no hurry to say it. They could pause five minutes and still the audience would not be afraid they had forgotten. Cora has an intelligent superior knowledge of her own technique. She does not believe in exact directing. "Let the actors read for a while, let the director get something from them, then fuse the two ideas," she says.

May 9: Marie* went to my play "Jig-Saw." Yessir, it was true to life—now that she was older she realized that most unhappy marriages were due to

---

*Marie Jeffers, who worked as a housekeeper for Powell with Louise Lee.

the mother falling in love with the daughter's beau, so the daughter makes a spite marriage or maybe never marries at all and nobody knows it is all on account of the mother and families break up and may never speak to each other again.

I am always amazed in tapping Marie's brain—the simplest imagery brings in reply a chain of clichés that cannot be broken off, old movie and cheap novel plots, legend and gossip, so that a real episode in her life—indeed life itself—is like a wire-walker stepping across the rope with this web of clichés outstretched beneath to catch it.

My plays have the difficulty of my short stories—an excellent real treatment of character and dialogue on a structure of contrived, exaggerated, and strained story. Except that "Big Night" wasn't.

May 12: A pleasant weekend with Joe—the sort we used to have. With decisions to make every day and excuses to think up for my decisions—to RKO and Paramount for not wanting to go to Hollywood, even for $1000 a week, merely because I don't want to. Am having difficulty enough getting my balance after my minor windfalls of the last few weeks—movie sale, etc. and play a half-success.

I am actually in a disturbed condition—unable to concentrate, unable to know my own thoughts—to plot or plan my new novel and play. I don't know what I am thinking or what my impressions are of this storm or that person—so steeled are my nerves against constant interruptions of pleasant things to do—decisions to make—sweepings of my other works—the need to make the most of this once-in-a-lifetime chance and the other counter-need to get my balance so I can work calmly at my next book. I am neither tired nor seemingly nervous yet my energy is all broken up into little spurts instead of one long drive. To read anything but scraps of things in newspapers or magazines is torture; to enjoy people is impossible. I am happy but in such a jumpy irresponsible way. Maybe a job would have been a good thing for me except for a queer psychological slant on the whole business. It represents failure to me, a public admission of vulnerability and defeat.

I think I need training in concentrated thought once again and reading might do it. If not reading, sustained study of some sort—an hour a day of Latin, say, to get my brain under control again. Perhaps I've had too long to think about my novel and play. They both seem slight and immaterial and unworthy to me now, a little false, though Lila needn't be. She ought to be swift, intense, violently real, moving as a brave, generous, gallant woman, eager to do things to help, bound by her life.

May 17: Began Elizabeth Arden exercise treatment, massage on Monday. Weight 148!!!

May 22: Tea at the Hatches—Elizabeth Arden exercises and massage till I'm knocked out. To dinner at Greenbaums and then Alec and Peggy and I (me drinking ferociously all the time) went to the Cafe Royale where Alec picked up two very dear Yiddish poet companions and was insulted that his wife, who should have been a perfect hostess to them, continued her absorbed whispers to me. Finally, Peggy and I went to her house and Alec, wounded to the quick at this affront to his honor as a husband, stayed with his chums. Hours later—as I was spilling my drinks all over Peggy's sofa, occasionally roused into consciousness by being very wet— Alec returned with his hat jammed over his head and his two dear friends, Bert Lahr (as he called him) and Mr. Sherman. Hands shook my shoulder—"Wake up, Miss Powell, I'm going to translate your works into Yiddish." It was Mr. Lahr, his glasses shining over two shrewd black eyes. When I woke up again it was 10 A.M. and I was in bed with Peggy.

May 26: At the Chinese dentist (Dr. Wing) he keeps the radio going full blast as he drills. Across the street the Brevoort porters in blue overalls sweep the *terrasse* and prepare for the big long Saturday lunch, though it is misting and people will probably rush to the Lafayette for good food rather than open chill air. The radio announces "Martial law in Bolivia! Strike in Bolivia! Armament discussion in Japan! Labor riots in Toledo; three killed! Labor riots in New Orleans!" Finally it switches into "The Goody Hour." "Let's all pretend"—as good a solution to the situation as any, except the ex-Secretary of Labor's solution—he merely died in the night as his suggestion.

May 27: To feel yourself slowly distilled into another sort of person—a weak, unchallenged, feminine hysterical—is so perturbing that my head swims in terror all the time. What new hurdles must I leap that I missed before, hurdles other people were never to have?

Certainly I might as well give up the plans I've made. Now I will do real people, relentlessly, truly, unmasked—now I have nothing to lose. I feel I will have Decker wandering about as a thread, even Morry and Jen. Characters of my old novels—perhaps Dorrie and Roger.

June 1: It is shocking to discover that after a few years one becomes more and more crippled—more crutches of "buts" and "ifs" and "anyhows"— till there is presently only a voice saying "Hear, hear, this is me. Don't look at what I do or the way I live; this is the real me, changed into nothing but a little voice, and if this wicked witch's body strikes you, don't be hurt for it isn't me. Just hear my voice saying how I love you."

Finally the voice is gone and the friends remember only the ugly deeds. The desire for Happiness complete—the Ideal—whittles down through shock after shock of truth grinning from behind horrid encounters to a simple acceptance of what snatches of momentary perfection come. *This* moment is true, *this* moment is all that can be said, and holding out for more only intensifies the precariousness of that little bit. You come back for it gratefully in the end.

June 5: These X-rays on the clot on my lung leave me shaky and upset.

June 11: I wish I could find myself again but alone I hunt for a familiar thought or clue through every door of my mind and there is nothing of me there. There is no inside to me, nothing but tactile sensations; this momentary presence is satisfying, its absence is pain but why or whither I don't know. It's as if a blowtorch had gone through me and left me outside the same, but nothing within but an utterly cowardly deathly fear of hurt. But even that is not like a human reaction but like a mechanical one whose very hollowness frightens you more than live quivering guts.

What happens inside people like me who are braced for certain challenges in life and then, spoiled a little so that their dikes weaken through lack of use, the storm, the ocean breaks in? We have nothing but our shock, no emotional equipment, nothing—so that the lightning plays over naked heart and bowels and no pain is left but the numbed nerves, the blank, the broken will, the broken back, the broken pride. From a person one turns into a sick dog defeating itself and its own happiness with every sick whine. I dare not even whip myself with my old whips— finish this or that. The lash no longer stings any more than the rewards appease. To wake and find this stranger inside me each day grows more and more alarming. My familiar surroundings strange, husband and child quaintly remote, my work foreign to me as if I had changed from human to vegetable and was only conscious of light and dark.

June 15: My novel seems formal and unsatisfactory—playing with silly people when real people are too monstrous, too horrible to be played with, and the more contact I have with life the more shocked I am at my boldness in pretending to deal with them.

June 16: I am angry at the repeated gougings—Marie and Louise and dentists and doctors. I've paid:

> $90—Miss Bertine for Jojo.
> $150—Dr. Lees (his dentist)
> Marie and Louise
> groceries
> My own X-rays, doctors and dentists

I have loaned:
> Dos—$500
> Bill Rollins $140 (paid back $20)
> given Phyllis $200
> LeClercq $100

Paid debts:
> Esther—$250
> Margaret—$500
> Francis F.—$550
> [illegible]—$110
> Louise —Jojo's camp $80
> Carfare $75

June 17: In Bailey Island with Jojo. Here blue sea spreads smoothly and majestically out ignoring the eager round little islands that pop waiting, their sandy laps held out for favors from this noble neighbor. The sense of being perched far up, immensely remote from cities or city life, high in the air—nearer Iceland than any state—is exhilarating and a little more of it would really cure me, I believe. This is the first hope I've seen for myself—a strange place—quiet—ocean—easy to be alone in for no one points—and new surroundings so that new reactions force the old familiar thoughts away and I can once again imagine myself writing. I ought to do this now—go away for two weeks and then have my weekends in Long Island. Work like a fiend and get novel in shape, but more than that—get sane.

June 20: Paramount wanted me to go to the coast again but I refused. Carol said it would pay $1500 a week—but money confuses me too much already.

June 22: I am lost without a novel—those plays confuse me with their hysterical bursts into my life. A novel is like a gland pill—it nips off the cream of my hysterics and gets them running on track in a book where they belong instead of rioting all over my person.

July 3: Up at 8. Worked at play, "Lion and Lizard," all day—time out for swimming, sunning, reading *Eastward Ho*. Letter from Jojo who seems to be happy at Bailey Island—if he gets on with the others it will ease our worry over the funny little kid.

July 5: This morning two young men came down to the cottage to sell me the *Delineator*. "Are you an author?" one said. "Pardon me but what is your name?" Then he stayed for an hour, largely because I offered him ginger ale—the first time anybody had offered him anything on Long Island, he said gloomily. He hated Port Jefferson. No girls between 14 and 50—where were they? He said he'd made as much as $1000 in six weeks selling *Delineator*—for every two-year subscription for $2.00 he got $1.75.

He said "Ah, Pennsylvania! What a state. Some of those mountains! I could take you places you could see seven towns from. And everybody offers you a piece of pie or lunch or something." His name was Lewis Andors. He was going to Teachers College but he was really interested in journalism.

Once he worked for the black evangelist, Father Divine, in Suffolk County. Four autos and an aeroplane, headquarters or "kingdoms" in five cities including Los Angeles. Four secretaries (one white) who write his sermons, all pregnant, all living with him. Those who proved their faith in him and "Brotherhood of Man" by turning over their insurance to him were called Angels. Angel Gabriel, etc. Each meal a "banquet"—but the singing got you, said Andors. He said Divine and his angels never said hello but "Peace."

He went to a house near Saratoga once and a woman came to the door. "Ssh!" she said, "I'm holding a meeting." Empty chairs all around where she collected Indian spirits who she said were ruining this country. She got them together, took them out on the lawn, put lye on them, and burned them.

July 9: Jojo's teachers write that he is upset as the other children arrive. Special measures have been necessary. Poor little kid—he does have a hellish time.

July 10: To "She Loves Me Not," the comedy of the ages according to all the critics and public. It was embarrassing in its simple, mechanical childishness. About three hearty natural laughs; the rest dowdy, pedestrian, sophomoric writing. One thing it did do—apart from embarrassing by its ham artificial adolescence—was make me realize that one need not wait for the perfect touch, or the natural outcome of character. Any trumpery is preferred by audiences.

July 17: I am so improved by the country and almost a month of very little drinking—suddenly alive and under control again, interested in matters away from self, and perhaps reassured in general. I was surprised at my indifference to the rather unflattering cracks about "Jig-Saw" in Sunday papers. I remember Ann Watkins saying "I've had to learn to be hard. So now things roll right over me. My feelings don't get hurt any more." In the arts if you cringed every time someone said you were lousy, or an imitator, you'd never go on—you couldn't.

July 18: 138 and 1/2 pounds.

Lost almost ten lbs. through exercise daily, about ten massages, and light supper. Chief improvement in measurements—four inches waist, four in thighs, four in stomach, about half in each calf. Ought to lose another ten by August 20th—down to 135 by July 26.

Auntie May and Jack and June* drove out to Mt. Sinai. I told Carol I would accept Paramount job—two weeks here in the East at $1000.

July 20: Coby talks so much about the necessity for doing more work like "Big Night" instead of lighter stuff like "Jig-Saw." This short story sketch could be a character play—very American in quality.

The Brooklyn Widow (Mrs. Flack)—very happily married before with average moron intelligence—to Mr. F, an Elk, O.F., K.P., K.K.K., ad salesman, proud of his home, its electric devices, etc. His death leaves her not grieved but the envy of the neighborhood because of insurance, etc. She, bored after awhile with mere envy, wants to do something gay with money, feels herself in class with Astors. Meets foreign orchestra violinist in N.Y.—invites him over—he comes, drunk, to scoff at respectability (she too is ashamed of it), ends by being earnest upholder of her dead husband's standards while she has no further chance at glamour. All the super solid things he had once asked, Juan now asks and she does.

Sickish from cabbage or heat or swimming or all three. Joe limp, too—he is an ideal companion alone—traveling with him would be great fun I imagine. Jojo writes worried letters about things Daddy said.

Wish I could buckle down to steady work. This hit or miss feeling is no good, even out here in the country, where I could stay now all week except that knowledge I'll have to come in queers everything. I must get a town schedule. At desk by 7:30, work till noon a few days and see what develops. That gives me a good three hour start on the telephone at least. More and more, I fear the early hour is the only one. Even 6 or 6:30 try. Nap afternoons if necessary.

July 24: Reading snatches this weekend of Nancy Hale, Louise Bogan, Kay Boyle, I was impressed with how women now made their art serve their female purpose whereas once it warred with their femininity. Each page is squirming with sensitivity, every line—no matter how well disguised the heroine is—coyly reveals her exquisite taste, her delicate charm, her never-at-a-disadvantage body (which of course she cares nothing about and is always faintly amused at men's frenzies over her perfect legs, breasts, etc.) What gallantry, what equalness to any situation in the

---
* Jack and June Sherman, Powell's young cousins, who were now growing up with Orpha May Steinbrueck in the same house where Powell was raised.

home, the camp, the yacht, the trenches, the dives—what *aristocrats* these women writers are, whose pen advertises the superiority of their organs. Fit companions and opposites to the he-man writers—Hemingway, Burnett, Cain—imitation he-manners whose words tersely proclaim their masculinity, every tight-lipped phrase shows the author's guts, his decency, his ability to handle any situation—insurrection (he is an instinctive leader or else too superior to show it), shipwreck, liquor, women. Through the words shot out of the typewriter clip-clip one watches the play of his muscles; one sighs to lay one's head upon that hairy shoulder.

Started job with Paramount doing over "Quarantine" at $1000 a week.

July 30: The plump manicurist—Miss Greenberg—who looks Lutheran and earnest and clean and so essentially good and sensible that she cannot ever get the hang of what her slyer girlfriends are up to. She catches a slang phrase or a new step and oh boy she's as up-to-date as the next one but her girlfriends and I'm sure the boys realize she doesn't know what it's all about. She wants so much to be jazz but there are generations of Lutherans in her fat little legs.

"At the camp there was these four fellas," she began, "and maybe you could give me some advice."

"Which one was it?" I asked.

"No particular one," she said. "They were all nice. There was this thin one, though. He asked me to go for a walk after supper and he asked me to neck and was very lovely. But next day he was very cool. Then we came home and he went back to Washington. And I was just wondering what to do. I was just wondering maybe if I wrote him a letter and let him see that at last he'd come up against a girl who wasn't going to stand for this sort of thing."

"What—the necking?" I asked.

"No—the being cool. I'd just like to write him and show him how little he means in my young life."

"If you wrote him, he'd realize you cared about him," I said, but this didn't make sense.

She held up a file dreamily. "I'd just dash off a note—casual, you know but just let him see! I thought I'd say something like 'On the train coming home from the Poconos the cinders flew so thick and fast that you couldn't tell whether I was Caucasian or Ethiopian'—something just sort of light and casual."

"I see," I said, and thought of the nights she'd spent thinking that up. "Well, you'd better write him, I guess."

She was full of the latest camp catchwords which she used with a great enjoyment of being right up to the minute—referring a dozen times to someone having "what is generally known as a belated spark of life." Everything was preceded by "what is generally known as."

September 9: Got a little into Act II, though it is mental acrobatics and needs to be done perfectly and brilliantly to make up for lack of emotion. I do not see any feeling possible here for any of the roles—a definite handicap—but the characters could have a dash more realistic detail to make them convincing.

September 15: Both on this novel and particularly the play my heart has vanished. I work by technique and where emotions once were there is merely a logical sense of justice. I click instead of breathing. This is from play and movie writing where emotions are whittled down to their operating value, where feelings are all reduced to a clean snappy click. A certain terror of feeling is also involved since instead of being warmed by them (as once) I am now burnt up and corroded by them in real life. In casting around for possible help—since I know no one I can appeal to anymore for professional and personal advice—I arrived at the conclusion I always have: return to myself. Free myself of any dependence on friends for amusement or relief, take a study or office uptown or downtown and set myself to an eight-hour day. A hotel room, perhaps. I hate a lease—about three months is all I can do in one of these places.

October 9: Dr. Rucker almost wept over Jojo—thought he was in such fine shape, a genius undoubtedly, a credit to everyone, etc. Miss Coffin is coming back to tutor him five days a week beginning October 15 for $18 a week.

October 24: This little room is loveliest thing I ever had. Upstairs here at night you see the towers of lower Manhattan lit up, the Woolworth, etc., and the voices of extra-news in the street, bouncing from wall to wall: "Russia—oom-pah chah! Russia—oom pah chah!" These sounds mingle with the far-off skyscraper lights, distant boat whistles and clock chimes and across the street in the attic of the Pen and Brush Club I see girls hanging out their meager laundry.

Royalty statement on *Country Boy* amazed me—less than 2000 copies sold. I need a build-up in name—serialization, probably, and foreign publication. Finish this Effie novel—a 60,000-worder is enough, I think—a bad novel will probably help to sell some good ones and excuse me for future good ones.

November 1: Finished "The Lion and the Lizard" play and turned it over to Hazel to copy.

November 5: Turned play in. Joe a little amazed but a little perturbed by it. Coby, to my surprise, feels it is much my best work. A play has no shape or merit of its own, it only assumes character through what people say of it so I have no idea of it, only feel tremendously relieved to have it done.

November 13: Terry Helburn called to say the Guild wouldn't want my play. I doubt very much if anyone else will take it then.

November 15: My life is so confusing—the design it once had has vanished and each day seems a blind step in the dark. Momentary reassurances, momentary confidence but underneath utter bewilderment and chaos. A novel has always been a steadying influence, if I can swim along with this one, writing fast and furious.

November 17: I find the Bacon-Brook marriage jolly but shallow, limited to its own very meager personalities, its own meager interests, each intense in its way and Alec enormously vital, enormously vigorous and hearty— but unstimulating, unsocial, frankly unconcerned with anything but their own getting ahead. Alec has the gusto, energy and actual gifts of a great man—he will probably be as great as Cézanne or Matisse though in a less original way. Peggy has the sharp minor talents of a small but shrewd personality—inherently snobbish, a little smug perhaps, a little vain.

November 18: I am afraid the play is really not good—wrong ideology, basically uninformed, and tomorrow I think I shall recall it and work it into a straight farce, cutting out all the features dealing with economic conditions.

Where I go from here is a problem. My novel reputation is so slight, so unpromising, dwindling away with each book (as the books get better) so that I feel the best thing for me is to center on plays. "The Brooklyn Widow" would be good but at the moment material is not sufficient so I have started a dramatization of *Dance Night*. I could use a collaborator on this.

November 25: Working on "Brooklyn Widow." Trying to use real people for models. Curious—as soon as I decided to write no more novels it was as if a door swung open and a treasure chest unlocked for my use that was to be saved for novels. Work on "Widow" to be as careful as on *Country Boy*—with charts, maps, etc., and steady at it. Must be done by Carol's return so that no one can bother me to do something else. The best idea I ever had. She must slowly blossom into a person under this passion—new warmths, etc. The play must have not only plot and character but the rich beauty of terrific sex awakening, flowering of love.

December 1: New novel must be burningly contemporary, even libelous if necessary—no words to be spared, no feelings saved, no recognition softened. This is to be the works. I think I will name it after Denny's own novel, "The Hunter's Wife." How much sharper and better to have the central figure a man rather than a woman—a man in whom my own prejudices and ideas can easily be placed, whereas few women's minds (certainly not Effie's or Corinne's) flit as irresponsibly as that.*

December 3: I think I will bring out the book anonymously so that I can get a new start on a career. As I look about at the people who have achieved great names or are on the way to it I see that all of them are not on the one hand a person and on the other an artist but that there is no division. They *are* their works, so that their everyday life is not divorced from their public name but is a constant advertisement for it. Jack Lawson, Dos, Alec Brook and Peggy—none of these persons have in their minds or hearts anything but their work, whereas with me I am always setting my person up against my work so that neither helps the

---

* Denny, Effie, and Corinne are the three main characters in *Turn, Magic Wheel.*

other. My friends, instead of being a relief from my work, should augment it.

December 31: To Catalan's Saturday night with Jolas and LeClercqs. Old Catalan sits by the fire, great face lined with anguish, huge body shrinking while wife Valentina cooks badly. For years she's helped him—she knows every recipe but she is a terrible cook. Ever since Catalan went back to Spain he's been a bewildered, sick man. His whole personality—Gargantuan, solid, arrogant—was based on knowing (indeed, on *being*) Spain in America. No revolution could ever succeed there—in Italy maybe, but you don't know Spaniards like I do. His dictums on all Spanish thought were final.

Presently whipped up by his own nostalgia (which was his backbone) and by friends' constant queries ("When you going back to Spain, Sebastian?") he goes. "In Spain you live on five cents a day—less." Now he finds it's so expensive he can only eat two meals a day. Revolution is succeeding—he's no longer a Spaniard—over there no one listens to the big Spanish authority Sebastian—his stomach gives out—he shrinks from 300 to 200 pounds. He comes back to America a sad, shrunk, silent, bitter man—neither American nor Spanish—unable to speak with authority about anything Spanish. He can only say, bewildered, when asked about revolution, "Why they want to kill? Why they want to hurt each other?"

To the Theatre Collective new house at Two Washington Square—any organization's dream. There Cheryl and Bobby and Clurman and Stella Adler and I to dinner and the last four to the Yiddish opera "Happy Family" where a most engaging little Polish comedian—Feld—won all of us. All the actors played to Stella—the great Adler; every joke was aimed at her. Feld had invented a machine by which you could talk to the dead for half an hour (but the dead cannot talk back). The author—Willy Siegal—writes 40 plays for Yiddish theaters (the best in China); behind us sat a man who played this part in Mexico City to an audience of 4000. Stella says Seagully is only 40, feels very inferior, kids about his work: "I'm the Jewish Galsworthy." On the stage a smart sophisticated Helen Morgan type was pointed out as the only Jewish Lesbian—spends her summers in Paris, men, women, drink and dope. Not at all Jewish in style or manner—looks more Irish. Probably "passes" all summer, then comes back to Yiddish.

1935

January 9: Lately—due to not working and due, too, to observing how much more prestige and authority other people with less ability carry—it seems to me, now that I definitely want rewards during my lifetime, that given a good talent, its recognition and elevation to great are utterly dependent on exploitation and outside funny-business, the personal approach. If someone doesn't do this for you, you must do it yourself.

Walter Duranty at Carol's the other day described to me Bolitho's* attitude toward this—sweep into a room no matter what your height. Above all, be a great genius to your friends—no man can be a great writer unless he is first a great man to his friends. Since I have always been disparaging about my work to my friends, I read a lesson in this. Observing elsewhere, I see how certain friends make good by sheer social contact—a flair for knowing who's who, for using these people without aggression. Success is a gift—like any knack for weaving something out of a few strings which to the rest of us are nothing but a few strings.

January 10: Head swimming with murderous rages again. Must keep away from people during this period as it is almost uncontrollable—never know where it will light.

January 29: I have made a decision lately—at least it seems a decision. Since I can write so fluidly and with such pleasure about real people and my surmises, it seems increasingly an effort to step from this reality into a storybook world. On the other hand, I hate to use real people and hurt them but I have reached the point where I must sacrifice my tender feelings

---

*Presumably William Bolitho, (1890–1930), English journalist.

for reality. It's a decision against personal life for the crueler pleasures of artistic exactness.

February 1: My writing career becomes an increasing problem. I have written in all directions in the last year, with the result that nothing is finished. Even the vignettes I have done are to no purpose but spraying out on all sides. I cannot let myself get flabby this way, particularly since I never felt better, more alive, keyed up to impressions in my whole life. No excuse, except diffused personal life which, if it gets too much in my way, should be sacrificed to my original intent.

February 19: Have been working on novel. Bad back again and bad general condition—not sleeping well, jittery over Jojo, insecure, etc., working late at nights. Believe, in spite of unusual facility in this new novel, that have something here rather unique.

February 27: Took up 44 pages of novel "The Hunter's Wife" with synopsis to Carol Hill.

February 28: Sailed to Havana on United Fruit boat with Joe and Harry Lissfelt.

March 12: Home from Key West. On the train, "Ef you want anythin,' jes mash the button" says the porter.

April 2: Disorder with Farrar and Rinehart resulting in contract washed up and negotiations under way with Little, Brown. Gave 72 pages to them. I think this is much my best book, expresses more of my own self than anything else I ever did and furthermore I enjoy writing it.

April 8: Took "Cheerio," a short story, up to Carol. This is a calm jolly period for me—no publishers, no money, so I can work with a freedom I never dreamed of before. I am very fond of my novel; hope other people are.

April 12: Little, Brown turned down my novel and I really feel rather sick. Hardly been able to do anything all week on it, simply wait for the day to pass and something to take place which of course it can't without my doing something. Looking forward to a weekend of nerves and jitters and the continuous realization that I have no longer any friend at all—no one I can confide in, no one who wouldn't be secretly delighted to see me in a disadvantageous spot. Carol out of town, of course. All I can think of is starting on my play if possible. Fear is such an utterly disrupting force—fears of no publisher, fear of cringing once more before debtors, fear of being trapped in the Middle West again and dependent on relatives—so that this panic creeps in my pen or typewriter, and nothing is possible.

April 14: With Harry and Joe to Lafayette and later 20½ Pell and then Moneta's. At Lafayette, Berkeley Tobey, 50, begged us to drink to Eloise, his very young wife, who is at last to have a baby. "Whose?," we all wondered, as we drank reverently.

Tobey began dwelling on his past (while Jacques and Edith silently fought with each other over Jacques' 4th drink) and he told of the time Mabel Dodge followed Jack Reed to Mexico and he put the rebel army between them so that she couldn't get across the border. Then once he (Tobey) and Griffin Barry were freezing up at Swann Island off Maine with a Henrietta Rodman, sitting up long into the night discussing theories, dazzling Henrietta with their thoughts on heredity which she combatted, saying environment could conquer any strain.

When they woke from a drunken revel, Henrietta was gone and a day later she reappeared with a child, legally adopted, with a syphyllitic gangster heritage. Griffin and Tobey named her Brace—Joan Brace. At 10 Joan had raped the neighborhood, stolen, killed, etc., and at 16 was on the turf. But, says Berkeley, that didn't prove anything either way since Henrietta's environment was a hell of a background for any child anyway.

At the Chinese restaurant then went to Moneta's for a drink. Moneta, a dissolute, degenerate old Barrymore-ish Balzac roué was weaving about, drunk as a Lord, and oddly giving the impression of being on roller-skates.

April 30: All publishers turning down my book contrary to Carol's absolute promises. I don't know why I never learn about these egotistical confident women like Cheryl and Carol. They don't mean to lie, it's merely their tremendous egos speaking. They can't believe they can't do whatever they like.

May 5: My domesticity persists, what with curtain-making, dressmaking and today a cake, a very good one, too. For some reason—either age or nerve-fag—I have been lately as near homesick as I have ever been. I frankly want to go see Auntie May in Shelby though spiritually all those trips away from home deflate me and discourage me—the surroundings, I mean. I think before it gets too hot I really will go—perhaps on Friday this week, staying till Tuesday, visiting Mt. Gilead and Cardington. Feeling the urgent necessity for refreshing myself—my own self—and perhaps it is because I am forgetting too much, getting soft and weak.

Every time in my life when I have no solution for present problems I escape to the past and new clear-cut pictures emerge—lately the Mantua vacations with Uncle Stein.* This little village, long a resort for cults, theosophists, etc., outside Cleveland. In the gardens they grew parsley, unheard of anyplace else, for parsley potatoes, and my cousin Gretchen, transformed six months of the year into her father's daughter, baked zueberkuchen, lebkuchen, salads and to the horror of the village every week a Blue Label or Blue Ribbon beer wagon backed up and unloaded a case of beer in the cellar. I was errand girl to fetch the bottles, properly cold, up for every meal. I remember the dress I had—voile with Irish crochet and the pink marquisette one, too—I loved them both. Uncle Stein's idea of a suitable beau for his daughter was a boy who could drink a lot of beer, so poor Ralph Allen had to drink his head off nonchalantly to keep up his end.

May 20: Fixed up novel with Stan and arranged contract.

May 23: Worked on novel all week. A fairy morning at Wylie's (Dwight's) with Tony or Effie. After Wylie's party (London favorite) someone softly going through London musical success on piano.†

Fairies as an oasis in midst of country villages; alone you find them—sure of some intelligent conversation and wit. Little cosmopolitan posts

---

*Otto Steinbrueck, Powell's uncle and "Auntie May's" one-time husband.

†Powell is here sketching a scene from *Turn, Magic Wheel;* her customary slang for homosexual was "fairy."

on the prairie, a little lamp. Here is conversation, here is imagination for the weary traveler, worn down by Babbittry.

May 26: To Gypsy Tea Room. She said November, December and July were lucky months; nine my number; Monday my day; Alice or Alma a name to conjure with; two umbrellas over me all my life; no door unopened in old age; and much hurry at present over work that should have been done before. To Esther she said an estate would be settled in five weeks.

June 4: This novel, conceived in essence six years ago, planned, replanned, main characters shifted and plot changed. Manner, too, changed—inasmuch as all literary manners have changed, mine particularly. The careful good English we were taught to write is out and in order to be considered good now one must publish first drafts, first thoughts. Possibly Freud's psychoanalysis has something to do with that. We want the seed, not the flower; the stammer, not the finished thought. Literature stutters now, gropes.

June 5: On 14th Street and 6th Avenue—Theatre Union, line-forming of the Comrades. They stood, jostling each other, eager to grab each other's seats, to make each other as uncomfortable as possible, blow smoke in each other's faces, step on each other's toes, trip over each other's knees. Let us all work together and let us all make each other as uncomfortable as possible.

June 11: Joe in men's washroom. Man says "Feel them muscles." "Like iron," says Joe. "Sure, they're like iron. I just put my arm through that door. See?" "Don't see how you did it." "Wait, let me show you the other side." "By God, man, you must be a prizefighter." "No. Not a prizefighter. I'm a lawyer." "Well sir, with those muscles you ought to be a prizefighter." "You don't believe I'm a lawyer? Here's my card. Let's have a drink." "Beer." "No beer for me, bartender, I'll take a real drink. Scotch." "Well sir, I would have said you were a prizefighter." "I'm telling you I'm a lawyer. You got my card there. Long and Lamburton. In line for a judgeship." "A judgeship? Well, by God, when you're on the bench and I'm on a jury one of these days and you hand down a decision I don't like I'm going to say by God, Your Honor, that's a bum decision." "You'll do that? Say, I wish you would." Shakes hand earnestly. "I certainly will.

Judge, I'll say, Your Honor, I don't like that decision." "Promise me you mean that. I want just that."*

June 14: The chef at the Shore Club.† Pale, bald, reddish mustache, reddish brown eyes, delicate long hands. In his chef's hat quite handsome but bare—he was bald. Read all night and coughed. T.B. His wife, older, pastyfaced, spectacled, smug, sure she could be a pastry cook. He was a good cook. Robert Louis Stevenson was his favorite, he said. When waitresses brought back compliments he sneered—"Oh, so she did, did she? She liked the lobster patty, did she? Well, isn't that *sweet* of her?" It was a cross silently borne that his wife's cooking was no good, particularly since she was so confident, more than he. Airily she squirted, in whipped cream, S.C. on the strawberry shortcake and always it came back with angry complaints. "We want old-fashioned strawberry shortcake and plain cream—none of this funny business." "Hicks," she said.

July 1: On the bus, two women: "It's the nights I mind . . . days are the same—he was never home days anyway, but the nights . . . if it wasn't for the movies and the radio I'd go crazy."

July 28: Wolfe's Pocket Apostrophe
      (of time and the river on my hands)

> *Oh Boston girls how about it*
> *Oh Jewish girls, what say*
> *Oh America I love you*
> *Oh geography, hooray*
> *Ah youth, ah me, ah beauty*
> *Ah sensitive, arty boy*
> *Ah busts and thighs and bellies*
> *Ah nookey there—ahoy!*

August 8: No work done this week due to family being in—Phyllis, Mabel, Edgar and Tootsie, Keith and Dawnie. Cannot tell about this book— so different from my others—it seems barish but not as bare as Tess Slesinger's stuff.

---

*Almost two decades later, Powell used this material in *The Wicked Pavilion*.

†Powell had worked at the Shore Club, near Painesville, Ohio, during her years at Lake Erie College.

August 9: [Penciled in later in Powell's handwriting: *My Home Is Far Away.*] The story of three sisters meeting for the first time in three years for a trip—the invocation of their childhood, their joint recollections recreating the stepmother, building up their families, their memories, their so different lives, meantime about them their first trip, a cruise into a foreign scene (Havana) yet all the while they carry with them the rubber stamp, the indelible impression of their childhood, their family reunions —put together the unfinished fragments of each till the fiend herself emerges whole. The stepmother, the sudden terror of attics, a glimpse of each one's life—of their husbands, one an Al Saxe sort of person, the step-mother has swayed her into communism, another the stage, etc.

Visit to Canton, Ohio. I was told a horror story. For two years M. was out of work, his father who had helped him was ill, F. was always getting sick or pregnant, no money for abortion so she tried to do something herself, finally went to an old doctor who did something but said it was O.K. Then M. got work, his first job in two years, had to get up at 6. An hour before, miscarriage started—she bled and presently a little hand came out but she couldn't get anything done—the cord was tangled. M. tried to cut it with scissors and the tiny hand got cold, but he had to go to work leaving her that way because it was his first job.

Next door were the lousy Swedes—neighbors insulted, tradesmen felt justified in walking on. F. waited alone till she saw Mrs. Olsen in the kitchen, then asked her over. She came over, examined her, used to be a Swedish nurse, sent for doctor, lifted her, cared for her, saved her. After that when neighbors insulted her—lousy, dirty foreigners, don't play with their children—F. stood up for her.

Phyllis* told me about a boy—Llewellyn—who shot himself at 22 over love for a girl of 15 whose parents wouldn't let her go with him steadily. Llewellyn played with toy soldiers till he was 20, dressed up in masks, made wigs, rang peoples' bells in half-pretty face, half beard. In Manual Training school each boy could make his mother a present as his semester's work. One made a dresser, one a table, one a chair—Llewellyn made his a wooden leg. When he died, he left several poems.

---

*Phyllis Powell Cook, the author's sister.

August 14: Weight 137 and $^1/_4$—lost 3 and $^1/_2$ lbs. in less than three weeks due to exercise again, light breakfast—much grapefruit juice.

August 21: Auntie May and Jack Sherman on hand—Auntie May looking lovelier than ever. Jojo played the piano—"In a Little Gypsy Tea-Room" —and in middle of it said "I love you, Auntie May."

October 3: Max Gorelik, having won the Guggenheim for stage design, a bitter avowed Communist, dropped in with his pregnant woman to ask about apartments here, definitely bourgeois apartments. He told of having just got a bargain in land—86 acres in Erwinna, Pa., for $1500—and his hopes to build when he came back from abroad. He raised his glass. "To the Revolution!" he said, and I said, look here, Max, you can't be working for the revolution and be a capitalist landowner at the same time. Or is it a graft so that when Gorelik, the revolutionist, wins, he takes the property away from Gorelik, the capitalist, and so nothing is lost? He said, good-naturedly, might as well make use of this capitalist age in which we live.

October 15: Have Friday, Saturday, Sunday to work—might do 18 or 20 pages. Definitely upsetting to have Jojo in house with his legitimate demands for program, attention, etc. Novel continually vanishes in scattered thoughts.

November 2: Finished novel late at night.

November 5: Marie said "I'm getting out of the washing and ironing racket."

November 9: I remember all the times Papa would come home, whip out a picture of a simpering but firm lady in bustle and say (collecting all three of us, alarmed at this unwonted burst of fatherly sentimentality, in his arms) "Girls, what do you think of her as a stepmother?" Each time it was different.

November 18: No word from Farrar and Rinehart and have curious sickness as result, something I seem to get when my work is affected, as if

work was a gland secretion and when circumstance blocks it, the phy-
sique reacts as to any disease—slight fever, aches, weakness, definite
mental vagueness.

November 20: Sickish but no longer tense, due to fine rage at F & R, so
wrote firm, angry letter to Carol about them on backbone engendered by
Bergdorf clothes, no doubt. Going up today to get evening dress. In that
place models wander in and out of dressing rooms. Perfume girl comes in
with trace of Matchabelli to squirt at you.

November 21: Figures on books.

Dance Night	reg edition	4972
	reprint	7500
Tenth Moon	reg	1932
		1089
Country Boy	reg	1842
"Jig-Saw"		281

November 22: In *Turn, Magic Wheel,* I believe firmly that I have the perfect New York story, one woman's tragedy viewed through the chinks of
a writer's book about her, newspaper clippings, cafe conversations, restaurant brawls, New York night life, so that the story is tangled in the fritter
of New York—it could not happen anyplace else. The front she keeps
up is the front peculiar to the New York broken heart; peoples' deeds and
reactions are peculiarly New York. "What? Our friend committed suicide—that's terrible . . . that's the kind of suit I'm going to get, there in
Altman's . . . She jumped out of the window? No!—are you getting out
here, why don't you get a gold belt. . . ?"

Publisher and critic (but not public which—once it can be reached—is
always more sane and sound than critical interpreters) would say these
women, discussing the deaths of their friends, must be hard, bitter. The
truth is that in New York, a city of perpetual distraction—where superficial senses are perpetually forced to react to superficial impressions—the
inner tragedies, no matter how intense, are viewed through the tawdry
lace of New York life.

November 24: Jojo, after tense day with very smug, self-satisfied Ann De Silver* was almost too wracked by her complacency so I asked him "How was Ann today" and he said "She's fine as hell!" then clenched his teeth.

November 26: Dreaming of the sea as I always do when concerned about my work—sea and houses. Last night I saw people skating on this huge, cliff-harbored sea. And frozen is the state of my work right now, too—not the creation but results. Stan says publication in February or March. Possibly parts could be published places—the Empire State one in *Vanity Fair* perhaps . . .

This year I have very little to show for my work, though it seems to me I have worked. Wrote only three short pieces: "Young Arnold By Night," "Cheerio" and "Artist's Life"—all sold for $450—pretty good, too. Two pieces for Dwight—"Venus and Adonis" and "Double Manhattan."

Ought to do enough stuff to come out during and after my book. All day stints as much as possible. Should not allow any time out for futile drinking—party drinking with reservations.

December 2: Lunch with John Farrar. He told me how fine my book was; it probably wouldn't sell, etc. Lunch with him is taxing for he is such a complete self-dramatizer. Even his face takes on a cartoon quality, a cartoon of whatever he's talking about—guinea pig—senator—burlesque queen. The flaccid features become these people.

December 10: Miss B.—very pretty but always full of news about her stomach. Eager descriptions make you see not her pretty face but the fascinating pattern of her digestive system.

December 14: Went to party at Rosie Miller's. Here a fabulous monument of a woman, Roman-faced, gray, diamond-studded, was introduced as Philip's cousin, Miss DeGroot, "an old aristocrat." Her pontifical presence, silent, impressive, moved people to conversations they would never have had, bolstered up Phil's contained class-complacency so much that he, to every one's astonishment, became offensively boastful of his high blood.

---

* Ann De Silver, Margaret De Silver's daughter, was, like Jojo, mentally impaired.

"You come from the lower middle class," he said to someone, "whereas I come from the upper middle class." He and his wife spoke of Miss DeGroot's millions, her jewels, her art treasures, her birth, as if she were a monument being unveiled and not a person. They nudged their guests—"old aristocrat," they said and pointed to her. Presently she was hoisted into a car like a Zorach marble and rattled off to the Museum, very likely to be loaned out to private parties again to symbolize royal blood.

Philip enjoys the peculiar pleasure of Gentile men married to Jewish women—permanent condescension. So worried is he by his marital lapse that instead of being trampled under by Jewish hordes he holds aloft a banner of super-super-Gentility, blue blood, Mayflower, etc., each new fear of being lost in Rosie's Jewish world creates new and purer blood for his ancestors, and finally her world unites with him to elevate him to High Goy throne. He is so lost in a Jewish world that he forgets there is any other goy and takes for granted that he is—if not the only Gentile—the only not of foreign immigrant extraction, the only whose parents went to school. A modest, slightly ridiculous figure in sheer colorlessness, he has taken on color and majesty against his Jewish tapestry, and has made of his very pallor evidence of superiority, of his aristocratic blood an ever ready whip to subjugate his too efficient, too vigorous wife.

December 16: Took Jojo to Medical Center for X-rays of skull to see how clot was placed and if ossified or calcified.

December 19: Johnny Mosher was over at Dos'. He talks and feels about himself as a very dear eccentric aunt and wherever he goes watches his own amusing reactions as if he were his own pet, too precious to be left in the baggage car but rather to be tenderly borne on the lap. When he went alone through Europe he was not going alone, he was taking that amusing fellow Mosher and taking him right, too. Whenever he saw some charming person—such as the little thing from Budapest in white satin blouse—he thought that once they got to Madrid he would ask her out for a cocktail but she talked so eagerly of the bullfights, the theater, the opera, that he saw a cocktail would only lead to expense and his own plan was better—one cocktail for himself, one ticket for the bullfight, one seat at the theater—so he never saw her again.

As for his friend, Miss Newell, he sighed, "Yes, we get along much better now. I'm too old for her at last, thank God." He is a faintly funereal wag, smelling of old ladies and moth balls, and Victorian parlors, expecting cancer with a smile, welcoming decent calamity with great good nature so long as it's something slow and fatal and respectable rather than garish and dramatic. He, like so many other gifted young men about town, slipped somehow into one of Henry James' lesser mantles, assuming with authority the role of Dean of Letters, without going to the bother of writing. This slight lapse in preparation passes unnoticed now, when others of his own generation have stopped writing anyway, so no one can be sure which witty critic once wrote a fine novel, a successful play or poem, and which never did anything but show promise.

1936

[*Undated*]

"Every object reveals by its lines how it would resolve itself were it to follow the tendency of its forces." (Painting of "States of Mind")

Gibbon said about the Christians—they professed a fine contempt for those luxuries which a wise providence had so fortunately placed beyond their reach.

Niles' report of Thomas Wolfe looming over a table at the Lafayette (with Clifford Odets, etc.)—"What I say is this, either you *have* talent or you haven't, that's all, either you have it or you haven't."

At the Playwrights' Dinner. How can we approach the "Bourgeois Press"? They enjoy making it hard and refusals make them think they're strong. They go at it head first, butting and rebutting, firm in their mistakes, attacking the invulnerable heart always instead of isolating and weakening it by picking off its surrounding weaknesses. Archie MacLeish and Lee Simonson both lashed in with original new points but the backbone, Albert Maltz and George Sklar, insist on their dogma and, pious little plain faces smugly aglow, wait with handcuffs of party clichés to imprison each fresh thought. Limited little minds find their only strength in clinging to four ropes, and pulling all free swimmers into the little pen.

January 1: The war of the two young brothers, one a Communist, the other a would-be capitalist, quarreling before their mother over which is going to do which. "I'll buy you a Rolls Royce"—the other says, "Rockefellers and Rolls Royces will all be gone, everybody just like us."

January 2: "What'd you think of the show?" asked Odets, firmly fixing me with blue eye. "You saw 'Paradise,'* didn't you?"

"Well," I said uneasily, "I can't say just what I thought. I was only sure it wasn't bad."

Group actors and directors took a step forward, like Gods of the Mountain closing in about me. I stammered more inadequacies.

"The reason I ask," said Clifford, "is that about ten of the leading playwrights are testifying for it in an ad, and I'd like to get you in on it. Some of the biggest people in the theater."

Later he talked of the Odets Plays, the audience joy over Odets Plays, as if Odets, the genius, was quite apart from Odets, the "modest" citizen.

January 3: Genevieve Taggard is changed. Happiness as a rule brings out the worst in people's characters. No longer afraid, they radiantly flaunt their smugness, small vices and worst sentimentalities. For years, G. was troubled by lack of humor and ponderous foot. A light conversation made her wretched, a twinkle in the eye made her aware of something going on that she was missing and, loud as she could laugh, she secretly feared her lack was conspicuous; strain as she could, she still missed everything and it depressed her.

But now, happy in marriage, secure in love, and conventional above all, she can say *what's so funny?* and *who cares?*; recklessly she can be pompous and patronizingly pedagogic. She doesn't need to see whimsy any more for she's safe above it. Fearlessly, she can leap into an old-style genteel lady's discussion of Art in Life, The Poet in a Crass Age. Her eyes flash ecstasy as she cries "But Art *is* Life! And Life *is* Art!" No wedge for the arty cliché is left ignored, her voice is raised in unctuous defense of Culture, a missionary hope ticks behind her words of bringing—even forcing—Culture, Art, Poetry, on the Man in the Street. Her clichés, her little pets that a sophisticated group of friends once shamed her into hiding, can all be brought out again, and she can stand bravely, self-righteously, up to a twinkle or light word, and bludgeon it down with Integrity, Sincerity of Purpose, Honor. Happiness has given her a sword; respectability has given her the right to be stupid.

January 5: Esther—gifted, but with the misfortune to be with people always of first grade genius. Without a great ego, work was impossible

---

* "Paradise Lost" had opened at the Belasco Theatre on December 9.

around them; at the same time creative urge almost satisfied by thorough dredgings of *their* souls. When they drifted out of her life she was rudderless, quite lost. Growing older, the gaps between the great who fed her became greater and she fastened on potential meat like a necrophile, or vampire rather, ravenous without its fodder, crotchety, full of righteous indignation and a philosophy: The World Owes Me A Thrilling.

Angry with promising talent of friends that came to never anything more, she wraths and storms when suddenly confronted with life among her peers—quiet intelligent people who feed on larger spirits, suddenly bereft in their community of king or queen or master mind, teacher-less. Lost, they nibble at each other's meager crackers, find only their own tasteless fare, storm, fume, brood. Even in love, they found others more glamorous and left their own pleasant fires to help a big blaze or thunderstorm; feed their romantic needs on other's romances; groom infidelities carefully as kindling for the big bonfire. So E., finding herself more and more only with nibbles, grows ravenous, furious, lost, vaguely indignant at the mental breast withdrawn, too old for weaning, too spoiled for self-feeding.

January 8: Long siege of grippe with accompanying cave-in of family responsibility feeling. Actual sickness has always come on me from mental or spiritual causes—pecked to death by duties, bills, plans for child, house, help, etc. Mentally strong, the surrender is physical, actual tonsillitis or grippe or female trouble.

Odd that I have no impressions of this *Turn, Magic Wheel* novel except that it seems more alive, more superficially compelling than any of my books—less change of mood from life required to enter it. Probably will annoy people as "Big Night" did, according to the way Carol and Halliday react and others. "Unpleasant, dreadful people"—what they always say when I have congratulated myself on capturing people who need no dressing up or prettifying to be real. But yes, people say, they do; before the reader will identify himself, he must be changed so that no one else will recognize him.

I think critics who have never given me more than a paragraph or two of dignified praise will suddenly, in attempting to describe their displeasure over this book, recall with delight my other great works. I expect unfavorable, even insulting, reviews, but long ones.

January 11: Coby was planning dinner for two people. How will you seat them? He didn't know, he said, it was such a problem he was having a man in tonight to work it out, a mathematician in fact, who thought he'd have to do it by the binomial theory.

Speaking of the new Chaplin picture, "Modern Times," he said there were conflicting rumors about it, one rumor saying it was good, and other rumors saying they didn't know.

January 18: Joe went to Oneida Community for weekend and returned with stories of the vital old grenadier women up there, all over 60, remembering days in the '60s and '70s when J. Humphrey Noyes was in full command, of the women in short skirts and bobbed hair, bronzed by the sun, serving excursion dinners at $1 per to tourists on the newly built O & W Railway, who stared at the "free lovers."

January 20: Mr. Cunningham: "Here I am—$52 a week. Eight years ago, I was worth $20,000—invested in the stock market. My wife had some money. Do you realize that stock went up 70 points in one day? 70 points in *one day*. I was studying to be a Certified Public Accountant. But I didn't take the examination. So the thing collapsed—our money went fooey. My wife says, if you'd taken that examination you'd be making $20,000 a year instead of $52 a week. We have a friend—Byrd. Certified Public Accountant. $20,000 a year he makes. Every once in a while my wife says 'Look at Byrd. If you'd taken that examination six years ago you'd be making Byrd's salary.' I like Byrd. He's a nice fellow. But you can't have someone thrown up to you all the time."

February 3: This is the longest period of Jojo being completely hopeless. I can scarcely remember any time since fall that he has put through a calm normal day. He requires the most intense control for from morning till night he bursts in, plants himself before me and shouts meaningless sentences over and over. Now I've decided to smack him or get Joe to. It's too horrible a life, waking up to the jabbering of a noisy maniac, a dreadful future for all of us to face—ten thousand days of hopeless work to pay for hopeless treatments.

February 7: Fine letter from Inez Haynes Irwin about *Turn, Magic Wheel.* Considerable enthusiasm in office. Have given it to: Mabel, Phyllis, Aunt

May, Ralph, Esther, Aline Bernstein, Louise, Niles, Dwight, Margaret, Eleanor Farnham, Coby, Dick Halliday, Kay Brown, Lloyd Sheldon, Dos, Lowell Brentano, Gene Jolas, LeClercqs, Charles Studin, Lawsons, Mary Margaret McBride.

February 10: The book is looking up. Robert Nathan, Rex Stout, Inez Haynes Irwin all read it and are enthusiastic. Mary Ross has too and reviewed it favorably.*

At Studin's yesterday the place was filled with charming sensitive, *passé* women, the saddest sight in all the world, except for the elderly men at parties. One once-beautiful woman of about 55, pounced eagerly on people, me particularly, and chattered lightly, vivaciously, of a million things, never pausing, alarming you now and then by a phrase like "of course my son is a raving maniac, has been in a State Institution for 20 years" and "don't mistake me for *Ethel Watts* Mumford, my husband's first wife and ruined his life, really, spent all his money, was indiscriminate to put it mildly . . ."

There was no graceful way to escape the incessant bombardment of her chatter, and just as I was leaving she said, ". . . of course it took all my own fortune and my husband's. I had to sell my diamonds, then my little boy insane. We tried to normalize him—in three months he went stark mad—only 14 years old. But you're such a dear child; why should I put this on you? Please don't look so serious—yes, 20 years he's been there and when I say 'what are those welts on his arm?' the warden says remember he is a Butterfield and a Butterfield can always upset 2000 people. Right, I said. Of course he can upset the other inmates, he's a Butterfield. They're remarkable people; his grandfather built the Pennsylvania Railroad. But the thousands I spent to begin with—as long as we had it—private institutions where he cut his throat and his wrists—a *private* institution, mind you—just a little boy, a fine, beautiful child, everyone adored him but no, they said, he could be normalized, so there he was, uprooted from his tutors, his house—he went to the boy's school, little Eton jackets, whippings every day—in three months he was mad—and me there alone to cope with it for four months. But don't let me burden you—why do you look that way?"

"You're not burdening me," I said. "My own little boy is 14 and we have been worried . . ."

---

*In the New York *Herald Tribune.*

"Oh, my God," she said. "It mustn't happen. You can stop it. I could have stopped Dan. Sit down."

It was a cocktail party for Margaret Widdemer and people were very gay. It was odd for two women in the middle of this confusion, sandwiches and martinis politely being passed, introductions to newcomers offered, to find that strange bond in common—a 14-year old only son—one 20 years ago and the other now—quivering on the brink of a nightmare future. I understood then her incessant gay chatter—for 20 years she had sparkled and chattered to drown the roar of her own tragedy, a little boy raving mad.

"Where do you come from?" Mrs. Dana Butterfield Mumford asked, examining me penetratingly.

"My people come from Ohio," I said.

"Nonsense, child, of course they did, everyone's people spent a few generations in the Middlewest but where were they *from?* Virginia?"

Later I went to lunch at the Womens' City Club, where she is chairman. "The old Butler home," she explained, whisking people in and out of the reception rooms downstairs, waving her program, accidentally spilling butter over her new dress while arranging the place-cards at the Chairman's Table. There was an odd air of Alumnae Day about the place, the women had the frozen, wizened masks of their young, athletic faces, the way women have now instead of the serene, relaxed middle-aged faces of their mothers at that age. Not made up but an inner seeking restless look that preserves but shrivels youth far into the forties.

In the dining room they gathered to hear speeches. "There is Portia Willis, a militant suffragette," said the woman beside me, pointing to a blooming Brünnhilde in red. "She used to be put on a white horse at the front of the suffrage parades. And there is Elizabeth Freeman, another militant, who was chained to the House of Commons one time . . . Of course we're not all militants. We're interested in Civics. Non-partisan. We even have one Communist—a friend of several of us, of course, or we might have hesitated. But in a way it's helpful having all angles. By the way, I wanted to ask about your book. My son died two months ago—and I don't like to read any books that might bring it up."

The women sat around, looking the way they used to look, then the sun shone in and the wrinkles popped into view, hinting the way they would look twenty years from now. Beside me the women listened eagerly to the speakers talk of glamorous worlds. They laid a place in their mental luncheon table for every great name that was mentioned; they drank in H. G. Wells, Pauline Lord, Ellen Terry, Bernard Shaw, David Belasco, Ruth Draper. They were on the same jolly pal basis with these great names as was the speaker. Here was their life, their outside world. From here, they returned to their more modest worlds, their sad worlds, too, with valentines from dead lovers, dead sons, dead husbands.

February 16: Jojo, beginning Italian lessons, as per his insistent request, is now very fine, very normal, very poised, stately, taking no pills, merely being bossed by Ann De Silver, and having his own way and a very busy schedule. Appointments make him feel important.

Dos and Coby at dinner. Dos bringing a present to me of whiskey, me having a Storm-tossed for him, and ending by my drinking the Storm-tossed, which I wanted really, and his enveloping the whiskey, shyly admitting "When people bring a present there's usually a pretty good reason for it. I personally feel the need of a little Scotch." So they drank and Coby reminisced. I have known Coby eight years and only in the last year have anecdotes about his life appeared; he's been close-mouthed but now out they come in long streamers as if they had been put in trust for him till he was 42 and now he's reveling in his inheritance.

He told of Bessie, the most kept woman on Whore's Row (Central Park West) who became more genteel with each diamond, more "rayfeened" with each new Chinese floor-lamp but no matter how refined she got her apartment remained inalterably whorish. She was constantly being bitched by her environment, which seemed to us a good title for a novel: "Bessie, or Bitched By Her Environment."

He told of the bearded girl in Denver, the sister of his friend. Six brothers, all hairy, blue-jowled boys even at 16, and sister unfortunately endowed the same. By this time Dos too was tight and radiantly delighted at the bearded girl.

"No! She couldn't have been really bearded!"

"Yes, sir, by God, had to shave every day . . . You'd see her at 10 o'clock in the morning and her chin would be blue!"

"No! Blue, really?" Dos, more and more amazed and delighted pouring himself Cutty Sark, Scots Blended.

"Blue as a man's! I swear to Christ! And pious! She was so pious. I remember she had a class in Sunday School. Christ, she was religious!"

"And she had to shave every day?" Dos asked again, pleased, rubbing his hands. "It was that bad?"

So it went on, with each drink the lure of the bearded woman getting stronger.

Coby also told of the minister who gave him a talk before he came to New York and told him never to dance with a woman, it roused the carnal instinct. So in no time at all, Coby, who had been unable to dance up to this time, became the best dancer in New York.

February 20: Inez Haynes Irwin's. Here is a big house filled with relations, pretty nieces, their husbands, their fiancés, a free pleasant house that no child would ever dare run away from, so kind a prison that one could scream of suffocation. The kind of warm, overpowering family house that even the casual guest enters with trepidation for there is no "dropping in" here; it is like joining a club, entering a term at college—permanence hangs over the vestibule like a hangman's rope. Somebody takes your rubbers, your umbrella; no getting away easily, you think desperately.

The pretty and fading nieces who wanted to go on the stage, be teachers, be this or that, sit about beaten by wise, understanding encouragement, look into their fiancé's eyes, lust licked by the broadminded arrangements of the family for them to sleep together undisturbed. They listen to their famous elders talk of their crowd, which they have never ceased to believe is the backbone of American *belles lettres;* they speak of the talent—or lack of it—of Kathleen Norris, Edna Ferber, Fannie Hurst, Charles Norris, as if any of these names meant a thing to the literary world today, for most people are under the impression these people are either dead or hacks. Certainly they never represented anything but normal, average intelligence and some hard work.

For hours after leaving this warm, wisely-managed prison I had the elated delirious sensation of having escaped and of thanking God I had no such sweet mufflers over my brain when I was growing up. Hooray for the kick in the pants as the mind-crystallizer, ambition-detector, wisdom-giver.

Alice Robe, Italian correspondent, was there, a heavy, Irish jolly woman, trying by tasteful clothes, reducing, quiet words, to quell the jovial good-time-lover that her Irish mug and laugh revealed. Her last 15 years have been spent in Italy which she feels is her home, where her lovers and friends are, her possessions. She wrote and sold a piece on Mussolini and now if she goes back she will be killed. She can never go back and, at 45, she says truth isn't worth it. She must be lonely and miserable the rest of her life because of her vanity in telling a few simple truths.

She told of asking Mussolini in her last interview how he reconciled urging the women to grow more babies with his warlike program. Wasn't it cruel to have babies merely to feed a war? Mussolini looked at her in silent reproach, hurt.

"Sentiti, Alicia," he said, "why do you ask me questions like that? Why don't you ask me how I keep so young and in such fine health? I eat fruit!"

Fine reviews of novel. In second printing.

February 26: "Realism" is the only completely vague word. "Satire" is the technical word for writing of people as they are; "romantic," the other extreme of people as they are to themselves—but both of these are the truth. The ability to put in motive is called satire; the ability to put in vision is romanticism.

A man endows a hospital in a small town; actually his *motive* is political and social advancement in the town. His *vision* is helping his fellow-men in their suffering. Emphasis on one is satire, on the other romance; both are true and truer than the middle course of "realism," just as frank radicalism and frank conservatism are more tonic, more constructive than the well-tempered liberal, who sees a little of each side without interpretation.

In my satire (except for stage satire which admits of little or no nuances) I merely add a dimension to a character, a dimension which gives the person substance and life but which readers often mistake for malice. For instance, take the funeral of a much-loved family woman, a mother. Treating this romantically, one writes only of the sadness in the people's hearts, their woe, their sense of deprivation, their remembrance of her. This is true, but it is not as true as I would do it, with their private bickers over the will in the garage, as they all gorge themselves at the funeral meals, as the visiting sisters exchange recipes, confidences (for they haven't seen each other in many years), as pet vanities emerge.

Yet in giving this picture, with no malice in mind, no desire to show the grievers up as villains, no wish more than to give people their full statures, one would be accused of "satire," of "cynicism," instead of looking without blinders, blocks, ear mufflers, gags, at life. Satire is people as they are; romanticism, people as they would like to be; realism, people as they seem with their insides left out.

March 2: The bachelors of New York in the Satyricon style. Do in swift fierce style of a race descending on the enemy—"The Joyous Isle."*

John Mosher, unattractive to women, silent in the home, finds balm in getting the pale silent young man in borrowed evening clothes away from Dwight. He has him in his home where he encourages him to go on with his cooking, gets him Escoffier, Brillat-Savant, Sabatini, Moneta, brings him home little gadgets, egg slices, canapés, entertains, proud of his pompano in fig leaves, his duck *a la presse.* John talks, educating him culturally; Dopey listens, says salad too wet. Gloomy, naturally ignorant, lazy, unattractive young man. They have a cat who is calling.

Dwight, the theatrical success, with the manager, etc., adoring people around. The young brothers quarreling over their Peggy Joyces and evading being collected at the same time. Gil's tragedy running through it, cut himself off from Ohio, from his roots, now free and lost at 40, a man of the world, paying for everything, paying for a friend to play the Joyous Isle. His friends go to their different menages at 8 or 9; he goes to opera alone. Turning on lights and finding book where he left it always hurts him.

John encourages Dopey to write cook book a la Brillet Savarin but week after week Dopey gets gloomier. Presently sees manuscript. "Cooking is the art of making something to eat. Everybody likes to eat. People mostly put too much water on in cooking vegetables." John's heart sank. "You ought to get out more," he said.

A town where all men are potential bachelors. A wives' town. On Thursday, they wander about, put out by wives entertaining former lovers. Free night—the women are in command of jobs and lives, the men scavenge frantically through the city for a life women can't get at, for pleasures reserved for them alone. The desperate back-to-the-wall fight for independence, for pleasure.

*This was the beginning of *The Happy Island;* Powell often modeled her characters on real people but rarely provided such a direct key.

"Yes, Mrs. Pudge, we Westchester women do like to talk over life in its bigger aspects."

March 8: Flagstad in *Fidelio*. What difference is there between a good voice and a magic voice? Sometimes no difference in tone, placing, or quality, but Flagstad's simple great voice flowers, soars, fills the ascending tiers—one voice enough to charm and fill with joy 10,000 hearts. It rose and grew (the great hall was not big enough), flowed through the orderly rows of light-struck EXIT signs, consorted with old echoes in shadowed corners, visited the old caged attendant in the Ladies Check Room, floated kindly over her proud book of autographs—Sembrich, Schumann-Heink, Tetrazzini, Caruso, Jeritza, Adelina Patti—and was reined in again by silence, a splendid echo left warm and unforgotten on the air.

March 10: The gal, Lilla Worthington, who died at the Brandt's cocktail party. The rainy day. The elevator strike so that streets were crowded with strikers, picketers, rain, cold, blowing off hats and umbrellas inside-out, taxis stuck for hours on sidestreets. By 5:45 only six people in the baronial Brandt living room to meet the Minnesota author, Margaret Culkin Banning, and those six ladies of little importance. "No one is coming to this party," complained Carol, looking with curious dislike on those who had been so common as to come.

In the adjoining dining room three colored waiters (one to every two guests) hovered over a table laden with seltzer, whiskey, sherry and martini mixes. They patiently and constantly passed the trays of little toasted sausages, the stuffed olives in bacon on the pretty colored toothpicks. People talked vivaciously to each other trying to be a crowd and eyes lit up when the bell rang and the row of too handsome young men from the motion picture offices came in. Carol looked pained with the bare bones of her ten percent party too obviously revealed—office employees and movie buyers, usually decently lost in groups of social and literary figures.

The pretty, sweet-faced Miss Worthington and I tried to remember where we met. I had never seen her at the Brandt parties as they rather dislike having their underlings in the home socially. A few minutes later she was standing talking to other people—a commotion, a slight exclamation, she was on the floor. Window raised, wet cloth brought, suddenly Carl picked her up and carried her into another room, her curly head dangling over his arm, strange animal gurgling noises coming from her, someone running along beside her with an inadequate little folded wet handkerchief. People looked at each other with expressions of mingled polite concern and natural distaste for the bad manners of the thing. The polite thing obviously was to continue to chat, forgive the rather vulgar interruption, and so groups closed in again. The several motion picture people argued about the value of Vincent Price's profile to pictures; those for him insisted that the photographer taking his tests declared "I don't know who this Price is but I will say this—he is without doubt the most gorgeous boy I've ever photographed."

Miss Banning moved about bravely, guest of honor to the end; someone occasionally asked about the girl inside; the three butlers passed their canapés furiously to get rid of these too plentiful supplies and then the Old Guard began to arrive—the three name old-time writers, gray, immense, evening-cloaked and furred majestic wives, old Cosmopolitan plots wrapped around their necks, ready for formal dinner and *Tristan* later at the Met, the Samuel Hopkins Adams, etc. Just then someone came out from the bedroom in the midst of this new cheer from outside and said we were all to leave, the girl was very sick. We left—but she couldn't be dead! But she was, and her last moments had been full of sweet little Southern banalities and she dropped off as if her name had suddenly thundered through the world—"Lilla Worthington—paging Lilla Worthington"—the first time in all her modest, kind little life she'd been vulgarly conspicuous, the first time she'd ever made a scene.

Later someone said her husband and relatives came—the great apartment with the three colored butlers, the untouched cocktails, the cold sausages and congealed toasted cheese—deserted, untouched and uncleaned. The hostess, still in her new hostess gown with trailing train, carefully matched slippers, rushed over to a hotel with mink coat over her arm. It was the dead woman's party, it was a home she'd never dreamed of having, a place she had often wanted to show her husband though he was never asked there. Now he could see the lovely rugs, the Sheraton cupboard and the gold Venetian bed she had often described to him; now he could see it for she was dead upon it. Taking her two little boys to school in the morning she had fainted, she had fainted other days, too, but she was afraid of the doctor. She couldn't be very sick; a doctor would scare her, would try to make something serious out of it.

March 21: Niles went to tea at the Whitney Museum—very drunk, ran through the rooms, tweaked an old gent's Van Dyke and pushed him into a chocolate cake. It was General Vanderbilt, no less. But what hospitality, he sighed—two footmen to each guest, pouring up your glass as fast as you could down it till they kicked you out.

A little resentful at leaving the sumptuous cellar, he rode with some socialites in their car. His radical side came out and he resented them saying "If we could kill all the Micks . . . if we could get rid of all the wops . . . if we could kill all the Jews . . ." "What about if we could kill all the Vanderbilts?" said Niles, very uglily.

The great man (Tolstoy) visited by pilgrims from all over the world—heckled by his wife and daughter. The only thing they feared was his diary. They bullied him in everything else but this one secret going out into the world frightened them and he used this weapon to full advantage.

April 8: At "Murder in the Cathedral"—we had to wait so long for it to begin Coby said, "Can't we do something to bring it on?" In restaurant he said about some woman "Sexually she was O.K. but spiritually she wasn't worth a f—k!"* And on his complaint of all salary being spent on liquor he was told he should have someone parcel him out $2.00 a day—which he agreed was a fine plan, he could manage on $2 a day in addition to his salary, only who was going to give him this $2 a day—would I? He wished he could go on the wagon, was outraged on being told he could do so if he had any will power. Will power? He had the most amazing will power in the world, it was *amazing,* that will power of his, the only thing was, it was completely futile.

April 18: Going to make "The Joyous Isle" a long book, perhaps 125,000 words. Try to do five pages a day—or average 25 pages a week. Should be flowing, fluid, full of good dishes as John and Dopey see them, life through a curtain of good cooking.

---

*Even in her diary, Powell never wrote this word out.

May 14: Twitted with not being Communist—why? He worked hard all his life—newsboy, waiter, garage mechanic, worked through college, everything open to him. Finds man who had ease and took it in youth; now, with other people's property behind them, lauding the Worker, as phony a sentimentality as the former awe of the Creative Writer, the Artist. The rigorous secret laws against anyone who derides a member of the Party (unless he happens to be a member of the Party himself); the self-deception, the acquisitiveness for property, passion for money and estate, the throwing of all personal feeling for fellowmen into a machine "Party" which exempts one from kindness, generosity, any form of idealism.

May 16: To Mt. Sinai. Planted flowers, marigold, bluebonnet, Japanese hop vine, hollyhock, mignonette, larkspur, delphinium, aster, moonflower, honeysuckle, morning glory.

May 29: To the Hickory House with Carlo where Wingy Manone plays with his orchestra "I's a muggin'." I went in the Ladies Room. The attendant, a thin, frizzed, middle-aged woman put down *Liberty* magazine and said "Well, the more you read, the less you know." I asked her what she was reading about, and she said politics. "I don't care what they say. I'll vote my straight Tammany ticket the same as always," she said. I said I didn't get around to voting much. "Well, you should, girlie," she said. "We women don't get much out of life anymore. Can't even get a seat on the subway since we got the vote." I went in the can. "How do you like this place, dear?" she asked. "Fine," I said. "Yes, I think so, too," she said. "It's home-like."

Outside the great round bar was arranged like a merry-go-round. Inside was the colored Wingy Manone,* radio trappings, an announcer, three bartenders, a bull fiddle and an orchestra of moronic faces playing moronic music. Home-like was the word.

June 4: Gretchen died.†

June 5: Left for Shelby to be with Auntie May at Gretchen's funeral.

---

*Powell to the contrary, Manone was white.
†Gretchen Quiggle was Orpha May Steinbrueck's only child.

June 19: Jojo very fine for a spell due to satisfied ego—weekend in country with parents. Confided that at night he felt sometimes that God had put a curse on his lips so he couldn't open his mouth and speak.

July 1: Read *The Beauties and Furies* of Christina Stead. Like [Rebecca West's] *The Thinking Reed* and Rosamond Lehmann's *Weather in the Streets.* These ladies (and Miss Stead is much the best) occupy themselves with the intelligent sensitive woman, the nostril-quiverer, the decent fine woman who falls in love with a married man, or else is married and in a paroxysm of decency falls in love with a single man.

Progress is so personal: "They" couldn't do that in those days. Yet George Sand seemed to have been able to hang around the cafes of Paris in 1830. There are still people who would swear no nice woman would go to a cafe alone, and others who would swear that nowhere today does such prejudice exist.

Everybody is traveling everywhere now. The voice of the people. Every young man has flashed through Russia and has reported the word of the people. That the inarticulate (when they do speak), the unauthorized, the naive are credited with being "The People" is ridiculous.

August 4: Exhausting dreadful weather, noise of riveting, etc., and house renovating next door—parties, radios, noise beats on brain like hammers, oompah of swing music goes on while ears are covered with pillows. Tired by night but prevented by heat and noise from rest; by day, the din of the workmen.

August 5: Mr. Sadleir* of Constable wrote pleasantly of the book in England. More impressive reviewers than here, due, I believe, to their intelligent approach to the book. Sent me a note of Helen Waddell's—whose *Medieval Latin Lyrics* have always pleased me†—saying "I have just finished Dawn Powell's *Turn, Magic Wheel;* it is the same kind of experience as watching Elizabeth Bergner act for the first time. Odd, to discover again the Comic Muse in Radio City, sorrowful, impish and wise. I do congratulate you."

Depressed slightly by bills, no money from England as expected, owing grocery, Louise, etc., and trying to provide house, food, supplies,

---

*Michael Sadleir, author and editor.

†See entry of June 29, 1931.

movies for Jojo and carfare for myself. Utterly disgusted with futility of my career if I can't collect more security than that. However, English reception pleased me more than anything for a long time.

August 7: The sweet, plump, fair, feminine, scrupulously cream-colored lady of 45, alone at the bar of the Albert, drinking Manhattans, carrying on a polite, low-voiced conversation with the bartender and obviously so genteel that he deferred to her before mixing anyone else's drink. Elderly, handsome gentleman at a table, amused and interested in her, willing to make fun except no matter how many drinks she took she continued well-bred, smooth, sweet and definitely not the type. He pays check, goes to bar for final brandy, starts talking to her. They drink together—five, six. She never seems to gobble her drinks, yet they disappear, no sign save for slight twitching of the mouth—the twitch of the dipsomaniac, as a matter of fact.

He becomes more and more the courtly wooer under her very definite role of prim lady. Presently she has taken a letter out of her pocket to consult him about. He adjusts rimmed glasses—he is already flushed and not so young-looking. He studies it; she looks at it over his shoulder as if it was a message she could not tire of reading—a prize, perhaps, an acceptance, good news of her daughter—but lonely, no one to share it with.

They were still drinking, his attitude more discreetly lustful, hers more bewildered little innocent protected wife without affectation, not a drop of vulgarity or humor in her, nothing but gentleness, childlike femininity, a consciousness and confidence that a woman's place was in the home, an ungrown-up sweet bewilderment in spite of a probable 45 years. I had a feeling that she was taught that a drink was all right by a husband she adored. He died or left her and she does the things he tried to teach her in his genial effort to make a cosmopolitan of her. By herself, lonely, a little alarmed by other women alone, she has no life but a vicarious one with dead Herbert. Talks to him, tries to read and be interested in his interests.

August 10: In "The Joyous Isle," begin with gay picture of crossed loves, perversities, night life, precarious fame of the city. The young man from the backwoods with his play ringing of truth, of bitterness, so that the town recognizes the ugliness of it, is disturbed, but rushes to praise suaver items.

September 14: Finished first act of play—very good. Now dallying with Paramount and Goldwyn on coast job—$1000 a week. Need a change for my mind. Too happy and contented—this is no good for my sort of writing.

September 28: Started writing for Samuel Goldwyn in Hollywood.

November 14: Paul Gardiene—the sour, curious, intelligent furniture man. "This is not an antique shop—this is a second-hand furniture store." Gloomily in soft hat, coat collar turned up, bandage over carbuncle on neck, he discoursed on his friend who died, all apropos of respectability. He suggested this or that mirror or chest for me. "It is not bad, it is not the best, still it looks respectable," he sneered. "To look respectable is something."

It reminded him of his friend, now dead. A man 60 or so. An editor. Spoke 13 languages. But bad luck—one thing and another—in spite of having $125,000 worth of paintings. Every day he came to the shop for 18 years. They had an old stove. He sat there, a philosopher. If he liked, he would get up and sell a piece of furniture. On his way to the store he would pick up bits of wood on the street, tie them on a string and drag them. M. Gardiene spoke of this to him: how could he drag wood openly through the streets? "I have no desire to look respectable," said his friend. "Furthermore, I have no respect for respectability."

On Sundays, his friend, who lived alone, came to the studios above the shop for breakfast. It began at 11 and ended at 4. They discussed life and philosophy. This Sunday he ate his breakfast as usual, bran muffins "we" made (as he no longer liked bread). He got up, said he seemed to have grippe, went home. In two hours he was dead. "The first thing," said M. Gardiene, "in any feeling of sickness is to eat nothing. That is the mistake people make. My friend, too. He should not have eaten. In any sickness, the first rule is to fast."

He examined a new customer gloomily. "It is not that I feel sentimental about death or that my friend was any better than anyone else who may die today. But he had just after years of depression begun to be a person of importance, an authority on painting, a figure in his own world. He was an unusual man."

This was the friend's funeral service—there among the broken chairs and mirrors, an elegy recited to a stranger, a portrait of a nameless "unusual man" for an unknown casual customer, words of appreciation he would not have spoken to any close friend but which were welling in his reticent, austere bosom.

November 26: In the furniture store, the quixotic Frenchman comments sourly "This piece for $25—a bargain, for if you ever wanted to sell it for $100 you could do so, if anyone had the $100." I said if at any time I was broke everyone else would be, too. "You have a certain humor," he said dourly, "things are not lost on you." I laughed and thought of a dozen pages of notes on him, his shop, his sayings. He might well say things are not lost on me.

December 4: Story of my father. A male "darling" who was devoted to whatever job or boss he had. Michigan Bed Company salesman. The Star Cookie Company. Cherry factory. Worked with Indians. A radical or a conservative depending on the boss. Widow's apartment—a history of his different bosses.

December 24: Virginia Pfeiffer is an odd person. I am perpetually surprised at my own stupidity about women and cannot really blame men for the same lack of perception. She has a sharp gaunt dark shrewd face, thin arrow-body (taut, about-to-fly), an automobile, big and black, a bare apartment, spending money, and an amusingly trivial retort. You are pleased mildly to begin with because she seems adaptable, able to fit into any scheme. Presently you discover she is illiterate and stupid and vain as any pretty girl, the shrewd black eyes mean nothing. She puts on an act of naïveté, believing it's an act, but what she doesn't know is that it's true. Bitterly envious of her sister's position as wife of a world-recognized writer and in touch therefore with the social and rich far more than the artistic, she believes in a bond between herself and the husband—I shouldn't be surprised if he occasionally gave her reason to believe this.

Like so many people who believe themselves unfairly treated by Fame, she longs for its recognition but lacks zest for its demands (whereas an honest fame-seeker loves the idea of accomplishment as much as the rewards). Virginia is ruffled every time she meets a name—immediately she must register her own ego by getting the name wrong, by asking what he does; she must show she doesn't care or know about his work. Sometimes this is true. Then she feverishly mentions other old-time names that are merely well-publicized and not connected with any but the most casual fashionable achievement.

I cannot understand why—when a person cares so obviously about Name—why, with her time and money, she doesn't study her own patter; read art and music news, some political, a few books; observe; maintain a decent balance about celebrities, since that is her obsession. At least study her own stuff—give something. Hollow and foolish, intelligence and conversation and merit are all lost on her; her only sensation is—it is *me, me* who is being told this fine story. A worthless woman who should marry and support some worthy gigolo.

December 27: A mistake to let Harold Clurman read my play. Anytime I allow anyone to discuss something before completion (regardless of what tact they use in criticizing), I see the thing can be done in so many ways that it seems a colossal, bewildering undertaking.

December 29: People wear and tear on each other's nerves so that I do not see how they bear up as well as they do. Particularly families: the family I was always running away from I now have for myself—the heckling of each other, the fumblings and demands and frettings of adolescence coupled with a violent temper, the baiting sarcasm of the parent, the perpetual nagging that is the basis of family life and the one thing that I cannot stand, the thing that will make me run away as it always has. Any barroom brawl is better than the persistent pinpricks of the happy little family.

1937

[*Undated*] Jacques Le Clercq was helping out the young man assigned to write an article on Dwight's early days. Edith was assisting. "Of course," said Jacques, "Dwight has always been a fairy. The only woman who ever really got under his skin was Edith. Dwight was really in love with Edith. As a matter of fact, Edith, if you'd worn pants, you'd be Mrs. Fiske today."

The two women at Harry's. The gaunt, tragic one, the cellist, a foundling, brought up, adopted with four other girl orphans by a woman doctor (unmarried, maybe Lesbian?). The other, double-lensed, overly eager, very smug virgin of 34, a pianist who leaps to the piano at the slightest hint of exaltation. She rolled and gyrated on the piano stool in an ecstasy, eager to give herself to each chord, anxious and waiting for one that was worthy but a pushover for any. When the little runs and chords came she conducted them primly over the piano as if on a leash, giving the little Pomeranian chords very motherly attack and keeping the bigger ones off the grass—always the disciplinarian but enjoying the romp. No matter how big they were, she was always the prim guide, never let them jump on her.

January 2: Coby is an ex-hero, it seems. At 14, he took the lady of his choice out skating in Denver. As she whirled off by herself, the ice suddenly broke under her and he was appalled to see her sink into the lake. He rushed up, held out a tremulous hand, when the ice cracked all over and he fell in too.

Once immersed, he had control of the situation and swam rapidly to shore but unfortunately left the lady totally forgotten, still struggling with ice and water. Triumphantly, having saved a life even though it was only his own, he looked back to reassure her of his safety and there was the poor girl of his dreams wading toward shore as best she could, finding the water was not quite up to her nose.

The odd thing about this story is that Coby remembers it. I asked him if memory of his conduct hadn't given him a big inferiority complex and he said not at all. On the contrary, it had given him a beautiful insight into human nature.

Anyone less realistic would have erased this record of their own frailty from their mind. Not Coby.

January 3: A wearing fortnight—nerves crackling, too much responsibility and no way out, no flight possible though in the slow drip on the brain it is as agonizing as childhood traps I have been in and later run out of. Nothing possible but surrender to life—sink under it, give up hope of fighting one's own tough-enough fight for a career and assume position as another woman allowed a brief use of her talents by fate and then clamped into her proper torture-chamber of domestic responsibility. Will this be my life now—driven, heckled and tortured as I was as a child? Hands tied by people—what can I do for them? how can I help them?— or is it all no use, a business of endurance, accepting the blockade of one's whole life as women have always accepted it?

January 4: Homes are bad places. Either they are so comfortable that no place else could offer as much sheer convenience, yet psychic and family connections are such that you can never enjoy these comforts—this cozy study filled with invisible foes, interruptions, responsibilities, worry, hatred. Or else you have no comfortable place in your home to work and in spite of privacy and other ideal personal relations are unable to enjoy it. Yet in both cases there is a hold that interferes with your life work, that bitches you, ruins you, sends you to the madhouse or the grave.

I have never before been so puzzled and balked for I do have very little money worry at the moment. I don't want to die, yet I see no other escape from the mess of my life. The responsibility for others who I have tried to care for has been useless—I might as well have forgotten about both of them. All that has happened is that they have—between the two of them, father and son—managed to tear my brain to pieces so I am neither any good to them or to myself.

January 6: Helen S. decided to have dinner for Mary Lena. She is a good woman and very conscientious. Have I had a greedy or an envious thought today? she asks herself every night. When she gave the dinner, she thought of Denny Wortman as Artist, me as Writer, and she strove to draw us out on our subjects.

How did Denny like the Surrealists show? Did he think it was Art? "Art? What's art? A lot of nonsense, either you like it or you don't, why have criticism of it or talk about it?" said the artist sourly, and that was a dead end. She turned to me. Didn't I love the Noël Coward things? I was a playwright so . . . I liked them all right only Noël Coward looked like George Arliss and Gertrude Lawrence like Fannie Brice and an evening of *nothing* was not good enough.

Poor hostess, stopped in both her little conversation starters, turned to the man on her right, to talk about the country, but he casually got up and stalked stiffly out of the room to the can. She made a few more brave starts, each one blocked by the individuals who did not have the faintest regard for how dinners or social events were run. Each seemed to think one gave a frank, even disagreeably frank, answer to a polite question instead of passing it along, with nice little cries of pleasure and suave addenda. Poor Helen's mouth drooped, circles came under her eyes.

Very well. Bridge. Quietly, during the coffee, she unfolded the bridge table; Mr. Davis checked the cards, adjusted the pencil, the score-pad. Now! "Do you play bridge, Dawn?" What—bridge? No. "You do, don't you Denny?" Oh, no—anyway I have to go down to a rehearsal of the Illustrators' Show any minute now. "You, Joe. Bridge?" My dear lady, I wish I could. Sadly, mouth firmly locked over the hostessy disappointment, Helen sat at the bridge table, her last fortress, with her Extra Man loyally at her side, the Man she'd called in for 25 years.

January 12: Leopold Atlas play "But For The Grace of God," which is a fine play. The qualities of a great play are definite, more definite than in a great novel. A great picture or work of sculpture must have the spiritual robustness of the artist. It must give life—show the creator's own abundance of power. A play, to show greatness, must show clearly the ruling hand of destiny behind a man's deeds. Not background, not enemies, not social unrest, not environment, not Marx—but Destiny. There is no thrill on the stage equal to the simple primary *theater* of the knock of Fate. Fate working through characters, not through the playwright or the exigencies of the plot.

January 31: Been sickish for weeks. Tired—sluggish—weepy.

February 4: Turning yellow—sick to stomach often. Jaundice.

February 6: Went to New York Hospital.

February 22: Came out of hospital. Still yellow and chastened, tired, not entirely well by any means.

February 28: Joe took Jojo to school. The freest, most peaceful day in years, with my great responsibility on new shoulders for the first time. Worked all day on—of all things—the play of *She Walks In Beauty* instead of the play I had plotted out with Sydney Harmon.

April 9: Virginia Woolf's *The Years* and F. Tennyson Jesse's *A Pin To See The Peep Show* read at once—what with rain and fairies and walloping bells at Oxford and Missie dying of love for Teacher with a dash of beans and fish with the lower middle class—impress one again with the constipation of English letters. They copy this sentence 100 times—"England is Jolly, Tea is Good, Rain is Nice, Oxford's Heaven, Teacher is Peachy, I'll be Buggered." Then they make their individual curleycues, Miss Woolf with air and sea and esprit at her command, others with mere patience and paper. The same things happen to the same families only it's Ron instead of Don and Winnie instead of Binnie. I do not know whether on this small island only a few patterns are possible in life for a writer to record, or whether people, well-read on their own fiction, dare not allow their lives to step out of fiction's prescribed patterns. It's a conventional country, after all.

April 14: The mellow wisdom of the "middle years" is no sounder or near Truth than the shrill intolerance of youth.

April 28: The PEN dinner was a banquet of faux pas. What with Whit Burnett and Martha Foley talking-blah-explaining to these old-timers that a novella was this and that, and Miss Foley getting all bogged down on her awards, saying she was glad to see that Mr. Poposch or rather Propoff or she should say Pokosch,* editor of *The Asiatics* (instead of "author of") was present. Further, she said that she had a hunch. The hunch was that the writers of the future would have a more *social* point of view—a hunch based on 10 years of experience, so it could scarcely be called a mystic vision.

Miss Beatty, the glad buxom chairman, then rose to introduce a saturnine gentleman, Count Roussy de Sale, and she introduced him in a most astonishing way. "Dorothy Thompson, our president who couldn't be with us tonight, told me Count de Sale would be frightfully flattered if we introduced him as Miss, she said if we called him Miss he would like it much better than if we called him Count, so I will follow her suggestion and introduce to you Miss Roussy de Sale—or rather *Mister!*" Agonizingly, she sat down, unable to excuse this strange mistake except by Freud.

We went up to the Colby's later and here was a curious situation. The two bedrooms were firmly locked by visiting daughter's family so bathroom was shut off. Fragile Lillian Gish-looking Helen Anderson was in agony, as was venerable Professor Montague and it was a most squirming group that gyrated about their seats with pained frightened eyes. Prof. Montague was further trapped by describing his indignation at dinner over Mr. Copland,† beside him, volleying out rage at the Spanish anarchists and the stupidity of the man, when I pointed out (as he blanched) that the gentleman was right beside him again. So he covered this up by admiring the tapestry.

Unable to bear watching his kidney pains longer I suggested home so he rushed me out like a bat out of hell, shoved me into one of the toughest looking dives you ever saw on the corner—as there were no ladies, I backed out, and he whisked into a tough but less so bar across the street where we then had a beer and highball under more relaxed circumstances.

Here he told me of the Inverse Square Law—that waves retain their power even though they spread out over a distance when a pebble disturbs them. He described the unknown law that short waves are more

---

*The name was Frederic Prokosch, the author of the philosophical novel, *The Seven Who Fled* (1937).

†It is possible this was Aaron Copland, who was active in radical causes in the 1930s.

powerful than long ones, electrons, the smallest atom, etc. He spoke of the atom as if it was a dear little Cupid flying through space, making statistics. The rowdies at the bar stopped dumbfounded in their roaring to stare at this venerable crackpot speaking of quantum this or that. For Christsake what was this, anyway? "The violet ray was the shrillest color in the spectrum, an octave higher than any other color," etc. It was odd watching him dive into this happy abstract world and breathe underwater and bubble and float—a world of his own. Other old people keep their youth by interest in people. He has that but what he also has is an endless joy in the atom, the electron, the measuring of the soul, the surveying of the abstract, it keeps him forever bubbling with joy.

May 26: Marie came in very happy today, knuckles scraped. Just beat up a man on the subway, she explained; boy, did she feel fine! Old man about 50 sitting opposite her exposing himself. She called a colored man over and he said lady, there's nothing I can do. Oh no? she said, well I can. So she sailed in socking the old boy, let her bundles and purse fly, everyone tried to stop her—men came up. "Let me handle this," she told them and socko, while passengers gathered round and said "Look at the little lady giving it to him. That old boy's getting the beating of his life. Let her be!" Conductor expostulated—she said "The law's on my side." A lady said "Something might happen." "Never mind that," cried Marie happily. "I can always offend myself!"

June 12: G-men all over Port Jefferson on kidnapper hunt for Stony Brook heiress.* The pretty waitress at Teddy's Inn was so excited. The place was full of newspapermen and G-men the night before. "But I didn't realize it was J. Edgar Hoover himself!" she said. "They were whistling for me when they wanted me and I said 'Listen, is that nice? I thought you were a gentleman!' Then the girls told me it was J. Edgar Hoover. After what I said to him! Was my face red! I was so thrilled I didn't get to sleep till 5:30 in the morning."

June 26: Jojo improved, calmer, less intense, more alert to outside conditions and people. Talks about Walton. Wanted me to buy Walton a present—say, a new suit. Told me he liked Mildred somebody best. "Is she

---

*Alice Parsons disappeared from her Stony Brook farmhouse on June 9, 1937; it is believed that she died of natural causes in the hands of her kidnappers.

pretty?" I asked. "Not very," he said. "Is she smart?" "No," he said, "but I don't care about that." "Is she a good dancer?" "She isn't so hot," he said. Then he added that when he first asked her to dance with him she refused, so he said, "Well you're damn well *gonna* dance with me," so she did.

July 8: How wretched human beings are! Last night I heard a woman's voice late at night and I looked out the window. All windows were dark so it seemed a bedtime quarrel and not a drunken one. "Get out of here, you dirty bum," she cried. "Get out, you low-life, I'll tell your mother. What do you think this is, a whore-house? Get out, you filthy bum, playing with yourself all night long in front of me, stop it, what do you think your mother will say when I tell her—!"

The voice was hopeless, wretched, uneducated in epithet, and the sinister misery of the black, hot city night left me frozen with horror. She went on wearily, a tone of such unhappiness in her voice that it was almost a sob, as if she was trapped and knew it, perhaps by real love that she could not turn to the scorn she would like, bewilderment and confusion over the monstrous sex exhibition, unable to cope with it, understand it. A dreadful night voice praying to a leering city night god.

Three taximen in front of a store on 8th Street. "You wouldn't know the girl now," said one.

"She sure has changed," said the next. "She used to be a nice girl, too."

"She's all right," said the third. "She is a nice girl. I don't believe you fellows."

"Listen, you can tell it by lookin' at her," said the second. "She *walks* guilty."

July 10: At Dwight's. He has achieved the complete victory over justice and truth, a victory of pure, strong personality.

When someone, perhaps me, tells a story, makes a pun or uses a curious expression, Dwight's stooges cry out, "Oh Dwight, you must use that!" and it is the accolade. The happy victim of the open robbery beams with complacency; his jewels were actually deemed worthy of the Master. Happy thief and happier gull!

Dwight told of the fat old New York couple at the Berkeley, that gloomy morgue of old New York ancient stuffies. The ancient husband locked his wife up in closets. The doctor said if she fed him chocolate it would soothe him and so all during the so-called social evening she fed him bits of Hershey bars and sweetly explained "The doctor says if I feed him lots of chocolate he won't lock me up so much."

July 20: I saw Norman Geddes about "Red Dress." First Michael Sayre was in his office, the young Irishman I met at Natalie Colby's. "I wanted to ask you," he said. "Is your play a comedy or tragedy? Four or five of us read it and saw it, of course, as a comedy about a nymphomaniac." I was as bewildered about the nymphomania as anything else but I stalled. Later, Mr. Geddes talked, asked me the same question. "Of course you meant it as a tragedy," he said, "a tragedy about a nymphomaniac." I stalled again since, tragedy or comedy, the "nymphomaniac" angle was the most baffling interpretation of any.

July 21: 146 ½ lbs.

Playing badminton at Arden's—also massage—thyroid and fairly starchless diet of grapefruit juice, steak, lamb chops, etc. Also exercising 20 or 30 minutes a day. Have lost four or five pounds since starting it.

August 26: A new family moved into the duplex garden apartment across the street. Last night they couldn't get "Louis" out. "Goddamn it, Louis," yelled the host, "what do you think this is, a foyer? Get the hell out now, Goddamn it!" Louis merely countered with "Guy is a stinker, Guy is a stinker, Guy is a stinker." The lady had a treble voice which kept squealing "Softly darling, *please.*" "Goddamn it, Louis, we're a young married couple, get the hell out. Does a man of my social position have to throw you out by the balls?"

All this was punctuated by a dog's squeal as someone stepped on him and cries of "Take those hamburgers away, Goddamn it!" Guest Louis said "Isabel stinks on ice. Isabel stinks on ice. Did I ever tell you that Isabel stinks on ice?" Darling replied sweetly, "Yes, I believe you did tell me once that Isabel stank on ice."

August 28: At the hairdresser's (Emile's) Marian told me of the lady with beautiful hair who went on a honeymoon. Before she was to be married she told Marian she was in a jam; her fiancé loved her for her hair, he had fallen for her on that account alone; they were to go on a month's cruise; how in God's name was she to keep him from knowing her hair was dyed, when it would come out after three weeks without a treatment?

Marian decided she would give the customer a bottle of dye in an Emile-Hair Tonic bottle. Since it was impossible to do the back of her hair alone, she would have to explain to her husband that he must help her with her scalp treatment in back, pulling aside the strands, dabbing the scalp, etc. This she did and Marian did not see her for three months. Then she came into the shop and asked for Marian.

"I could kill you," she said. Why? Because she had done as Marian said. After three weeks, she explained to her groom she must shampoo and tonic her hair; he must help. He did. He loved her hair, after all. So this simple tonic helped the beautiful hair, did it? He vanished while she was letting it dry. Where was he? She went to look. He was "treating" his own hair!

The truth came out and he wouldn't speak to her. He weighed 200 lbs. and looked fantastic with pink-lavender hair. He had to take a month longer cruise to let it grow again; furthermore had to have 26 oil treatments to cure him of dye-poison. But after three months he forgave her.

August 30: Alice (at Emile's) is a beautiful Swede. She says her best friend is Ellen. Ellen is smarter than most girls. She has a boyfriend but won't marry anyone because she doesn't see why, if she does all the work, she shouldn't spend it on her own comfort instead of supporting a husband. The other girls in the shop all have husbands but you know how it is, men can't get work or they don't get paid much, so a girl has to go to a neighborhood movie where 80 cents buys two tickets instead of to Radio City by herself. That's why Alice admires Ellen so much.

The most fun, though, is girls going out together, without their husbands. They leave the shop about 7, and stop in every bar along the way, pretty soon end up in Greenwich Village. What kick do they get there? Oh boy! The men dressed and made up beautifully like women, the women dressed like men. Perfect! If one could only buy one's husband a suit like the Lesbians!

September 13: In the bus (Riverside) the heavy bilious man finally recognized the two fat women. What was he doing now? Playing bridge all afternoon. That's all he did. He played at the best place, the Union Club, 74th Street. What a business, what a business! Fifty couples every afternoon, a hundred and fifty in the evening! Did the ladies play now as much as before? Yes, she did, she played every night. Where did she play? Home, she said. Home?—he asked as if he had never heard of such a place. Yes, home. He was rather reserved after that, as if she had said she played polo at home. Both ladies became voluble in their excuses. "She don't like to play them clubs," one said. "Too much smoke, too much excitement! She likes better to play home!" "Yeah?" he politely said, unconcerned, and then shook hands with them and got off. A play could be written about a bridge club—a melodrama: crooks running it, contrast of boresome bridge-playing innocents with an underworld background.

Riverside Drive is still the loveliest, most glamorous place in New York by night, particularly now with the drive opposite.

September 17: The culmination point of another dreadful, futile year, the high moments being what in normal lives would be the worst. The only good time was jaundice, when at least I was too physically sick to take the mental and emotional socks lying in wait for me. Hanging over the hospital can with not a care in the world but whether I could stop upchucking was the gay carnival of my year.

September 19: The Legionnaires in town. Manager of a theater where they made noise protested and was swung down a manhole till they relented.

In Lüchow's I was reminded of old days there with Katherine* and called her up. In no time at all she and Cynthia arrived. Cynthia is a big striking-looking girl of 16 who looks 25 and, after years at the Professional Childrens' School, even her youth is acted. Katherine beamed exquisitely across the room. I looked around and saw some respectable Legionnaires staring at her, bewildered. She waved again until one came up to see if he recognized her. Then he spoke of seeing a nurse friend. Katherine said she and I were both nurses. She said—for still no reason—that Joe was from Boston. (Later Cynthia asked why I said we never saw any warfare when Mummy had told her she'd had soldiers die in her arms. On the spot, to defend Mummy's romancing, I said yes, perhaps that did happen but the soldiers hadn't really *died*.)

---

* Katherine Chapman, Powell's friend from the Naval Reserve.

Then Katherine insisted that Baby join the Legionnaires at their table, a baffling adventure for the restaurant and the soldiers. They were at first pleased with Baby as a hot number, then confused by her insistence on chocolate cake and apple strudel instead of champagne. After all, they wanted wild women, that's why they left their wives at home; they didn't want to look after other people's kiddies. Cynthia pretended she was Peter Pan and twinkle-toed about to their surprise. It was an amazing night for the elderly Legionnaires.

October 3: Coby, unfortunately for his own good, is superbly funny on a long binge. Saw him in middle of one. Yes, he missed his old Rocky Mountain home. Just a native son. "The beautiful old home still there, of course, full of memories, even the pictures, the beautiful collection of etchings, shown to generations of women."

October 4: Bunny [Edmund] Wilson called up from hotel. "Come over here right away," he urged. "I just had a dream about you and I want to go over it with you."

October 30: Turned in third version of "Red Dress" with revisions still to be made of minor nature on Acts II and III. Feel that the Geddes tyranny has finally justified itself by my being able to turn out good play, much better than original version and more saleable.

November 6: Came out to country to close cottage. Though I dreaded coming, as one dreads going under ether, once out here, perspective became slowly normal once again. Suddenly the work on "Red Dress," the insistent torture of it—a baby that will not go to sleep—seemed ghastly in its insignificance. I have never put in so much and been dominated so much as by this—one more change to make, one more scene to switch.

December 10: To *Manon* at the Met, with Bidu Sayao, the Brazilian soprano, and Richard Crooks. "Adieu, mon petite table." The Gavotte—Le Rêve.

1938

[*Undated*] Lou feels that a cold wife who has a headache is a pure one, a high-class one.

In 1931—wrote play, "Walking Down Broadway." Sold it to Fox—$7500. Wrote 93 pages of novel *Tenth Moon* ($^1/_3$). Received $6850. Short stories. Sick—fatigue year and a turning point.

In 1932—wrote $^2/_3$ of *Tenth Moon*. Rehearsals of "Big Night." Rewriting two Dwight pieces. Received $1996.

In 1933—wrote one play, "Jig-Saw"; one novel, *Country Boy;* six short stories; six Fiskes. Produced "Big Night." Received $1980.

In 1934—wrote one play "Lion and Lizard." Two shorts for Dwight. Two weeks Paramount. Produced one play, "Jig-Saw." Published one novel, *Country Boy*. Movie of same. Received $13,845. Started *Turn, Magic Wheel*. Miami. Nightmare year. Changed to Carol Hill though all sales were from Watkins office.

In 1935—wrote three stories; four Fiske stories; one movie original, "Mandy Blue"; one novel (except for first 40 pages) *Magic Wheel*. Published five short stories. Received $1346. Bad professional messes. Havana. Misunderstandings due to Carol Hill misreading contract.

In 1936—wrote nine short stories, all sold. Two others sold. Wrote part of play, part of novel and movie work. Sold all stories (11), reprints to 4. Published one novel, *Turn, Magic Wheel* (also in England); seven short stories (two reprinted in England). Received $6208.

In 1937—wrote one play ("Red Dress," dramatization of *She Walks In Beauty,* three complete versions) $^1/_2$ novel, four short stories, six Fiskes. Received $1056 and yellow jaundice.

January 2: Jojo went back to Devereux. 5 ft., 7 in.—119 lbs. He is awakening, is much improved generally, though plans for a future must be made with a general line to be followed.

January 3: After listening to Greta Keller I think I could write a waltz with these words: "Gelieben sie—ich liebe—du, du Sehnsucht—immer allein—Frühling—glücklich—du, du—Wien—mit mir—immer allein —warum nicht Alma—wo wohnst du—nur Sehnsucht und du—was is das—Strazzi Bund sehen sie, gehen sie, lieben sie, blieben sie, glauben sie, stauben sie—heh-heh—Daddy."

January 4: The amazing anecdotes of Lejaren Hiller, photographer, with his clown's face, gravity, Scotch accent. The time he was on the train through Bavaria. It stopped, at wrong place, Nuremberg. He gets out, looks for a Gasthaus, there is none. He finds a Burgomeister who will let him stay. He does—no train till Saturday. He scrapes acquaintance with the clock-or-bell-ringer at the Cathedral, where the clock brings out the 12 apostles.

Here he finds a village feud going on. The bellringer (who turns the wheel controlling the apostles) and his family have feuded with the Burgomeister's, so for revenge on the latter's town pride, the bellman broke the apostle John. Then, contrite, he had to dress up and take its place at every hour and quarter hour. It was very boresome. Well, says Hiller, I'll take its place. So he dresses up in a tunic and for the two days he was there came out with the Apostles whenever the fourth (John) was called for. All he had to do was keep feet moving fast on a trudgeon, but one time the thing stuck and he didn't know what to do. He couldn't get on, he couldn't get off. He had to keep behind Luke, because a crowd was gathering below. Finally, he gets tired, rushes to rail, says "Hi, everybody!" and runs off. The machine went on—he had been standing on the cable.

Another time, having gotten drunk at a village artist's, he was called next day during a hangover. "We'd better go right down there," somebody says. "Oh," he says, not knowing what is being said. They find their recent host has committed suicide; he left no will and his wife and mistress are fighting over it. Taking a shower, Hiller finds writing on his chest. In the mirror he sees it backward: "Whereas I, being in sound mind, do hereby—etc." He is a legal document. He is evidence, has to be probated, etc., and that, too, is a true story that must not be laughed at.

January 6: Party at Studin's. Norah Hoult, Irish writer, whose books I like, came out with me and we drank up all my Xmas champagne. You aren't just malicious, she said, you just open the veins and let the blood run out.

Lunch with Ginny Pfeiffer—to Murphys afterward with MacLeishes, etc. Archie had his passport from Washington back for South America. It said "waiter" instead of "writer."

January 17: Read Djuna Barnes' sad brilliant book *Nightwood*—a great book. Neurotic subject matter treated not with usual thin sugary sneer but with vigor, as classical writers dealt with it. Its spreading evil grows like a night poison in the mind with its beauty, its sadness for all love.

January 20: Bunny Wilson is funny. He appears to ask questions but pays no attention to answers, though later they emerge. Now that his mind has enlarged into such a vast organization, it's as if conversation has to wait in the lobby till the message has been routed through the proper department. Sometimes it has to come back Monday.

January 23: A session of the Group Theatre, with Harold Clurman, the absent-minded, slender, well-dressed leader. The "taking an adjustment," the "getting the spine of a part." The life from morning till night in improvisations. A world of make-believe, a cult. Bowed head. The dismissal of lines; the *feeling* was the important thing.

January 24: In the taxi coming from the Geddes I saw the driver's card with "Uzweld" as the name. I asked if he was Russian and he said no, Swiss, but his grandmother had been Russian, his father German (named Oswald), which seemed to make him a Swiss. I asked about Swiss wines, especially the valley wines, and he said, "Lady, you should drink a good red French wine, a Bordeaux." He explained that there were few white raisins in Switzerland, so he came from the district where they dyed the red ones white and this dye made stomach ulcers. Why bits of information from taximen or porters seem so authoritative I don't know, when so often they are ignorant, bundles of hearsay and superstition. But whatever they speak of seems pretty final.

January 26: For no reason at all I hated this day as if it was a person—its wind, its insecurity, its flabbiness, its hints of an insane universe.

Rosie Miller told amazing story of worrying over her small son's anti-social nature and "broodiness." She said it could lead to a breakdown. Then she explained why 30 years ago—she was 22—she had a complete mental collapse. Jumped out a six-story window without hurting herself, except for a wrist still scarred. She had delusions, feared she would be caught for setting fire to houses or stealing bosses' money. Finally had to be put away for a year, completely batty. Her sister had done the same thing and been put away before. Rosie had come home from school to see her sister muttering and brooding to herself, talking nonsense, finally getting so they took her away. The fear was in the whole family and even though now some were 60 they were in a panic when a disappointment made them brood, for fear it was their turn now. Knowing there was this weakness made them all the worse. They gave in as soon as it began, or else got hysterically happy.

February 1: Saw John Farrar regarding novel and he substantiated Coby's remarks and my own feelings. The people exist but are not supported or mirrored by enough human evidence. The position of Jefferson in relation to the group shows him weakening, giving in to them rather than firmly holding out as I intended. He needn't be so slapped down or such a complete ass—more Steinbeck than Odets.

Seeing Francis' [Faragoh] play last night reminded me of how hard I must work. He is older than I and here is his first Broadway play. There isn't all the time in the world at 40.

Charles Studin talked of meeting the ex-mistress of H. G. Wells, who turned to him at a dinner and said "Do you know, you interest me more than any man I've met since I left H. G. Wells?" Then, to his chagrin, he heard her say this in his presence to three or four other men, paying no attention to the fact that the others heard her.

February 4: The two drunks coming in the Blue Ribbon about 7. Joe has the table by the phone booth. Says one, "You call her up, you tell her I'm detained on a conference and won't be out." So Two reluctantly takes the nickel and calls up a White Plains number, while One goes bumbling off to can.

"Hello," says Two. "Mrs. Busby? This is Tod calling. Ethel. I wanted to say—what? No, I'm not doing anything over the weekend. What time? Why sure, Ethel. I'll come out of the 6 o'clock then. Say Ethel—what? Lunch? Sure. O.K. I'll meet you at the Stork Club, then, at one. O.K. Oh yes—Ethel—Bob won't be home for dinner. Goodbye."

February 6: Reading Henry James' *The Sacred Fount.* Stately, carefully cadenced sentences like Proust and delight in detail the same but no senses, no smell or sound or geographical sense which enrich and place a person as much as his mental processes do. Even his intense absorption in psychological apparatus is not a novelist's interest in a human being but an engineer's interest in how exactly his own apparatus detects and finds the subject's mental apparatus. A *reflected* interest, much the same as these amateur radio-operators who spend long hours trying to reach far-off stations but with nothing to say or hear to or from such a station, merely to find out if their own apparatus is strong enough to reach the other. The strange pattern of dialogue, like stage scenes without scenery or music, but only one prop at a time. Two can converse, but no more; sometimes a third appears—if there are more they function only as one person, as a conductor from one dialogue to the next or as a key or tempo modulator.

February 19: Ouija board session. Odd. Dangerous, not because of spirits you unloose from dead but those you unloose in yourself.

March 17: On the warm day today my antique dealer, dour philosophic Frenchman, sat in front of his shop on one of the satin-upholstered Chippendale chairs reading the paper while an itinerant bootblack shined his shoes.

March 19: Stories of Carl Ruggles the composer and his early struggles. He was told he could get $25 by lecturing to the New York Women's Club on Modern American Music so he went up and spoke, looked around the luncheon table filled with women and said "I have been asked

144

to speak on Modern American Music. There is no such thing as American music and what passes for Modern American Music is just a lot of god-damn crap. Shall I continue?"

Next he was invited to play at the Gracie estate on Long Island. He was threadbare and broke, but could get by if he could dash at once into his Tuxedo which, as a performer, he had to have anyway. He got there and was shown to an elaborate bedroom and told dinner was at 8. He waited, then rang a bell and asked for a highball. It was brought and the footman said they were not dressing for dinner. Mr. Ruggles saw this as an affront to his poverty and rang for another highball. So they weren't dressing for dinner, eh? Well, by God, he was! So he got out his clothes and dressed, only to find he'd forgotten his studs. He rang again and the footman came. "So dinner is at eight o'clock?" said Ruggles. "Yes, sir," said the footman, "dinner at eight." "And so Mr. Gracie is not dressing?" asked Ruggles. "That is true, sir." "Well, I am, and will you please bring me Mr. Gracie's studs?"

May 31: Finished *The Happy Island* at 6:25 this evening.

June 1: Jacques Jolas broadcast, cocktail party at LeClercqs, then the Sweeneys, then dinner at the Czech-Slovak place, Sokol Hall (76th Street) where on every floor girls in gym suits were practicing health, horizontal bars. It was here that another one of Dr. Cook's students passed out. Dr. Cook is part of the new university tradition that is sweeping the country, in movies and fiction. Before 1929 the world of teachers might seem very fascinating to the teachers themselves but to other people was a world of prigs and masked gentility. Then in 1929 came the boys who would ordinarily have gone into business or a profession and, unwilling to conform to the priggish rules, made their own, so a group of wenching, drinking, Big-Appling professors came along.

At a Studin party I went out for another cocktail with a few N.Y.U. teachers and a couple of pretty students. One student had a tousle-haired boy student friend she was forced to bring along, mainly to show how close she was to the rather drunk good-looking teacher. At the bachelor-professor's apartment (a pronounced fuddy-dud fairy) more martinis were served and suddenly the drunk young profs found two superior men from Columbia or someplace desirable and tumbled the two pretties off to the boy student, forgetting them in a scramble to make an impression on their superiors and, if possible, be recommended for an advanced position. The one little girl hung around, finally said good-bye. "Oh good-bye, Miss H.," absently said the young man teacher and eagerly resumed his good-impression making, while the little boy student kept his arm around her all the way out.

It was the same with Dr. Cook. At the Sweeney's very beautiful terrace over the East River, a tall, hard, model-looking girl was being made much of. Dr. Cook, very virile head-hunting gent, was demanding Jolas' time, then decided to go, and as he passed the girl suddenly started kissing her in a big way. She was delighted. He left. At Sokol Hall she was in the can, passed out, while the hearty, bloomered little Czech girls looked on in disgust. I took her for a walk around the block and she said "Boy oh boy, do you know why I'm tight? Because Dr. Cook kissed me! Listen, I've been in that man's classes for two years and he doesn't know I exist! All of a sudden he starts kissing me—well, I just had to get tight!"

So she got a little sicker and a Greek named Poppadocky took her home. Then Mrs. Sweeney said the distinguished Dr.'s other student had passed out before. He brought one to her house, then she began getting pea green and Mrs. S. saw her out where she said, swaying into the elevator, "I've forgotten my notebook." Then, this being produced, she shyly said, sliding to the floor, "I had a pencil, too." Then she passed warily away.

Later we found ourselves at a huge benefit on top of a Riverside Drive roof, crowded with people drinking for Spain.

June 4: John Farrar read novel and says it's fine. "Terrific," he said. "The end is so—well, I'm so excited about it I can't talk."

June 20: Bobby Morrison was in. He was sick with nosebleed two weeks and lost his job at the Apex School of Beauty Culture for Colored. So he was going to be a "pin boy" at the Paradise Recreation Club, a beer-garden and bowling alley on the Grand Concourse. Run elevator and pick up pins for $10 a week, four cents a game. A 20-alley place. He had to give somebody $3 for the job, though. Where was the place? "Up on the Grand Corncob," he said.

June 27: Marie spoke of how fine the two curtains looked that my brother-in-law sent me. I said he worked in that business. "Too bad he can't send them to you for the whole house," she said regretfully, "but I suppose it would look like too big a bundle to be carrying out of the store."

Jacques LeClercq spoke pleasantly of an old friend whom he had seen again. "He's done awfully well," he sighed. " I saw him today on Broadway —beautiful new false teeth and a fairy on each arm!"

June 25: Went to Canton to see Phyllis. We drove to Massilon to see her crayon and oil pictures in the local exhibition. Very good—the show quite as decent as any other art show—Glyn Jones a sort of Currier and James Rutledge a local Benton. Phyllis' three kids very smart and appealing and self-amusing due to their lack of funds. Canton home of Timken Roller Bearing Co. Timken worth 55 percent of $100 million firm. He is a social-ist but "doesn't think the country is ready for it."

July 4: Said Marie of "Flatfoot Floogie with the Floy Floy" (words of which are just those repeated with "floy doy, floy doy" variants): "What do you know? The fellas that wrote that piece is just a coupla kids!"

July 13: Jojo went back to school. Three weeks home and very improved. Contact with the family was good for him; he had constant conversation and said "I like a big family around me." Jojo hated to go. "I like to be with my father and mother," he said. I told him to just remember wher-ever he went and whatever he did his parents were right behind him. "I don't want my parents behind me," he said. "I want them *with* me."

July 26: Louie, the old waiter at the Brevoort, was not his usual red, whiskey-burned self. So I said, "What's the matter, Louie, you're so pale?" He shrugged. "Ah," he said bitterly, "I been away on vacash!"

July 29: Cunningham, the little man who was nearly a Certified Public Accountant, fancies himself as a great Don Juan, always tossing off re-marks about how many women he has. When wife went away he gets room at a Village hotel on advertising exchange and finds this makes all his boasts come true.

Calls up office from Third Avenue bar one morning, been drunk all night and all day. Why? Because last night he got a "cherry." It was won-derful, only it wasn't anything like his wife's. So, after all these years, he was suspicious that his wife had put something over on him, and the more he drank the more he was sure. But how go and accuse her now, when the way his doubts came to him were so guilty? All he could do was drink.

Coby said he could never love a woman who had no social conscience because he had such a honey himself.

August 17: Harry Lissfelt tells of his old German aunt in the south side of Pittsburgh. After some years he returns from New York business success and sees her.

"How is Hilda?" she says, beaming at what a fine big fat fellow he had become.

"She's studying music in New York," he said.

"That's too bad," she sympathized. "And you, I hear you've got work and all."

"Yes, I've got a job," he said.

"That's fine," she said, "and are you happy in it, have you got a good foreman?"

August 18: The story of Niles' grandfather, who was doing so well in the crinoline hoop business in Pawtucket that he decided to come to New York and branch out at the close of the Civil War. Which he did, after much weighty preparation, exchanging of letters of introduction to New York merchants and backers. He arrived, carpetbag in hand, and presented his proposal for a big New York hoop-skirt headquarters.

"But my dear Spencer!" exclaimed the New York merchant. "They're not wearing hoops anymore in New York!"

"Well, they are in Pawtucket!" snapped Spencer, closed his briefcase, and marched out, back to Pawtucket where, as usual, they were sufficiently behind the fashion to make him profits for several years to come.

August 26: Louis, the old waiter at the Brevoort, is often tight. With hard times they try to dismiss the old waiters but Napoleon and the rest won't go. Having had 35 ryes, Louis tells his life story—born on the Rue Madeleine, mother used to dance, etc. So Pierre, the head-waiter, half-annoyed, half-amused, said "Hey Louis, write a book, write a book!" Louis was insulted. "I have lots of enemies around here," he said, "plenty, but I fight them all, because I love the Brevoort." To soothe him, I said, "Well, you really should write a book, Louis. Why don't you?" "Money!" he answered. "What do I care about money? I live my life! Money means nothing to me."

September 3: On the pleasant porch at Lake Boniseen, Esther, Margaret, V. Pfeiffer and I sipping our idle whiskeys at noon, facing Mr. [Alexander] Woollcott's private island guarded by the Doberman Pinschers and having been these two days exhausting our minor gossip, nothing was left but the Larger Aspects of Life.

Why, demanded Virginia, did we want to be on the Loyalist side when it was a side waiters fought on, and all high-class people were on the other side? Esther, indignantly (about to come into her third $10,000 inheritance) declared *she* was "low-claws" and further that Ginny was "middle-claws." Ginny said she was *high*-class and how else explain her father being the leading citizen in Piggott, Arkansas (a town of 2000) and the whole town bowing to her and her family like royalty? In spite of having lived in Paris and every place else in the world she had an astoundingly complacent provincial satisfaction in her minor station.

Esther remarked that money didn't make high class; well, hastily amended Miss Pfeiffer, she meant you had to be intelligent, too—the *cultivated* class, she meant. Ah, said Esther, calming down, you mean the aristocracy of the intellect. Exactly, said Virginia. Margaret, who had been gently dozing, nodded full agreement, and allowed the Funnies to drift to the floor and everybody agreed happily. "The aristocracy of the intellect, that's my idea of the high class," said Virginia. "No waiters in it, either."

No one had even read a newspaper for days. They aged in their own rotogravure covers until ready to light a fire with them, but a book on the table, and a magazine a week in the mail and one in the bath gave confidence in a gigantic intellect going-on.

September 5: I'd love to meet him personally and shake him by the neck.

September 18: Felipe Alfau called, now a Francoite, as ostracized as a Conscientious Objector in the war. He originally was thrown on the rebel side by simple animalistic reasons—his brother, a mayor in a Spanish town, was assassinated by the Loyalists. Another brother intensified Felipe's vengeance necessity by accepting a Loyalist salary to live on, in spite of the family honor. All very Spanish. From then on he was pushed into more drastic Fascistic positions than before—anti-Jewish talks when all of his friends had been Jewish. He is a Latin and naturally intellectual, so gravitated automatically to the Jews. They are the ones who start war, who start persecution, is his point. His life is worth nothing, he says, why not go fight if Europe is in war? He would join the Nazi army of Hitler's.

When he was first here, he had an uncle teaching at Wisconsin University so he went there. The bouncing, athletic American girls thrilled him but made him "walk his love away," he mournfully said. There was William Ellery Leonard, the old poet with the Locomotive God, who has a phobia—he can only go five blocks away from his house. There he has wife after wife, of varying degrees of youth. "One is always there, packed, ready to go," said Felipe philosophically, "and one ready to step in. But imagine—a man, an intellectual, 60 years old, with such a phobia. I tell you in English strange things happen, terrible things. Only in English could such things be. In Spain, the little boy who was nervous would be spanked. Here, he is drawn into conference with his parents, later the teachers, later the psychoanalysts, the doctors. Conferences! In Spain, the professor would have such respect paid he would have no need for his little game, or else people would jeer at it. Seeing him walking his little five blocks, they would look out their windows and say 'there he goes, the big liar!' Or else from house to house the professor would be led by his nose, here with some red peppers frying with a little red wine, further with goat cheese and a small bottle of port, all for the great man, and so his ego would be fed with no other need. But in English these dreadful things happen and if Prof. Leonard could only translate himself into some other language—Russian, of course, or Latin—he would be a very fine man and much happier."

At Lavatoria, the cheap Italian restaurant, where we had devilfish and white wine, the waiters, proprietors, and one guest played peanuckle rummy. One made some remark in Italian and Felipe said, laughing but serious, "Heil, Mussolini! Duce! Heil Hitler!!" The youngest boy turned gravely around, his cards in hand, and said, carefully, "But I do not like Mussolini! I do not like Hitler! They are bad." Felipe, his strategy recognized, shrugged and smiled. He is now so definitely a Fascist propagandist that he must meet every casual opportunity for finding out who stands where.

September 29: My plan has always been to feed a historical necessity. In the Ohio books I was not interested in making up romances, but in archaeology and showing up people and places that are or have been familiar types, but were not acceptable to fiction, because of inner wars in their nature that make them confused human characters instead of standard fiction black and white types—good, bad, strong, weak. In my last two books I have not deviated from my original purpose—the Provincial Out of Place, or the Provincial Attacking a Cosmopolitan Problem. My moral is always present, though never in black and white or concerned with criticisms of my characters' activities. In *The Happy Island* it is a picture of people ordinarily envied as Glamorous Idlers and showing up—not their immorality, which is always fun—but the niggling, bickering meanness of their life—not the great gorgeous Cecil B. DeMille idea of corruption, a pagan rout that any imaginative person would like to get into, but a story of miserly, piddling souls without one great, generous glittering vice to their name.

In the new book, I propose another provincial angle—the businessman on planes, trains, buses, private cars, whose business axis is New York; whose homes are Iowa, Chicago, Detroit, Pittsburgh, Alabama.* These men have their wandering minstrel, gypsy lives, in and out of hotels— the Stevenson, Chicago, the Fort Sumter, Charleston—tornadoes, wrecks strike them, a life of adventure, a code of their own. Strict love code, romantic within rights. Barney's nightclub remark—"He used to run around but now he's settled down. A very settled man—same wife for the last five years, and the same mistress. Getting old, maybe."

Coby spent the evening at the Players' Club, drinking. I asked him if the members did much drinking and he said well, yes, but real drunkenness is frowned on, so everyone sits there frowning at each other.

October 16: A ham session over amateur radio. Friends all over the world. The Amateurs have done everything in radio. Government turned over the five-meter band and said—see what you can do with it. They tinkered and compared notes and fussed, then when they've got some ultra

---

*This would seem the beginning of what became *Angels On Toast*.

high frequency perfected, the government takes it back. They have ham picnics, give directions over the air and invite everybody.

October 25: Ed. For all his life, a fat prissy little mama's boy, cowed by his terrific Bostonian mother, sister, brother, etc. Lived wretchedly this austere, apron-string life, then—in New York on business—had a Village apartment—sailors, black girls, Filipino boys, whores, Lesbians—stayed out in dives under Brooklyn Bridge all night, had a regular Dr. Jekyll-Mr. Hyde life. Then mother, old and sick, demands even more, denies the possibility of this outlet, he must be with her constantly and ever more supervised, till she becomes a paralyzed, dithering old idiot, when he avenges himself, removes her to New York—a place she has hated all her life—puts her in great Park Avenue apartment, has his friends capering about in girls' clothes, black singers, etc. Old idiot woman in other room —Woman Who Would Not Die.

November 15: Dinner with Pauline Hemingway. Jo Davidson, conceited, warm sculptor says—on being reminded of his beard—that he is just a "flying old man on a dying trapeze."

December 18: Jojo home after further treatment at Gladwyne.

1939

January 4: For short story collection: "Day After Tomorrow"; "Wise Guy"; "Slow Burn"; "Enter Two Girls, Laughing"; "The Comeback"; "Feet on the Ground"; "Cheerio"; "Blue Hyacinths"; "A Letter From Peter"; "Gentleman Lost"; "Sample Size"; "Lovers Again"; "Florida Limited"; "Here Today, Gone Tomorrow"; "Talent in Her Little Fingers"; "Ernest's Experience"; "Artist's Life"; "Such A Pretty Day"; "Every Day is Ladies' Day"; "Adam"; "Ideal Home."

January 12: The Chopin scherzo—Barere playing it. The immaculate madness. The one melody—grave, aspiring, pure—Man's purpose. But all around the exquisite forays into sin, sometimes combining them into an evil duplicate of the True, though it rings out stronger and stronger. The murmuring rebellions carry him away.

January 16: Heard Myra Hess and Budapest String Quartet in Mozart Quartet in G minor, Haydn and Beethoven. She looked like a Wagnerian soprano or a harpist with her flowing sleeves, large arms that seemed mighty but were for tiny dainty precision work, agreeable feathery runs, delicate attacks on the piano nerve centers rather than mighty forays into the guts of music.

January 22: I told Marie I dreamed of rushing out in the street and saving two little children from an automobile and carrying them to safety. "What a wonderful lady," said Marie.

January 24: To dinner for Mary Margaret McBride and later to Casa Mañana with Ben Gross, radio critic on *News.* He said banks owned most nightclubs now, which were operated on 77B. This was a banking law which allowed that if a club fails and cannot pay bills it does not have to go into bankruptcy but goes to bank for a representative to manage. International Casino was Farmers and Building and Loan Trust Club. Also hotels are in hands of bankers and even Hearst is. Warner's dropped Cosmopolitan because they refused to star Marion Davies in any more pictures.

January 26: End of ten years.*

If anyone likes truth—and it seems to me the most beautiful form of art in the world—they not only like to get at real motives and the real character of other people but there is a release in finding out something about themselves, or even finding old clichés true. After a while a number of things unfold—the reason for the banalities of best sellers, the popularity of platitudinous books on living. Platitude is the stuff of life, the core of living, the cure for heartbreak, the ultimate answer to "Why?" Underneath the woes of the world run the firm roots of platitudes, the song cues, the calendar slogans. "Darkness comes before daylight," "Tomorrow is another day," "Where there's a will, there's a way," "Jesus loves you."

There is nothing permanent, nothing for the mind to fall on but this old bed of clichés after it has stormed through life trying to find its own answers, its own solutions, and finally its own heartbreak, its own stone wall. What comfort then in "Into each life some rain must fall, some days must be dark and dreary"? Little—but all there is.

There is an overwhelming kind of love—not born of habit but a love of the person's nature, mind and very self (apart from a physical attraction which should be present)—that enables one to want the best for that person because they deserve it, to want it even at one's own expense. This is a truth not many people find out because it is hard to find a person one admires, enjoys, loves, likes and lusts for all simultaneously.

January 30: Bernard Shaw says every man over 40 is a scoundrel.

---

*This private entry—and the meditation which seemingly grows out of it—is still mysterious.

February 2: Ginny tells of Simon Barere, the Russian pianist now playing so marvelously, that he never had a break before. He was a boy prodigy and could think of nothing more wonderful than playing in the cafes to bring home money enough for his parents to eat—then, at most, to be a teacher in the Moscow Conservatory. Now he practices always naked but in winter gets cold and puts on long woolen drawers. He never knew how to work a piano stool; all he knew was the piano, so he fusses on the concert platform over the stool helplessly, finally gives up and moves the piano.

He hates playing the Baldwin and he gets worried he is sick. "I feel seeck," he moans, "I doano, I feel seeck. Maybe I have not eaten enough. Or maybe I have eaten too much. If I have eaten too much I will go out and walk through the Park for one hour. But if I have not eaten enough, then I will go to a restaurant and eat for one hour. I doano."

Philip Loeb for lunch. He said Shirley Temple was doing a heartwarmer picture and he was called in for a run-through of one terrific ham scene which was a tear-jerker so he wept even though the scene stank. Next day, the conference. "Boys, it stinks," he said. "It's impossible. It's out." "What's so bad about it?" they asked. "What's so *bad?*" he jeers. "Alright, I'll tell you." He starts to describe the lousy scene and the tears again pour down his face, just telling it. "The scene stays in, Mr. Loeb," they assure him.

February 4: Insecurity is often the basis for stable affections. The feeling that any moment this person may be gone forever keeps their best points always before one, just as the feeling that someone is permanently committed to someone else raises the question of the other's merit daily. Is such bondage worth it?

February 5: The Rachmaninoff Concerto in C minor. He wrote it under hypnosis or a Coué form of Christian Science psychoanalysis, after believing he could never write again. Every day he went to the doctor who repeated "You are going to create; your new concerto will be excellent" and finally he did it. It is mental music, intellectualized, icy Tchaikovsky, icily invigorating, majestic as the Alps—brave, haughty music with dignity and no heart. The theme: "I was unfaithful to you, dear, but it was my heart that broke."

February 9: From "The Knights": ". . . to steal, perjure yourself and make a receiver of your rump are three essentials for climbing high."

February 16: Griffin Barry, sad, dried up, desperately miserable at 54, once a pretty boy, once the lover of all the famous women and even of their lovers—for he took Edna Millay from George Slocombe and at the same time slept with Slocombe—he appeared at 10 o'clock, forlorn, somewhat drunk on Pernods. He had been weeping over them at the Lafayette. "I sat there with tears streaming down my face," he said dismally, "and a young man came up and asked me if there was anything he could do. He seemed to be connected with the Oxford Movement, though when I referred to it he denied it. I usually dislike it when the young people from that Movement come up and butt in on your troubles but tonight I really would have enjoyed talking to him about God. But he said, when I tried to talk to him, that he was not connected with any religious organization at all. He simply wouldn't admit it. He went out but I followed him to question him, because if he was the spiritual adviser there I really felt like talking about God, but finally he said—Look here, I'm just an employee of the hotel and I didn't want you to get sick on the floor."

The young man, he added, had a mustache, and I recognized him at once as the hard-boiled bouncer of the cafe, very much a "dese and dose" guy and tough as they come. I can picture his astonishment and suspicions at Griffin's questions.

February 18: Felipe Alfau, brilliant, dazzling mind, witty, Jesuitical, a mental performance similar only to Cummings, but a scholar—erudite, fascinating, above all a romantic about his Spain, fiercely patriotic, a figure out of a medieval romance, a lover of Toledo, of old Spain, valuable surely to his country—talked so brilliantly of Totalitarianism that is based on human weaknesses, human error, human conduct, that it almost convinced me. Certainly its admission of individual woe and personal problems is wonderfully relaxing after the Communists' rigid belief in paper theories and a love of masses that excuses them from making personal loans or any emotional duty to a wife or friend; their uncompromising belief in theory excuses their startlingly variant lives, their greed, egotism, callousness and personal brutality.

February 27: There are odd lines that convince and deny by a word such as: "I will never forgive you, dearest; I will hate you for this as long as I live, sweetheart; this is one thing I will never, *never* excuse, my darling."

March 1: Wits are never happy people. The anguish that has scraped their nerves and left them raw to every flicker of life is the base of wit—for the raw nerve reacts at once without any agent, the reaction is direct, with no integumentary obstacles. Wit is the cry of pain, the true word that pierces the heart. If it does not pierce, then it is not true wit. True wit should break a good man's heart.

March 3: Meeting the Archbishop Francis of the Greek Catholic Church in his rich brocaded robes, small red hat, etc. at Charles Studin's. Fragile, vital, calm, eager, pleasant bird-like man of 40 or so. "I should like you to come up and see our incunabula," he said in the manner of someone asking a lady to look at his etchings. He likes dogs as pets in the abbey but not cats. "Cats look at you as if there were something they could say and then they don't say it." He should have a cat because only the other day he saw a rat in the refectory. He does not mind but it embarrasses one when guests see it too. I suggested that he teach it to waltz and then it would be a matter of pride to show off his waltzing rat. He said yes, but he was afraid one day it might appear without waltzing, and again and again— revealing a horde rather than one gifted pet.

Winchell says—"He worships the ground she staggers on"; also, "He came in like a lion and went out like a lamp."

March 11: Ginny [Pfeiffer] and I, resolving after the Ivens film "400 Million" not to drink, compromise on one highball at the Blue Ribbon which, with great regard for each other's resolution ("Don't have another because I know you don't want one but I do—") rattles out to three. Then, carefully walking to Fifth Avenue, we were obliged to go to the Algonquin Ladies' Room, passing the jolly-sounding bar. We are not drinking this night and merely glance at the place, but oddly enough we put on all new make-up in the can, for going home on bus to early bed. Then Ginny finds her hands are very dirty for going on a bus, and we carefully wash our hands. Then her hair needs a little fixing for bed and my coat must be brushed for the bus home. Then, our resolutions still intact, we silently walk into the bar and drink like fish till 3:15 and the scrubwomen are underfoot.

March 14: A woman should attempt to be as sympathetic, amused and understanding of a man's vices as his favorite bar is.

Yesterday with a fever of 102.5, my mind suddenly made a tremendous shift and said—I'm not happy, I'm not making use of my life, I'm not even using forces that could make me happy. It's all the bunk, this resignation to the Blue Plate. My mind is coldly working on a plan of change.

March 15: Bumby Hemingway, tall, handsome, decent guy of 15—in fact, ideal boy—on way to Key West, Fla. It seems when he was 5, in Austria, he was by nature a sport-loving outdoor boy but his mother was musical so he wanted to be, and he cried for a violin so much they finally gave him one which he proudly toted, in its case, all over the countryside skiing, bobsledding, etc., and never would stir without it, finally finding it very practical in banging the local village children over the head.

March 16: A person is like blank paper with secret writing, sometimes never brought out, other times brought out by odd chemicals. In Cardington, Sam Kahnheimer, a New York Jew, appears in 1890 in clothing store—attends dances, etc., is taunted by local boys that though he may dance with these girls he would never be able to marry any. So he bet he could marry the prettiest girl in town—in fact, the daughter of the richest man, Mr. Singer. He did, though old man Singer swore the family would disown daughter and him, which they did.

Because it was a small town, Mr. Kahnheimer's house for his bride was only four doors from her parents but they never spoke. He brought his own Jewish mama and she stayed in one side of the house and never spoke to anyone. They had no friends. He went to Washington and left them there to fight it out, coming home only once a year.

The wife, Ella Singer,* no friends, developing an odd Jewish accent and raising her children to be Jews—Miriam, Flora, etc., teaching them music. A fine rich household with hundreds of books where I read, where I learned to play the piano when my stepmother refused to allow us to

---

*This is most likely the model for Mrs. Gross in *My Home Is Far Away.*

play, where I learned about Grieg—"Anitra's Dance," Mrs. Kahnheimer played, and advised me to read *Adam Bede*.

All the time, three houses down the street, the old Singers lived, lonely, with a wild adopted daughter Verna, and never spoke to their other daughter. A brave woman, Mrs. Kahnheimer, who braved all for love and a cheap stranger's gaudy bet, and had neither love nor him, but her own dignity and the rich cultural life she built up for herself. All by herself she had to defend the Jewish race against this one invasion of the little town.

March 22: Coby and I ran into Griffin and Lady Hastings again and more politics. Finally I urged him to stay all night as a house guest which he did. In the morning Joe came in and said "Who is that in the living room?" I said, in surprise, that I didn't know, having forgotten. Later Coby said he woke up with no idea where he was, then out of one bleary eye saw Joe and wondered what he was doing in his house, then what he was doing in his house in a bathrobe.

April 4: "I hope someday I have enough money to enjoy economizing."

April 5: Desire makes its own object worthy of desire.

May 1: Bobby Lewis said Saroyan's egotism came from his grandmother. An Armenian, she settled in Fresno, California and remained thoroughly Armenian all her days. Commenting on her next-door neighbor she said, "She is so stupid. Think of it. She has lived next door to me for 28 years and still can't speak a word of Armenian."

He wrote a play about two people which he hoped the Group would produce. Saroyan, his hero, is in bed onstage with a woman, in darkness. On screen behind them are pictures of waves breaking.

"You're the best lay I ever had," said the prostitute.

"Not only that," he answers, "but I'm the best writer you ever had."

After a silence, one enormous wave sweeps all the others and the screen blacks out. Lights go on as woman gets up naked and crosses stage to bathroom. "The greatest play ever written," says Saroyan.

May 4: Frederick Kiesler—a penthouse at 14th and 7th, overlooking the river and New York. 60 guests coming and going, Russians, Tunisians,

French, Germans. Buckminster Fuller, neat, gray architect-engineer of 60, carries official Naval Ordinance book around, book on ballistics, pointing out that the first two pages are in verse—The Elongation of the Pressure and the Velocity—etc. Gorky's grandson, tall, mournful, black mustached, essayed a Russian dance. Later, in a small room, in darkness I saw him earnestly talking to the tall, exotic, stagey Russian from Hollywood, with daisies for earrings and a handsome red spangled shawl. "Permeet me to say," he was saying, "permeet me to say that you are like so many dead feesh."

"No! You deed not say it, Arshile! You deed not?"

"I said it," he repeated stiffly. "I said—permeet me to say that to me, I said, you are like so many dead feesh!"

I left and went inside where the Frenchman, the Viennese doctor who had been beaten up by the Nazis, Noguchi the Japanese sculptor and a French Tunisian were all in an open-eyed dither over the blondeness of Peter Jack's wife. The Tunisian was particularly blunt. "How do you do?" he said. "You have a beautiful bosom, do you speak French?" Later he saw her again and reached out his hand. "How do you do, will you come on the terrace?" he said. Peter was jealous, not only of her but more because *he* was the one who should be flirting. He is a strong masculinist.

May 12: Finished play, "Every Other Day," and left it at Brandts.

In this wave of nationalistic frenzy biographers are discovering more obscure Americans who were "powers" and absolutely changed public opinion, so that history for schools in the future will be very involved indeed. We had Lincoln and Washington before, with a sentence for Aaron Burr, Alexander Hamilton and Jefferson. Then presidents of all kinds were dug up, vice-presidents, small-town mayors, etc., men who ran and lost offices, unheard of "powers." You could do a biography of your Uncle Bill and pin any offices or honors on him you chose without anyone objecting since we are used now to all sorts of strange histories we have to believe on faith.

Characters in the past had one word—Carlyle: dyspeptic, Mrs. Carlyle: shrew, Disraeli: Machiavellian, Barrie: sentimental. Now all these simple categories have been housecleaned and shrew is glamour girl, dyspeptic is benevolent sage and, as Coby says, the "not-at-all-biographers" hold sway.

May 14: Dwight's summer in New York. Tired and bored, he said to his chauffeur—let's not go to Sands Point today, let's not go to supper at Piping Rock, instead let's see New York. We will be alone in the city, we will explore, we will see the city we have never seen, we'll wander.

So at 11 o'clock on Sunday, he rose and put on his finest tropical tweed, a yellow tie and said "Frederick, don't wear your uniform, I will sit with you. We'll just bum around the city." So they rode through the park and the trees were all perfectly green and the flowers were blooming, though not so profusely as to give offense.

"There are not so many visiting nurses out on Sunday as during the week, are there, Frederick?" he said, and Frederick said no. "But there are many more fathers out," he said, and Frederick said yes, there were. He thought of going to his favorite restaurant but on Sunday it disappeared and so had all the places. They went to the Battery, got out and tried to see the Aquarium. Nothing to see—a standing line, which was perfect nonsense because they were people who must have seen the fish dozens of times; certainly, it was free. A little cross, he went back to the car with Frederick.

"Let's wander up the East Side," he said, for he hadn't been there for ages. Streets were wider but suddenly there were crowds and crowds of people, hanging out windows in undershirts, dirty—drive a little faster. He felt blue. It depressed him. "You shouldn't be so soft-hearted, Mr. F," said Frederick. But do they have enough to eat, he whimpered, do you suppose they have beds to sleep on? He felt a dreadful lump in his throat, he was much too soft-hearted.

The noise was deafening—radios, radios, radios. How do they have money to buy radios? "That's just it," said Frederick. "You don't need to worry." Frederick was right, when you stopped to think. If they had money to buy radios, they had enough to eat on. He felt better.

May 20: Niles and I sat in Lafayette and discussed Alec Brook and Portia LeBrun. Alec has been gone so long now that there is nothing left to say but the good things; we fed each other praise of him until he no longer existed and became a fabulous legend, too wondrous for even us to ever know personally. And Portia—the girl he loved, what a little queen! Suddenly we looked out the window and there they were. They came in. We had invoked them and it was embarrassing to have a pair of legends sit down and order drinks like ordinary people; besides, they had no connection with the characters we had just invented.

May 22: Harold Freedman called up and stated—in regard to my tender, sentimental, slight little play—that it was structurally excellent, except for the second act. Hard, unpleasant, brutal people. I said I thought it was a slight, sentimental story, gay—and I find no gaiety or wit that is not based on truth. For me there is nothing delightful in blindness, in people being gay because they do not admit facts.

True gaiety is based on a foundation of realism. All right, we know we're dying, we know we're poor, that is off our minds—we eat, sleep, make merry but we are not kidding ourselves that we are rich and beautiful or that Santa Claus and two blondes will soon come down the chimney. There is only sorrow in people making believe—sorrow and sordidness in stories of invincible, Peter Pan fairy-godmother world. Gaiety should be brave, it should have stout legs of truth, not a gelatine base of dreams and wishes.

May 28: At the Brittany after quarrel with Joe. On way out this morning I looked at apartments and Miss Lundgren said a lady with a divorce was just taking it. "Her husband left her to marry a younger woman." Terrifying words to be inscribed on every woman's tomb. There will always be younger women, and men will always want them.

"He say he wanted children," said Miss L. with shrug. "Always some excuse." On the third floor is a divorce, too. He, too, wanted younger women. In one case the wife was 40 and attractive. In the other case, she was barely 30.

I have been wondering if there is anything comparable to that in a man's life—any fear in love—and it probably is this: she wanted a richer man. In both cases, the person can do nothing about it. Beauty can sometimes be achieved or substituted by chic, money, wit, charm, clothes, hospitality, but youth is youth, and while riches seem attainable, they are less and less so, and certainly can't be whipped up at the drop of a hat. A woman is not old until the man she loves falls in love with a younger woman. At once there are wrinkles, gray hairs, pouches, all the middle-aged signals, no Arden or Rubinstein can retrieve her then. At 40, a woman should not gamble; she should bend all her energies to retaining whatever she has, if it's family, marriage, job, etc., because from now on the losses begin and the diminution of courage.

June 1: Donald Ogden Stewart is a really funny man. I warned him that
the mint juleps he ordered at Longchamps would be all ice as he applied
himself to the straw. "That's all right," he said. "I'm blowing back in a
couple of drinks I had last night." We congratulated him on the deft way
he wove in and out of parliamentary rules. Is the speaker speaking to the
motion? I beg pardon, the chair has not granted you the floor. Mr.
Chairman, I object, we are not ready for the question; the motion has not
been seconded. Very well, we are waiting for a second.

Stewart said he had never been anything but dazed by Roberts' Rules
of Order. In fact, Roberts must have been a nasty little man. He thought
Mrs. Roberts must have had a terrible life with him. He thought he
would write Mrs. Roberts' Rules of Order. He surmised that Mrs. Roberts
had spent all her life waiting for a second.

June 7: Coby went to telephone at the Brevoort, being quite tight. When
he returned he was ushering to our table with a courtly air a figment of
someone's imagination, a character invoked from a bad novel, a woman
of fifty, dark, almost theatrically modest, cheaply dressed in black, almost
a companion's uniform.

"He could not find his number so I helped him," she said, smiling.
"You see, I had my glasses." Yes, she would have a drink—anything he
suggested. In a carefully smooth, soothing voice—the voice of a medium
in a dark lace-curtained parlor—she said she was expecting to fly at
Mineola that day; she was not a good flier but fair, but her friends had disappointed her. She said "I have been a person outside myself since 1925, I
do not think of my own lives, I live other peoples' lives." She had the
veiled suavity of a dressmaker to the rich, someone of low connections
who had made a life of pacifying and serving the rich, trying to be overly
genteel, overly lady-like, almost fawning.

"You are soothing," she said to me. "You put everyone at ease—an
inner peace"—and then I noticed an odd thing, that, while mesmerizing
me with her flattering words, she was quietly stroking Coby's arm up and
down, and, since there was no lust in her manner or face, but the veiled,
burned out mask of a person without interest in herself or anyone, the polite, meaningless hull of a woman without soul or desire, it occurred to
me that she was a whore—the *born* whore who is not one through tu-
multuous dreams, vulgarity, or gaudy tastes, but through negation of life,

indifference to feeling, complete absence of desire. Behind the genteel masquerade was a cipher, a sinister blank.

June 14: Driving out to Port Jefferson, Coby, who never sees the country, was perpetually amazed by it. A middle road between Babylon and Huntington seemed to have no inhabitants nor houses, but every cottage was a bar—"Harry's," "Annie's Bar and Grill," "Myrtle's," "Bill's Place," "Joe's," "Tommy's Bar"—and peering out the car window Coby kept exclaiming again and again over this little rural settlement that had nothing in it but bars. "They must take in each other's drinking," he decided. I sometimes think that a writer could become immortal merely as a chronicler of Gilman.

July 1: Jojo, thin, only 120 lbs., but very good. I read a chapter of *David Copperfield* a day to him, explaining points of conduct, geography, history, character, ethics, etc., and it seems a means of awakening him to realities. Dickens read aloud shows how far afield we moderns have gone from duty to readers. The reading mind is a 12-year old mind just like the movie mind. It requires a gentle introduction to its story, characters slowly and definitely introduced with major physical descriptions since no movie was anticipated; noises, backgrounds, voices, all clarified since no radio version was planned. If authors continued to pander to every sense, as the old writers did, instead of pandering to their own egos, books would still be greater than radio or movies.

July 20: Finally decided that my stern attempt to first-draft my novel at the typewriter instead of in pen and ink was what was delaying me, so took up pen again.

July 23: John Woodburn and wife called. He was with Doubleday Doran —blonde, ruddy, cynical, fair knitted brows over wildly blue eyes. At Woodstock once, broke, he hung around his wife who had the Western Union office, read all the telegrams, and later, at parties full of strangers whose lives he knew only through their telegrams, he astounded them and embarrassed his wife when he, after a few cocktails, said: "How do you do, Mr. Peters? Glad to meet you. Too bad Mary couldn't meet you in Saratoga but I guess she really did have a cold . . . Well, Miss Jones, sorry you've been having such a tough time with Dan, but after all if his wife's coming home you know there isn't much he can do," etc.

He also said that in San Francisco he wanted to be tough western and, looking at the menu, ordered a dozen Bear's Claws for breakfast, only to find they were a Danish pastry with jelly between five points.

August 8: The door opened and a stranger appeared. He was, he said, Bacon of Key West and was looking for Esther. Come in, I said, have a drink, stay for supper. I will, he said, and in the kitchen, as we squeezed limes for a Collins, Coby suddenly appeared, having passed out previously and, still dazed, looked helplessly at this stranger. This is the doctor, I said, the doctor I told you was coming. Oh, are you the doctor? Coby said, eagerly. Do you want to look me over right now, doc?

Introduced them by name. Bacon, said Coby—are you any relation to Leonard Bacon? His nephew, said Ed. Coby was delighted. Leonard's brother was my best friend, he cried. Old Will Bacon out in Denver, a damn sight better guy than Leonard. I read some memoirs of Leonard's lately, infinitely lousy. They're in book form now, said Ed. They ate for a moment till Coby looked up and made a gracious gesture toward Ed. "Pardon me," he said. "I didn't get your name. My name is Gilman."

August 9: Carl Van Doren's and Jean Knight's colored maid said, on the day she was told that after 12 years of illicit love they were to be married: "Congratulations, honey. I only hope it will last as long as it has."

August 25: Broadcast.* "Three Little Fishies." Cut off air because of war broadcast.

September 30: Traveling on train to Josephson's for weekend. Suddenly there is a stop—State Insane Asylum. The lamps swing in the rain outside. Men in raincoats—hats pulled down, lonely dark station, but acres and acres of a huge interminable building, lit up for night, and as train screams by, figures appear in every barred doorway, desolate prisoners at every iron window, and your heart stops. There they must stand or crouch, hour after hour, at windows or doors, knowing, like wild pets, that the trap door is there and someday it will open to let them out as to

---

*Powell had begun scripting and contributing "song analyses" to a radio program called "Music and Manners" starring Ann Honeycutt. No recordings are known to survive.

let them in, night all around them as it is in their torch-lit mad minds, the train blazing and screaming past them in the night no more real than the other images.

This is the picture the passenger sees in the seconds' pause at the institution, this is the picture on his eyeballs, on the windowpanes, tattooed on backs of people sitting ahead, so that the sleeping Catskills, winding brooks, village churches, the river and the whole quiet countryside for miles to come, all cry of murder.

October 21: At Port Jefferson. The plump, humorous-faced little man, contentedly sipping his beer at one end of the bar—shabby, working clothes, but coat on and soiled felt hat. A young man in garage mechanic clothes, big Sinko sign on back of shirt, came in. He looked at the clock. "Ten minutes to five," he said. "I never can drink till five. Never till after work."

"Saving to get married, eh?," said the plump man. "Can't have a beer until after five, eh?"

"Yeah, and what'll we do for that good Czecho-Slovakian beer now that Hitler's got my country?" evaded the young man.

"Hitler and Roosia," said the little man.

"And Mussolini."

"Ah, Mussolini is too smart," said the little man.

"Like Stalin, they wait till Hitler's got his moustache shaved off, then they step in and divide it all up."

"Roosia. There's a country I'd like to see wiped off the map."

"Mussolini'll fall in line soon enough," said the little man, "then us."

"Hitler don't want us or the Eyetalians; he don't even want the French," said the young man. "All he's after is the limeys."

"He wants to knock the handle off Chamberlain's umbrella," chuckled the little man.

"Not only Chamberlain," said the young man. "He wants all the limeys. Those limeys are what gets his goat."

"Sure, Mussolini'll fall in line," said the little man. "Then our boats will be sunk, then we'll fall in line. I wish John Pershing were a little younger, we'd have nothing to worry about."

A traveling salesman, blue suit, gray hat, blue tie, with beer at other end of bar, spoke up. "The brains is still there," he said.

"That's right. The brains is still there."

"He could run a war from here, if the brains is still there," said the young man, and looked at the clock again.

"Saving up to get married, eh?" teased the little man, watching him fondly. "No beer till five o'clock. Well, Johnny, what about it? You got no country now, Hitler's took it away. You got no country, like a Jew. What're you going to do now?"

The young man lazily unwound himself from the stool, yawned and stretched.

"Well, I can always go back to Brooklyn, where I was born."

"Brooklyn's a good country, alright," said the traveling salesman.

"Nothing the matter with Brooklyn," said the little man.

"Brooklyn's all right."

October 28: Coby, drunk, tie awry, coat half wrong-side out, hair tousled, inspires a "Good God!" from group. Why? he wants to know. "Go to a mirror," they suggest. "Just take a look at yourself." He shakes his head complacently. "I look alright," he says. "My genitals are covered, aren't they?"

1940

January 20: [Phelps] Putnam filled with constant rage and moral indignation over Gilman's constant drinking, which should by all decent laws be punished by social ostracism and unpopularity. Complacent, certain that drinking disqualifies one for social as well as business advancement, it annoys Putnam constantly that it is the loud, over-drinking Gilman who is invited to the best places; it is Gilman who is doing all right with the big names.

At night he discusses this with people. "Too bad he drinks so much. He could be such a nice fellow." And when he hears that Gilman was here or there, he frets that social judgments should be so faulty. He conducts imaginary talks with Gilman, showing him how mistaken his success is, for it exasperates him that the march of moral justice should be so slow.

Finally he himself was drunk and it was unfortunate that it was in this condition he should see that renegade Gilman, cold sober. He asked him into a bar, where Gilman had a Coca-Cola, but Putnam had brandy and, from this regrettably unconvincing pulpit, delivered his sermon on drinking, punctuating it with more and more drinks, prophesying moral and social and business collapse for such a wastrel and lashed on to both more drinks and more moral frenzy by Gilman's insistence on Coca-Cola. As he reeled out, he stumbled and Gilman must take him home. The crusader fell asleep on the floor, snoring heavily.

January 22: I dreamed of sending out cards to an Execution Celebration. The execution was the butchering of a bull. There was the struggle to conquer the bull when his horns broke off with no trouble and made the celebration seem silly.

January 24: Jojo to doctor and then to Brooklyn Hospital. Obsessed this time with Ann, and very close to serious breakdown.

January 25: Portia's broken heart would be more to be sympathized with if she were not so picturesque. No pose, no artificiality, yet everything about her is so fabulously fictional, even medieval, that her woe becomes an exquisite old miniature to be admired and laid aside.

At her huge loft, for which she pays $25, she achieves an air of regal luxury. Lace tablecloths, gold candelabra, grand piano, rich paintings, canopy-bed, pink Italian walls, tiny antique mirrors, great vases. Here is luxury—a dinner with wine, spaghetti, coffee, a lavishness based on no money. In the midst of this, Portia, in blue evening dress, red gold hair caught up, wanders like a vague Ophelia, bewildered by her lover's departure, lost, wearing her broken heart with sad grace, as if it was a locket. Her little laugh—tiny Chinese bells. She walks through today's grief not knowing she has been dead a thousand years and the little blue wax flowers in her hair are from her own long-forgotten grave and her forlorn sighs are not for a lost lover in a tweed suit but for Kubla Khan deserting her for war.

January 28: How soon and how easily ideals are corrupted. Here is this radio program—originally good and fruit of my own perfectly good mind, but in Honeycutt's tiny little destructive and determinedly trivial paddies it becomes an embarrassing nest of archly wooden banalities, clichés, unfunny attempts at banter. The effort to ignore all past radio stuff is appreciated by a new audience but firmly pushed aside by little, stubborn Honeycutt—capricious, uninformed and certain that no one knows more than she does, even though she is often rather startled at her own ignorance. Inefficient, erratic, occasionally enthusiastic over some small corner of an idea and eager to enlarge the little corner—never knowing that it is the little corner in proportion to the main idea that makes it good, so she must tear up ideas to messy bits like a child destroying a chicken. After the first dismay and anger at having good ideas destroyed comes resignation. There is no fighting mediocrity when it is in authority.

February 3: Bobby Lewis and his cute little Mexican girlfriend Maria de Ferreira took me to an Aviators party and then to a benefit in Harlem.

Maria is tiny, childish and naughty-faced, and tonight she was an irresistible item in cerise silk with white top, silver slippers and a white gardenia in her long black hair, blue eyes penciled upwards. Bigger, less beautiful and gayer, she would have been a bore but with her combination of clichés and delighted laughter, she was a charming toy.

"Look," she screamed in the taxi. "Look! That man behind us, he is speeding. He should not do that in the park where there are childrrrren!" (It was then midnight.) "He has a Cadilla, a beeg car with a weak motor." She relapsed in a happy drunken state to singing, then leaned forward.

"There is that beeg car with the weak motor again." She saw a bus. "That has a Ford motor. All the busses have Ford motors because they are so cheap and Mr. Ford makes them by quantity, not by quality." The conversations of all her lovers stuck to her mind like swamp moss to be happily torn out at a given cue, though she seemed never to remember anything but the banalities. From time to time movies came up. "Was it a Goldwyn picture?" she eagerly asked about six times, then entered into a speech: "Goldwyn makes B pictures and spends meelions and meelions of dollars on them so they seem good. Goldwyn has never bought a good picture. He could have bought a wonderful picture, a perfectly wonderful story, but he did not. It was about an aviator. . . ."

Drunk, eyes shadowed with pure childish fatigue, she fell asleep in the cab, gardenia still fresh in her hair but drooping down over one eye.

February 6: Last broadcast—very good and final tone pleasant since all was mine, Honeycutt having gone to hospital with general nerves.

February 7: Visited Jojo at Brooklyn Hospital and we went for walk through Fort Greene Park. Say what you will—there is something superior in a child who stops breathless, glowing-eyed, before street intersections, figuring out where they come from correctly, wondering where they must lead, wide-eyed with the thrill of it. This was along Myrtle Avenue, crossing Willoughby Street, Ashland Place, etc. Full of Italian stores with Sicilian bread, two cents a loaf. He was better than I ever knew him—in the thrill to his mind his walk changed from institutional shuffle to perfectly normal.

Coming across Manhattan Bridge by taxi at twilight the city again looked magical, ever challenging, ever unconquerable, and yet always alluring. Part of this was that the six months radio job was over. The strain of being another person spending infinitely valuable hours and nerves on trivial radio matters was over—the strain too of knowing the medium need not be so ridiculously trivial. Like the old silent screen, it deliberately sets up its own limitations.

February 9: "I have just learned," said Coby, "that you cannot use the word 'irregardless.' Of course if it's incorrect I shan't use it; naturally one cannot have an outlawed word in one's vocabulary. But"—he looked very wistful—"I don't expect to get anywhere without it. I owe all my skill in debate to that one word. Irregardless. You can't prove anything with re-gardless. But take irregardless. Why, you throw out 'irregardless' into the argument and you win, hands down. Nobody can talk back."

February 18: Heard Quintinilla talk at the New School on fresco painting. He said Giotto called the colors Brother Red and Brother Blue; that Paolino in the 16th century wrote the definitive work on fresco, that he said fresco painting is a man's work, all other painting belongs to women. That in colors earth-green cannot be bought at any price; black is danger-ous but beautiful; red is a pitfall changing itself on the wall to whatever grade of red it chooses, thus mocking the artist.

Quintinilla said as a young student of fresco his professor gave him the tile roof of a church built in Giotto's time and praised him for the beauti-ful face he painted on it but when it dried the face had erysipelas* and the professor could not explain it. The mason was called in, he came in inso-lently smoking a bad cigar, keeping his hat on. "I told you a dozen times, professor, those tiles could not be painted on, they are so thick with mildew that the artist is painting on mildew, not on a wall." The fresco professor could not explain this so the next day Quintinilla left him and went to study under a new teacher—the very mason who at least knew the most important part of fresco-painting.

March 10: George Davis at party, slightly drunk, angrily defends himself against Peter Jack's insinuation that while in Paris he slept with Cocteau. "I never slept with Cocteau," he declared. "With Norman Douglas, yes, because he was an old man and what can you do? But Cocteau—never!"

---

* A bacterial infection of the skin.

In the bedroom he folded his handsome muffler about his rather naughty-boy rosy face, before a mirror. "I was just looking at the wreck of what was once a very pretty face."

He said when he last visited Ford Madox Ford in his bare, cheap little room at 10 Fifth Avenue, opposite the Brevoort, where once he had been king as he had years ago in his great days in Paris, Ford said to his wife, "Look out the front window, my dear, and see if people are dining on the *terrasse* tonight." She looked and said "Yes. They are on the *terrasse,*" and he said, "Then it is warm enough for us to go to our own little restaurant," and they bundled him up to go to his cheap little outdoor restaurant on 8th Street, "Main Street"—a tough taxi-driving dive where he spoke French to the waiters.

March 14: Dwight had told me before he went south his plans for gaiety in Miami and Palm Beach and cruising, then to his secret hideaway in Key West where there is no society, no temptations, so he would just creep into the little hotel and sleep. I asked him if he'd had his Key West sleep when he got back and he threw up his hands. He had gotten into Key West at 4:30 Saturday and found, instead of the sleepy dead stillness he remembered, a screaming, yelling, whooping crowd of sailors and sailors tarts. The Navy was there, and tarts had come from all over America to service them. Bars were jammed. The Rendezvous, the Havana Madrid, Sloppy Joe's, the Garden of Roses, all were jammed and the town screamed day and night.

At first, Dwight made the rounds and was amused at the language, the whores and tough sailors. Then he remembered he was here for sleep so he went to his hotel only to find a drunken party in the next room whooping it up. He seized the telephone. "Manager, this is Mr. Fiske in 204. Will you please tell those bastards in the next room to shut up?" The manager merely laughed. "Sorry, sir. This is Saturday night. The sky's the limit." Dwight was furious. No reverence for the great name at all. He threw a boot at the room and said "Shut up." They said "Shut up yourself!" and threw a chair back. It went on till five when they all fell in a groaning heap on the floor and Dwight got up and with trembling fingers found a timetable—how soon could he get out of the damn place?—and was out by noon.

Story here is of famous man, tired of flattery, secretary, etc.—anxious for the peace and quiet of anonymity but he finds no peace in anonymity. No wifely and secretarial protection, and without it he is helpless.

March 17: Ann Honeycutt told of Lucius Beebe, the fabulous gourmet and epicure who arrived in Bleeck's the other night around 8 or 9 very drunk, sat down with them, too inarticulate to speak, but ordering another drink which he spilled and drooled and belched over, until Ann said "Lucius, don't drink—you must eat something" so he said stiffly "Very well, I will" and thereupon produced a large sandwich from his pocket, which he proceeded to wolf, while all around waiters and customers rose from their tables to see what new rare dish, accompanied by what rare wine, the fussy Beebe was working on. Eyes were popping over the spectacle of the sandwich. Finished, Beebe brushed off his crumbs, rose, and stalked out. Next day Ann called him up and said "Lucius, where did you get that sandwich?" He said "What sandwich?" and he had no recollection of the entire episode. It seems that while he sports his exquisite exterior man, the inner man is a crude fellow, a prankster, who loves to betray his other self.

March 23: Coby's jitters. How big? Well, very small. Hardly hand-high, but very bad. Getting into his joints and head. The way to cure them, he says, is this: when they come around you courteously invite them in, offer them a drink, then if they are still there, offer them another. Then, if they start getting rough, just say to them, "Look here, I've treated you like gentlemen, if you can't act like gentlemen, then out you go." Then you throw them out.

March 26: Gene Jolas upbraids Americans for not appreciating their own best talent. Any type of writing like French or English cultivated prose is "bad" if coming from America—where writers should be crude, phony Whitmans or instructive about their own country. Also, since he moves either in exclusively Cocteau-ish circles or exclusively bourgeois family circles, he never hears of the run of the mill writers, and when he does fancies they are precious and little appreciated in their own country. Carl Carmer (a best seller and lecturer) is an unappreciated native genius, he thinks. Margaret Widdemer (five serials running at once and *Ladies Home Journal* poetry) is another unknown brilliant poet.

March 27: Sad day. Jojo went completely berserk and Joe beat him and even though I held him in my arms calming him for hours afterward he went off again and Joe took him to the sanitarium at Gladwyne. It is true that one person, near delirium, drives everyone else in, too—otherwise I cannot account for my own insanity.

March 31: The thing about the gifted little children of the King Coit School is that in spite of their utter concentration on the theater, acting, costuming, etc., they are "unspoiled, natural, childish." After "The Tempest," in which Tanaquil LeClercq, thin, wise ten year old, was Ferdinand, we went for cocktails to their apartment. Presently Edith (the mother) came in with her little unspoiled prima donna, the latter still in make-up, bearing a coffin of flowers large enough for herself. She put the flowers on the floor. "I wonder who," she said, examining the card with a pleased smile (upside down, incidentally, since the talented child knows Racine and Corneille but not how to read, at least only with difficulty).

"Miss Tanaquil LeClercq, Guild Theatre!" she reads pleasantly. She opens the box, the envelope. "The Tinkers. Isn't that sweet?" They were enormous tiger lilies. She sprang up to put them away then had a second thought. "No," she reflected. "I think I'll just leave them open like this on the floor, so that when they come in they'll say—oh, the darling child!"

An elderly man came in. "I liked you in the love scene," he said.

"Love scene. Which one do you mean?"

"Where the princess kneels and says his kingdom is yours for one sweet glance, and you say then I do love thee."

Oh, she says—"You mean the pony scene. That's the pony scene. Of course there's not a real pony but I step down this way as if I was getting down from a pony."

"But it's a love scene" he said. "I didn't realize you were supposed to be on a pony."

"I don't see what you mean calling it the love scene," she said. "It's always called the pony scene."

She arranges herself in an imitation of childish naturalness on the floor. She shows pictures of herself in other performances. "I was just a *baby* in that," she says. "You can see how tiny I was."

Finally off to bed. In bed she must have Charles, a rather dilapidated doll, whose sailorsuit she has removed and replaced with a nightshirt. At

last here was a child. The guest, relieved, says "Goodnight, dear—you remind me of myself. I always liked my boy-doll best."

"Oh this isn't a boy doll, Mrs. X," she explains, covering him up carefully. "This is Charles Boyer."

April 2: Reading Marjorie Fleming's (Pet Marjorie's) journal, the only
thing that seemed worthy of the exaggerated fuss made over her was her
pious self-admonition: "We should not rejoice at the death of a neighbor."
Otherwise, an unusually barbaric but normal child of bright parents.

April 3: Recalling Selma Robinson's episode with the rich Clare Boothe
Brokaw,* whose book *Stuffed Shirts* she was publicizing. Like any other
young ambitious woman, she was flattered at having lunch with Miss
Boothe. A real person. Nothing phony about her. Hates her whole crowd,
just like we do, despises society, just a real girl. Chums. (Meantime Clare
milking Selma for publicity, has her up to meet people, tells her gossip
about them—hates them all, a real, genuine person.)

Little gifts are displayed ("I admired this vanity—she gave me one just
like it," etc.). Would Selma like to go to a little party with her? Debu-
tantes, etc. and, incidentally, the Grand Duchess Marie (that old bitch).
Selma, eager and delighted at such insolence to royalty, tells anecdotes
from publishing angle re: the Duchess. Clare refreshingly amused.

At party all girls get up and curtsy when Duchess enters but Selma
smiles, stays seated, leans to catch Clare's sarcastic eye over such rubbish,
is surprised to see Clare rising and curtsying, too. As they leave she realizes Clare is angry with her—when she suggests lunch as usual tomorrow, Clare frowns. Selma starts wooing her back by panning the group—
the Duchess, etc.—and Clare says nothing except finally "My dear, you
really should have curtseyed to the Grand Duchess. *Really,* my dear!"

April 7: Coby said gloomily, "All my life I've arrived at the station just
after the Orient Express has left."

April 10: Dorothy Farrell came in. "I thought you were going back to
Chicago," I said. "I should have," she said, "only I went on a three-weeks
bat in Harlem instead." I was startled. "Yes," she said. "I've always admired

* Later Clare Boothe Luce.

Stuff Smith—the colored bandleader at Hickory House—so I went up there and I just lived with him up on Sugar Hill." I was almost speechless but managed to say, "Well, isn't he a little old for you?" and she said, "No, he's only 31," and I murmured "Oh, that's alright then." She said the place was full of guests all the time and she drank all the time. The Negroes drank gin with a layer of port wine on top of it. Mr. Smith made her go on the wagon for three days finally. She referred to him reverently always as Mr. Smith. She is not really the type to do these things—it's just that she is trying to do all the things the husband who left her was fascinated by. She is sort of a "darling" and still wonders how and why she lost James.

On a bus with Coby, a very pretty and richly dressed girl got on and everyone was silent with obvious admiration. Coby turned around. "I suppose you're going to sit with her," I said. "Yes, do you mind?" he said. "No, but just how will you start the conversation?" I asked. "I will simply bow, doff my hat to the ground," he said with a courtly gesture removing his battered hat—"and say, 'Pardon me, have you seen my new hat?' "

April 12: To Diamond Horseshoe. Always New Years Eve at the Follies, 1900. Fritzi Scheff in her 60s—still bitchy, strange face—singing "Kiss Me Again" with the throaty sexy quality in her voice. In the powder room the matron so busy rounding up the cigarette girls selling their rubber dolls, etc., that no customer could get in. She went in one cabinet. "Frances, you've been in here. I can always tell it's you because you always pee all over the place." Frances, in ruffled costume and mere fraction of a skirt, stood at mirror putting purple eye shadow on. "Mary, you always blame me for everything," she complained. "Can't I wee-wee once in a while? How do you know it was me? I'll bet you had a man in here. Any men been in here lately?" "Listen, if any man got in here, believe me I'd know what to do with him," muttered the matron. The girls laughed, then the band struck up. "Come on, girls, you're on," yelled the matron, and they dashed squealing out.

April 27: Went to Ohio. Spoke at Shelby dinner.

May 13: This novel is about love and ambition, two cliché ideas. Different kinds of love—different kinds of men and women, different kinds of ambition, and the rubber relationships that are not rubber but sometimes break instead.

May 24: Lunch with Max Perkins. War everywhere.

June 3: Tea with Max Perkins. Perkins thinks there should be emotional education—but how? Reason is a separate factor, a crossword puzzle to mark time until the final burst takes place. It does not do anything with the emotions, it occupies them only till they have found some other emotion to feed on. The analyzed does not cure herself of frustrated love by analysis but by falling in love with the analyst.

June 4: My feeling about the war is that Germans are made for conquering by nature and go to pieces, suicidal or insane under defeat, whereas English are made for dogged hang-on endurance which in the long run conquers. One terrific defeat for the Germans and they will go to pieces, hysterical—the mechanized machinery of war will be no good under their personal defeat confusion.

July 27: I still think a book of American stories—covering last 75 years—would be valuable. And American Literary Primer.
   A *pas de deux*—Cat with Clothespin.

September 15: George Davis—ruddy, clear-eyed, frankly homo but untroubled by it, honest royalist, honest snob, but his clarity about it removes it from sophistication.

September 18: In spite of pleasure over Max Perkins' editorial work on me, now that the book is to come out the usual deadly hopelessness and weariness comes in. The lack of any ad or announcement, the silence from publishing end, the all-too-familiar signals of another blank shot, and once again the weary packing up and readying another book—never understanding why I am unable to follow the arrogance of my writing with an arrogance of personality or why the luck should so unfailingly fall elsewhere.

September 19: A book about two men living together in New York, or two women (one like Helen—cold, uncommunicative, department store head, once married, child taken away from her). Ferocious woman, en-amored of the newspaper-man life, Bleeck's.* Nobody can make a shrew out of a jolly woman quicker than a newspaper man. The lives of my last three books might easily converge, as they really would in New York.

September 20: There is the possibility of doing a second book on Dennis Orphen. There are so many kinds of fame for a writer that it is astonishing the number of us who never achieve even one.

There is the writer of magazine serials, whose huge financial returns make her or him a fit companion of the elite and dignify a suspect profession by the solidity of their finances. These famed ones may affect wit, chic, high life or pomposity, their success excuses the drivelings of their pen. Publicly they are always Kathleen Norris, the writer; Alice Duer Miller, the writer; Arthur Train, the writer. Never are they what they really are: Kathleen Norris, the banker; Alice Duer Miller, the broker, etc., etc. A more legitimate cause for their fame (with a vast body of less attractive people) is the honest escape and dream goods they offer the consumer: 25 minutes of Cinderella as respite from poverty and cure for tired feet. Here, their service is to be honored, no less so because it pays.

Another fame is the famous writer whose writings are few and possibly erudite, but whose prestige in society, banking or educational circles makes his name well-known, regardless of his writing. Then there is the famous writer who is touted to fame by journalists, whose actual work is of no importance but rides on personal notoriety (Dorothy Parker, Oscar Levant, and dozens more). And then the famous writer of talent or genius who never makes money and whose shabbiness and usually accompanying bitterness, profanity or simple rudeness make him regrettable in the society which makes or breaks artists. These are the men who must wait for death (instead of money) to make them socially desirable, to make their wit and wisdom collected, their lives exploited by weeping biographers and others who find them more palatable in death than in life, more glamorous as misunderstood geniuses dying in garrets than as living, bitter talent with no tuxedo to make their presence acceptable at the PEN or Stork Club.

---

*The Artist and Writer's Restaurant, known familiarly as Bleeck's, a midtown Manhattan hangout for journalists from the *Times* and *Herald Tribune*.

September 23: The increased pressure on the spirit, weariness of soul, that comes from something waiting to be done and an utter inability to do it, a weary dependence on luck. This is the matter of Jojo, ready to be removed from the sanitarium and put in school or brought home for a period but no bills paid at either place and increasing inability to do anything about it, as if 25 years of work merely ended in one final proof of inadequacy.

The one thing my own childhood taught me was that a child should be freed from the cloud of debts and indifference of parents. The sad end is that my own child is worse off than I ever was—with me hand-tied, and Joe ever romantic and elocutionary about ideals and not about reality. For years I have faced it that I could pay for myself and Jojo's care modestly and without debt, but with Joe's big salary nothing is ever paid but extravagances. What a waste of blood and spirit this has cost one little boy, innocent and undemanding! $30 and $40 Joe pays for one day of parental call—I do it for $7—when that gesture-money could be applied to the poor child's bill and see that at least he was respectfully considered. I used to average $3000 a year—lately barely $2000—but if Joe would pay $60 a month (a fourth of his weekly salary) I could take Jojo someplace myself and look after the two of us decently. But I doubt if Joe would do it—he would prefer to take him to the Rainbow Room once a month for $150.

September 29: Fear is a primary factor in life—either one begins courageously with no fear and slowly learns to cringe, or one begins fearfully, so afraid that bravado is necessary for everyday routine, a shell eventually serves as well as genuine courage for meeting the monsters of life. But, unless the shell is constantly rebuilt, it melts like some Dupont imitation glass, and then one is too old for new bravados. One can only quiver and hide and scamper finally to a grave where They cannot find you.

I never realize how lost my defenses are until the crisis comes and now I only want to run and hide. A new book coming out no longer rouses any hope. As the day approaches, I look at the book section and think with a sudden horror that this is the last Sunday I will be able to look at a book review without sick misgiving—no review, bad review or the patronizing review of another illiterate lady reviewer. There is a dreadful week now of the usual worst fears ahead, and after that the nervous, weary effort to pick up and begin again after another disappointment.

October 8: There are, I have now learned, rigorous rules for wit. Wit is not wit unless directed above or below. There is nothing funny in a property holder. The middle class is wit-proofed. Wit directed here is never "good-natured" as the jolly shafts directed at shanty Irish, East Side Jewish characters, drunken panhandlers—nor good-natured as the jibes shot at the rich man's bed and board. The middle class must be decently dull, and if they sin it must be at least 50 years ago and even then their sinning must be done without laughter or happy abandon but with remorse and Biblical incantations and anyone who has observed anything else is a bitter satirist.

If there is to be satire it must not bite at the bread-winner—but at those who interfere with his getting ahead. The rules for satire as laid down by reviewers are purely materialistic. Let no mockery interfere with the budget! Flay with "good-natured fun" the antics of the poor or the rich, but never say the pleasures of the middle class are a little ridiculous, too. The middle class comes in large families, and if you must record them, say they are earnest; say they eat simple apple pies and honest roast turkeys; say they till the soil, quibble over wills, snub new neighbors, juggle their accounts, cheat their partners (through family necessity), disown sons for unsavory marriages—but show that these vices are necessary, and are accompanied by worry, harassment and groans, never by laughter. Say that these sins (if sins they be, since they are at least *solemn* sins) are done with dignity, unlike the sins of the rich or the very poor.

October 12: Accidental prophesy seems part of the writer's job. After *Turn, Magic Wheel,* Ernest Hemingway's married life began turning out that way. After *Happy Island,* then Sheila Barrett, nightclub entertainer, told me of having thrown out her woman friend who lied to her and then a day or two later, her accompanist dropped dead in her house. Now, in *Angels on Toast,* I changed my nasty refugee Trina to look like pretty, sweet little Mexican Maria, flowers in hair and all, and by thinking of the character as Maria, instead of the shrewd, self-centered original model, was able to make an attractive person, unhampered by author hatred.

At Maria's this night, I was therefore startled to hear her talk in Spanish over the phone to someone Bobby jealously explained was Maria's Cuban bandleader—for that was exactly what I had invented for her in the novel. An author, observing and listening and living long enough should, I suppose, be able to complete an X line from two known points in a character's progress, either alive or imaginary, but it is startling to see it work out infallibly.

October 13: To the Murphy's at East Hampton, now a background for the Dos Passos' fatty degeneration, for they live and eat well, their beds are good beds, they are not idle rich but busy, good-living, intelligent, idling rich; they are understanding and not personally fortunate. But what is a writer and observer of mores doing napping luxuriously in that cushioned shelter? A Proust would thrive here, a mathematician, a historian —but not a live creative mind in 1940. Here is the great temptation of all middle age—comfort and security—but the surest death to the artist if accepted wholly.

The Murphys dash to Nassau—Dos goes; they sail the St. Lawrence— Dos does too. Gerald's mind is alive, witty and intolerant of any but artistic unconventionality—a mind to be enjoyed but not trusted, just as their life is to be enjoyed but not trusted. It is this trust that is to be suspected, not the enjoyment, but Dos both trusts and smacks his lips, sops up the gravy and finds reason for this having been the right life for him— a Jesuitism that is dangerous for an active mind. It is thus that priests and philosophers are betrayed, and Dos is part both of these—half ascetic and half sybarite.

October 22: Harry Gousha. His wife read *Angels on Toast* and started accusing him of being the model. At the train a special telegram waited him: "Why are you always so secretive about your trips?"—first indication of suspicions roused by character.

"Hell, she's always been suspicious," says Harry, "letting herself go, lying around in a negligee one week to the next, thinking up things to be the matter, no makeup, her hair wild, eyes popping out. Jesus, she looks like a witch! I come in from after a six week's trip—'You never take me anyplace' she says, looking wild. 'Okay,' I say, 'let's go haunt somethin'.' Nag, nag, nag, why do I spend money on restaurants when there's the cook and food at home—it's extravagance. Nag, nag, I'm a sonofabitch, a bastard, the lowest thing on earth—that's how it begins as soon as I get in the house—no matter how long I've been away. Last time I was feeling too goddam good so I talked back, wouldn't let her get started. 'Listen,'

I says, 'please bear in mind I'm a sonofabitch and a bastard of the first order and lets have no more argument about it. Now will you shut up!?'"

October 24: E. H. perturbed and conscience-struck over having left first wife (in spite of her second marriage). He finally forces himself to call up after a couple of years and says "This is Ernest" and she says "Ernest Who?" Meantime he has played on present wife's rich uncle's cultural passion, so that uncle upbraids niece for not holding him and is set to receive the supplantee of his niece and thus add to the cruelty.

To Libby Holman's for the weekend with Bobby and Maria Lewis. Auriol Lee and Bob Wallsten there. Auriol, angular, red-haired, sharp-faced, shrewd, monocled, dozing off into snoring naps in the middle of conversations—because, she explains, she doesn't want to excuse herself and go to bed leaving the nice party, but if she naps then and there she is delighted to wake up and still be at the party. "Dear Baydie," she says, "I do adore him. Poor darling, he's such a bore, bless his heart . . . Ruthie is a darling, she's a lamb, not a brain in her head, bless her heart . . . Mary is a doll, a perfect little doll, so pretty with those great blue eyes and her dark hair—rather a mess, though, I wonder Frank doesn't tell her, but then he's in such a tizzy about her, after all there *is* that fortune and all, he'd hate to risk losing that, naturally, but a darling, really, I wonder where she gets that wretched voice."

About Libby—a generous-spirited, genuinely kind person, once in a murder case and close to trial for it—she explained that Libby said it was worth those months of torture to discover at the end that there was justice in the world if you could find it, and she had.

October 29: Book.* New York during the invasion. Eggs thrown at Willkie in Detroit. Accents on the bus. Waking up with pressure on head. In London there is bombing. 87 children lost. A story of ambition against a background that is constantly torn down. The young men—idle, poor, no jobs to look forward to, drinking a little beer—apathetic because what chances are there for optimism? None of the "Welcome To The World, It's Yours To Conquer" of other days—playing mandolins, recorders, a permanent standing away. Their girls more and more going over to older men, their own fathers, because they have the money.

---

* *A Time To Be Born* begins with a similar meditation.

November 5: The somber, dignified high-school youth, not just a scatter-brain. What do you expect to do after school? What is your main interest? At the present time, he somberly answered, I am chiefly interested in per-cussion work. Percussion—I repeated stupidly. Yes, he said. I hope to be in the school band next year when the present drummer graduates.

November 6: Listening to Anton Bruckner's regular breathing. If he could carry a tune, he'd love to imitate Beethoven but as it is all he can do is pre-liminaries—getting his pitch and blowing the dust off all the instruments and as soon as he does this he has a good nap.

November 13: Fritz Kreisler playing the Beethoven violin concerto—extraordinarily kingly man, standing superbly on the stage, violin and bow at side, blinking slowly at audience, then at conductor Barbirolli with lion-like eyes, indifferent to the mob and to the keeper as if he were and had been for years a prize lion, knowing he had no equal, occasion-ally watching the violin group with a faint flicker of interest, secretly conducting them with a brisk nod.

November 26: I saw the sea—a blue lake—last night again in a dream, always a good thing for me.

November 27: Visiting the Greenwich Prison—Women's new House of Detention. Top floor for rehabilitation work where in one room a little colored girl was drumming at a piano, trying to learn; another room had a history class (all prostitutes); here was a group rehearsing the Xmas play; here was the ward for social diseases; here was the kitchen where the girls did the cooking, sewing, etc.; here was the library; here was where they talked to visitors (through closed windows and amplifiers so no tools could be exchanged); here were the locked doors everywhere; here were the little bunks, stockings being dried, *Screen Guide* on a bed, but barred doors and windows; here was a cop bringing in two new streetwalkers, one colored, one drab white, and here, coming from one assembly hall, was a chorus of incorrigibles lifting happy voices in "Hark, the Herald Angels Sing." We heard them as we went down the hall, the matron unlocking one heavy door after another on our way to tea at her private suite.

December 31: Depressing year but not as depressing as the thought of a new one, and the weariness of perpetually beginning at the bottom. From the appalling lack of momentum in my progress I gather I must have originally started several ladders below bottom and have not yet struck bottom rung. There is an effort, certainly, for those who must keep their ball rolling uphill, but that is nothing compared to the ever-increasing work for us whose efforts keep nothing going up, merely keep the ball from crushing us in its downward roll. Every book, every play, every story, seems to have less chance than ever, and the factor of luck seems to have nothing to do with me—merely work to no avail.

1941

[*Undated*]* The moving from Mt. Gilead to Shelby, where Ma lived. The rented surrey, and on the 30-mile drive the stops at all the relations—the young couples like Olive and Chris. Chris, with pipe, telling something and Olive kneeling on floor chattering out the story. My father: "She tells the story before Chris has even got started." The grocery store where you got chocolate mints for a penny and every other one had a penny in it. The "corn," niggerbabies, shoestrings, jelly beans.

In the country at Uncle Will's—the sleigh-rides, the walks to town with hair skimmed back, later loosened up to be more pretty. The ten cents not to be spent on useful objects but on sky rockets and Roman candles, carefully shot off at dusk all alone since Uncle Will and Aunt Bessie busy in barn with chores, and after supper was bedtime. Practical family that did not believe in pets or holidays or unnecessary labor. The paper dolls—cutting out dozens and naming them, having them act out stories. The pleasant (still pleasant) feel of the slip of paper, the high-buttoned shoes, the natty blue coats and muffs. The expert's joy in a flawless figure—i.e., one that did not have half its arm or foot cut off in severing it from the group. Some of these dolls are still vivid—taken from *McCalls* and *Butterick* and *Delineator Fashion Books,* also *Fashion Quarterlies*. Miss Muhlbach's works on shelf, also Mrs. E.D.E.N. Southworth and books on Quaker mysticism. Old socks. Falling down off Father.

Father and stepmother rage over damage done to new coat. "They wouldn't care what happens to us so long as the coat is saved," we bitterly say. They walk silently and angrily in front, both with quick short steps,

---

* Probably written on the morning of January 27 (see entry).

heads high. We are filled with unreasonable glee in getting home more because of *going* someplace than really getting to our dour home—no more books because we daren't touch them, no paper dolls for it's a mess, no organ playing because piano belongs to stepmother and no one dares touch it except for her loving dusting of it. On Sundays, dressed up in her expensive trousseau bolero suit she bangs out a few chords (all she knows), then shuts it up. Yes, the parents—he about 36, she about 31 or 32—hurry ahead after meeting on train, their frowns as they hustle us off the train, a candid warning not to expect any words of welcome. The gossip and excited news of our good time freezes on our lips, we trudge silently behind them, knowing how unwanted we are and muttering resentfully to each other.

The visits from our favorite aunt, before whom my stepmother cringed, thank God. How annoyed she was when we embarrassingly followed out stepmother's rules for us—*Never* Come in the Parlor—*Never* Sit in the Living Room Chairs—and if unavoidable because a guest urges this violation of property, Do Not put Sweaty, Dirty, Leprous little hands on the nicely polished wood or allow Filthy Shoes to brush the nap of the rug, and above all Do Not Stand in Doorway, looking with anxious terrified eyes at Said Stepmother, thus revealing the horror under which you lived. The daily chilling misery of being unwanted, in the way.

Stepmother burns my "trash"—the notebooks in which I write my poems and stories, throws Phyllis' crocheting and needles away (gift of a kind neighbor) because it "makes her nervous" so instead Phyllis sits biting her nails and sneaks off with string and hairpin to crochet and this, reminding the Stepmother (Christ, what a thoroughly mean, evil woman) of her cruelty in throwing the real needles away, makes her yank these imitations away from Phyllis. When Papa came home from the road (he was traveling then, which burnt her up) Phyllis had nightmare and walked into their bedroom saying "Why did you take my string?" until, bewildered, Papa asked for explanation and Phyllis burst into tears, being wakened.

Finally Papa's funeral—and the new little girl, with her piano lessons and 12 pairs of slippers to match her 12 dresses, her Pink Room. During last days all the Stepmother's belated heir Virginia does is show her three older stepsisters her clothes, change from one to the other. Harassed as she is by Papa's year-long illness, Stepmother smiles pityingly and says "Poor darling, she's too young to realize"—Virginia being twelve, the age when the rest of us were persecuted out of her house. The death rattle lost its real horror for Stepmother in her anguish that by mistake somebody had called in Virginia at the last moment and she was too sensitive, too young for such horrors.

Twenty years or less before that, Stepmother's greatest joy was in making us go downtown on errands with no hems in our ragged calico skirts (and forbidden needle and thread to sew them as Waste) so our schoolmates would sneer. Another sadistic treat for her was to make us come out on porch on Monday morning and run wringer or washboard in worn-out Sunday dress (instead of cute bungalow aprons like other girls), in full view of the children playing in the schoolyard so they could mock us. Even when we asked to make "hot-water soup" with hot water, salt and butter, she refused because we *wanted* to.

In his mill-clothes (she'd made my father give up the road and work in the mill but was again humiliated by his floury clothes) Papa sat at table over burnt oatmeal, scorched potatoes, soggy bread, lifeless chicken with lumpy gravy. He discursed on this spoon which he picked up at the Palmer House in Chicago—left there at 4:22 and got into Columbus at the State Hotel, etc., etc., all records of his years of travel.

The time one girl had tonsillitis and Step M. put rag dipped in coal oil around neck. In night anguish of fiery throat so great all three girls wake up but with one accord did not call Step M. to do anything as they were so resignedly sure this was her intention. In the morning she tore off the cloth, part of the skin coming with it, and she giggled at her mistake in not putting Vaseline on first. She hummed hymns in a hollow voice when she was happy. The charm and goodness of Cardington—a fine little village. The quarter to spend at the Fair and one buys a silver whip which Step M. hangs in kitchen. "I'll give you your whip alright," she'd say— and she would.

January 1: To Bobby Lewis' and then Edna Exton's where surrounded by small rosy fairies (at least ten) she begged me to repeat the compliment someone gave her about her hands, which I obligingly did for about the tenth time and then, extending the pleasure, she gazed tenderly at her hand and implored me to name what was the special beauty of her little hand and why it charmed him. I said, "because it was full of money," and so began my new year as I ended the last one—with insult.

January 2: The avoidance of contemporary manners in modern writing. In the last century, Thackeray, Dickens, Edith Wharton, James, all wrote of their own times and we have reliable records. Now we have only the escapists, who write of happenings a hundred or three hundred years ago, false to history, false to human nature. Among contemporary writers, only John O'Hara writes of one very small section of 52nd Street or Broadway. We have Hemingway, who writes of a fictional movie hero in Spain with the language neither Spanish nor English. When someone wishes to write of this age—as I do and have done—critics shy off—the public shies off. "Where's our Story Book?" they cry. "Where are our Story Book People?" This is obviously an age that Can't Take It.

January 4: The Borodin 2nd Quartet in D major (Pro Arte Quartet).

The idea of making a musical out of *Angels on Toast*.

The idea of writing "Brooklyn Widow" now—more timely than ever, since my plots for plays are nearly always indicative of a future trend.

Novel. Get up early or else start writing nights on novel as of old.

I want this novel to be as complete as if there were no modern imagination-savers (as radio, movies, etc.).

It should have a concerto form like the Rachmaninoff Second—with the mischief theme sounded in one movement, as the ideal is also sounded, and then developed thoroughly later on. I want the heroine simpler than any of my others, not jaded. Realistic, yes, but not soured, still subject to pain and joy and sentimentality.

January 7: No sleep can give rest when each day brings news of previous work refused. So why—now up and glancing through your failure's mail—do anything to increase your fatigue? Why work or drive yourself to add to some next week's or next month's morning disappointment?

January 14: The young woman sent me by Charles Studin to advise her on how to get a play produced. Small, dark, nice black eyes, and like most literary women the first impression is quite good-looking but second glance shows the firm chin, the determined lines around the mouth, the deviations from any beauty standard, the fretful bitterness of the too watchful, material-chasing eye. She was a quick, observant, intelligent girl—anywhere from 24 to 36—but handicapped by great gaps of ignorance about stage. Thirsty for it but poor and not knowing theater people, she gets excited over a "brave little group" (consisting of Russel Crouse, Arthur Kober, Antoinette Perry and other hardboiled commercial experts on Broadway) who are going to conduct the daring experiment of No Scenery!—the play Read By The Author!—and other devices that Winthrop Ames in 1902 and Gordon Craig and all the others had worked on for years.

January 18: Gilman had called up his office already on two hangover mornings to say he was "sick with grippe," but by Friday's hangover it seemed too unconvincing so he didn't even call. Whereupon the office called him and asked nastily, "Mr. Gilman, are you sick again?" Thus challenged, he said cheerfully, "Why no. I feel perfectly fine. I just don't want to come to the office today."

Later someone reported a sneering query to him—"Are you mice or are you men?" "Tell him we're mice and proud of it," he answered. Late by two hours for an appointment, he was astonished and righteously hurt to find the lady furious. How could she be so unfair when the only reason he was late was that he had been in a bar singing her praises with a friend?

January 19: Listening to White House reception program on radio. Charles Chaplin gives his speech from "Great Dictator"—appeal for humanity which was knocked by critics and everyone. However on radio it sounds singularly effective—a terrific job of mounting excitement. "Soldiers, you are not cattle—you are not machine-men to be driven by machine-men—I appeal to you . . ." There, as his tongue gets twisted Chaplin says "I'm sorry, my throat is dry? May I have a glass of water? . . . *Is* there such a thing as a glass of water?" There is a long pause. Obviously a signal for applause is given to break the astonished silence. Then Chaplin begins—a paragraph back, mounting once again but all magic is gone. All that can be remembered—and this with great poignancy from the speech—is that Chaplin wants a drink of water for his throat is dry. Here is a new effect learned by dramatic force. One simple irrelevant interruption in the middle of a perfectly good political speech. A mounting speech—possibly bombastic—and the sudden breakdown—"I am hungry" or "I am tired."

January 27: Unfortunately my fever brought back so many childhood memories with such brilliant clarity that it seems almost imperative to write a novel about that—the three sisters, the stepmother, Papa.* This is bad because the new idea is so much work and the old one now seems wooden. Wrote a start from 3 to 5 A.M. in bed with temperature.

Coby was reforming for a week because he was drawing blanks. He broke down and went on a binge but just a little binge, he said. I asked him if he drew a blank and he said "Oh, no indeed—at least not that I know of."

Niles perturbed over being thrown out of Brevoort. At a party at a gallery some women asked his theoretical opinion of steel engravings and he said he would have to see them to judge. She asked him to her place to look at them and it turned out to be the Brevoort. It was after midnight so, as he got in the elevator with great dignity, the room clerk came tearing out demanding angrily "Where do you think you're going?" To which Niles replied coldly, "This lady has asked me up to look at her steel engravings." The room clerk gave a scornful snort. "None of that goes on here," he said. "Come on out." So Niles had to exit with dignity.

February 7: Coby said, when trying to tell an anecdote to my interruptions, "Listen, Dawn, when I tell an anecdote I want you to be all ears instead of all lip."

Later, when everyone chattered and he strove again and again to tell his story, he complained loudly "Now will everyone please be quiet because I'm telling an enormously absorbing anecdote?"

February 11: At Hassoldt Davis'. Alice retreated to a small side room to whisper "I think the woman in beige is a new girlfriend. She is welcoming everybody, getting them drinks and so on. I can't stand it. And above all she said to him 'Bill, shall I feed the dogs?'"—the care of the dogs being a specially intimate thing. In a few minutes as she was worrying over this obvious usurping of her own place as dog-tender, a girl in a red dress thrust head out of another door saying, "Davey, shall I feed the dogs?" and scarcely was this done before a third woman inquired "Hassoldt, how about the dogs? Have they been fed?" All three had their own nicknames for him and all were obviously familiar with the house.

---

*Powell began *My Home Is Far Away* on this date.

March 3: Life in New York begins in strange ways and at strange times.

March 15: Sidney Lumet, child actor, now grown up to 15, still jumps in older actors' and actresses' laps. Says he has now grown into long pants and "Tobacco Road" (no one under 15 allowed). Says Professional Children School boys have all dyed hair red, hoping for job in "Life with Father," where four boys must all have red hair, but keep growing out of parts and so do their subs so young hopefuls dye hair red. Said he went to Zionist boys camp last summer. Nobody agreed—Left Wing Zionist, Right Left Wing Zionist, Right Right, polo Zionists, visionists, Trotskyite Zionists, Norman Thomas Zionists, etc.

March 17: Drama critics of New York have lived together so long that (like married couples) they think and look alike. There should be little uniforms for them to wear. The fault is not that they know little about drama, it's that they know so little else. "Life-like" is a word they use for a form of life they have seen sufficiently on the stage for it to seem normal to them. They never disagree—they have an adolescent fear in differing one iota from their associates. They permit one playwright a year to enter, and one actress. Century Club technique of membership.

March 20: There are two things essential to best creative work—one is overweening egotism (a quality seldom allied with any sense of humor); the second, exaggerated public reception. The chances of a man being spoiled by early praise are not as bad as his being ruined by adverse criticism for the personal sowing and inward-doubting, the fatal element of hate for humanity, is ruinous to the blooming of an artist. So a person like Hemingway—indeed, most of those I recall as being overpraised in their beginnings—are protected from annihilation and self-corrosion until they sometimes accomplish that which they are already credited with having done.

March 31: The way fate in its infinite justice works. The ones originally praised for some mediocrity continue to receive bouquets and gold medals since the critics do not want to admit they were ever wrong. Fate balances this careful nursing of her pets by an equally steady lambasting of her bastards. There seems to be no creeping out one door and coming in another one disguised as a pet.

"High strange beauty" new critical word, taking place of last year's "richly rewarding" and "heartwarmer."

April 3: Fear is the basis in love loyalty. Fear to break off for fear the next will not be as good or as permanent or that the old will do too well without you. Women don't leave a drunkard as often as is reported. The drunkard, being maverick, can always get other women and besides there is the maternal he arouses—also the sex interest since he is likely to be a different person every time.

April 21: Bobby Lewis wants to start new theater with Elia Kazan and for this needs plays. I promised to have one done during the summer. This could be one of two—the Brooklyn Widow one brought up to date, or the Louis Bromfield idea one. A musical beginning with the characters making their favorite entrances—leading lady rolling hoop and just home from boarding school—the leading man, a Guardsman, making his favorite speech about justice. Players' Holiday—each doing what they like, using their old costumes.

May 30: This is a period of no compass, no base, no program of ideas for work, no courage to see them through. A complete play ready to be written but a panic about using the time for such a gamble—as if time was on a budget and must be properly apportioned. Short story ideas get started and fumble as memory of past flops make brain uncertain. It is a period where if the full, well-fed ego is not present, then a director with authority and faith should be.

June 12: Worked all week on tentative outline of musical show for George Hale, etc. Also sample scene. Louise away—several dinners and lunches. Jack L. in town. Wrote review of Brontës for *PM*—very poor due to hasty reading on book which should have had thought.

After Alice appeared with extraordinary handsome, crooked-eyed, drunk, rude young man, the men of the party, instinctively recognizing an attractive rival, began to tear him to bits and this made the women automatically rise to the defense of the rude stranger. This is how women create their own rivals and, seeing men naively do the same, the lesson was clear. The man had been stupidly insulting to almost each woman—

"Dish-face," he called one—and if the men had cleverly defended him the women would have shouted derision. But the fact that the men innocently hailed him an obvious superior by their jealousy was a build-up for the guy. The men's jealousy testified to their certain sense that here was a *man*. Women should learn from this to pay as little notice as possible to their rivals since it is this attention—the spotlight of jealousy—that gives a perfectly mediocre woman her glamour.

June 14: Coby, looking enviously at an apartment costing about four times what he could afford, said "If I had this apartment, I'd be a rich man."

Weaving about, very tight, and in a mood of rather reverse graciousness, he said "Would you be good enough to bring me a cigarette . . . I don't want to seem importunate, but my dear host, will you please bring me a fresh drink? . . . Pardon my interruption, my good man, but would you be good enough to light my cigarette. And by the way—not to seem rude—but there seems to be a shortage of cigarettes."

Very irritated, I cried, "Why don't you carry your own cigarettes, anyway?" He was aghast at this suggestion. "The reason I don't carry my own cigarettes," he said patiently, "is because I'm afraid they'd blow up on me."

One time he was going home and saw the apartment door beneath his wide open. An own-business-minder, he marched past, then a budding sense of neighborly responsibility overcame him. A fleeting glimpse out of corner of eye of something not quite right. He went on down, aware that this sort of gesture was completely out of character. On the floor, half obstructing the door closing, was an enormous body of a man, rolled up in a rug. Coby thought at first he was murdered, but heavy breathing said the man was alive—perhaps knocked down. Lamps, etc., were overturned.

Unresourceful as he is in any such emergency, Coby did a master's job of dragging the man to a rug, slipping a pillow under his head, throwing a blanket over him, and shutting door so thieves couldn't get in. Next day on way home he wondered if all was well and rang bell. The Body and a rather elderly woman were at dinner. "I live upstairs," said Coby. "I just wondered if you were alright." Courteous but cold surprise marked the Body's face; the woman merely looked annoyed at this stranger's intruding. Gathering that he was very *de trop,* that it was he who seemed the

Drunkard rather than the man—Coby mumbled some embarrassment and hastily retreated, the good Samaritan driven quite out of him.

July 15: Unbearably depressed by this usual play business—delays, hard work, no check (here the goddam Dramatists Guild steps in and gouges out of their small fry whatever they can, and it's always me). Money owed and promised back to friends—heckled by everything—cat sick—icebox on blink.

September 10: Historic occasion. Beginning of good luck feeling after weeks of downs. Jessie Matthews likes script. Frank Swinnerton likes novel. Movie money for production raised. Frank Swinnerton said in London *Observer*: "Brilliant work, merciless in its precision. No wonder many English novels seem vapid."

September 13: Started to take 3 o'clock train for country, bought ticket, got on train, felt violent impulse to get off and did, just as train started. When I came home I was puzzled to receive phone call from Carol, asking me to go to Hollywood, via stratoliner, next day, at $500 a week, dialoguing "Du Barry Was A Lady." Actually wanted to go—just to get out of general mess, but Hale would not let me off show. Just as well, probably, as there would have been trouble getting ready cash, etc. on Sunday to take out there.

September 16: Jojo in beautiful form, except some Ann talk—off to Gladwyne for week's examination.

September 24: Incredible cheapness of musical comedy field. Cruel exploitation of egos. All men engaged in it mercilessly make use of their advantage, call in girls for auditions—or boys, if that's their taste.

Story of 2 or 3 men friends of composer or producer dropping in apartment and auditioning his list.

October 13: L. has been in New York at least 35 years, with only occasional weekends in her cherished New England. Yet no matter what goes on she believes herself a temporary visitor here. "On the Cape we don't believe in steam heat, we have hot bricks in bed at night, we don't care about electricity, we prefer oil lamps, we like oiled paper at windows, organs instead of pianos, we make our own cornmeal, hams, dried corn, flour," etc.—in short, her "home" is not anyplace at all but the world of small villages in 1906, though this she would never admit. On the Cape they have only one dress a year, they go barefoot with dignity, they do their own work, they live handsomely on $10 a week and have none of these "New York" ideas of automobiles, etc.

October 21: The gray busy rainy sky I love, and would like to be out under. But weather, sky, night, sun, wind, rain, or friends are forbidden when there is not money. The invitation of a morning must be ignored for it is a reminder that money must be made—therefore work must be attempted. Actually, there is the empty purse too—a walk, an impulse to use a phone, a bus, buy a newspaper, and these are impossible. I never see autumn anymore without the feeling that I have missed summer—out of doors so forbidden to the poor and the desperate; for us, there is no time, no sun, no daylight, but the endless crouching over a typewriter, trying to keep it from its own will, forcing it in a dozen suggested paths to fortune or at least security.

October 22: Never believing in regrets I have regrets lately. I wish I had finished my novel (which I would have by this time) or else done a play of my own. I wish I had stayed out in Mt. Sinai minding my own business doing nothing but vacationing perhaps. Anyway, it has been a long time since summer has been summer. A summer revision for Geddes and Dwight, a summer of radio, of finishing novel. I still have a secret passion to live alone and work. I could do as Esther does—live in a $12 a week furnished apartment, live on $25 a week altogether instead of this massive overhead that Joe and I run up.

1942

January 6: Date of Time on Novels
   Whither
      October 1922 to June 1924 (16 months)
   She Walks In Beauty ("The Dark Pool," "Rooms")
      September 15, 1924 to April 12, 1925 (after moving to Gr. Village)
      (7 months)
   Women At Four O'Clock (short novel)
   The Bride's House ("The Truelove Woman")
      December 1, 1925 to July 17, 1926
   "Women At Four O'Clock" (play, eight months)
   "Walking Down Broadway" (play)
   Dance Night
      July 1928 to June 15, 1930 (including hospital)
   Tenth Moon
      May 1931 to April 20, 1932
   Country Boy
      November 30, 1932 to December 12, 1933
   Turn, Magic Wheel
      (notes since 1930) About 1934 to November 2, 1935
   Happy Island
      May 26, 1936 to May 31, 1938
   Angels On Toast
      September 1938 to July 3, 1940
   Time To Be Born
      Started January 1941

January 23: Last night Bobby Lewis here for dinner. Then we went at Latouche's request up to the 1-2-3 Club where L. T. table-hopped, chatting with everyone and doing a very busy celebrity job. I was shocked at the rather naive opportunism of this very charming boy.

January 26: Strange wave of novel-admirers following "Lady Comes Across" flop. First the new president of Metropolitan Museum an admirer of *The Happy Island,* finding it a fine picture of museum life and museum fairies. Then Richard Sherman, successful writer, same night, says it was best novel of Manhattan he'd ever read. Then this morning comes amusing letter from a Rickey Austin, Paseo de la Reforma 219, Departamento 9, Mexico D.F., who says the same about the same book.

If these things happened at time I needed them for encouragement, a lot of my time would have been saved. I would not have felt my novels were private luxuries and failures so I had to desperately search for other mediums and flounder around.

January 30: Wrote short story, "The Audition," 3300 words, in about four hours or less. Seems pretty good.

February 1: The trouble with "dashing off" a story as I sometimes do in an afternoon, is that it takes two or three days to get over it. 3300 words in one day is a four day gamble, in which I might have done 5000 words on novel, which is no gamble and which is harder than ever to get back into.

It is incredible how hard I have worked in the last five years to get nowhere. More and more there is this desperate necessity for haste—haste—haste—since nothing I do has any power in itself to keep moving or make any registration. A novel takes months to finish and is through almost the day it appears. No sense of accomplishment—it might be a newspaper piece, finished one day, cast aside the next. Amazing the sustained ever-bad luck with plays, considering the praise they've had. This musical took most work, though the Group waste of time was somewhat same, also the Bel Geddes torture machine and usual business.

Short stories—admired later—suddenly are not sold and no use. Radio job six months waste. And now this book review job for *Mademoiselle*—something of no importance even 22 years ago. For what? For $75 a month, incredibly enough—rush to read books—write—rewrite—possibly please, more likely not. And double rush to finish novel, desperate need to get up earlier and earlier—yet merely being up 20 hours a day doesn't signify the creative process is working, more than likely not. No real day of rest but stolen ones. Hangovers—probably deliberate, since knocking self out obtains brief reprieve—guiltily made up for afterward.

February 9: No work today. Every day I don't work means questioning the quality of what I have already done. It's gone fast, true, but my inner desperation is not to be trusted. There is an inner clarity that comes from an idea long simmering and finally able to pop in a single burst, but the frantic need to make Jojo secure has led me to years of most futile, damaging labor, and when I finally turn back to novel which, poorly paid as it is, is the least gamble of all my work, my need is too desperate to have the creation trusted. I have seldom mistrusted any large work of mine so much. It could be good, if time could be given, but there is no time. Time is for the people whose single effort brings them fortune and security. Then the relaxed brooding essential for a solid work is easily arranged.

February 16: Feeling sickish, probably because I wanted to. *Mademoiselle* still has sent no books, yet I have a deadline for a 1500 word review of about eight or ten books in eight days. My eyes hurt—a deadline on my novel of April 1—bad enough to be late or always rushed on your own book without having the employers deliberately rush you. More and more I seem to be obliged to meet challenges, which, when met, get me nowhere anyway. Terrific inferiority—too fat, sense of being watched and criticized for the most ridiculous things—clothes, hair, figure, shoes—and inability to do anything about it. Novel seems desperate, helter-skelter, fictional and the business of taking benzedrine, thyroid, wild hours of 4:30 A.M. to 6 P.M., one day working and knocked out for week—seems to give a nervous garrulity to the book. It reads like an effort by somebody to write so much a day to fill a column.

My dear Dr. Witt died, a warm, born doctor, too much a human being not to suffer over his deaths.

February 23: Suicidal period—rare for me—but based on curious conviction that my fate was offered me in 1936—three years in Hollywood —$1250, $1500, $1750—and on rejecting it I must pay forever for not being commercially opportunistic. Not the faintest thing goes right,

either in finance or in prestige—with result grinning reminder that the
money gods are right—grab the money and you win artistic success and
everything else.

February 25: Heart hurt for first time in years.

April 5: Devastating how one neurotic in the house can destroy everybody
else in it, no matter how calm and normal. Wonder if I can ever get back
to book in really organized way or if it's ripped completely to shreds by
this responsibility and frantic problem, financial and human and emotional. Thought of renting house or farm cheap upstate or near swimming someplace and having Louise there, a dog or two, maybe chickens,
garden and letting farmer farm it for half the supply, also providing company for Jojo.

April 9: Jojo ran away this morning, no coat in freezing rain and snow,
with no money, intending to look for a job at employment agency. Ended
up at Bob's soaking wet. Went berserk in afternoon, had to give him epsom
salts bath, luminol, icebags, etc.

April 10: Jojo back to sanitarium—ran away, went berserk again this
morning.

April 25: Wandered over to 23rd Street, suddenly coming upon the
Metropolitan Building where I used to wait for Joe and where Mary Lena
and I used to confide. Recalling in the downstairs hall going out for coffee
with Paxton Hibben (now dead) who said—first of all when you marry
Joe, take out insurance for all of you. (I wonder if he did.) Where was the
10 cent store? The American Art Galleries was gone where Miss Stoner
and I used to wander (I believe she is spinster in Kansas City). Where was
Mission Bell, the restaurant we sometimes went, or the Persian one,
Palais d'Orient, and where, too, were Joe and I and the old excitements?

It has been a long time since I had leisure to think. I work all the time.
Days pass, Sunday, holidays, and I have fruit juice and coffee, maybe benzedrine, and curl up in my office chair with my work. I grow dissatisfied
with novel—which is not like me. But it is the longest, most expansive
book I've ever attempted and I'm afraid I have not the actual capacity for

handling this big a theme. I still like it and feel cheated that I can't linger more over it and make it richer, which is what it needs. The title ought to be changed to a more provocative one—"Almond Tree Shall Blossom" not so bad.

Sensitive once again to impressions, after months of dullness. This is due to taking up walks around strange territories by myself, getting out occasionally in daylight instead of working till night, then going out for cocktails.

May 18: Finished novel at 4:30—page 402.

May 19: Turned in novel to Carol. Read books for *Mademoiselle* reviews.

May 22: Lunch at 68, cocktails at Dos', blackout night (Murphy's) with Alan Campbell and Dorothy Parker.

June 8: Think I came to serious decision last night affecting future. Decided, in short, that I *did* want money, and that I will get it. The quest for it has always seemed such a deliberate block in the progress of real ambition that I have always shunned it—almost with a complacent rich man's theory, as if there would always be money anyway. There won't and never was anyway.

July 28: Signed up to rewrite book for Peggy Fears. The book is a difficult one for many reasons. It is feeble and dated to begin with and the heroine has no charm, either cliché Cinderella or what not. My usual hard, sophisticated line is out of place here, as it should be delicate, sweet, with lovable people. Even the bad ones not really bad but acting according to their own mistaken lights.

Glenway Wescott wrote Latouche an odd thing that leaves me puzzled. He wrote that he wished he had drawn me out in conversation more—that he found me a "touching and distinguished person." I don't get the "touching."

August 1: Making character and general contour analyses of book for Peggy Fears and see possibilities. Must retain lightness and charm but another quality must be injected—suspense, and a transforming of character.

August 13: Turned in 46 pages of Peggy Fears' show revision last week but as usual very much in doubt. Have not the courage to declaim my perfection—a necessary value in the theater.

August 16: Came in last night to work today. So exhausted my hair is all wool, and sleep is filled with Wish-Fulfillment dreams of idle countrysides, meadows, rest, instead of these vacationless summers where I have to keep driving to get something done I never get anything out of. Actually more encouraging than ever with cash returns, however small, and pleasant associations. But constant work. Have to rewrite lousy sniveling piece for *Mademoiselle.*

September 1: Dream of being in strange house by sea with Jojo. In the night I ran down a sandy dark slope to the sea which was a misty, blue-black fog with huge ships beached on shore. Even in my dream I thought "Is this a good dream—ships beached?" but suddenly a lovely ghostly figure beckoned me on—a fair girl in white with cape, who kept pulling me onward right into the misty sea which immediately was transformed into a shadowy meadow filled with blossoming trees and more gay ghostly figures danced in and beckoned me on while the branches shook with blossoms. I did not want to leave and all the time my mind kept querying "Does this mean my dreams of my work are being changed from sea dreams to meadow dreams and does that mean a change in work?"

Book came out Monday to unexpectedly encouraging start. Three reviews—big ones—in *Times, Tribune* and *Telegram.* Macy's sold out at once. Then David Selznick offered $1000 option to buy which I refused. Then next Sunday paper has rave in *Tribune* and long, less enthusiastic piece in *Times.* Also *Time* magazine does it.

September 6: Country at Esther and Margaret's. As usual country is no rest with people to talk to—only rest is silent type weekends where no effort, drinking, or conversation is necessary.

Latouche came out Saturday and Sunday and left me exhausted. He is so multi-gifted that he seems to leave people as worn as if they'd been to a circus, and while he shoots sparks in all directions, in the end it is the others who are depleted and he is renourished. It is the same with talented people who do not use their talents and, having no outlet, feed on those who do use talents, and have the plucked bones to rejuvenate themselves as best they can. Being younger and suppler, LaT. is able to feast himself so well that I actually have scarcely been able to do a thing on these two assignments. It is unconsciously deliberate on his part. He wants people not-to-do, just as he doesn't-do. He likes their doing well—no envy there—but it is the actual *doing* he minds.

September 28: Moving to duplex at 35 East Ninth Street, which is considerably cheaper but much more deluxe looking in a sort of modern-improvement Central Park West way. Old battered furniture looks very startled and terrible here but I will not give in to this place and pleasure it with that white decoration sort of thing—the bare tasteful simplicity of the places meant for bare, tastefully bleak personalities.

October 15: Saleslady in Saks: "Do you want me to be perfectly frank with you, Madame? That dress will either be perfectly terrible on you or perfectly wonderful!"

October 16: Did broadcast in Schenectedy on WGY—discussion of my book. Stayed overnight at Van Curler Hotel hoping for rural rest but hotel in middle of square so noise all night and wakened in morning by parade in fancy uniforms of drum majorettes and band from Draper High School, Peacock High School, etc.

October 17: Apartment a source of delight to servants—incinerator, porters to do heavy work, parquet floors, white kitchen—and as dreary a dump to live in as I've ever seen. Quite charmless, with pitch darkness day and night and no privacy because the delighted servants prance in and out of places with things to put in special Shoe Closets, Hat Closets, etc., and my bedroom-study window looks out over blind brick walls. Too noisy to sleep after 3 A.M. when trucks and street noises begin, and too dreary a sight to open the eyes to in the morning.

Louise's room on roof is very beautiful—probably will start going up there.

October 23: Made broadcast to England over British Broadcasting with John Brophy. Mr. Brophy stopped proceedings to talk several minutes to me on how much he admired my work and how sure he was that my new book was "going places" in England. It was very cozy and like a party line.

October 25: Listened to rebroadcast of BBC and sorry to hear Mr. Brophy's flattery deleted from record by censor. Did *Mademoiselle* piece which was better than usual.

November 5: Had luncheon coffee with Pauline Hemingway. Pauline seemed sharp-edged, too eager, brown and desperate. Her confessionals, her rosaries, that kept her head up during the bad years (so that she amazed everyone with her poise) do not after all fill the major gap in her life and give it a frittering quality that does not flatter. She should have a cause, beyond Saks-Fifth Avenue, and a philosophy, instead of a religion.

November 13: Bought third thousand of John Hancock single premium life insurance which makes $3300 payable in 15 years for $2200 payment. Have paid all these other policies through 1942, bought one $500 Class E war bond, due in 10 years for $375, and put $1075 in savings bank, paid Dr. Witt's estate bill of $115, paid up on Jojo's Gladwyne, and $500 on money due Esther.

Yesterday spent at 68 William Street, arranging trust fund with Margaret De Silver for Jojo with lawyer.

November 14: Story about Phyllis' fortunate friend who boasted of her husband—not many men like him—so good to her. For her birthday he gave her her choice between painting the upstairs or new linoleum in the kitchen. She took the former because it was easier to paint woodwork than to lay linoleum.

November 17: 160 lbs. Metabolism test. Also started Elizabeth Arden body massage with Miss Carlson and Face Youth treatments on West 56th. God knows why, except for a sudden impulse to make myself over.

November 22: A consciousness of sudden happiness—not exhilaration but rather of sudden orientation after months of circling. Actually nothing to cause it but an atmosphere of things suddenly being right, of an ability to command again, rather than to be preyed upon, an ability to choose and create, actually to hope. These moments, so rare, are also astonishing in their revelation of how deep your confusion has been up to that moment.

People, without active grief, are a lifetime unaware of their unhappiness until happiness comes to them and they say, with wonder, "Why, I have only half-lived until now. I have been unhappy all my life without knowing it. How strange! And why did I cheat myself of the reverse pleasure of conscious woe? The orgies of tears and self-pity I have denied myself!"

November 27: Went to Shelby. Max Eastman gave me his poetic novel *Lot's Wife* to read on train.

November 28: Arrived in Shelby. Struck by tremendous heat of houses and the horror with which out-of-doors is viewed. This is how America always hugs its Improvements. The automobile, for instance, is converted into a complete necessity; to walk is to reveal poverty. No one is on streets, as a two block walk is viewed with alarm and the car must be used. The children cannot possibly walk six or ten blocks to school but must be carried to and fro by car, and the maid must not be required to walk five or six blocks from her streetcar. Furthermore, under no circumstances may one go outdoors to get into car, for air might creep in lungs and poison the system; one must creep from kitchen into garage to enter car, thus avoiding the air. "Where do you want to go? Jack can drive you." "You want to mail a letter at the corner box? Someone will drive you there." There is no idling around, no opportunity for surprises; people go to a definite place and then return. You want to see your old schoolhouse and the yard—very well, we'll drive past. Proud of their central heating, so they overdo it, to show how perfect their heaters are the house must be sweltering—90 to 95 degrees. At night, gasping, you try to open window but find a new invention there—a double window for Air Conditioning so that instead of air you have two eye holes covered with screen which permit a teaspoonful of air to percolate in. Moreover, everyone drinks coffee steadily—with every meal, for supper and for bedtime. Their skins, from coffee and heat, are usually dry and inclined to wizen.

Charlie and Effie* drove up from Columbus with rabbit which Charlie had shot. They shoot rabbits and pheasant around Cardington. Everyone

---

*Charles and Effie Miller were relatives of Powell's.

seemed more prosperous; even the poorest relations had spruced up and having been jobless and poor all during Hoover's and Coolidge's administration are sufficiently prosperous now to berate That Man In The White House.

Hillbillies in defense works (Cycle company now makes 14-inch shells) bring new problems. They complicate Group Insurance by not knowing how old they are; they carry knives; they are unbeatably ignorant and dirty. An ordinance in Shelby forbids any colored person to spend the night within the city limits—also true of Shiloh, so colored help has to take streetcar out at night. Much talk of Catholics—the mother's heart breaking because son marries a Catholic. In Cleveland, Negro population one-tenth, with a colored welfare and art movement. Expect 60,000 women next year to replace men's jobs, 40,000 never having worked before.

Phyllis and I wandered downtown and behind the B & O Railroad Saloon saw Grandma's house where it was moved and now is a lumber storehouse. It is a good house still, with dignified old Colonial doorway. We visited Mrs. Starr in a four-apartment house on East Main (one bath for all of the four). Here, four old ladies, widows or spinsters, live in apartments costing about $12 a month. They sit on porch or lean out window and gossip.

To Cleveland with Phyllis on Tuesday and Mabel and Marie Reycraft took us to University Club for lunch—then to photographers for Marie to show me pictures of her daughter's wedding. Tootsie* going to be married, said all of her friends were pregnant. She felt if they had to do it, it was alright but why get caught? She gets up at seven to go downtown to Business College and gets home at six. Everyone talks Red Cross First Aid, hoards coffee, and prospers and says how happy the boys are that are in the army. This is because on leave the boys put up a front of "wouldn't live in this dump for a million dollars" though they actually are homesick enough. Also the parents are so relieved to have Elmer off their hands that they want to believe it is all for the best, regardless.

A lady called up Mabel while I was there. She said she was Peggy's mother and Peggy and Tootsie were such friends; what a shame Peggy had to get married! What a problem we mothers have. It is only luck, she said, that Tootsie isn't in Peggy's condition. Tootsie gets redder and

---

*Dorothy Pocock Chapman, Powell's niece.

redder as Mabel repeats this. "I think love excuses everything." Mabel says the woman is crazy. She chases Peggy with a butcher knife.

Mabel showed me her diary from 1909 on. In Cardington there were meetings of the B.L.G. This turned out to be Buckeye Lark Girls. "Met and raised Cain," said Mabel. Later B.L.G., after due deliberation, changes its name to U-Know-Us-Kids. Her beau Heinie. "Heinie came and we went to show. Heinie came," etc. Then, "Heinie and I had fight." Next entries are: "Stayed home." "Nothing doing." "Stayed home." "Finally Heinie and I made up. Went to all the shows," etc.

December 9: Slept 10 or 11 hours for two nights since my return from Ohio and realize how long it's been since I felt sane. Must have effect of sleeplessness in new book. The strange progress of fury and revenge and rasping disagreeableness. Away in provinces, I missed Latouche, since he impersonates New York itself—alive, eager for every phase of the city, foreign to, but eagerly interested in, the provinces. This is what often makes love—the absent one is missed not for what he or she is but the life they represent—parties, first nights, music, conversation, tennis, drinking, slumming, travel, or whatever it is. In a sense almost everyone is a Boat Acquaintance—fitting into the loneliness of the traveler, answering the demand for merely amusement, instruction or padding the hours. Sometimes the trip is long enough, important enough, to be the biggest thing in the traveler's life, so these Boat Acquaintances, representing Triumphs and Travel and Happiness, are treasured as if for some value in themselves. The value has been poured into them by the Traveler himself and the virtue he finds in these strangers is his own ego, embalmed.

December 12: Continuing baths at Arden's which slenderize by taking out bloat. At Freeyouth, Constantine, the Greek masseuse-sculptor-photographer-dancer, out of boredom decides to annoy his partner by threatening to have his hair dyed red. "Business is bad enough as it is," says partner despairingly, "without you looking like a freak. Red hair! Those fancy glasses! Next a beard and permanent!" "Well, I am getting a test curl," says Constantine. Partner red with anger.

December 17: A cat is the soonest corrupted by luxury, even more than a snobbish servant. It has one more room, a downstairs and upstairs, a new plush chair, and out of sheer snobbery it is ready to throw the owner out and claws are ready for anyone (owner included) who takes away the open fire, the new sofa, the chair. A cat is the fabulously interesting symbol all completely luxury-loving creatures have for the other kind.

December 19: Dave Bibenao, lieutenant in navy, says rescue belts are so weighted down with handy ideas as to sink at once and incidentally look like Xmas trees. Rickenbacker was saved by jumping quick with only four oranges. A shrewder person would have arranged the life raft so they all would have sunk with their supplies.

Letter from Latouche, the naughty fellow, who immediately projects himself by letter so I can do no further.

December 21: At 5 A.M., after usual curious night of not quite being asleep and not quite being awake, woke up and had feeling of tremendous exhilaration—the kind that usually ends in tears but I willed it not so, with my old-time power to will. But nothing beyond a marvelously constructive idea to quit this incredibly silly and kindergarten job at *Mademoiselle,* which I did because of George Davis, whom I like. Then lunch and this usual but new business of people *I* know but am sure don't recognize me waving to someone behind me and bowing and finally coming over and saying "Well, well, *Dawn!*" I am still so amazed at the brazenness of people—completely New York people—who only remember you when you've gone into your fourth printing.

December 23: Fire in beautiful new sofa due to Joe's falling asleep with cigarette.

December 24: Strange dream of Hassoldt Davis back and phone talk, with him rather bitterly telling me that I had been ruined by making money, and that one of these days something catastrophic would happen to me. He compared me to a friend of his, James Aldrich, who had perfected a wonderful invention, modeling iron or clay birds and leaving them in fireplace to bake so they were decorations. This was intended as a reproach for some reason and, very embarrassed, I said I believed I'd met the man at a restaurant on 19th Street and Fourth Avenue years ago, but he said irritably that he didn't see how I could have met him. Then I realized an open window had blown in piles and piles of sand, which the dream book states means many small vexations.

When I went to bank I found check account below $300 which made me realize my windfall was evaporating. Yet I felt strangely exhilarated by the news—as if now I could get down to work, with that load off my mind. Mixed with this was odd apprehension of skulking around without paying bills. The only way to lead unconventional life is to have admitted financial security to excuse it.

December 27: Dinner at Gerald Murphy's with Dorothy Parker. I told them about Latouche's letter describing the lepers of the Congo and Parker thought it might be a good idea if Touche came back with an All-Leper revue called "No Faces" (since all are called "New Faces" now). She was delighted with this thought and pursued it to having Mark Cross put out a special Leper Leather bag to be opened with no fingers.

Terrific fatigue continues—perhaps the sleeplessness of the first few weeks in the new apartment and now no motive for getting up. Look badly—fat, exhausted.

It is hard to know what work to buckle down to. There is the Griffin story. There is the Dr. Martin story. No dash to write them. Should resolve to do so anyway, also resign from *Mademoiselle*. Last night I dreamed of gay music and dancing.

1943

[*Undated*] Aristotle's distinction between the poet (dramatist, novelist) and the historian. Poet is more philosophical because his picture carries the conviction of general validity and is universally true. Historian is only reporter of events which may be freakish occurrences of highly improbable possibilities. The philosopher prefers probable impossibilities.

January 5: I could write a novel about the Destroyers—a third for *Turn, Magic Wheel* and *Happy Island*—that cruel, unhappy, ever-dissatisfied group who feed on frustrations (Dorothy Parker, Wolcott Gibbs, Arthur Kober, etc.), all spending their lives preventing each other from working. They challenge each other by being seen at certain parties, places; they are each others' sores and are half-fascinated, half-repelled. They are ruined by not being able to want what they individually want, but must want inevitably what the other wants. They are spoiled nursery children who really want to go on playing with an old clothespin, but seeing Brother happy with an engine, must fight for engine. Winning it, they are discontented, ill-natured.

Most of all, they have perverted their rather infantile ambitions into destruction of others' ambitions and happiness. If people are in love, they must mar it with laughter; if people are laughing, they must stop it with "Your slip is showing." They are in a permanent prep school where they perpetually haze each other. They destroy their own happiness by being ashamed of whatever brings it; they want to be loved but are unloving; they want to destroy but be themselves saved. They are afraid of being used, even while they use. As Dorothy Parker (fed, housed, traveled and clothed by the Murphys for two years) said, "You know, they feed on me, I realize that." Two kinds of feeding.

Wrote story of Griffin. First short story in years. Coby pointed out spots for clarification. Dinner at Murphy's with Dorothy Parker and two RAF flyers from Canada. They spoke of the thrill of going up on a bad day and going for 15 minutes through black clouds and finally coming into the beautiful blue day of the borderland between stratosphere and troposphere. When they left, Dorothy was very moved, in a certain excessive Irish tenor way she has, and kept proposing toasts to them. Later she said "I'm sick of those little poops. I've had them on for two days, doing my Goddamndest to entertain them. I fell over my poodle and knocked my head on my Bechstein, so I think I have a concussion of the brain for them—what more do they want?"

Dreamed of new house, with iron railing stairs up three floors, of sea beyond—as always a very consoling, reassuring dream.

January 6: In another printing of *Angels On Toast* I would like to print my plans for the mood, etc., from my notebook.

January 13: Carlo assassinated at 9:50 last night.* Incredible that at last this should happen, yet it is the perfect end to achieve his aims, for now the police will unearth many Fascist spies and actually he will have the law working for him, carrying on his wishes. Instead of dying of cerebral nosebleed as he almost did last year, when he would have had only a few lines in the paper ("at one time a powerful figure"), now violence gives him death as it gave him his life, and there is a triumph that should be in every death for it sums up and puts a spotlight on all his past work, gives it perspective and importance, justifies him and his entire career. Everything is *explained.* For this justification, men would give fortunes and, indeed, their lives.

January 16: Carlo's funeral. Here were thousands of "best friends," people from everywhere who sincerely loved him—and the curious oratorical drumbeat of Italian calls to action, which no other language has.

It seems impossible Carlo can be gone. A vital person, always to be remembered when something curious happens, someone to tell it to. The

---

*Carlo Tresca, a leading Italian anti-Fascist and the lover of Margaret De Silver, was murdered as he left his office on lower Fifth Avenue. The crime was never solved.

cortege leaves the packed hall, travels downtown from 34th and at 15th and 5th lies a blanket of roses where the killing took place and then, as it travels eastward the chimes of St. Mark's in the Bowery, ring out exactly as the hearse passes—for an unbeliever. But Guthrie (the rector there) never believed in the church anyway and, years ago when strikers were locked out, Carlo went to him to throw open the church to let them sleep there.

January 24: At Peter Jack's, where his class from the New School English Literature night school came in. Very earnest in their desire for the exterior of culture. Peter discusses various books he hasn't read; class earnestly sops up this bird's-eye culture.

January 29: Did nothing this week, and therefore was largely in mischief. Working on two novels: the one of the Destroyers, the other my bastardized life. The latter can be done anytime for next six years. Technically it is from Dickens, particularly *David Copperfield*. At the beginning, it is written as for a child—words, images, etc., are on the table level of their eyes; everyone is good to the three sisters, their pleasures are simple, their parents good. As they grow, the manner of writing changes—the knowledge of cruelty, divorce, disillusionment, betrayal—the anguish of adolescence, of not being wanted, of struggle for survival. The world growing up as fast as they do, the political wrangles and changes in sophistication. Sisters coming together (Gretchen) not on virtues but on vices—each with lover, drinks, husbands cheating, money grabbing. "Three Children" could be its title. It seems like an endless job—three volumes anyway. The early separation of provinces and New York; the way vices as much as inventions brought the two parts of America together, and vices, inventions and corruption brought America and the Old World together.

January 31: I have two novels again, as I did at 106 Perry Street, when I had beginnings of *Tenth Moon* and *Turn, Magic Wheel* both. In between the two of these I wrote *Country Boy* and the play "Jig-Saw" and changed my style completely which had followed in a conventional straight pattern from *She Walks In Beauty* on, then switched in middle of *Turn, Magic Wheel*. Now I have a contemporary novel of the Destroyers and a general history of 42 years of disillusionment and life—innocence to grave—with some characters preserving innocence, others embittered (failure and success do this equally well).

Heard Toscanini in broadcast studios—all Verdi—and for once convinced that an artist can be "created" by his interpreters. Frightening to think of the dependence of the artist (that is, a playwright or composer) on his interpreter.

Reading Tacitus with great pleasure.

February 1: My two books as usual have me stymied, one a warmer, richer book than previous but binding in opportunities for off-record discussions, etc. However Coby feels this is by far most important and, if I could regain some energy, could be done as easily as breathing—which, due to my increasing cold, is not so damned easy after all.

February 7: Movie of *Time to be Born*—really wish I could do it because of actual new feel to it. Time for all the self-promoters to be dismissed and the millions of anonymous patriots to be promoted to stardom.

Saturday Peter Blume—handsome, sweet, good and, as a painter, the genius of our age—and his wife—also childishly good and devoted—had an enormous cocktail party. Two famous wits were present—James Thurber and S. J. Perelman—and this is the waggish dialogue that ensued, with me as buffer.

(Enter Perelman.)

Perelman: Dawn, I hear your book is going like blazes. How many copies sold?

Me: (lying) Why, I imagine around fifteen thousand.

Perelman: Ah, here's Thurber. You know Dawn.

Thurber: Hello, Dawn, how many copies did your book sell? Fifty thousand?

Me: Well, more like twenty.

Thurber: Understand you got $15,000 from the movies. Shoulda got more. Would've if you'd held out.

Me: Well, it would still all be gone now no matter what I got.

Thurber: (glancing around, though almost blind) Big party. Musta set Peter back about fifty bucks. What'd he get for his picture?

Perelman: Do you realize that bastard Cerf takes 20 percent of my play rights, same as he did for "Junior Miss"?

Thurber: Shouldn't do it. Harcourt never took a cent off me. Had it in the contract.

Perelman: I'd like to have lunch with you and discuss that, Jim. Jesus, Jim—20 percent!

Thus does the wit flow from these two talented fellows.

February 13: I have a first chapter done on London Junction and feel there is a social importance in the idea of a family of early 20th century, poor without being aware of it (since no one had any more than they did), loving each other (since everyone had to make the most of what they had and opportunities were scarce)—growing up as the century grew up, into bitterness, cruelty, hatred, war.

A picture of a little girl—"your great-grandmother"—eager, laughing, with a ball held up to play. But she was to have four babies, one stolen by Indians, others dead, husband killed, hard work. Brother laughing and dear—ending up a postman with two families, amnesia, razored his sister and self, insane asylum, tied to a ball and chain. This hung over Marcia's mind: that laughing youth should grow up into terror and horror, that one of them might go mad.

After Clare Luce made such evil use of her new Congressional power* I was glad I had slashed her in my last book and realized that my immediate weapons are most necessary and can help. The lashing of such evil can only be done by satire and I am the only person who is doing contemporary social satire.

February 15: Suddenly did a lot of work on old Mrs. Carmichael in Cleveland and also Shelby, with sudden wave of pure revisualization of that Cleveland period coming back.

February 18: I am very exhilarated over the fun of remembering the Cleveland episode. Once a memory is encouraged, as one must encourage it for writing, strange negatives develop in my mind and a chain of pictures of people, backyards, rooms, smells, etc. emerges more real than reality.

There is almost no fighting the success of combined wealth, looks, chic and aggressiveness. Columnists—the fawners of all time—work on

---

* Luce had publicly attacked Vice-President Henry Wallace for his internationalist views, calling them "globaloney."

them, rebuild them, tenderly nurture them, though later, if they are on skids (usually financially) they say "Drink did it" or "Women did it" or "Overwork did it" or "Social climbing did it"—in fact, all the things that made their success are accused of being the causes of their downfall.

March 5: In the new book, I want to trace corruption, private and public, through innocence and love—possibly learning that only by being prepared for all evil can evil be met.

March 18: Have done some revisory work on book but very little and am afraid of mistaking garrulity for realism. Actually I want to do a simple American story, the idea being that in these early simple moments of a child, a community and a century, the seeds of future happenings are seen. In a sense this is a mystical idea—it is also an old man's idea, for the old remember the seemingly trivial in their past as it added up to final events.

The ideas here are the basis of fascism, cruelty, personal careerism, etc., to make up for early frustrations but—as in *Tenth Moon*—I had no plot, only a mood to explain, and could not therefore map out an outline—this one, with an idea of seeds inevitably developing, cannot be crystallized as yet into a synopsis.

I looked over my journal for *Tenth Moon* but first I read the book. I seldom can read very far in my own works even if I don't recall them but to my amazement this particular book which I despised as a mere tour-de-force and wrote to save my own feelings (because I put so much heart and emotion into *Dance Night, Bride's House, She Walks,* etc., and was so crushed by their indifferent reception that I vowed I would choose a theme completely mental which did not involve a drop of blood or tears) —anyway, I was actually absorbed in it and read it all the way through weeping and moved to my depths! The fact is that it is a beautiful book— the best writing I ever did and technically flawless, with the most delicate flowering of a relationship that grips interest far more than my dramatic plots such as *Country Boy.* I then examined my notes in my journal and found all the way through references to the pleasure of writing something that left my emotions absolutely uninvolved, a mere craftsmanship job, a literary joke—okay, critics, I won't give you a pound of flesh, I will cheat you. Result: a quivering book filled with pain and beauty.

March 23: Reading for the first time a fine book (Flaubert's *Sentimental Education*) I am again impressed by the importance of satire as social history and my theory that what reviewers call satire is "whimsy" and what they call realism is romanticism. But *Sentimental Education* gives a completely invaluable record of Paris, its face and its soul, its manners and its talk of 1840, and no realistic novel of the period remains. The best sellers, no doubt, were the freak books—as now (war in Spain, fun in Johannesburg, Civil War) but these are worthless journalism for posterity. The only record of a civilization is satire—Petronius, Aristophanes, Flaubert. True, in *Sentimental Education,* there are also remnants of Balzac's *Lost Illusion* and *Provincial in Paris.* These are so valuable that they are timeless.

April 2: Cocktails with Bunny. Just reading *Sentimental Education* myself, I find Bunny a great devotee of it, though he feels it loses in translation, being, like poetry, built on the cadences of its own language for rhythm and dramatic phrasing. Then we had breakfast again today and cocktails and dinner. He told me about looking over his own journal for notes on a certain ten year love affair he had and that he found it was 100 typewritten pages and a masterpiece—his comments on the woman and his varying opinion of her. An invented character, he said, would have to be so consistent it could not be described in constantly varying lights but a real person is seen by another in ever-changing lights, perspective, etc. He said he had put down everything she said, they did, etc., and result is the "greatest love story ever written," in pornographic detail, so that he cannot publish it till after death. It was exhilarating to spend time again with a sharp, creative literary mind, a balance so necessary in the hoodlum world I live in.

April 7: Drew out $75 to send Phyllis who is having difficult time, husband not working and unable to paint anything for the May show. This is the most pleasure I've had—but also a duty, inasmuch as Margaret taking $10,000 for me in insurance for Jojo makes me duty-bound to do same.

Curious effect a day with Bunny Wilson had on me—balanced me so that I remembered again the natural pleasures of the mind—reading, thinking and working, all of which are canceled by drinking.

April 14: Borrowed $400 on life insurance to pay State Income, the accountant, and some general debts. I can't tell whether my Ohio family novel is good because I enjoy it myself or whether it simply seems good to me because of complete recollection. Since it is episodic rather than plotted, I am not sure of it at all; since it is sentimental, I am not sure it is not simply an elderly softening of the brain.

April 26: At the new nightclub—The Blue Angel—with Peter and Jane Jack, both extremely tight but eager to applaud their friend Sylvia Marlowe, entertaining there. Also their friend Max Gordon runs it—he ran the Vanguard for years. Gordon is a rather heavy, fair, half-intellectual/half-football player man—a unique, shrewd, sensitive man with a genius for human beings. Could be a politician except that he prefers keeping in background and making the strings work.

Peter was delighted to see a young accompanist (male and French) there so they spent their time shushing all other tables who talked during a performance and talking themselves during performances. Jane scolded a table nearby which asked Sylvia for a number, and said they knew nothing of harpsichord music or the finer things of life. All during Sylvia's playing, Peter was making up to the French boy Rudy, comparing hand sizes, etc., and Jane was loudly admonishing hecklers.

Afterward Sylvia begged them to go home while I stayed with Max Gordon. "What's the matter with this place?" he asked. "People are having a good time outside but when they come in they start whispering. They don't even go to the restrooms. Another thing—everything here costs a mint of money but nothing is nailed down. Any drunk can knock over anything here—those pink candelabra, the plaster-paris curtains, anything. The bar—black patent leather—sure, it's alright. It looks sinister. A bar *should* look sinister."

A big man started a fight with the bartender, asked for the manager, but Gordon in a low voice ordered the bartender to be nice. On our way out the doorman told us that the big quarrelsome guy—now on the best of terms with the bartender—owned half the block next door. If Gordon had not intuitively sensed this the man could have made a nuisance for the club. I spoke of the Vanguard. He said "How would you know? You were only there once in the ten years I ran it." He had met me long ago without my knowing it. A curious, interesting man—lonely and philosophical and sensual.

May 3: One of the greatest sports in life is killing the goose that lays the golden egg. It's a bastard goose, anyway, and the pampering of it is a form of cowardice and human degradation. All integrity is sacrificed on this fear of the Queen Goose—business is built on it, art is slaughtered on it, truth tailored for it. Aesop was a fool, a ballyhooer of chicanery, a propagandist for cupidity and Man's lowest standards. All my life seems to have been spent killing geese that lay golden eggs and it's a fine decent sport— superior to killing small birds, horses or lions.

May 10: Reading over my book I got very depressed because it seems vague and bare, and this sort of thing ought to have sharper characterizations to tie it together since there is no plot. I must not lose sight of my original plan—i.e., to let the story grow up as the children themselves do—let their perceptions grow more acute through their experiences, finding themselves different from each other and being amazed. The slow formation of character and tastes—the total difference between Lena and Marcia and Fuffy,* yet all open to some heredity and environment. All three separated now—different friends, different lives. Marcia —hard but gallant, humiliated and mortified, lonely, in love with the married man, goes along the street, past his home. There is no home for anyone ever, she thought, never any home.

June 23: Too hot to sleep, and with scenario on mind, especially. Decided reason for Ohio novel is propaganda—duty—to show there was another America, not just the present one of war and woe. Also to show the things possible to learn—that in a small radius of 100 square miles in Northern Ohio there are a half-dozen different types of civilization—a Finnish town, a Dutch town, a rubber town, steel town, and great grain farms, fruit farms, German towns, etc.

June 25: To Gurney's Inn near Montauk with Ann Honeycutt. Mrs. Gurney—Christian Science smile. Little children yip around. Young man of eight—large, fat, handsome—sits alone at table and orders lunch. Waitress horrified at order: fresh shrimp ($1.50), creamed eggs and asparagus ($1.50) and chocolate ice cream cake ($.60). Doesn't he want to

---

* "Fuffy"—Powell's sister Phyllis's lifelong nickname—was later changed to "Florrie" in *My Home Is Far Away*.

1 9 4 3

join his parents at another table? No, he'll sit here. He gazes around pleasantly, speaks to next table: "Is that the Pacific Ocean?"

Another gentleman of ten appears. Will Durham play with us this afternoon? Durham (says guest of ten in low, significant voice) can't come out as he is being punished. He took his mother's lipstick and rubbed it all over his face and said he was sunburned. Now it won't come off. Both gents look gravely out the window—typical of Durham to do the wild thing, just as well that type of person is kept in, not our sort and all that.

Gent still eating chocolate ice cream sandwich. Presently he said "As soon as I finish supposing we play this: I throw the ball against the wall and you catch it on the bounce and throw it back to me." Guest considered this and allowed it might be a very good game. They went out solemnly and in due course were heard yelling and screaming like hoodlums.

In window, three-year-old forced to take nap presses nose to window and calls "Hello, want to come see me?" to everybody who passes.

July 16: Went to Shelter Island with Ann Honeycutt—stayed at Oxford Hall, drove to beach in horse and buggy. Very charming island. We drove all over the place looking at estates and houses with a deaf real estate man. The Wren estate—huge, fabulous place with private beach, eight or nine bedrooms—$500 for rest of season or $25,000 asking price.

August 5: Arrived alone at the cottage at Mt. Sinai which I rented by telephone for $125 per month.

August 9: After 12 hours sleep alone in this house, things settled considerably regarding my work. The Ohio book needs clearing up in early chapters (to take away itsy-bitsy effect) and more color later. It is very good when it gets to Grandma, and in spite of the averageness of the story it will be alright when it covers the mother's death and the beginning of cruelty—the finding out that growing up is not a slow and certain approach to rewards but an unfolding of Life's mask to its cruel face.

August 10: In calm mood for arranging novels yesterday due to 18 hours alone with no one demanding me, but at 6:30 Louise and Jojo came in just as I had my mind clear and bedlam began. Exhausted, to bed at 10—not a

wink of sleep, desperate with fatigue, self-pity, general injustice, etc., and
hopelessness of battering down an unkind fate. Crickets made hullabaloo
and I thought of a fake Aristophanes play—"The Crickets," a musical,
with cricket chirps as metronome for musician, telegraph operators, machine gun, etc.

August 11: Title could be "My Home Is Far Away" or "London Junction."

August 26: New suit for Jojo and he went back to school ten pounds heav-
ier, handsome, poised, well-dressed and, except for obsession about
military life, fairly content. My hunch is to rent a house this winter for
him—let him have regular bachelor life—give him $200 a month check-
ing account to pay rent, groceries, maybe a Filipino servant to teach him
language, if Louise uninterested. Give him responsibilities which will develop him and make him strong against possible pushing around after
war when institutions are overrun with shell-shock.

September 23: Started work on musical version of "Taming of the Shrew"
with Irvin Graham and Al Margolies as producer. Idea sounds provocative but on reading the play it seems hellish hard work, wondering how
much to leave and how much to change—either complete freedom or
imaginative production of original.

September 25: Went with Joe to visit his mother. Exhausted to begin with
but wanted to get acquainted with Jojo's relatives. Impressed with calm,
happy family life, content with their home—comfortable enough, too
and much more than we ever had, but vaguely oppressive. In these small,
complacent, nationalistic circles I am far more ill at ease and inferior-feel-
ing than in wealthy places, for they are the ones who are safe and secure
in the low-ceilings of their imagination. Even their material ambitions
aren't much—they are so smug they would not admit themselves unable
to get anything they wanted. Nothing to want except what they have seen
next door; no aim except a nice roof with a slit for a chimney to let the
pennies drop in.

October 10: Supposed to work on outline of "Shrew," I became interested
in my novel instead. The frenzy of exhibitionistic work such as radio or

stage always drives me to drink, whereas the novel medium (apart from the feeble reception mine receive) is completely satisfying in a dull, unobtrusive way.

Bunny Wilson wrote me a letter depressing in its way. Men really dislike a literary woman (especially if she's good) and prefer not reading works of their women friends, hoping and even saying they must be bad. Now he is reading them and finds them good. I myself read *Angels on Toast* recently and found it remarkably good and valuable as a picture of Middlewestern types in high gear and sudden wealth. I was glad to find I enjoyed something of my own—and this one a book I wrote fast and intensely since the mood had to be preserved.

October 29: I am conscious increasingly of a desperate crowding and narrowing of my life, of being on several tracks at once with no engineer. My room is a testimony to my desperation. The file cabinets with all of the things in them I never have time to revise, the lost account books, household bills, stories that need just a little calm work (secretarial, largely) to be disposed of, the novel notebook and the half-copied part, the plays I want to write suddenly fall out of notebooks, the immediate assignments—reconstructing somebody else's play, a book review, or some other strictly-to-order work which I should never have gotten into—piled up with carbons (always one page missing for my efficiency stops glaringly short of itself).

My actual mood has been one of imprisonment for three years with almost no psychological let-up in spite of much party gaiety. I set out to revise that musical "Lady Comes Across" for the rather despondent reason that if I made a success of a hack job in the theater, I would not only be allowed to write my own plays with the critical acclaim reserved for those who have pleasured the box-office, but be received in the publishing world reserved for those who have made a success in some other field than books. This has left me with half an engine or less for each of my activities and even that enfeebled by responsibilities about Jojo, money, etc. Moreover, the psychological imprisonment feeling has been enhanced by this apartment, which is dark—no sun ever enters and, except on very bright days, very little light. The sense of day and night is lost here, so work seems spread out fitfully over 24 hours of twilight.

Actually what I like is still the same: a pleasant, sunny, quiet floor in an old house—in fact, the place I almost took on 11th Street, impersonal yet intimate.

November 14: I am beginning to see some value in this novel. So elated over finishing play ("Taming of Shrew").

November 15: Dinner tonight at Helen Hoke's—mostly strangers and wonderful food. A George Annent there, cartoonist and F.B.I. man, told of a fellow yachtsman visiting home of Irénée DuPont, who is deaf and has whole room wired with amplifiers so doesn't have to wear gadget. After dinner, dirty stories are told, booming all over the place. Asked next day how he slept, the guest said fine, he hadn't even turned over. Irénée then said, "We shall find out about that" and took him to basement where a seismograph such as records earthquakes was placed, with chart recording all movements of the guests during the night.

November 20: Coby read what I had written and said it needed enriching with facts as I originally told them. As it goes along, it gets more and more fictionalized which is not good at all since its only value is documentary and ought to be true. It needs styles, talk of the period, new household fancies—pillowcases, etc. When I get to stepmother, it will be better—the housekeeping, the books locked, the notebooks torn up, the whip used. Papa saying forlornly—well, you've got to love somebody.

December 1: Reading *Whither* I was horrified at how completely hopeless and utterly devoid of promise it was—far worse than what I had written at 13. On the other hand a re-reading of *Dance Night* persuaded me it is my best book—material, mood, prose and structure by all odds the best.

December 2: Dinner at Mrs. Mabel Cochrane's on East 81st Street. Usual baiting about my last book. In most of my intimate groups I would not gather that anyone either read or cared about my work. It leaves me taken unaware, therefore, to be attacked, quizzed, etc., by strangers who appear to take a deep, profound interest in the novels, and I sound utterly dumb.

December 4: My Home Is Far Away: Although I set out to do a complete job on my family, I colored it and, even worse, diluted it through a fear of embarrassing my fonder relatives, also a distaste for throwing away my own privacy.

A writer, for purposes of future collecting of material, needs personal privacy and disguises. Since telling the truth is merely a version of events anyway and nobody else's "truth," the essential thing is to convey similar effects, similar emotions and in my own case arrive at artistic truth by artistic means, instead of handicapping myself by withholding some facts and enlarging or distorting others. Better to fictionize all—more pleasure and more freedom. Deciding this, I believe I can achieve much more interesting and worthwhile effects. *Dance Night* was completely fiction as I was working on it. Yet it is more autobiographical (with facts translated into their own value emotionally and structurally) than any autobiography I can imagine.

December 8: Claire Luce* tried out for shrew part at Irvin Graham's. I remember her as a delicate blonde pink ballerina type, Dresden doll, in a "Follies" soon after Marilyn Miller. Today, close up, she looks and acts sex incarnate. The high nostrils of the horse type, slender arrogant body made for writhing, handsome chin and superb throat, blonde hair and wide blue eyes, strident hoarse voice, the combination of arrogant slut and sluttish queen, and an atmosphere of theater about her that is more aristocratic and raises more barriers than the atmosphere of family or riches.

December 10: Party at Gloria Vanderbilt de Cicco's apartment. Graphologist said my life was simplified by the complete division of heart and mind—and no worry on my part of reconciling them. The heart might break but I then turned completely and blithely to mind at risk of seeming unfeeling.

December 15: At cocktail party for a Dr. Decker, President of Kansas City University. Ann Watkins and her husband, Roger Burlingame. Roger complained that Ann now keeps meeting people and saying she used to go to school with them. Ann asked jealously about Carol (who had taken

---

* American actress, not to be confused with Clare Boothe Luce.

me away from Ann) and then Selma Brandt, who also hates Carol (because Carol took her husband away from her). They had not seen each other for about twelve years or more and though bound by the same enemy, did not recognize each other till Ann said, "Didn't we go to school together?" They were still trying to figure out where they'd met—there *was* something familiar, they granted, very puzzled; maybe they had lived in the same town. This is how relentless people end up with their carefully hugged animosities—eventually there is something vaguely familiar about the face of the enemy.

December 16: Carol called to say she "liked the new book very much." Maybe after the second part was finished she could tell more—"and then the first part could be cut."

December 17: Elation over this little room upstairs which I feel is saving my life and nerves.

December 23: What I want to do in this book is to make it as rich and fruity as an attic trunk of the late America before the war.

I want to show the Montague-Capulet war between two families— Aunt Lois* and Papa warring over a poor dead woman, accusing each other, blaming everything on the death of Daisy. This hatred mounting, use of the children as a football (against both of their real natures—Aunt Lois is warm, generous, aggressive, exciting; Papa is hot-headed, impulsive, laughter-loving). Both betrayed into cruelty, revenges, etc. and hate themselves for it—but, hating themselves, blame it on others.

December 25: Jojo home, very good, absorbed in Latin which he studies by himself because he says it puts him in another world. He visits the Cloisters because it reminds him of ancient Rome.

December 28: As usual, this theater business has me stymied. I should never get into any of these "to order" jobs because life is too short and I am not a good hack. I have lost years doing such stuff. Now that Perkins is pleased with my novel I am anxious to concentrate on that, but producer has been unable to get backing so blames it on script. I have ideas

---

*Aunt Lois, the adult "heroine" in *My Home Is Far Away,* was closely modeled on Orpha May Steinbrueck.

of how it could be done but run into stipulations of music and of Shake-speare and the doubt (born of much lost blood and sweat) that it makes any difference what I do.

1944

January 5: Wrote resignation from "Taming of Shrew" and hope I can be firm. In the past, I have often been badgered to the point of writing a letter of resignation but then I didn't send it, and the badgering went on. Looking over old letters I see how much simpler my life would have been if I had sent them—eventually in all cases it was the other party who cut the deal or else continued to make life miserable. So I hope this was wiser; I hope I remember not to take any further hack jobs on plays or magazines.

January 11: Anniversary of Carlo's assassination.

January 13: Busy "reconciling" and drinking with Peggy Bacon. She is, like Portia, best in her own home, of which she is enormously proud the way some people are. A combination of acid indifference to everything and an unexpected sentimentality to make up for really not liking anybody. Everyone is a "honeybunch" or a "sweetums" suddenly, but this spurt of sugary tenderness is not accompanied by any spark of interest in them or their problems—indeed, a complete callousness protects her from wearing out any energy over others. She talks meltingly of her children but would not lift a finger for either of them. Belinda had a beau coming (rather, she had commandeered him) and when he arrived Peggy explained that he could not have any cocktails as there weren't enough for us as it was.

January 17: Very bad chest cold like old times. In fact this is same cold I went to Dr. Martin for over a year ago and he was so determined to have me have ulcers instead.

February 2: Pleurisy. Temperature stays 104.

February 3: Sulfadizone brings fever down to 97.4 but leaves me a wreck.

February 7: Went out today for a little while. Letter from Hemingway very cheering. Said I was his favorite living writer.

February 8: Felt sufficiently improved to begin to be depressed at idea of what good health means—worry about Jojo, money, novel, etc. Very depressed about book unless something helps lift me and it by bootstraps. Applied for insurance loan. Bare chance of some sort of major encouragement (never happened yet) to corral my top energies to pull book together. No life urge or spirits left or even doggedness. General licked feeling. Look like the devil, too.

February 12: Work on book upstairs and I feel at last completely in it, so much so that it goes running along in my head all the time—editing itself, correcting and planning.

February 16: I am in a curious position about this book, for I haven't the faintest notion of whether it's good or bad but at least now it is going very fast. It pours out spontaneously now that it is more fictionalized. The purity and loyalty of Florrie must be brought out more; the mixture of arrogant selfishness, pride and bravery of Lena; the complete retreat into dream world of Marcia with surprised shock of contact with reality.

February 22: First day I felt approximately normal, without the dread of friends nibbling at my strength. Still have some cagey desire to spare myself unnecessary social or physical demands. As for book, have reached what seemed at onset an important chapter but now seems to break rest of story up, so to avoid being stymied probably had better drop it.

February 23: Dr. Amsterdam's report on X-rays of chest show dermoid tumor (what Dr. Witt used to call interlobular sac). Now about half size of lung. Will start in short-wave treatments.

February 24: Actually bored by my book and eager to get to the other one which permits the special kind of writing I like. The time element is always a whip—so little time left to write the important book which gives most of you. So here I am on page 185, and tired at the 200 more pages that stand between me and the next book. Also dispossess notice, no dough coming in, not feeling good, and curious lack of prospects.

March 8: There is no pleasure like the artist's pleasure. "Hardest work in the world" is a lie except for those not naturally endowed, who have taken it up as rewarding more materially than the clerical work for which they are adapted. Hardest work is motherhood, care of your own children, because the worry, responsibility of future is there adding to the routine exhaustion. Housework, office work, factory work—all unsigned drudgery with few unexpected rewards but the boss' respect, romance, outside consolation. Artist with even moderate acceptance in world of arts or letters has elation of new inspiration and of a work accomplished—rewards of unlimited possibility in addition to that—immortality; contemporary attention, if not fame; respect; the vanity appeasements from the other sex always due publicity (even murder publicity) and even riches.

I'm just beginning to think this novel may be of value. I enjoy writing it now. Page 200 or so. I write and rewrite each chapter half a dozen times with pleasure—perhaps because the material is so limitless. There is always more to say, to touch up. This is again proof of the advantage of doing by hand instead of typewriter. The latter always seems so final I hate to change the pretty neat page, and a certain magazine style creeps in.

March 18: I have never paid attention to rumors of my friends' fine social or financial background but take them on basis of how they appear. If they are social or well-born or rich but behave the reverse—economical, stingy or ill-bred—then their behavior is not softened, excused, or even made amusing by contrast with their rumored rights. It is part of a superstition that a college man is entitled to be dumb because he is educated; that a rich man is entitled to be stingy because he is rich; that aristocracy is entitled to be rude because it is aristocracy. The rest of us have to perform the difficult reverse—be generous because we are poor, be polite because we are peasant-bred.

March 20: Up here today with a private blizzard on the roof—sky and roofs white (through my windows, dove gray). Lately my novel is a football I am carrying down the field against tremendous odds—no support on my own team and a stronger opposition team—friends, responsibilities, dates and debts who tackle, trip and grab. If I get to goal it will be a triumph indeed.

Female friends are the greatest hazard in a working woman's life for they cannot be casual. Talk about men being little boys growed up—women are little girls not growed up or little girls are old ladies shrunk up. I am glad to be friends with Peggy again but I have the desperate, haunted feeling I have with Esther—no place to hide or think. Esther of course is more closely tied with standards and memories. Peggy demands little emotion or real life-blood but a call returned, an invitation for an invitation, flowers after a kiss, a birthday remembered, a compliment on a hat. These are the difficult things in life that fritter away a writer's nerves and affections.

Writers' wives and husbands are successful only so far as they learn to ask nothing but murder, money and mentality from them.

A. is an attractive girl with enough intelligence not to try to understand anything. I realize more and more that age and experience have taught me nothing but to pretend they have.

March 21: Panicky with fear of burglars from childhood, I have ripened into someone afraid of everything—debtors, enemies, a knock at the door, a telephone call (these all represent demands on time and courtesy), teachers, doctors, admirers (these may be disappointed in me), my clothes, my work, editors, strange houses, familiar houses (I might get trapped in them), invitations, no invitations, businessmen, friends of friends, other races, dumb people, head waiters, elevator boys, mirrors, political thinkers, musicians, women and children. Nothing in my life has ever reassured me. My mind is as filled with terrors as my closet is with moths. I am not afraid of criticism or death or pain.

March 23: For a writer or artist there is nothing to equal the elation of escaping into solitude. The excited feeling of stolen rapture I feel on closing the door of this little room up here, knowing no one can find me, no one will speak to me. I look over rooftops into sky and far-off towers. This is exactly like my sensation of sheer exhilaration as a child when I got up into the attic or in the treetop or under a tree way off by the road where I was alone with a sharp pencil and notebook.

At Margaret's, Lewis Gannett* flung an affectionate arm around me and introduced me: "Dawn's a good girl except she drinks too much and one of these days she's going to do a good novel."

"If I did, you wouldn't know it," I said. "As for drinking too much you've seen me at these parties in the last five years where you were drinking more than anyone. That's why you can never be a writer or know good writing when you see it—generalizing about a person's habits from public performances instead of private understanding."

He was mad and I lectured him that if I ever wrote something he considered "good" I would know I was slipping. A touch of horticulture, a few recipes, some nice people he would want in his drawing room—in fact, his idea of a good book was one that could run serially in the *Woman's Home Companion*.

March 24: Sent Part II to typist. Very important to avoid the usual cliché, wrong side of tracks stuff of which only adults—and not many of them—are conscious. Not the real trouble here anyway.

April 3: Exhausted by friends—not so much by revelry as by the responsibility of friends who are so happy to gnaw away at the bones of your energy and talent. Peggy is almost as bad as Portia used to be; she doesn't want to work any more than Portia did. Like 90 percent of women and small boys, however, they do like to pester people who *are* working.

I like writing better than anything but it sounds as conceited as "I love my own beauty." So I feel guilty when caught enjoying writing.

Perkins and Carol think a trilogy is a good idea for this book and while they are not enthusiastic I think it is because the pattern itself is not clear yet but should be at end of Part III. There is no reason why I shouldn't do a speed-up on this—as fast as *Angels On Toast*.

April 5: How can one distinguish between tolerance and indifference? The sharp edge of youthful prejudice wears down and because it can no longer cut pretends it doesn't want to. This is tolerance which, unmasked,

---

*Gannett, an early friend, was now book critic for the New York *Herald Tribune*.

is indifference, leaving once more prejudices which are senile irascibilities, defenses against more powerful enemies.

April 11: I am at last promoted to insomnia. I am exhausted by dull friends who get from me more than I could ever get from them. My heart hurts and seems bleeding and I'm sure it is.

What amazes me is friends' fond determination to kill you, no matter how you beg mercy—to kill, destroy, impoverish you so they can leave you without regret. If you are tired, then they insist you must come see them because they feel fine, if you have a passion to work they must keep you from it at any cost and if you are in debt they swear they must borrow from you or go to jail. I end up wanting to hit or scream at them and the more devoted they are, the more relentlessly they insist on your blood. What a waste of everything my life has been.

April 14: Just diagnosed my savage reactions to the slightest annoyance as anemia, so must start on iron again. Easily exhausted by demands on conversation, energy, I finally fly out in a self-protective rage at nothing more than my own fatigue, in the same way people coping with one unbeatable problem (a lost love, financial worry, an inherent inability to leave some tie) strike out unjustly at whatever can be struck, since they cannot strike at Fate.

I would like to visit Ohio for a few days again soon.

April 22: Went out to Port Jefferson and looked at beach cottage.

Shack so beachy and wood-sheddy it was funny but at least it was open and sunny—the two lacks in all country houses even more than in city houses and the things that have reduced me to frenzy. Curious how this beach, very familiar as it is, seems strange and new when considered as a base.

Each neighborhood in this village offers totally strange views and points of view in living.

April 30: After long despondency over novel, my own future, past and present, I veered at 5 or 6 yesterday and felt myself again. I suppose main difficulty was in being on wrong track so long in novel. I nearly always go off-track after I've submitted a section of a work and gotten a reaction.

This was the worst—almost a month's work wasted. I believe I recaptured it finally. At any rate I suddenly felt as if at last the wind had stopped blowing against me and the intense fear I've felt not only of Fate but of all life and people.

I have spent most of my life being an adolescent cringing with painful inferiorities based on others' opinions of me—and leaping out of them with bravado.

May 2: P. B.*—to be approached as some people are, as slowly as if one is about to be locked in a closet. Not a mysterious closet either, but the same musty smell of old velvet in camphor balls, the smell of darkness, dankness. She gives claustrophobia—as some people do—a person who has used her own life, her own prejudices, as armor-proofing, and nothing goes out, nothing comes in.

May 15: Hemingway down all day yesterday—exhausted by his immense gusto—someone who gives out more in six hours than most people do in a lifetime—leaves you groggy. Latouche at night. Fond as I am of him, he drags the last drop of blood out of you—seems tiresomely juvenile in his sober moments—fonder of teasing his prey than of eating it, teasing his thoughts and plots by talk.

Exhausted by my novel and not sure of it, even. Too tiresome. Only thing is that most successful books are tiresome.

May 16: T.† has way of pronouncing all corny humor, old time whimsy—straight facts even—"surrealism," the way English claim every loose island for England. It is done with a great air of discovery and daring, and actually is about as intelligent as saying "and stuff" at end of every sentence to make up for fuzzy observation. Almost as boarding school a classification as "perfectly adorable," as meaningful as "darling."

May 18: Book back on right foot—up to page 260 now, after throwing out a great deal—forty pages or so. Working on typewriter now for clarification purposes and to tense up plot, which sprawls forever over pen and ink.

---

* Powell probably means Peggy Bacon.
† This may be John Latouche, known as "Touche" to his friends.

May 19: Went to Metropolitan Ballet last night—saw "Tallyho" with Gluck music; "Pillar of Fire" with Schoenberg music (Anthony Tudor choreography and Freudian undercurrents); "El Amor Brujo" with de Falla music and excellent dancing; and Jerome Robbins' "Fancy Free" with Oliver Smith sets, Leonard Bernstein music, and Bernstein, the new wonder-boy, conducting. This gay work, spontaneous and arrogant, made me aware as I constantly am of the factor of luck in art—the confidence, super cock-sureness of early success, accidentally being friends with powers-soon-to-be, learning early the manner of success. I have always felt that the *manner* of success came first—the inside later, if at all.

June 17: Awful wakening early with consciousness of bouncing checks and nothing to be done. Tired of borrowing—also awkward as no reason for person in my professional position having to borrow, or for that matter to say "Sorry, I cannot afford to buy my own dinner, let alone yours."

Off to country where shack turned out to be heavenly. All bright sun and sand and sea air—everything I miss. Marvelous view, comfortable beds, clean. Bed at 9 with stars looking in window and waves lapping like music and late the strange sound of planes very low overhead.

June 18: This oppressive novel never seems to get anywhere in spite of many good things in it. It is like a child that takes so long to grow up and look after itself, like a cancer in that the only thing about it is that it's my very own.

June 19: Here I am, feeling rested, calm and completely empty, so I look on my novel with a feeling that here is this immovable rock to be pushed (without its ever moving) and I have no energy or hope about it. What is that law that some people must always have an immovable block between them and the public—and others have all roads greased and even perfumed? The tons of plays, etc., I have written—the wasted labor would dig a grave halfway to China.

July 15: To Henry Billings for weekend at Rhinebeck. Count and Countess C. called. Decided that rich refugees' rage at Hitler was not sympathy for Jews, etc., but same as privileged class' rage at Roosevelt—a danger to their private wealth. His racial and personal cruelties they would have approved if he had only left their fortunes alone.

July 24: To Murphys' at East Hampton for wonderful, restful weekend, returning last night with notes for ending of book.

July 25: Turned in last of *My Home Is Far Away* to Perkins. Pleased with ending and other features of end more than beginning or earlier part.

August 5: Went to country, having stayed at Margaret's while house was repainted. Working over play, "Every Other Day," for Leonora Corbett.

October 19: Worked steadily for past two months rewriting play, with Leonora Corbett's intensive analysis of each line. As she lost idea of play and thought in terms of star part, I feared it was going overboard. Then George Abbott came into picture as co-producer, made brief general suggestions—all anti-star—and restored balance. Abbott hates "vehicles" and a vehicle is all Corbett wants. News of [Samson] Raphaelson play being exactly like it seemed to doom this and, as usual, the day came when the whole thing was off. First utterly crushed, I swung back with an elated feeling that, by God, with producer and star out of picture, I'd do what I damn pleased, rig out a version that would please me alone. I did a fine job and actually have complete confidence that it will come through. Result—Corbett liked it immensely.

Worried about book which is due out in a week and has no advance publicity or anything.

October 20: Leonora Corbett called last night to say she was determined to go ahead with this play—that I was a great playwright and I shouldn't waste any more time on books. Actually I don't remember any time in my career having done such a superior job as I have in this play, due primarily to Corbett's interest in it and flagellations, then balanced by Abbott's generalizations. I suppose this confidence comes from the steady support and admiration of two people at the top of their branches of the theater— Abbott as producer, Corbett as actress, both hardboiled. I could have done a great deal more if I had not always gotten mixed up with tenth-rate people who didn't know as much as I did so they frittered away my plays.

October 30: Publication of *My Home Is Far Away,* which I now think is one of my best books. On rereading it my first feeling was of queasiness over the initial establishment of a distinctly autobiographical flavor, but after a while the characters became wholly fictional, increasingly round, and with the full reality that only created characters have. Certainly few facts are here.

November 3: Unusually fearful over book, largely because the skeleton is so close to life and I hate to bring myself out so openly for censure, also to expose the family. It made me cringe today when review called it pathetic, etc., good-for-nothing people.

November 13: Up on roof in spite of Louise being still away so I may be missing phone calls. Dr. Wing says my swollen face is not teeth but mumps. It is certainly not attractive but I seem to be too tired to care.

Marie once said a wonderful thing: "Nothing rests me like money."

November 17: Shopping at Saks, I ran into Leonora Corbett, looking very beautiful, who insisted I shop with her and collect her new-made hat—a towering, black affair she declared she was getting especially for the football game. Sitting with her while she tried on many hats of ice cream cake, red violets, etc.—all made by the Russian Tania du Plexis—was Mrs. Gilbert Miller, described to me later as one of the world's best-dressed women but off-hand in her tidy discreet well-massaged way she might have been the governess who was allowed to dine with the family. They talked of Noël and his gaffe about the Brooklyn boys in his Mid-East diary. A dreadful book, said Mrs. Miller, and so like Noël—the Sun God, little Apollo driving his chariot across the world and spreading sunshine, having champagne with the General and getting a little bit tiddly.

The furrier came through and told of some marvelous new Russian sables just in from the Russian government to be sold at fantastically low prices. Leonora at once asked how much a short sable jacket would be and he said "$12,000," and she said "I don't call that cheap. But let me see it." He went to get it out of a vault and she asked Mrs. Miller then if she might borrow Noël's book ($2.50). Mrs. Miller said yes, but she had loaned it to Carol. Leonora said she could hardly wait to read it and hoped Carol would return it. This is why furriers are richer than authors.

Nothing happens about my book—not even ads anymore—so I am waiting as usual for the Great Review that will put it over. Meantime George Abbott called to ask me about play for Zasu Pitts. He is so exceedingly considerate and respectful of my ability that I would do it.

Mrs. Humphrey Ward (me) and Professor Ernest Wigmore (Bunny Wilson) carrying on scholarly correspondence. Not drinking for a week gives the world a strange opium dream quality. I realize that I drink to make the fantasy rattle down to reality.

November 20: Curiously enough, Leonora Corbett called to say she loved my book—so did Esther—and the few people who have read it seem very sincerely pleased with it, much to my surprise.

I went to a party Friday; first time I drank for a week and actually the reason for drinking is extreme boredom and lack of interest in anyone. To be even civil to others you require some false stimulus. Through the entire party I could hear the tired, pompous, patronizing voice of Paul Peters saying about this play or that book—"I thought it had some awfully good things in it" or "It had some very nice moments in it—very nice"— "Yes, I rather liked it. There were some good things in it, I thought."

I began working up an intense contempt for this stingy, cautious appraisal. If he cannot give himself wholly to something he doesn't deserve even "some good things." A capacity for going overboard is a requisite for a full-grown mind. I am so grateful for "some good things" in a book or play that I gladly dismiss the drawbacks. For that matter Dickens, Tolstoy and all the great writers had "some good things" and people were damned lucky to get even the bad things.

November 21: This is a wonderful day—rain and snow and sleet and a curious hangover that settled suddenly my new novel.

November 23: For past few days I have finally been living in Book II* and have a secret, unresolved, unarticulated sense of being home, though I cannot put down in definite words the course of this book. I know I must enter into the agony, self-consciousness, coldness, breathlessness of adolescence and youth—the secret immense confidence and egotism, the outward embarrassment and fear and fumbling. The cat-like cold contempt

---

*A quasi-autobiographical follow-up to *My Home Is Far Away*—usually referred to as "Marcia"—on which Powell would labor for much of her life but never complete.

for everyone and fearful embarrassment at good people; the wild animal fear of kindness (of being tamed, actually); the avoidance of understanding and goodness.

November 24: Perkins writes that *My Home Is Far Away* has sold 4500 copies so far—three weeks after publication. This is better than expected. I think it will do around 10,000 at Christmas.

As for the new one—the first book dwelt on the clinging to remnants of tribal sentiment and loyalty—the security and warmth of the little family, the bewilderment and shock of its wreck into separate fortunes, the dawning realization that this *was* a wreck, and there was no safety; each person must sink or swim by himself, snatching from each other whatever rafters floated by. A frightening thought—that in your very dearest there is no hope or safety, to expect nothing so that the disappointment will not be too great, and to insure yourself special delight and joy when unexpectedly something does come through.

Book II should have a name indicating the forming from all sorts of crude clay a figure—a person who is either a work of art or at least a stout instrument for withstanding many experiences—a name hinting at the forming of youth, the harnessing of wildness into personality, the focusing of daydreams and longings into a plan for action, a plan for life.

Marcia is particularly representative of the wild, untamed, unlimited cold intensity of adolescence—the fierce longing for Everything; the stony contempt for fatuity, pretentiousness, adult stupidity, goodness, kindness, etc. The intensely mental inner life of an intelligent youth, anxious for happenings, even bad, or change rather than cozy routine security. Marcia develops into a person always more mature than the elders, pitying them for their self-deception. The intense, voluptuous pleasure of books—wild joy of library. The warmth of the cold world—the welcome sword—almost the preparing of the young warrior. The strangeness of this—the recognition of talent, etc.—anywhere but in family.

November 28: After 21 years or more of writing novels steadily with inch-like progress I am about where most of my contemporaries are who wrote one play, one book, of moderate success, and basked in increasing glory, prestige and (in some cases) affluence, ever since. They took care to nurse what fame came on their one outburst—they cultivated the rich, the publicity spotlight, and discussed their literary and artistic perceptions so avidly that no one ever forgot they were permanent stars. This perpetual going over the finished deed prevents them ever building new deeds, but this is no handicap to their mounting success.

If Bunny's review* had been offset by a powerful, favorable one the book would have gotten off. As it is, it is very discouraging to have someone (who actually has told me I'm infinitely better than John Marquand and equal to Sinclair Lewis at his best) do me so much genuine damage. I have enough damage done me already, merely by the desire to write and my pleasure in people and strange angles of life rather than the English-class models.

---

*Powell was deeply upset by Wilson's mixed review of *My Home Is Far Away* in *The New Yorker*.

1945

January 9: For two days I can do nothing but sleep, be seasick and doze off again. My insides seem jaundiced but it occurs to me it may be paralysis because of the weakness in the legs, the refusal of the stomach and the dizziness even in my sleep, so that I dream of dizzy people.

I have been trying to do the Marcia book but the reaction was so slight to the first one that it will take a great deal of health and egotism to continue. So I wonder about starting the other one, which God knows gives me a brilliant opportunity. In spite of what Max advises I believe I will do this. It may bring back my energy and interest. I have an idea I can do it in a very short time, whereas Marcia requires a long time. It is possible to do one part of the trilogy, then a modern satire, then the second part. Begin today and see how far it goes, if it gives me back my springs. Write in longhand—maybe by night since I don't sleep—and see. I feel better already.

January 29: Harry Lissfelt died today. It is the first time death has touched me so closely. There was first the surprise, the shock, and then an impression of pure unpleasantness—as if someone had brought their child to a gay drunken revel, the revel being Life and the child being Death.

What amazes me is the after-exhilaration of other people's death—the reaffirmation of your own life and loving, the deep breaths you take, the expansion of interests. There is the same renewal of gaiety as when someone, no matter how well-liked, leaves the party—everyone has another drink and feels all the closer. Fred Lissfelt and Joe had a warmer, closer time than ever—Harry bequeathed as much warmth and geniality as if he'd been present. A curious purpose in death which I never realized:

even the poorest, dying, leave a heritage of thoughts to their heirs—what do I mean by living?

Death is a fertilizer. It suddenly seems the only clear clean use of life—all of the muffled meanings and intentions suddenly are focused into this great flowering and the pattern of the dead person becomes clear to everyone. The curious wave of high joy that follows the shock of his departure is not forgetting him, but coming into the full understanding of him and the little wisdom that he bequeathed. Conversations and explanations obscured his own meaning. When they stop, the whole figure emerges rich and brilliant and so it becomes true that death is the triumph of life—Harry's especially—bright, clean and luminous with his own peculiar radiance, as Carlo's was a triumph and declaration. But the deaths of boys on battlefields are defeats.

February 2: Made new start on novel about Marcia but having same inertia I had on *My Home Is Far Away*. Must remember value is of reconstruction of period so that it lives and breathes and *is* again, and in this the breathless expectancy, mysticism and hardness of adolescence.

February 5: Jojo restless at Gladwyne. Believe I will go down there and stay at Valley Forge. Fortnightly visits there or home may help.

February 12: A good idea in Sunday, January 24, 1943 journal. The teacher in the Canned Culture courses so prevalent at NYU, New School, etc. Six weeks course in Contemporary Literature where students visit drunken teacher and whole course based on *reviews* of books since teacher too bored and too tight ever to read them and students only want an opinion on everything. Class regrets it can't discuss the book, having missed the reviews, so innocent as to say this, never dreaming some people read the books—but when they did, how did they know whether to say it was bad or good? Therefore the course. One person read the book—everyone astonished—but he reads a lotta books. Likes to. Likes 'em all. Just likes reading. Kinda takes up the time. At first impressed, others finally contemptuous because he can't discuss—he has no opinion.

Teacher: "Dos Passos, the writer of *42nd Parallel* and *Number One*—what about him?" Class: "Good on general ideas but his characters not real people." "Right," says teacher. "I read it," interrupts boy. "I liked 'em all right." Always interrupting.

February 14: Vernon Duke called up asking if I would be interested in original New York musical and I said yes.

Meantime Jefferson Lightfoot Calhoun, a half-grown alleycat, arrived to tease Perkins* and enjoy the furniture. A personality cat and if I could have managed I would have kept it. Felt bad at seeing little thing carted off to new house.

February 15: Went to "On The Town," a beautiful new fresh musical with sets by Oliver Smith, book and lyrics by Betty Comden and Adolph Green and rest by Jerome Robbins and Leonard Bernstein. Sets and new operation of scenery were masterpieces.

Wonderful thing about the theater is its utter lack of logic or consistency. One day last year I was sitting with Latouche (in the Algonquin) and some friends of his—Paul Feigay, Oliver Smith, and someone else probably called Manny. They were discussing their ideas for the musical production of "The Firebrand," wanting Latouche to do the lyrics—very much as if he were W. S. Gilbert himself and the project would be ruined if he didn't consent. As for the music, Latouche suggested Lenny Bernstein. No. They liked Lenny; Lenny had talent; but he had no name. This was big stuff, see—no amateurs. Latouche protested—Lenny would be all right; why not go over to Lenny's place and listen to some songs he had written—really good. Well, sure, they'd let Lenny have a try but they had too big a production in mind for little Lenny.

The very next day, to my amazement, the front pages described the sensational debut as conductor by Leonard Bernstein in Carnegie with the Philharmonic, last minute substitution for Toscanini or Stokowski.†
It was the talk of the season, and a few months later his music at the Met for Robbins' ballet "Fancy Free" was the next sensation. Next we have Mr. Feigay and Oliver Smith producing Mr. Bernstein's musical "On The Town," telling him, no doubt, that they always knew he had it in him. Meantime, Eddie Mayer, author of "Firebrand," decides Feigay is not big enough name for him so he signs with Max Gordon for the musical.

February 17: Dinner at the Murphys'. Archie MacLeish was staying there and came in after Chinese banquet where he sat next to Nicholas Murray

---

*Powell had named her cat Perkins after her editor, Maxwell Perkins.
†In fact, Bernstein had replaced an ailing Bruno Walter.

Butler, who is almost blind now. He toyed with an apple, cut it in two
and put it aside. Later, fumbling around blindly, his hand found the half-
apple and he muttered "Good God, what's that?" as if he had just stumbled across Mrs. Butler. "Your apple, Dr. Butler," Archie reassured him.

Archie proudly displayed the watch the librarians at Library of Congress had given him on his exit. I said "Wait till you see what the State
Department gives you when you get out of that." "Yes, they'll tie that to
my tail," he said.

We went down to Jo Davidson's studio at the Beaux Arts and looked
over his sculpture, portrait busts largely. Very few women, as he seems romantic about women, making them smooth, empty and beautiful.

February 23: Took pages 18–45 to Max. This book must not be merely the
story of an "interesting child." It must show the adult which is already in
this child and her impatience with the delay, her fighting off emotion as
something which will impede her. It must have that sense of being an
artist each artist is born with—a sense of destiny beyond the present.

March 26: Childrens' party for Miranda Marvin. All seated on telephone
books at table. Miranda wearing crown as birthday queen but very disappointed to see that other children have same (not less) favors as she. Finds
horn and blows it—others do same and Miranda looks on in grief, blowing her own horn, drowned out by others. Cries "Mine doesn't blow!"
and sobs bitterly that hers is not the loudest. All put whistles in mouths
and close eyes puffing in complete utter ecstasy as noise issues. Mothers
upstairs and fathers having drinks finally stuff their children into leg-
gings and other accoutrements. Little boys told to kiss Miranda good-bye
and she runs after them, highly pleased, for more kisses.

April 11: Roosevelt's death.

April 12: Contracts signed with George Abbott for play to be done by June 1.
I do not really care for Zasu Pitts as lead—she has been a star so long that
she has star-muggings.

April 30: Long period of utter uncreativeness, mass of practical duties—
money, income tax, Jojo, etc., and boredom with limitations of both novel

and play. Really exhausted and, though up early and working all day, no drive. Used my drive on useless works.

May 7: Began series of tests for Jojo with Dr. Portia Hamilton, psychological consultant. Jojo himself less spastic from insulin and emotionally more localized. Spent entire week without upset. Problem now of where to spend summer.

May 23: Beginning this play again and again and sort of nibbling it to death. I think I need to do a fast modern novel like *Happy Island*.

June 1: To Murphys' for weekend. I had the charming pink room next to Sara and Gerald's but a charming old grandfather clock bonged out the hours all night and I was shattered to the point of actual sickness not by no sleep but by being *prevented* from sleep. Next night I dreaded, knowing it would be the same—so hoped to stay up late. We did. We went to a movie in East Hampton. Its name was "The Clock." That night was the same as before so in spite of luxury and coziness in every way I came home a wreck.

June 9: Left for Ohio.

June 10: Met by Mabel at 55th Street Station, picked up Phyllis in Canton and on to Shelby.

July 9: I think my great handicap and strongest slavery is my insistence on freedom. I require it. So I cannot make the suave adjustments to a successful writer's life—right people, right hospitality, right gestures—because I want to be free. So I am tied down and now in middle years almost buried (so far as my career goes) by my freedom.

July 18: The longest period I have neither written, reacted, or felt guilty about not writing. Mostly I feel curious and surprised for I cannot recall any time in my life being reduced to such average dullness. I know what it is to be an uncreative, unimaginative person, not very much interested in anything, not even in beautification or parties. I am tired out from the curious direction my former energy takes—domesticity.

True, it is somewhat like my first two years of marriage, pregnancy and baby. In the shack at Mt. Sinai, I knock myself out trying to make it palatable, though the truth is we are stung. I cook in town, make different stabs at arranging things, take a vast interest in the rigmarole of household tricks, feel extremely indifferent to all literary life.

This all has happened since February 17 when I visited Dr. Ruth Fox and started taking the strange combination of gland, appetite, Benzedrine vitamin pills. At first wrote ferociously on novel for three weeks—as ferociously as a wheel spinning fast on momentum before dying out completely.

Then everything stopped. I lost weight steadily—20 pounds finally—and hardly a thought passed through my head beyond the immediacies of life. I spoke to the doctor about this and she was not interested—very few doctors are interested in curious side-effects of their pills. They know that this cures a cold and the fact that it makes the teeth fall out or hair grow on chest merely confuses and annoys them. *This* is a specific for *that;* no blurring, please, of a scientific rule.

Another discovery is the way tradespeople and taximen scorn people they think have means for living in a beach-house or tent merely because they love water, sky, nature or something that doesn't cost anything.

July 25: I wrote Jimmy Quiggle, Gretchen's son, paratrooper in the Pacific, when I returned from Ohio and he answered that this was one of the several surprises waiting him on his return. The big one was a letter from his fiancee back home saying she was no longer such. "There is no one else," he said. "She is a swell girl and I don't blame her." This, he said, was happening to so many G.I.s that they had formed a Brush-Off Club. To be eligible, you produced the letter jilting you and picture of the girl jilting you. Then the Crying Committee took over—the letter was read out loud and everyone cried as loud as they could.

Dorothy Parker said there was another brush-off club, too—the men writing their wives that they were not going to come back but were going to settle in Australia with a nurse, etc. A short story about the two meeting each other.

July 30: Feeling better than in some time due to good weekend with Coby and Peggy Bacon in country. A girl came up to me, said she was writing a novel—her name Henrietta Weigel.* How a novice would react to the visit to the dismal shack in the dunes where the old-time writer lived I don't know. Be discouraged from writing forever, I should think. Or regard the oldie as cracked.

Silly to think money does not change a person and his whole point of view. Suddenly he is conscious of being "used" for his money—he thinks everyone is aware of his money and he must not unduly excite envy or greed in those less able to moderate their cupidity than himself. Neither do stomach ulcers affect a man's point of view—merely make him dislike gourmets, good cooks, drinkers, conviviality, in fact ulcers have not changed him except to transform his whole attitude toward life and people.

On the train, two girls. They carried a small Victrola and as soon as they got on the train began playing innumerable records. The object was obvious but they had hard luck for no soldier or sailor got on until we were at Huntington when the two GIs got on and were astonished to find themselves so attractive they were able to crash a conversation with the two girls.

Behind them sat a desperate looking little dark girl who had watched with desolate yearning—longing to be gay like that, have such a good time, as if the little Victrola was a badge of permanent beaux, dances, bars, nightclubs, mailbox full of letters. Presently she gave her seat to the two soldiers who were very foxy, they thought, in requesting numbers from the girls. The girls proudly played, never letting a moment elapse between numbers, looking gravely responsible as if they were the modest but nevertheless admirable custodians of a gifted animal and as if the needle and record's collaboration was every bit as worthy as their own genius in winding the machine, selecting the records and humming the words sometimes.

Then two other hearty, earthy young women butted in, asking for numbers, trying for the GIs and a tired, amusing-faced little Red Cross nurse or maybe marine stood modestly in the doorway. One soldier—tired, handsome, unhappy-looking—asked for "Always" and you saw that they were asking for their own distant girlfriends' favorites. By Jamaica, where the men got off, the two girls had made no progress beyond having their music accepted.

---

* Henrietta Weigel's *Age Of Noon* was published by Dutton in 1947.

August 7: Decided (or re-decided) to do New York novel and out in country began notes again on it.

August 11: Charlie, the long-faced little eleven-year-old in the cottage behind us, whose sole passion is to run to the beach after breakfast and get to work throwing stones. Then he sits, lonely and thoughtful, staring at the water. Another boy and he went out in a canoe with the dog and, when it upset, his father scolded him, forbidding him to go in the canoe again. A little while later the two boys were very purposefully and secretly lugging a large table and logs along the beach. I said "Have you nails big enough to go in that log?" and the little boy's face lit up rapturously. "Do you know about it too?"—the "it" being the raft in progress. "We need rope and logs and an anchor now" he said, reciting happily what the bigger boy had told him. I gave them the rope I had found on the beach and after that he waved joyously to me when he saw me and when I was swimming he cried out "You can climb on the raft if you want to."

September 29: My dear cat Perkins died today—very sweetly, very quietly, daintily, a lady wanting to give as little trouble as possible. She took sick Monday, with chills and bladder trouble and threw up her fish. She knew and I knew that this was it. I cashed a bad check to take her to Speyer's where the vet gave me pills and medicine to give her which she hated. She could not eat, either. Nor would she try. Finally she lay on the balcony, exhausted, in the sun. I heard her choke, and she was in a convulsion, but I picked her up and put her in a chair where she managed to fix her sweet eyes on me while I held her paw and moistened her lips with water. It was unbearable.

Joe was in the country. I read Mrs. Trollope* furiously all night, loving Mrs. T. for coming to my rescue. I hated even to give up the little soft dead body lying in the chair but fortunately the SPCA came in at Ann Honeycutt's call and took her. Otherwise I would have done away with myself. Perkins seemed the only lovely thing in life that cost nothing, asked nothing, and gave only pleasure. At least she won't have to have this operation now, which would have been fatal, and at least she didn't give me the prolonged anguish of running away or being lost.

---

* *Domestic Manners of the Americans* would become one of Powell's favorite books.

Adopted Perkins on July 3, 1940 after turning in *Angels On Toast* to Perkins, my publisher. Took kitten out to Mt. Sinai, where Alice, Tootsie,* etc., were all delighted. Her major service to me was curious—she cured me of the disease of night fear. I stayed for weeks alone with her, hearing her rattling around the house. Very dainty from the start, she waited like a modest bride till I was in bed with the lights out, then washed herself and leapt softly onto the bed, tucked herself in my neck and nuzzled off to sleep. It was wonderful to be unafraid.

I forgot my debt to her for this until the night after she died when I was alone in the house and suddenly every sound once more became sinister—the escaped lunatic slowly turning the doorknob, the big brute creeping up the stairs. My cat analyst was dead and my phobias came plunging out of the pits and closets where they had been locked. I cannot have another pet—it would be unfaithful to my little dear who liked no one but me, knew no other cats, no mice, no love but mine. She thought she was my mother—was ashamed and outraged if I was noisy or loud-talking, slapped me if I was blah, avoided me scornfully if I was drunk, approved if I typed. She was the first pet in my life.

October 1: Being slowly weaned back to writing after my blank months. I think I should go away for a week of concentrated work on my book. I don't know where to go, however. Maybe Atlantic City again.†

October 4: Still curiously-mooded about my cat. I have a pang eating all my bacon instead of decently saving some for her. I miss her ears pricking up from deep in the yellow blanket of the bed as I stir in waking. Actually I felt the exhaustion of her death week as if it was a contagion. It seemed unendurable, getting up all hours night after night to try to feed her or do something for her but mostly just following her around, wringing my hands. I felt the heaviness of her death on my bones as it was on hers, so that I could scarcely have borne another day waking to her patient, doomed, motionless wait.

October 11: Bunny Wilson returned from Greece a few weeks ago and I saw a lot of him. All relations with Bunny are dictated by him—he is

---

*Powell's nieces, daughters of Mabel Powell Pocock and Phyllis Powell Cook.

†Powell regularly checked into the Hotel Traymore in Atlantic City during the 1920s when she wanted to do sustained work.

the one to name the hour, the place, the subject of conversation. After knowing him slightly several years I finally realize he is not at all what he seemed—he is totally unaware and violently allergic to whatever is going on. He is mystified and annoyed by the simple process of creation; he is furious at the things he does not understand—furious, blind and bored. What he does not understand is all life that is not in print, so he sees people, invents a literary category for them, then locks them up in it, occasionally peeking at them through the iron bars of the peephole to say: "There you are, you in-love-with-father, hate-mother type, reacting exactly as your type does and any other way you act will not be observed by me."

Freud served a purpose for this type of anxious-to-know-what-they-can-never-comprehend intellectual, for they can fasten a ready-made label from the printed book on anyone without even trying to study them. Bunny resents women being friends with each other, and since he is positive they cannot be friends, he tries to make trouble between them by resorting to such a bludgeoning type of bitchery that it unites them against him. He likes all conventional things but fancies himself a revolutionist. There is no popular opinion he does not share, no unsuccessful artist or writer he does not berate, no Book-Of-The-Month he does not praise. He wants to see his ladies alone so he can attack them, leave them chastened and feeling limp, hopeless, unloved, unattractive. He has told them that they are looking well, that usually they look so unkempt, so dowdy; he has told them on seeing their latest work that he always felt their best work was done when they were twenty; he has told them that everything they like is impossible; everything they dislike is perfect and a test of intelligence and taste. He beams with joy and well-nourished nerves as he leaves, like a vampire returning from a juicy grave.

October 17: Coby said "I must be off now for I'm a breadwinner. Most breadwinners bring home the bacon but I bring home the wool because I'm a wool-gatherer." When he came in to the party there was nothing but a row of middle-aged ladies looking like a women's club so I said "Ladies, this is Dr. Gilman, the speaker of the evening." He said "Yes, and I have some very good things to say to you ladies today because I'm an optimist—that, so far as the future is concerned. I find it very difficult to be optimistic about the past."

October 20: The pleasure of Dickens. Young eager readers find philosophies of conduct and life reported; allusions to social-mores, history, culture, which set a match to future investigation. Old readers find these printed words check with their familiarity with the world and recognize their truth.

October 21: Ever since Esther has been visiting Margaret all parties are bevies of middle-aged women either raucously bawdy and potentially (though unconsciously) Lesbian or painfully materialistic, ignorant, inexcusably silly. Helen Culbertson's was a peak—with everyone shrilling away about bargains in auctions, the Lazy-Susan that was such a bargain, the passion for anything money buys and the assumption that this is what interests all civilized people—so I am anxious to balance my prejudices with my customary new friends. In the middle of conversation which we had found was impossible to deflect from the utterly silly, Coby arrived and with a few boulders mowed the whole conversation.

One lady said the uniforms of the men made their slim hips look so fine and Coby said "Nobody but a lecherous female would notice that. Slim hips, for Christ's sake! Who cares whether hips are slim or as big as Brooklyn Bridge?" "You don't mean women's hips can be that big?" "Sure," he said, "women's hips *ought* to be as big as Brooklyn Bridge." He complained that all the younger men he knew—pallid, nearsighted chaps —had gone to war, been lost in jungles, in prisons, wounded in combat, riddled with jungle fever, pellagra and Bombay duck, and come back looking better than they ever had in their life—an argument for war as a health measure.

October 23: Josh Billings, aged 42 or so, separated from wife considered social climber, turns into something far worse than she is. At restaurant, he put his medicine on the table (as he thought he was getting a touch of a cold), tried to laugh at everything we said to show he had humor (which he hadn't) and in an effort to "make" somebody young showed the stiffness, sterility and barren desolation of his mind. He has amoeboid thrifty characteristics—that is, he is attracted to people who have such an overflow of life and enjoyment that he thinks if he stands beside them some of it will drip over onto him.

All these years he has been separating his friends of talent, juice and guts from those he wished to identify himself with socially, but actually all those social people liked was his connection with the talent. (How did such a pallid, decent, queasy fellow with nothing but polite manners to recommend him ever make the most difficult group of all to meet—the talented bohemia?)

So he tries to act as they do—use bad words, etc.—which do not become him, sit oddly on him who is so careful that everything else must fit. But if he uses these words and says these things, then surely Society will take him up since he has the added (he does not realize canceling) virtue of table manners.

November 23: Carl Brandt said why not write love story? A disturbing stinginess about this novel, for I almost willfully cut out love whereas I am not sparing of any other matters.

November 30: The way one falls in love with someone, not at first realizing it is not with this person but with the person he reminds you of.

December 25: Esther Murphy at Gerald's—tall, gaunt, in tweed suit with folded cravat, regretting the necessity of a body whose needs interrupt her conversation, studded with statistics on Third Empire, Economics, and European politics. Statistics occupy her as if they were rare jewels; her contact with the human race (she is concerned with only its major figures) is in shy revelations made to her that the great (in diadems of dates and robes of sparkling statistics) also were interrupted by body or mortal demands. She talks constantly, on nothing trivial, not as an exhibitionist but as a tireless defender of her own privacy. Some alien hand might intrude or pry in a silence, so barriers of statistics must be piled up like sandbags to protect the small shy bird within. She talked of the practical accomplishments of this generation—she herself could drive a car but with no knowledge of what made it go or what made it stop beyond gas. What was under the hood that made trouble she never even guessed. "For all I know," she said dreamily, "it might be a little cherub."

1946

[*Undated*] Important and basic to have New York geography.
1. Nightclubs and Restaurants
    Blue Angel, Oak Room (Ritz) Plaza, Lüchow's Bar (Men's), White
    Turkey, Spivy's. Jimmy Savo (Black Magic), Irwin Corey (Blue Angel
    —Autumn, 1943), Dwight (Versailles, Dec. 1945–Jan. 1946), Tony's
    on 55th Street, Barney's, Chauteaubriand (E. 53rd?)
2. Joints and small restaurants
    Palais d'Orient—Ticino's—San Remo on Bleecker—(Mills Hotel
    man with shoes)—Hofbrau—Bklyn. St. George Bar—fish place—
    Pete's—Bleeck's. King of Prussia Inn.
Name New York Novel
    "O Strange New War"
    "Prudentius Psychomachia" (Battle of the Soul)
Masculine novel— "Promiscuity Recollected in Senility."

January 3: Blocked and locked in Marcia novel. Started New York one,*
which seemed to flow and like a good psychoanalysis cleared up the reason the other book was blocked—i.e., the damming up of all adult
observation, the inability to use anything in my daily life in New York
today, yet a deep personal necessity for such an outlet.

January 24: Jojo had an attack like epilepsy. By great good fortune both
Louise and I were here. He had made his own breakfast—cut grapefruit,
fried bacon and eggs, for first time, and said proudly to his father "I guess
this is the day you've been waiting for." Then he went to Italian barber by

---
* *The Locusts Have No King.*

himself, came in and said "Oh, I feel sick" and, looking frantically at ceiling as if he saw monster there, fell back rigid in chair with look of terrible adult pain on face.

Louise came in—he fell to floor—rigid, then with eyes closed lapsed into a kind of sleep-like unconsciousness. I could not get doctor—finally got police who commandeered ambulance with intern. These arrived as he came to. Afterward he slept off and on, exhausted, with pain in head and neck from rigidity. He said he had three in 1943, four in 1945 during insulin treatments. It was the day army radar touched the moon and he has always been affected by full moon.

Later he described other patients at Gladwyne. Miss Livingston, whom he likes, was a patient of Philadelphia General Hospital after divorce, then came to Gladwyne and works as scrubwoman for treatment. In his dormitory a 70-year-old Dr. Pike (long the urologist there until affected) sits and says "Just give me some scissors to trim my nails and I'll be all right." Another boy came in November, had electric shock treatments Tuesday and Friday and was cured by January. Jojo spent one night before the attack figuring out when Easter would be in 2040.

January 29: Did chapter on Moonlight on Rubberleg Square. 5 pages.

February 10: Party Sunday at Rumsey Marvin's for Dos. Later to Bunny's with Nabokov and Auden, etc.

Reginald Marsh at Peggy Bacon's, looking pale after a hernia operation and flu and four months on the wagon. He spoke of the pleasure of illustrating the Limited Editions' *U.S.A.,* for which he had done 442 drawings. (Dos delighted with the whole concept.) He had been interested in his operation—had taken local anesthetic and had mirror above so he could watch and later sketch his own interior. Said sadly: "But now I have no navel. It's a funny thing not having any navel. What about the beach? I'll look funny. And your ancestors. After all, it's the tie with your ancestors, isn't it?" He had not been scared during the operation but only when he thought—"Suppose the bastards stop in the middle of this and decide to go out and have a drink—leave me all open this way?" He had gone on the wagon because of his psychoanalyst. No, it was true he never drank a great deal, didn't care much about it really, but had terrible hangovers whenever he did drink, so why did he do it? The analyst said he drank to ingratiate himself with people—make rich people like him. So he stopped, saying "I'm not going to ingratiate myself with those sons of bitches. If that's why I drink, then I stop."

February 12: Mayor O'Dwyer shuts down entire city for tugboat strike. English war-brides arrive on Queen Mary and some are not claimed.

March 9: Examination by Dr. Norman Pleshette reveals necessity for operation—fibroid tumor. Scared me for while, then decided to balk same by hot salt. It might account for fuzziness in head.

March 11: This novel, now typed to page 42, should show the breakdown of a love affair and its reconstruction as new, after its seeming destruction has broken each person into his and her basic cells. Patches of love left. Now it is a work of art—a mosaic.

March 16: Clothes from New York can no longer be sent; folks back home have everything. Sentimental aunt who still thinks homefolks are barefoot.

Reshape first chapter showing more dream quality. Frederick like White Rabbit in a rush, not knowing where or how, already late.

Age of airplane crashes.

March 28: Heard Latouche and Jerry Moross' dance operas—very stunning. "Davy Crockett," "Willie the Weeper," "Susanna and the Elders" at Touche's apartment at the Chelsea—strange, elaborate, Gothic chambers, stained glass doors dividing odd halls.

March 31: Blew up Saturday night and quarreled with Peggy. It seemed outrageous at the time but I feel free and wonderful again. If she stays mad, I won't have that burden again—sort of a wife you have to do everything for after you're tired out from day's work. A calculating, shrewd but not happy operator who knows how to wheedle whatever she wants out of people but is not smart enough to know what to want.

I have often gone off-balance with someone after years of sizzling behind their back and burst out in what seems most unreasonable, unforgivable attack. Actually, it is all that saves my life. Instead of feeling guilty after my swing at Peggy, a great burden seemed off my mind. I regret being obliged to be a monster in order to preserve my sanity but I had to do it. Result—mind free and active and released again.

April 14: Met Mischa Resnikoff who was experimenting on hangover cures at Romanoff's. Alka-Seltzer, tomato juice, coffee, coke. Finally, baffled by stolid clerk, he says "Well, what do *you* do for a hangover?" "I just don't go there anymore," said clerk innocently. Later he said he was married and a married man didn't need to drink to have a hangover.

Mischa told of George Wettling, drummer who has taken up painting. Thinks it's wonderful. "How do you work?" Mischa asks. "Who taught you?" "Never had a lesson," said the drummer-painter. "I just go at it like I would go at my drums. Take the brush and go boom-da-da-da-da-boom-da-da-da-da and there's the picture." Somebody took him to the Modern Museum and he looked over all the paintings and said "I never knew there were that many drummers."

April 19: Large cocktail party. Someone took George Dangerfield's hat—left another. I asked Coby if he got his hats at Callahan's and he said, no, he got them at Dick the Oyster Man's and if they had none to fit he got them at Lüchow's. I heard he had been banned by Cedar Tavern and he said indignantly "No, I'm in very high odor there."

LeClercq said that all over Europe and Africa he ran into Ron Freelander and new wife. Rivals for Ron's first wife, they were thought to be friends and invited to all the same parties. Jacques said the habit of putting horns on Ron was so strong that he could hardly keep his hands off his head.

May 22: Freedom at last. Could not sleep for marvelous exhilaration. Good God—how long have I been a dope and how really stupid not to understand what has been obvious for at least 12 years! Now I can write.*

May 23: Off to Provincetown with Margaret. Colonial Inn. Stopped at Red Coach Inn, Middleboro for dinner.

June 29: Niles said he had a bad night. One thing he could never stand

---

*This entry remains enigmatic; certainly, there were no obvious immediate changes in Powell's day-to-day life.

was a dripping faucet and when he went to bed, maybe a little tight, he couldn't sleep because the goddam woman in the next room hadn't turned off her water. Angrily he called up the desk and asked them to ring up the next room and make her turn it off because he couldn't sleep a wink. What made him so sore at the hotel service was that next morning when he woke up the goddam thing was still on.

June 30: Atomic bomb test 6 P.M. Bikini. Bill Downs (NBC). Palms still waving. Words as bomb went off—"Bomb Away??" and "What Goes Here??" The tremendous fuss about "sharing our secret." Curious that all the to-do of our increasingly bigoted, money-mad, culture-hating nation about the atom bomb was not about the outrage of spending such billions on a gambling chance—this appealed to the gambling, wasting nation. But "sharing the secret with other nations"? The affair, badly broadcast but elaborately prepared for, might have been arranged, sponsored and paid for by our own big News Reel companies, broadcasting companies and newspapers. It appealed to Comic Strip public, a Buck Rogers, Li'l' Abner public, never outraged by folly or waste on such a gigantic scale but only by fear of a nation that dangerously prizes art and culture and brains—Russia—sharing and understanding it.

July 25: Bikini bomb again.

August 9: The book is a love story, the New York love story of a triangle marking time. The love story is serious and important and tragic to the people in it, but a matter of cosmic burlesque to all casual outsiders. Therefore the book has a serious main story in the setting of ageless laughter.

The human comedy is always tragic but since its ingredients are always the same—dupe, fox, straight, like burlesque skits—the repetition through the ages is comedy. The basis of tragedy is man's helplessness against disease, war and death; the basis of comedy is man's helplessness against vanity (the vanity of love, greed, lust, power).

August 30: Jojo returned to Gladwyne in very good condition.

September 30: Operation on uterus and tumor at Doctors Hospital by Dr. Norman Pleschette. Went into shock six hours after operation. Nurse called house gynecologist Ingraham, then Hartman, then Dr. Jericho, then my doctor and Dr. Powers—all surrounding me with plasma and my own blood—RH—in transfusion. I gather change to 76 over 46 very sudden and ready to slip out, then wild pulse up to 160. Pleschette, a witty sweet man, prepared to stay all night but I rallied. Knew I was low but confident of recovery in spite of ominous surroundings of doctors and nurses.

October 12: Out of hospital feeling fine.

October 14: From the nurses and my own memory of far-goneness and surrounding doctors a few hours after the operation, I deduce that I was near slipping overboard for a couple of hours or so, but the conviction of it comes now that I am fine with the enthusiastic triumph of waking every morning—a look-who's-here-look-who's-alive feeling by which the body itself betrays how close it was to vanishing.

The chief change in me, which is something I was despairing of, is a sense of command of destiny and material, a sense of freedom and arrogance. It is probably only natural that the body and hence the mind should be slowly weighted and oppressed by a foreign burden such as the tumor was and attached to the reproductive organs it crippled all creative and self-constructive faculties. Cut out I feel equal to anything and prize this feeling more than anything.

October 15: The complete meager spirit is Peggy's, though it is not a fault any more than you could call chill blood a fault in a fish. I have never heard her or known her to help any artist or human being or to advance their career one iota. In her cups a refreshing pure spring of hatred wells up for everyone's work and love and life but mostly this lies hidden under a demure mask of politeness. Her professional lady-likeness wins her everyone's help. Someone is always offering to get her an exhibition, to write good reviews of her, to get her lunch with publishers, to get her jobs, but she has never done any of those things for anyone else.

I recommended Elmore Lindsay to arrange insurance and annuity deals for the sale of her house. She took mild pleasure in confessing that she had been rude when he called and had said she needed no insurance, had a lawyer to handle her affairs and could not be bothered. I granted her right to rudeness but felt annoyed I had let Elmore in for this.

Yesterday, however, she called and told of having finished the sale of her house and making marvelous complicated arrangements for the money to go to her children. Mr. Lindsay had been wonderful about working out these deals and been most helpful. She made no reference to my having suggested Elmore and had indeed forgotten it—she had followed her usual amoeboid practice of ingesting the good people could do her with no feeling beyond complacency in her fine powers of ingestion.

November 13: Stanley Kent back from Europe—war-work in England, etc.—after 12 years. He remarked on Joe being fat and I said "Certainly he's fat. Don't you know there's a war on?"

1947

January 27: High blood pressure, sleeplessness, wound up as result of four months hospital and worry and desperate sense of inadequacy in every detail. Again facing hopeless years of good work never properly presented so that best years seem a riotous waste.

February 17: Did a great deal of work on novel with feeling of confidence and pleasure in it that I hope sustains itself. Also must do this year "Brooklyn Widow" play.

February 18: Very good writing day with new insertions clarifying the whole situation amazingly. I think this will be a really fine book and it is not handicapped by plot since the movement is human relations.

February 22: Reviewed wonderful book, Malcolm Lowry's *Under the Volcano*.

February 26: Went to meet Malcolm Lowry and wife. He is the original Consul in the book, a curious kind of person—handsome, vigorous, drunk —with an aura of genius about him and a personal electricity almost dangerous, sense of demon-possessed.

February 27: To Lowry's hotel for wine. Wife Marjorie in control—news he invoked voodoo god "Bucket of Blood" and ended up with hemorrhages and doctor saying he has hole in lungs.

March 2: So saturated with the violent contact with extraordinary devil-angel-demon-child Lowry that I made Joe go out in gray, snowy, rainy day, down through the deserted palaces of Downtown, to ferry, where fog wiped out Statue of Liberty—strange, desolate, After-The-Judgment-Day fog that rearranged distance.

Coby's new zipper doesn't work but he doesn't care as he says most of his friends are nudist swimmers anyway.

March 9: Up Riverside Drive. To Bretton Hall, where dreary new bar had P.A. system paging anyone. A foreign land here with accent Yiddish—much changed since 1920. Rules of conduct are different, pastry and ice cream shops jammed, ladies not allowed at bars in some places but must sit at tables.

March 11: This book today seemed dry and cold and dull though frequently it seems fine to me. Time to get it typed again. I believe clear division of chapters and parts will illumine it. Furthermore, there is little awareness of the city, in spite of descriptions. Smells, etcetera, are much lacking and I again sense the kind of work done by an afraid person, someone so disabled by fear and insecurity and other lacks as to make expression more and more desperately painful.

March 22: The German mother in Lüchow's who said "I hate my son. He was 18 pounds—I was in such agony. I said when they showed him, so you are my Pain. I hate you."

March 24: Days of Homer and Langley Collyer* case—the old home on Fifth Avenue. Could be, in complete purity, the Artist's Story. What series of professional disappointments did Homer have? Rival artist hermits have stacked their paintings in the barn, painted on and on—with the sympathy of their other paintings, their brushes, their canvases, their paints, their sweethearts and comforts—till the barn is filled with old sleighs, canvases, experiments in painting, hay, musty oats, dead animals, rotting stalls and the body of the artist.

---

*Homer and Langley Collyer, reclusive brothers, had been found dead in a Harlem townhouse so cluttered with papers and debris that it was compared to a rabbit warren.

March 25: Nothing makes you so infuriated as to have someone prefer friends who appreciate his virtues to you who can point out his faults.

An anthology for Temperance might be put out—Jesuitical, of course—pointing and quoting scenes of drinking in all sorts of work that explain the crime. *Under The Volcano*—Consul drunk. Without drink he would be prime minister. Norah Hoult's *There Were No Windows*—obviously old lady got mad through alcohol. Then comes a feeling of anger at the author who is so shrewd and sensitive as to spot vulnerabilities but has the harshness to expose them without real understanding. You feel suddenly "I like this old lady. I do *not* like her author. Her author is cruel to her." Once disliked, an author has a hard row presenting his case either way. In *Under The Volcano* you love the author for the pain of his overwhelming understanding.

March 29: The way all formal parties seem a masquerade.

April 2: The universal wish that this poor or drunk person could die—removing his personal nuisance value—so one could send a guilty enormous funeral wreath indicating appreciation of basic fine qualities.

The satisfaction mental cases and ignorant get from routine and meaningless rules.

Drinking very little past two weeks due to excitement over novel. Should have what I have typed and ready for Max by end of next week.

April 9: Looking over manuscript back from Perkins for new inserts, saw for first time note on envelope "O.K. so far but hasn't she overwritten as usual? Weber." "My friend" Mr. Weber has been fired and evidently Max has always disliked him—he was presumptuous, etc., lost manuscripts, wanted to be editor instead of business and occasionally went nuts. So his comment I'm sure annoyed Max as much as it amused me—Weber's tastes being wholly for detective stories.

April 12: This novel is a Hogarthian record of the follies of our day—Post War. Therefore more careful pictures should be given of apartment difficulties, rationing, conservation.

April 26: On the bus the Jewish voices—talk of someone "cracked" who writes poetry. Of how they wish they could get hold of $500 and then go over there, get black market prices for it and "live right." The longer the war the more cynical the individual becomes until, winning, all is lost. Actually, if the strength was not gone, the individual is now really ready to fight but this time for the cruel tangibles which are all the war has taught him.

April 30: Remember—this is a New York novel: city demanding success and rewarding it nobly, the fairy-tale city recognizing no age limit for love or success. Also a new technique of characterization of two lovers, showing what each thought of each other, of themselves, what their friends and mocking strangers thought of them. Make Rubberleg Square more clearly a voice above the main characters.

May 3: This technique of characterization is in real life—gossip of enemies, our own impressions, reconciliations as near life as possible, indeed the ideal I had once on West Ninth—that the person is so well-known as to be recognized in a crowd.

May 22: Had party for Lloyd Frankenberg's award from National Academy. Very good except no one to help serve. M. C. (whom I had met years ago creeping in and out of S. G.'s bedroom) kept saying in corners: "The idea of Dawn Powell giving a party for the National Institute of Arts and Letters simply *kills* me." I gathered that as a paid weekend lady she herself was in a better position for such activities.

May 26: In doing Marcia II it would be helpful to outline entire book with chapter subtitles as in Dickens novels.

June 4: Managed to do good job on Caroline's party chapter. This is really a fine book and it is fine to be able to believe it for a few seconds every few months.

June 14: Pete Martin is discovering that lumberjacks, stevedores, etc., are not—as is romantically assumed—inarticulate poets and silent sages but inarticulate bourgeoisie, silent stuffed shirts, uneducated reactionaries.

June 16: One of the most unreasonable and avoidable signs of age is the loud fury over some movement or philosophy that is *exactly* the same as that one you knew 20 years ago. It is necessary to remember your own happy adolescent shouts of Freudianism, surrealism, free versism, Coué-ism, etc., to a sour indignant cry of "Exactly the same thing as that 1903 theory—16 to one!—free silver!, etc., etc." Coldly and contemptuously you withdrew, for this time it was different (and it *was*). Something was added, something left out, and moreover, like a classic read by one person in varying situations in life, each time it had new meanings—its meaning is relative to its interpretation and its interpretation is dictated by conditions of the convert's times and added experience.

June 17: Max Perkins died. We had talked only a few days ago of Ernest Hemingway's troubles about his son Patrick.

June 22: Visited poor Portia again at Medical Center. She looks lovely and gay and since I have not seen her anything but tight and inarticulate for years I was ready to believe her present amused condition was encouraging instead of beginning of the end as doctors say. "Oh dear," she cried as pills arrive. "I get more pills every day."

June 23: Cosmo buying "White Tie," which I relabeled "Every Day is Ladies' Day." This—as sale of "Ideal Home" to *Story* indicates—shows what a lazy thing loyalty is. I should have the guts to send my stories around myself regardless of fear of interfering with Carl.

July 7: Jojo went back. Flying disks sighted.

July 8: I would like to do a juvenile story about a day nursery in the Marcantonio* district—people out on $25,000 bail—garment industry—waiting for the parents. Could be a movie. Crap games in street. Dark. Raising of money.

July 9: "The Loneliness."† Mrs. Vroon on roof in curlpapers talking across ramparts to "Jersey City girl"—an old lady across canyon in apron.

---

*Congressman Vito Marcantonio represented East Harlem, then a largely Italian neighborhood.

†This became "The Roof," one of Powell's best short stories; she also referred to it as the "Troupial Bird."

Mrs. V., a Staten Island girl (77 years old). Jersey City girl loves to bake apple pies. The life on the roof of the Devereux Apartments was a life by itself. Maid's rooms but very few maids. People's mothers-sons from away, father. Just give me some scissors to pare my nails and I'll be all right. No cigars, no cigarettes. Plants. Dog. Bronchitis. Boy with asthma. Sweatshop across. Garden. The two old ladies talking of past days in green fields. Point of view of shy old man—knows he keeps people awake but drinks in green fields through their conversation. The loneliness.

July 21: Traumatic Surgery school begins at Beekman-Downtown Hospital. "Flying Saucer Inn" opens in Hollywood. Dutch soldiers in Indonesia. U Saw displaced by British in Borneo and arrested. Nine assassinated. Gangster Age—not atom.

August 31: These are really numbing years, as if early years were unknowingly spent in a danger that pounces on you in middle age. The danger is not new—the tiger has always been there, the hot breath sometimes on your neck—but you managed to avoid it blindly. There is no longer any belief in your ability to cope with any problem—you see the defeat but must struggle as if you had faith. Indeed, you see the whole futility of struggle in a world where luck is king. Now the Income Tax has battered me down, the bank has expelled me. I cringe in stacks of notes, etc., confusion that could be helped by some single clear defender or believer—but nobody believes in anything now, not in themselves or in any other person. Is there no dignity left? no freedom except the freedom to buy a stranger a drink in a low bar? nothing you can do for any other human being except tip a waiter 10 percent?

September 6: Out to Murphys' for wonderful weekend of restoration chiefly through experiences of these miraculous two people. Gerald did a superhuman analysis job of getting me to brave ocean breakers—go out past first two without terror and this conquering of the deep is something. We did nothing but laze over stacks of *The Tatler* and *Sphere* and *Illustrated Sunday News*—all panning American films and drugging us with smiling pictures of the royal family.

September 9: With my usual contrariness the kick from the bank seemed to give me momentum and after a stimulating weekend at Murphys' I feel the first stirrings of excitement and certainty.

September 13: The dreadful news of the Dos Passos' auto accident—Katy killed, Dos losing an eye. Again the death news releases curious exhilaration—we are not dead but for that moment doubly alive, swooped up to heaven for a second with our friend's own spirit—to be crushed and saddened later. Was Dos born to be lonely—the lonely love child—finally snatching at the girl who was herself disappointed in love—no children (which he would have loved)?

September 21: Boston—Hotel Lincolnshire. I half-dreaded this trip to see Dos—poor eternal Orphan Monk—but the town itself beguiles me and the hotel Margaret sent me to is at Charles and Beacon—old Boston filled with old houses and Never-Changes, a beautiful, steadfast city, holding history and age and death in highest reverence.

This morning was Sunday. I walked across the Public Gardens (almost the only person there). A brilliant sunrise over the gold State House Tower at daybreak made me forgive the noisy, sleepless night. Coming upon the swan boats, their drivers like gondoliers, waiting, only a handful of children around. I thought of Katy and the swan boat as the funeral barge she herself would have picked.

Then I turned and came down Mt. Vernon Street—filled with great mansions, senatorial chambers, the Calvin Coolidge Law Schools, Barristers Chambers, Probate Bonds, with (down the street toward the river from Pemberton Square) a drunken man and a battered woman, indicating the secret of the Bostonian character—family home, dignified profession, whorehouses, taverns and churches, all in half a block.

Down Mt. Vernon Street—magnificent, silent (like Wall Street on Sunday or at night), no face at any window, the trees swaying like graveyard trees, slowly as if rockabye-baby ghosts were in the tree tops and dust must not be raised. A lawn bloomed on this gray lovely day with blue morning glories and I heard hidden organ music coming from the still green earth and trees and the great houses themselves as if all this was a gravely joyous welcome to a sweet, much-loved lady ghost, telling her to have no fear—here was an august ancient company, honored not doomed by death, and here was joy everlasting, a prize she was deemed fit to win. The wind carried off and then brought back the fragments of distant church music and there seemed a delicate consolation in remembering that she was an odd, fey creature, never to be wholly known or even guessed. Living, she had the quality of a lost legend, someone whose essence could not be captured, mercurial from imp to child to sphinx—as if, even when alive, she had been a visiting Soul.

In my room, church was over but a clear trumpet sounded in the lovely street below—hinting of Salvation Army without drums or song. The trumpet was a good one and it played "Redeem me, oh redeem me," I believe. I looked down and saw Major Barbara herself—a beautiful Titian-haired young girl in a gray, jaunty officer's hat, a strikingly chic figure in immaculately fitting tan jacket and jaunty skirt. Then another young girl with more brown than red in her hair but the same smart cap, figure. Sisters, I thought, when a third appeared with redder hair but the same Rockette figure all with collection plates and looking up with pale slender faces. Finally, what must have been the youngest appeared—very bright red hair and a striking blonde wool coat but the same fine legs and figure. Who was their father? What beautiful fallen woman had he married to produce these glamorous children—and how did he keep them in the Salvation business? I heard the trumpet long after they left—it seemed to carry on the funeral fugue for Katy and I cried, to my great surprise.

September 24: Boston. With Dos to "Man and Superman." Moved from charming room at Lincolnshire with its lovely neighborhood to Vendome —a gloomy, ancient Civil Warrish place with everything in the same tempo as the ancient hiccuping elevator.

Important thing in novel is the message that anything done for love is in itself enough reward and nothing is too much to do.

September 30: Decided to work entirely in my room for a while—breakfast there and start work early before any necessity for human contact. However this did not do any good beyond some revising and general going-over. I think the fault (not mine, of course) is repeated evidence of the lassitude and indifference of my publishers. Max was fond of me but really never pushed me—almost as if I was a relation he felt self-conscious about. Royalty statements say only seven copies sold; things like that discourage handing over new manuscripts to them. Must collect statements re: old novels and send to French publishers, also Russian.

Coby read me his review of Gide and it was brilliant and scholarly—belonged in a scholarly magazine rather than *Post*. He was very happy about this outlet and should do more—a salvation for him. How about anthology of America—Mrs. Trollope's impression, *Chuzzlewit,* Mrs. Stoddard, Rebecca Harding Davis?

October 4: Some people drink to make the people they're with turn into the people they *wish* they were with.

October 5: Trollope's autobiography interested me at last in his novels and he seems witty and adult, beginning as I am in *Phineas Finn.*

October 11: Gerald got back from England today very low and depressed. The finger of death which I saw on him (and which he saw) seemed deflected to Katy. In some ways I think G. has a pact with the devil, whom he admires as clear-cut, swift, a man of taste and matchless discrimination, a man of organization, whereas God is a lumbering, trial by error, dowdy person who drools in His beard and wears cotton neckties. Gerald believed England was sunk and he has such instinctive respect for form (indeed it's his lifeblood) that it made him sink.

October 19: Walking over to the East River Drive with Joe at night in rainy mist, seeing new houses of Stuyvesant Village rear up against old tenements, new stylish drive cutting through old streets, then the huge power plant—dark, oppressive, like a medieval forge—on to East River Park Drive. Silent boats and tugs gliding along, a body of man in doorway. This is set up for the "Ideal Home" story which would make a play.

October 20: Hollywood Investigation largely made up of Menjou pictures.*

November 4: Cocktails at John Wheelock's. In two meetings I feel closer to him than to Max or any other editor I ever had. Max was an admirable institution and of unquestioned integrity—even his enemies admitted it—but toward the last I had my private opinion that the word "integrity"

---

*HUAC had begun its investigation of subversion in Hollywood; Adolphe Manjou, a passionate anti-Communist, was an enthusiastic witness for the prosecution.

so universally applied to any businessman means that he has never done anything to jeopardize the firm's money. The word indicates a life run on fear—fear of losing his professional position; fear of making a financial error; fear of not showing an annual profit; fear of giving in to a brave artistic impulse. He always put a book's financial possibilities before anything else. His good judgment (primarily appraisal) lay in his strength to dismiss a manuscript of sheer artistic merit instead of plunging and employing his talents to persuade backing. How strange that his financial caution and his labor over such trashy works as Taylor Caldwell, Marcia Davenport, etc., should have given him the reputation for high artistic courage.

November 9: In the city of New York in this year 1947 it is still confusing morally and embarrassing to see a man or woman in two guises—sometimes with the lawful mate and sometimes with the lover. The small-town snicker, shock or curiosity is always present. The loyalties are stirred whether one knows the sinner well or not at all. The sense of the mate being wronged is always with us and if we know enough about it to side with the extra-marital set-up we feel a glow of revolutionary pride.

November 10: The Matthiesens, Fadimans, etc., somberly riding geniuses —the clumsy, overweight jockeys on the delicate Arabian steeds.

November 11: The moral of the story is that love must be guarded against the Destroyers, and that fidelity is romantic. Even unasked and unrequited, it is the great true romance, more compensatory and personally enriching than revengeful flurries and escapades which momentarily stroke the pride but only curdle the memory of what was pure and genuine in the true love.

November 16: Have been typing direct last chapters. Should have done it before since this book shows the danger of loose large pages and pen—no sense of permanency or responsibility since typist will type it and then I will change it again. Great waste of sheer physical labor and expense and sprawling of mind. Never work this sloppily again.

November 17: The old man's story (July 9). Memories of the war (in basement, Jap shortwave, numbers). My son came up to see me last week.

Escaped canary. Boys back from war. New teeth. Looks at painting left by artist to pay for new teeth.

November 20: See end of novel clearly now—day of atom bomb (Bikini). Lesson—cling to whatever is fine.

November 24: Jojo came home Saturday, looking fine, very set up over making money.

Josie Herbst's* reviews in Sunday papers were very close to me, though our writing is (God help her) not at all comparable. But there is a similarity in our themes this time—i.e., evidently critics find in her flaws of the kind I fear in my own present work.

November 28: Evidently life gets incredibly more terrifying—the childish "foolish" fears of the bogeyman waiting in the dark are sounder than any hope. Beaten—head bashed—knocked down—and the monster face at last revealed was my birthday present today.†

December 5: Stunned and frightened, Dos got me doctor, neurologist. Head no better. As if all forces, particularly treacherously loyal ones, were bent on keeping me from finishing book already at printer's. Too battered to raise willpower yet but hope to.

The accident happened on my birthday night—actually a culmination of controlled desperation and hysterics that would have led to some crisis anyway—stroke, pneumonia, etc.—for I had hysteria a week ago, feeling almost beyond my powers to go on alone.

December 6: St. Luke's Hospital. Lovely room—419. Arrived last night. X-rays this morning. General condition better but head more painful, especially horizontal during sleep when I had finally to have hypos.

December 7: Dr. Thomas (Samuel) is a charming, sweet, perceptive man. He says I was in very bad nerve condition quite apart from everything else when he saw me—my veins flat, my reactions bad, rock-bottom point of fatigue. I told him I knew I was from the curious shock-color of my

---

*Herbst's *Somewhere The Tempest Fell* had just been published by Scribners.
†Whatever happened to Powell on this date remains a mystery.

face and the odd, realistic images of my waking mind. He was very inter-ested and said these were exact observations of nerve fatigue—the clear, non-moving, images very different from the hangover illusions—the shock color—all of which told him of a bad case of shattered nerves.

December 15: Still in this wonderful hospital. Allowed company yesterday so had nightmares screaming in night and turned off guests today.

When (if?) I finish this book I want to do a quick play. Before that—or after finishing book here—I must figure out some kind of rest or deci-sion. I believe this is out of my hands and can only come through some restoration of sense of self-sufficiency.

December 22: Came out of St. Luke's Hospital. Woke up weeping at the prison of darkness—never day, never any view, nothing. Story here of woman with obsession, always polite but saying: "So dark—so dark—I find it very dark."

December 23: The difficulty of making people believe their eyes and ears. Faragoh (on a bus with me) called me a liar when I marveled at a lovely bright-eyed woman who suddenly got up and showed everyone her locket and said in a pleasant, conversational tone: "This is my son—imag-ine, only four years old—this is his picture—only sick a day—hardly four years old—he would have been four today—only sick a day—we had no idea—his hair was light but you see it looks dark in the picture . . ." She showed it to everyone, smiling quietly and got off the bus.

I was absolutely struck dumb by the implicit tragedy of the lonely lovely woman—Ophelia herself—not really convinced in a way except by the words repeated politely but without meaning as a child saying I'm sorry. There was the second marvel that nobody seemed surprised or in-terested; they might have been dead; they were like the ones in *The Lady Vanishes*. I wanted to run after her and say "How did it happen? Tell me about it if you like and I promise my heart will break too." I saw her hur-rying along the street, nicely dressed, slender, a bright, sweet smile fixed on her face the way they had told her to behave and I said to my writer friend excitedly "Good God, that *woman!*"

We went to someone's house and I described the strange, typically New York episode of the woman whose son had died—long ago or just now—and her gentle madness, and no one believed it. Francis said "This woman is the damndest liar."

I said, "But you saw her—you heard her—"

"All right," he said resignedly, "sure I saw her but the woman was crazy; she didn't know what she was saying."

"You saw her showing the locket," I persisted, completely bewildered that he should deny a fact he had seen.

"Sure, I saw that, too, but the woman was just crazy—why do you pay attention? It happens a million times a day." He persisted in calling me a "liar." I still am mad when I think of it and wonder again that we could ever have been friends, though friends are like food—one's palate and capacity and preference changes with education, travel, ulcers, and better opportunities for choosing.

1948

March 6: Arrived in Port-au-Prince *par avion.* Plane over Caribbean the most tremendous experience I ever had—all trivial things seemed explained in mountains, ocean bottom and the still, frozen surf. Death by air did not matter so long as it was in strange sea and mountain and clouds—a rainbow underneath. Marvelous Hotel Oloffson run by two Maurices—Maurice De Young and Maurice Morency (*noir*) with a mad Maurice in the kitchen, fed and cared for by De Young. Mad Maurice looked like a mad monk—eye-rolling, muttering and praying—washing hands gesture perpetually. De Young once in a while outfits him in clothes and mad Maurice says he will have to have a better place to live now that he looks so well.

April 2: Arrived home from Haiti after stopover in Miami. Difficulty in connecting planes, but at least time to clean up for New York and buy things I missed having in Haiti. Back home, dined at MacLeishes'—Dos and Murphys there.

April 9: I read my book with apprehension and was astonished to find it an admirable, superior work—no holes of plot as in other works—and a sustained intelligence dominating the farcical and exaggerated so that it had more unity and structural solidity than anything I ever did. In fact, a unique work, showing indubitable development. Advance sale is 3,000 before New York.

April 26: Book published today. Advance sale over 4,000. Lunch with Wheelock.

April 29: Dorothy Speare had party for me, very pleasant. Maurice De Young arrived from Haiti and came to party. Orville Prescott had given me fine review in *Times* and was there.

May 4: A long period of Not-Doing and very wearing indeed, for the exhausting business of friendly daily exchange takes ten times more out of me than ten hours of solitary writing. Women—good God—telephoning, yapping of nothing—just to keep somebody from working. Knowing it or not, the general ambition of all women is to prevent somebody from working. In order to duck these exhausting, grueling telephone demands I daresay I must get up earlier and get up to room before they nip into me completely. Have enough interruptions of my own choice without being prey to all these others.

May 6: Johnny Faulk, Dorothy Speare, Dr. Bob Feldman and others came in. Doctor looked at my peeling palms which have buzzing numbness and he said "leprosy"—numbness and lesions are sign of it. However it takes four years to incubate.

Reports of next week's reviews—*Sun, PM* and *Times* are very favorable. Most important of all, I sat next to Van Wyck Brooks at "Inside U.S.A." the other night and he said he had just read *My Home Is Far Away*—thought it was a perfectly wonderful work, and description of funeral was one he could never forget. I was so dazed by this belated encouragement of a work that almost threw me completely by the indifference of its critical reception, that I found the very bad, noisy but genial show very fine.

May 24: Gist of criticisms (Diana Trilling, etc.) of my novel is if they had my automobile they wouldn't visit my folks, they'd visit *theirs*.

Again there is the shaking of heads over not writing about "nice people—people one likes." *Who* likes? *I'm* doing the work. I write about people *I* find interesting, largely because they are often representative. My readers and critics never recognize themselves. I find this country monstrously hypocritical—absolutely unable to stand the truth. A sort of ignorant belief in Party Manners for book people. It is only within the last years that the speech of fiction characters even approximated life. Our reader approach to a book was much as it was to a sermon in the wilderness on the sins of the city—we would have scalped a minister who spoke of the sins of the wilderness.

Mrs. Trollope wrote of America in 1830s, said our men spat tobacco over floors, ladies sat in one room while men had good time, etc. All very good reporting as borne out by everyone but we were in a fury about it, implying the truth as it did—that the body of our population was a rugged, pioneer lot, without education. So we scream "Lies! Lies!" 75 years later, Mark Twain does the same thing but it's then Great Humor.

May 26: If I were a child today I would certainly never read anything handed to me as "in my age group." The only use for juvenile reading discipline is attractively dissembling castor oil of geography, arithmetic, and government. The point is that attention of censors, book clubs, parents should not be wasted on readers but on people who don't like to read. They should be subtly cajoled by selected books into pleasures of reading—once there they find certain authors or subjects that appeal and seek them out of an undictated field.

Ever since *Lady Chatterley's Lover* it has struck me that the forces of censorship are not against the immoral suggestions in the book but against the high literary quality of the work which enrages certain readers, forcing them to face their impregnable ignorance.

Here is the real outrage: that there are mysteriously privileged people who find inexplicable delight in books—consolation, laughter, comprehension, beauty—and the Censor or Proctor does not. He is sure of the only print that has ever stirred him—the four letter word; unable to arrest his superiors for pleasures he cannot dream of, he arrests them for the one he can. There has seldom been a period when so many "lusty" books have been printed and published; only those with intellectual qualities palatable to superior intelligences have been in trouble—not the masses of others bumblingly produced for non-readers (the drugstore-bookworms, that is, who expect contraceptives and bubblegum thrown in with their books).

Actually, the attack is on reading. You find it constantly. The chronically stupid mother or father or teacher, incapable of concentration, is driven to frenzies of temper by the clever child's absorption in any book. The parent is prepared to rage at the child's indifference to righteous book-learning; he is prepared to beat an education into his young, a position that still allows him his superiority. But what can be more galling than to find the child constantly demonstrating the independence of his ideas? Therefore, the books must be suspected, destroyed or hidden. For the intelligent, eager reader, no evil suggestion carries any force unless the entire literary tone of the work appeals in other ways to his critical eye.

For the naturally perverted child or adult no censorship can prohibit or protect. They will find phalluses in every chimney, a "September Morn" in every cloud.

May 30: Weekend at Libby's place Treetops in Stamford with innumerable leaping, squeaming lads—Latouche, Bobby Lewis, etc. The dogs. The playpen. The lovely Clarice (English refugee girl who looks after children).

June 7: Only recently, after prodding, goading, lashing myself on for years, have I reached a wonderful Nirvana—there is no hurry; there is time to think, to read, to study, to observe. Only in the actual practical building of a novel is there need for haste.

June 16: The artist who really loves people loves them so well the way they are he sees no need to disguise their characteristics—he loves them whole, without retouching. Yet the word always used for this unqualifying affection is "cynicism."

A self-made writer outlines a plot with a point he wishes to make already laid out in his mind, oblivious to the freedom of character development and conflict. The genuine novelist thinks of one item and it magnetizes a thousand details of sky, earth, reflection and connecting links that give it richness and the radiance of life.

July 12: Weekend at Margaret's at Niantic. These ferociously exhausting weekends are wonderful because there is no possibility of thought. Consequently, the unconscious works and now I believe the second Marcia novel can be done. Most important is to arrange its capacity for standing on its own. Above all this must be more than nostalgic as *Home* was. It must be as powerful as *Dubliners,* say. The growing powerfulness of the main character plotting to control fate as a Disraeli plots to control an empire.

July 17: After these weekends, a weekend in town is a luxury, selfishness itself. The travel to and fro, the housework, the drinking, is not so much but the incredible exhaustion of three or four days without one minute, day or night, of real privacy—being a hostess or guest every minute, like a long-distance dance marathon, waking to the trivial exchanges, the talking with no mind, the impossibility of thinking and the struggle to survive not the hostility but the friendship of others.

The greatest prize the world has to offer is the privilege (without the obligation) to be alone. I don't think anyone who pretends to know me knows that solitude for at least five hours—no human interchange— is my iron lung, without which I could not get through a day, let alone any work.

July 18: In spite of half-promising both Jed Harris and Paul Streger that I will do *Locusts* play, I do not feel like going over same material.

I would like to do the American Widow*—the bereaved widow of a solid, stodgy Babbitt; his death releases her; she hides travel folders, records to which she dances rhumba alone. Everything stranger tells her she applies at once. He can be a quick Broadway type—instead of thick type. Everything he does quickly and casually changes her—from quiet cool virgin to ballerina.

After he has changed into Elk, etc.—and discouraged her from her brief fling ("Don't use this or that; fix your hair"), she is puzzled—back to early obedience but somehow sad. End with her playing gay record and dancing. Husband objects. She says "But Harry used to like it." "Nice," he says. Or else she weeps—"How I miss Harry!"

July 20: The bus stopped, held up by driverless bus filled with colored people in middle of Fifth Avenue and 14th Street. On street lay— sweetly—a pretty, painted young colored girl, eyes open, covered with blood, face bloody, pool of blood beside her. Big shirt-sleeved colored man, hands held up—cop with notebook. Perhaps big colored man is driver. Eyes open, still, perhaps dead. No one must touch. In an accident the victim is immediately the guilty one—as well as the quarry.

The girl's body—gay in five o'clock, after-work, date clothes—stayed with me. Everyone from then on stayed colored and I wanted to say:

---

*This is yet another version of the "Brooklyn Widow" play, which would obsess Powell to the end of her life but was never completed.

Laugh, shop, select the paper cocktail napkins for the party but Flora—your sister, your wife, your daughter, your neighbor—lies in blood in the middle of 14th Street and nobody dares move her, it is the law. So here is her audition, her picnic, her date. Continue jostling, arguing over the dinner—pretty Flora will not be there. You do not know the truth and so she lives a little longer, cheating a little.

July 26: Thought of ruination of material through immediate "angling." Short piece on someone disgusted with their own country's bigotry and unfairness they tentatively decide to go live with foreign friends but find foreign friends just about to approach *them*. This point could be brought into the Widow play. However, here the pay-off is that the foreigner does not realize that neighborhood children call him (or his nationality) Hunky or dirty Swede. End play with his already becoming American enough to say—we don't want any foreigners. Widow ends slowly chilled; he has turned into Harry. This is very good. Should be mapped out and should be done.

Incredibly discouraged and bleak about everything, including novel. What use doing another when entire Scribners outfit so oblivious? No real life anywhere—except from reviewers who praised, but no decent proofreading, editorship or anything else. A few weekends with friends have exhausted me; all fairly ignorant, so there is no intellectual stimulation.

August 1: Trying to do *Bazaar* article in a state of frigid hatred toward everything—due, I now see, to humiliation of no longer being independent. It affects my whole ability to write anything. To be in the same position that I was at 12—unable to have haircut, soda pop—ridiculous at my age; ridiculous to be unable to help anyone, to repay a kindness, buy a jar of cold cream, to have to ask always. Moreover, the August month is usually horrible and I no longer have capacity for dealing with it. The only sure thing is this article, which must be done with arrogance or not at all, yet even my words I spend cautiously.

August 2: At this point Carl Brandt telephoned. *Today's Woman* had bought "Devil's Grip" story for $900. Immediately the town looked finer than ever, and the prospects ahead for August even finer.

September 14: Took Seconal last night and slept late for first time in ages, waking up calm instead of rigid. Important for creative process since it is continuation of dream and when sleep is tense, *working* half sleep, there is no change of water.

Thought of gentle story with Haiti overtones as new novel. Odd how eventually you say you've met someone fine and old friend says "What? George Frank? I knew him 30 years ago!" As if in time, as we change our groups, we filled our hands with our friends' discards.

November 2: Sat up listening to Election results.

November 8: For hundreds of years (it seems to me) I have wished above all to be where I love with those I love doing what I love—and, after that, let us have the professional respect of those I respect, few as that may be. After these last, bitter, hundred years I find that no quality or achievement is respected or loved unless it brings money. I have doubtless bent my wishing powers to the direction most scorned by the gods. The desire for money with its attendant power is paramount for respect.

Above all I do not want to end like Rosie, fearing one thing—insanity—all my life, getting secure and far from it, then, sure enough, there comes the childhood bogey which has lurked behind every curtain waiting for the final weakness—that final sense of security—when its dread familiar face conquers at last.

The curious pleasure of age for the writer is in examining mistakes. I admit mine at last—it was the fear of vanity. I should have been more vain and shouted my merits to the skies. I have been outsmarted by my own peasant shrewdness and am not sure there is any chance of change.

Considering the horizon now, I see abstractly that certain gestures would have been wiser—appearance in *New Yorker* oftener, solely to impress New York editors since I question its worth per se. I feel it has ruined more authors than it has made.

November 9: Examining all my Marcia material and decided too confused—due to rhythm of writing interrupted by many desperations. High point to remember is that this is to be a female *Jean-Christophe.* Trying all kinds of careers for her. It is obvious that the type is primarily writer—but my repugnance to the writer-heroine is largely that fictionally they always win a prize and their triumphs are in limousines.

The kind of writer I am should write fast and with complete immersion—not coming out so often for recapitulation, criticism, etc. What I should do is write steady on Marcia—conceivably planning to finish it by February 1.

November 15: I was thinking it takes an awful lot of material to make a good tailor, a lot of dead men to make soil, and a lot of good playwrights spoiled to make a successful producer or director. Anyway, when I look at successes by Cheryl Crawford, Harold Clurman, etc., I realize how well they fed on me as their laboratory guinea pig. As they are infinitely inferior individuals, they can only learn by laying waste (as they almost did me and others) first-rate talent; in this manner they learn, in a shrewd sub-normal way, how to succeed themselves.

November 16: Turned in short story—"Too Old To Change"—to MCA. Not very good except a light, likable, farcical story with reasonable base. Would make a movie—also would probably sell to several kinds of mags.

I slept wonderfully, dreamed of all the dead—the Mulligan sisters, Gretchen, Grandma, etc. Telephone insistence finally woke me and I read at *Scarlet Letter,* being astonished at something never mentioned—i.e., the sheer workmanship, research of it, the long-range creative process behind it so that a town in 17th century New England could come alive like a genre painting.

One reason for my writing difficulty is my final weary surrender to the enemy—the insistent telephone early in morning when the modulation from sleep to writing is being made. For years I have made scenes at Louise's morning chat; I have hidden, sulked, but finally fatigue forces me to be polite and then the dream life is blown to bits. I even assist in it now and can spend hours telephoning myself. The enemy has won but I may win again if I have money or any minor triumph that gives me the confidence to be rude.

November 18: In the dream the man said "Now I should like three pictures of you—one standing up behind the chair, one sitting down in the chair—"

"And one sitting on myself on my lap," I said, the three selves in the picture already all clear to me.

November 22: Almost the only privilege allowed by Scribners publishing me is one of using their store where the clerks are unusually nice, presided over by a fine, huge, book-loving Belgian who knows more about literature than anyone in the editorial department. I bought Melville's English journal, in which I was fascinated by his references to the greatness of DeQuincey's *Opium Eater.* Home, I read *Opium Eater* and found it wonderful—simple, mounting dramatic story told in a style that now is modern again, like the Oxford Movement confessions or *Lost Weekend.* A good thing for a magazine to run old novels whose manner or matter has become fashionable again. Clear, living, inherently dramatic but superficially simple and unpretentious—the undercurrent of fantasia makes it an *Under the Volcano* in reverse.

November 27: Sylvia Marlowe's concert. Later Stella Adler's—Stella looking lovely and vain as she should. Portrait of her in bedroom in rococo, luscious (almost lush, almost blowzy) style, and I said "Very good of you." "Why is it good?" she angrily demanded. "Because it looks lush and arrogant." She almost stamped her foot. "I am *not* arrogant. I'm only a little Jewish girl in a big hat!" she stormed.

The professional Jewishness struck me again. She was going to be the poor little Jewish girl on the East Side, the Jewish intellectual, the Jewish pushcart, the Jewish banker and the Queen of Sheba—claiming as her personal treasure everything Jewish, bad and good. Actually, she is above all the Actress (not very good and seldom on the stage), just as Leonora Corbett assumes everything British as her private due, when she is not anything human or national or racial—but Actress.

November 29: Dream of a talking dog, a tan, close-haired dog with spaniel face, standing on hind legs and desperately trying to tell me something. "All right, if it's so important, speak," I challenged, thinking of course I know this is a dream but here is where dreams end, when it gets tough. But this dream dog was very clever. He moved his mouth and I saw he was forming words and not making a fool of himself by *speaking* so I was obliged to lip-read. "Dawn, Dawn"—his lips moved and his forehead was wrinkled with a colossal effort. He said something which surprised me in the dream though it was trivial—something like "Keep your powder dry"—but I could not carry it over to waking even though I woke myself at once.

December 1: Sore throat. Have been taking walks and getting out alone in daytime (I daresay sore throat comes from that) and with tremendous effort have decided that part of anguished writing of past few years is due to staying too close to it. For a long time I have stayed so close to my work that I come out like a mole frightened of any new face, scarcely able to get around in a simple ten-cent store. The outside life becomes a tremendous effort, a tightrope—what clothes do people wear? how do they say how-de-do? Now I go out almost every day—usually to the East Side, marketing. Vitamin pills help, too (niacin and thiamin chloride).

December 2: Cato the Elder (Plutarch's Lives) says there is great difference between a reasonable valor and contempt for life.

Sybarite says no wonder the Spartans are brave in battle; death releases them from their arduous privation, labor and wretched food.

Thoth (the Greek Hermes) discovered the lyre by stepping on the tendons of a dead tortoise.

Primitive flute fashioned from bone of an Irish elk. Whistle of reindeer bone. Carlos of Guiana—jaguar bones for flutes. Gamelan—Javanese bells sounding like string orchestra.

December 5: This year and last have been age of the notebooks and journals—the promissory notes of the artist, as in international lending operations. James Notebooks—Trollope—Wharton—Delacroix—Melville. The Hasty Age (big business and Hollywood influence): we buy the prospectus because we have no time for the finished work.

December 7: I Shot My Arrow / Into The Air / It Fell To Earth / I Know Not Where—so I, spent Bow with lost, futile arrow, have no alternative but sleep.

Should follow old procedure of two pages a day during doldrums.

1949

January 1: Jojo went back to Gladwyne after week being better than ever at home.

January 2: Friendship in youth represents sympathy without understanding; in age, understanding without sympathy. ("I know too well all the sorrows and frustrations of your life, old chap, but they're no worse than mine and at least *I* deserved better.")

January 8: The enemy (for a creative writer) is the tired tolerance born of fear of middle age. More and more perfectly deserving people demand more and more time, energy, expense and sheer justice and one asks one-self—with the cosmic judicial sense of the grave's nearness—is one's own work worth more than these importunations?

But the truth is, it *is*—and making oneself a blotting pad between others and their certain destiny serves no good to anyone. More sheer waste in the exhausting give and take of trivial daily contacts than in a thousand nights of revel. In these, at least, one is lost and therefore preserved.

This year I am determined to keep Louise from ruining each day. It doesn't matter what happens after five—it's the easy modulation from dream into waking and working that matters to the writer.

January 9: Read *Daniel Deronda* last night, with astonishment at the mighty grasp of mind and sheer character-novel technique of George Eliot. First, the mature super-intellectual avenue to the story—the masterly handling of character growth, psychological balances better than any other writer, showing bad and good equally and dispassionately. Then, once story and people are in motion, the superb storytelling—equaling Balzac and de Maupassant, Dickens and Thackeray—but more educated, more profound and searching, less plain padding and driveling—and less charm. More formidable and, now that I near the end, less memorable, less important characters with somehow more mediocre fates. I wonder if she connected with Disraeli at any time—for *Vivien Grey* somehow suggests much here.

January 22: Persistent headache, buzzing and numbness which makes me wonder if some clot is there. Luncheon—very jolly—with Jonathan Cape.

February 19: The doctor. If you don't drink, then a little whiskey. If you don't take barbiturates, then do. In fact, take everything so later it can be taken away.

February 24: Since February 3rd, lost in pain of pleurisy—broken ribs— pain—then Feb. 20 broken finger and more pain. Either pain or codeine. Pain killers deadening brain to complete sub-cellar.

March 27: Came into St. Luke's on Dr. Robert Solley's say-so and feeling near well on sheer confidence. Whatever happened dulled the senses so much that I continue to be about 200 percent below normal mentally and for first time understand boredom, empty-mindedness.

March 28: Reading Mary McCarthy's *Oasis*—a curious book and a curious talent. Characters (though report has it taken straight from life as to names, jobs and physical attributes) are strained through her earnest studies in literature till they are only well-turned phrases. The well-dressed words consort with nature and philosophy, curtsey, fence and draw sawdust from each other (if not library dust). It is a dry, juiceless gift, intense over trivia, conscientiously literary in unliterary situations among unliterary people. The drive is the agonizing one of earnest, sincere people striving desperately beyond their decent mediocrity toward some vague heaven of mind they are incapable of even imagining. Whether McCarthy, limited in imagination and human understanding, takes characters and situations as trite and trivial as possible so as to give her words the stage (conveying images or communicating warmth does not interest her) or whether she is ignorant of values, literary and human, I don't know. Curious how blank and dusty this well-written piece is.

April 4: Operation for chest cyst. Five hours on table, three transfusions, oxygen tank, infusions, etc. Nurses very nice.*

April 20: Returned from St. Luke's Hospital to home. For first time as I sat in living room looking around a wave of realization engulfed me of what had happened to me and what had *almost* happened.

May 2: Third day of feeling like work. Telephoned Phyllis to find out about Mabel who is having bad time.

May 16: Pressure of women pals calling and whoopee involved drives me fortunately into work-mind. What about a play? Dreamed last night of Terry Helburn at a table in large wings of theater discussing play. To show what she wanted she had a play done for me—a huge Romanian hotel was pushed up and costumed figures emerged in songs.

Thinking of my constant wariness of being drawn into the smart, well-dressed life. It is really not fear of its demands but the knowledge that when your work is important you choose love, friends and social life that leaves you free for your work. Certain groups require you to think about clothes, accessories, hours, appearances and manners that by themselves would take up all of your time and prohibit the work of your choice.

May 17: How little people change their views and how strangely their views suddenly take living shape and dog the person. I recall my views on the family, my anguish as a child over anyone scolding or nagging and at that time I saw more young scolding the old—Gretchen vs. Auntie May, Mabel vs. Grandma, Papa vs. his father—than parents vs. children.

When the other children were saying how many children they were going to have (as we skipped rope) I said "I don't want any children. All

---

*The growth on Powell's chest—variously diagnosed throughout her life as a heart attack, a cancer, and a tumor—was finally revealed to be a teritoma, a tumor with vestiges of teeth and hair that had been growing within her. It was removed. Powell always believed the tumor to have been her partially formed twin.

they're good for is to be mean to you when you're old." Later I wrote themes on how the State should look after children since parents were bad for them and they should always be institutionalized. So what? My child is in an institution.

I learned (from family berating others in family I loved) that nothing endangers a child's peace or balance more than disparaging remarks about people they love. It bewilders them: "You love me but you do not love this other person who belongs to me, who is good to me?"

June 5: Arrived at MacDowell Colony after night in Winchester, Mass., with Margaret.

June 7: A title would be valuable as nudge to novel.

June 15: MacDowell Colony. Wood Studio.

Must remember that my creative brain works only when it's working, not when it's thinking. Writing begets writing.

July 2: Party at Bunny's with Isaiah Berlin, an Oxford don, Geismars, etc.

July 8: Coby very depressed, surprising in view of his change of office from seedy Third Avenue to 45th Street near Times Square. Finally he broke down—he was very near tears—and confessed. He said the old place—under the Third Avenue El near 42nd Street—had depressed him each morning when he went to work because everywhere lay the bums drifted up from the Bowery, lying sodden or bleeding in the gutter or in shop doorways, bandaged heads, ragged or, if well, begging. Something the matter with everyone in the area—paralytics, idiots, lepers, hunchbacks, dwarves, all desperate and grim.

"But I *liked* them," said Coby. "I understood them and I pitied them. But in this Times Square neighborhood it is much more depressing. For a while I couldn't figure out these long lines of people, some going that way and some this, all standing in line at 9:30 in the morning. But it turned out they were just waiting to get into a movie—any movie. Some were reading newspapers, or watching the sights, but none of them seemed nervous or excited about waiting around. They were just happy to be there standing in line like everybody else to see a movie everybody else was seeing. Now, when I get up—no matter when—I'm tired already and all I have to do is go to an office. But those people get up at crack of dawn and come from Astoria and the four corners of the world to sit through an awful movie at ten o'clock—in the *morning,* mind you. I've tried and tried but I just don't understand it. The Bowery bums I could understand but these people I can't and I feel as if I was in a world of monsters and I hate it."

July 12: It is important in Marcia novel to make it alive, undated—not a period piece. Not only do I have no desire to read of things relating to past (dead) but I freeze in my tracks at idea of writing it. This is undoubtedly one major difficulty with Marcia. To offset this, emphasize character and emotion and interrelation of same more than anything else.

Moral:

1) Those you idolize betray you—you must always expect betrayal.

2) Circumstances and other conflicting laws oblige you to betray those you idolize.

July 14: The month at MacDowell did one thing which I must have known instinctively it would do—it allowed me to revise beginning of novel and see where it might lead. The introduction and the thousand desperate, exhausted revisions had set it in dull tracks and prevented the mood and quality I demanded from emerging.

August 15: Broke with MCA on finding they had lied or got mixed up on where my stories were. Said the one had been at *Today's Woman* for two weeks but hadn't even been sent. Had it copied and sent up myself.

August 19: Finished story "The Mermaid in the Punch Bowl" and took to *Cosmopolitan.*

August 25: Peters sent notice of "Blonde" story, check for "Women's Own" from National City Bank. Heard *Today's Woman* had bought story. Big day.

September 11: Louise away so I sleep—constantly elated. Decided to put short stories on market and having them typed now.

September 23: Wheelock turned down short-story collection. Am confident it will sell with proper presentation but do not want irritation and necessity for upsets, arguments and defenses by publishing elsewhere, involving switch of novel publisher. However do need some support.

October 10: I have so often thought of Alfred Downing Gray and wondered what became of this promising lad. Some place in China, perhaps, or doing very well on a Caribbean isle. At seven, he was the child prodigy in Shelby. Later a figure of ridicule because of his arty and theatrical side, yet there he was—a potential Bing Crosby or Maurice Evans. A novel about him, perhaps.

October 14: It occurs to me that I have been "winding up" for the last few years and not very well at that. Partly personal hidden desperation but mostly the lack of support in my writing. I could scarcely buck the Scribners indifference—and yet I do not seem ready to change.

October 16: Possibility of short novel based on Brooklyn widow. Change locale—near Yonkers.

October 24: Today I decided to deny the barrier between me and my proper home—the novel—by giving up this formless second Marcia book as so much petit point to be done another day. It is not necessary to do the nostalgic child book. Max was bad for me in that way. I cannot feel at home there. I *am* New York—this minute—now. I know more about it than anyone—not historically but momentarily. I must do a New York novel to be happy—one in the *Magic Wheel* series. Suddenly I remembered meeting Glenway Wescott in the Lafayette and he said how much he liked *The Locusts.* "No one but you," he said, "is doing for New York what Balzac did for Paris." It illumined my whole disorder.

October 26: Mabel died at 9:50. Yesterday morning I was waked by dream [entry breaks off].

October 29: Mabel's funeral.

October 30: Shelby. Home from Galion.

November 7: Sara's birthday. Dinner and "Kiss Me Kate."* Dr. Solley in A.M. and novocaine daze.

November 8: I should like to do a love story because in this country love seems disappearing. Our books are defensive and guilty books, but not love. One story like Henry Green's *Loving* from England shows the marvelous freedom and exhilaration that comes from that topic. In self-consciousness of the material solidity of this country, novelists write first of simple working man; then, with pompous head-shakings, of racial equality; then, let us return to God and the Vatican and do good in slums with prayers—but nowhere is there love. *Tenth Moon* showed what could be done.

November 11: Weekend at Snedens with Murphys. Marvelous weekend. Heavenly river—elated. Gray day—the undersea feeling, the black trees stripped to the black-rot roots of hell itself—the Gerard Manley Hopkins poems. Wonderful. Send my roots rain.

November 17: Odd thing about a death in a family—the values shift and become topsy-turvy; truth long-lost emerges or is, until some other death, submerged. Mabel gone; suddenly Phyllis—hitherto seen as anti-Mabel or everything I chose to imagine—has the eccentricities I used to fasten on Mabel.

December 13: Did revisions on Marcia beginning. Remember early conception of her willing her own destiny. Captain of my soul—the *willing* and *shaping* of a person's destiny.

---

*What Powell thought of this enormously successful version of her old "Taming of the Shrew" musical idea is not recorded.

1950

[*Undated*] Minced some four-letter words.

The infallible rule—when one is below par, apprehensive, harassed, one resents time wasted on anything or anybody but the finest. A feeling of complacency enables one to relax and even delight in common pleasures and inferior companions—assuming one's superiority is acknowledged (instead of envied or resented as among one's peers) and one's presence is bestowing wondrous joy on awed yokels.

January 7: To Snedens. I had read the Mizener Fitzgerald biography,* mentioning Murphys many times—once regarding their "wealth, great charm and social position." I was impressed but less so as I heard Gerald refer to this very phrase for what was evidently not the first time. This is what happens when people withdraw, tired of their glory—they have to spend all their restored energy telling new people about it.

Sara was cross because Gerald had told so many stories about Scott that put him in such an unfavorable light—the one about kicking the basket of nuts for sale off the poor old peasant's head. "You should have told the end of the story," scolded Sara; when I asked, she replied "Why, Scott went back and *apologized*." But the argument grew more complicated as Sara stubbornly declared she would not read the book because of unfairness to Scott. "I'm sure Mizener got most of his stories from other sources," Gerald defended himself. "After all, Hemingway was one of his best friends." "Not after he got tired of Scott breaking into his apartment and wrecking it," Sara retorted. "You know perfectly well Ernest had to throw him out."

---

* *The Far Side of Paradise* by Arthur Mizener.

"Of course Mizener is by no means a perfect reporter," admitted Gerald. "In the story about Scott throwing the ripe fig he neglected to say it was at the Princesse Cassini—the whole point of the story." "I don't consider the story worth repeating," icily stated Sara. "Scott was always throwing ripe figs at people." (This story could be combined with the steady resentment each person has about other friends appropriating a dead celebrity.)

Sara's persistent defense of Scott—"But why didn't anyone tell Mizener how much he liked Thomas Wolfe?"—revealed how rarely he liked any other newcomer, how envious and vain he really was probably. The way one tells of Katherine Cornell hiring private plane to rush a Vineyard fisherman and wife to her New York opening (how generous! how simple!) though she would never consider giving free tickets to a poor suburban neighbor or young actor.

January 11: Anxious to get into novel with both feet. Must remember that I do not write by planning but by writing. Loving does not come by waiting for an object worthy of love but by loving.

Lunch with Dos and I gave what I considered a cheery talk on New York gossip and gaiety at end of which Dos said "Good God, Dawn, you make my hair stand on end."

January 16: Large letdown after exhilaration of new typewriter and agent and stories when Ivan called to say stories too slight to submit. However *Today's Woman* asked for them and I recommended *New Yorker*—after that, *Cosmo.* An underlying sunk feeling too great to even be faced. When I look over this novel I enjoy it but get no further—lucifying past chapters, whittling really. Some kind of outside support is really needed to give me confidence. If I cannot write—if that pleasure is crushed out of me—then I might as well have been finished off by my operation.

January 29: A lovely, remote time at Murphys'. They spoke of Elsa Maxwell and how she raised money for Russian Ambulance in World War I, absconded with money, then returned to social success after three years. How a friend, Lily Havemeyer, had a caller who brought Miss Maxwell to lunch. Elsa looked over place—marvelous for party—said to Lily (first meeting) "You go shopping for the day and leave me your servants, your house and carte blanche and at night you will find yourself with a party all Paris will talk about." "No" was all Lily said.

Sunday, Gerald played irreplaceable records—"Le Bouef sur le Toit" of Les Six—Poulenc, Milhaud, Satie, etc.—and novelty comic records of Florence Desmond, Budgery Carr, Arthur Marshall, etc. Very gay. Apples in bourbon on chafing dish and artichokes.

In life of Edward Young, biographer says Young started to deliver sermon but so much noise and conversation that the vain man "in pity for their folly—laid his head down and wept."

Gerald reading Sir William Maxwell edition of *The Creevy Papers,* which I glanced at and became fascinated, especially at Mrs. Creevy's letters to her husband from Bath in which she refers to "that Wicked Pavilion"—the place everyone enjoys till after midnight, drinking so they cannot get up till noon, and then with heads.

January 31: Started novel about Cafe Lafayette. Wrote seven pages. Called *The Wicked Pavilion*. If this goes it will be due to Murphy weekend—early bed in strange, river atmosphere and without the dull callers. The Murphys are superior, intelligent, superficially liberal, gay, resourceful people, but only when alone or with old friends of known gaiety. They would never *impose* gaiety.

February 4: Free enterprise. Coby sees laundry boy taking all his laundry. He says "Have you brought the other?" The boy says "Have you the money?" "I have no money," says Coby, and boy takes off with clean and dirty alike because under free enterprise no man says the truth—"I can't afford" or "I have no money" or "I'm drunk." They say "I'll send you a check tomorrow. I have one in the mail," etc. And, even knowing it is a lie, the other is appeased. But there is no place in our American economy for the true word. It comes like an insult and a defiance.

February 6: Delighted with new novel—*so far*—as it seems to have already been written in my head waiting for the title (and focal point of the Lafayette) to release it.

How wonderful to feel it again—the wheel beneath the hand, the chariot leave the ground. Even though there will be the certain colossally depressed days one is happy over that initial sense of power over the instrument.

February 7: I dreamed of the crow—a slow flying bird in trees across from 121 North Broadway* at Auntie May's. It seemed a huge bird with a long, plumed tail, as big as an ostrich, not at all sinister, flying, slowing, hovering and sometimes backward or still in the air like gulls. Charlie and Effie and Auntie May noticed him—and Phyllis. He came over to us, a soft friendly bird, so we fed him, but Phyllis gave him all the fried ham in the icebox and I was against this as his awakened taste might remind him of vulture ancestors and he would eat us.

February 19: "Yow." A cat book. Two-leggers were always after things, anything that moved. Also they (two-leggers) like anybody who feeds them, have no real affection. Like cows because they feed them; like mothers because they feed them. Change affection according to who feeds them. At least we're better than humans who kill for no reason.

February 24: Later life of woman is beginning of friendship and enjoying female companionship—indeed missing it if one is domestically tied to old husband. Man's capacity for (and pleasure in) friendship dies out in old age. He wants Mama, being spoiled and eunuch pleasures: children, food, family, etc.

February 25: Bop is "music with a hole in its head." It is otherwise the reaching out for sounds in modern life to be musicalized—the riveter, plane and fire siren to add to the babbling brook, river, waterfall and waves of original shepherd music.

March 1: At Bunny's, where S. N. Behrman told many interesting stories. He represents a special kind of Oriental politeness, civil to the point of obsequiousness. He told of Victor Hugo. In his old age, Hugo was asked at dinner whether he was aware of his own great fame. Do you realize what a great name you have? Yes, said Hugo, in the last week he had finally been made aware that he was famous. He was returning from dining out and, what with an excess of wine, he rang his concierge's bell furiously to be let in, for he was an old man and it was hard to contain himself. But the concierge, too, was old and deaf and did not come. So, in his desperation, Hugo was forced to relieve himself before his gate, when he felt a

---

*The address of the Shelby, Ohio house where Powell grew up.

violent hand on his shoulder and a passerby was gripping him, shouting "*What?* In front of Victor Hugo's *house?*"

March 3: Bunny came in for lunch.

This novel (New York) started out in exactly same way as *Locusts* did (see 1946): "Blocked and locked in Marcia novel," so went into New York novel for which all my notes seem to have already formed a pattern.

March 20: In the perverse way of authors, the Leon Edel "Ghostly Writings of Henry James" with interpolations re: James' theatrical aspirations—all futile, vulnerable, vain, foolish, wasted time—inspired me to write play once more.

April 2: Remember to do cat book for Julia Ellsworth Ford juvenile prize. About 35 pages or 10,000 words.

April 4: Anniversary of operation. Margaret gave me round-trip ticket to Paris—*Ile de France.* How this is to be managed I do not know but hope for some return on my last few years work. Good God.

April 5: New Pavilion novel—idea is of the far-reaching outposts of the Pavilion—as if it was the New York center with radiations to city's fringes.

April 6: Maurice De Young called. Told stories of exploitation of Haitian primitives by the Caribbean fairies.

April 27: Thought about Auntie May's last visit to Mr. L.*—his new red tie, the new dressing gown, her escorts of the two boys. Wave good-bye, we're saying good-bye to our old friend for the last time. The idea of all it meant—the constancy based on absence—both really family people and raising other people's children. Moved me so.

May 13: In the matter of the human ego, I note that the political ego—desire for power over fellowmen—is accompanied by sexual vanity and

---

*Charles Lahm, a produce representative from Cleveland, was originally a boarder at Orpha May Steinbrueck's house but became, in the words of Jack Sherman, "part of the family." Sherman believes the two might have married, had it not been for Mr. Lahm's wife and children in Cleveland.

pride in conquest apart from love. The artistic ego is often compensatory for sexual or love disappointments and is more apt to be combined with love (i.e., the sexual pride comes from personal love, too). Sometimes the artist—whose artistic ego must always first be gratified—deliberately if unconsciously sabotages amorous success so that his work can gain all the double force of unhappiness and frustration. Balzac had some reason in feeling that they were incompatible.

May 16: Jojo and I exploring Riverside Drive—water's edge. He is momentarily in better condition—says due to intravenous glucose.

June 2: Re-read part of *Locusts*. Decided it was over-written, due to habit of revising, and over-detailed and repetitious without adding effect. Should fight tendency to rewrite and revise every day instead of slamming through as in *Angels On Toast*.

June 8: Made up mind Paris must be the answer and must work to that end—not touring but *living* there, working, and changing my luck. Must organize for that purpose. Possible two months absence?

July 17: It is necessary to have the character of Jerry real—from outside and inside. No one has done this completely New York woman—opportunism, a kind of combination male-adventurer/female-lusty trollop, creatively powerful in the old Roman courtesan and Paris *saloniere* style.

July 20: Preparations for Paris—must have play organized, copied, in agent hands. Stories, etc., on hand with record of same. Should have novel shaped up to page 75 by July 29.

July 21: Have been organizing *Pavilion*. I wish to convey the complete vivid details of New York life and varied characters not in conventional fiction guise but with the *complete* reality of the 18th- and 19th-century letter writers who told all the inside scandals chattily, informatively, real places, real names, etc.—and a kind of special woman of the last two decades, as peculiar to this age as certain Balzac types.

July 24: Reorganizing novel—well, I believe. Other conditions of work would absolutely devastate me if I dared be devastated, but have switched to anticipation of Paris as a tonic step to shake walls of doom away from me.

July 30: What I wish to do is to know my own country as well as possible before traveling, since I always am bored by foreigners, however intellectual, who are limited in knowledge of their own country.

See Leo Lerman for *Mademoiselle* article. Type "Broadway" article. Make will. Type birth affidavit—have Joe sign. Take certificate and Joe to 630 Fifth—have passport picture taken first.

August 3: I dreamed of Gretchen and going into a field—large and grayish—seeing some men come towards us, silently, heads down, guns over shoulder, and then behind them two others, equally silent. I was frightened vaguely as they walked very slowly, heads bent, purposefully toward us, but then I thought they are French (I have in the back of my mind the idea of going to France) and they passed us without looking at us. Next day I went to a French movie uptown at Thalia about a country estate hunting and there was the field—gray looking and dreamy because of the faded film—and the two men with guns, heads down, followed by the other two. I have these geographical previews of where I'm going often— i.e., the dream of colonnaded pink adobe building and palms. A week later I passed it in Pasadena and recognized it exactly.

August 10: Advice on Paris. George Davis—get in touch with someone you know so they can get you out of whatever place you go first and don't like. Esther—go to Venice *at once*.

August 11: Week of Jojo—second week of Joe's vacation.

Good thing about intensiveness of Jojo visit is that no conscious thought of novel is possible. Result—subconscious suddenly has decided to return to Marcia theme.

September 10: Pete Martin and wife in town and we had party.

Now that I seem to be really going I have my travelers' eyes already and observe the usual here with a foreign eye. While I wake with a sick feeling of homesickness for my cat—and the security of men friends who are not available anyplace else but New York—I realize the knowledge of departure is a shot in the arm. My mind and imagery focuses, as a deadline obliges such focusing, and when I think of the places I've tried to work—MacDowell and Hollywood and Snedens—I realize it is impossible but still to remain here also is slipping. People should go away to keep up their value. Moreover, I feel released and free to tell more frankly the true New York stories.

September 11: I would like to write about French women—what they do with their day—above all, what do they do with their ambition . . . why are they not transportable? I may take an apartment so I can fiddle with cooking if I like. Take "Troupial Bird" story along. I do believe in this trip.

September 12: A novelist should not study the idiom of science, psychiatry, etc., since his work is to communicate images and ideas to the public, not a private, already primed group of experts. He should express himself originally, combining to his own taste complete expression of himself with grades of communication for others. The idiom of experts is a lazy, inept apology for not assimilating and reissuing the idea in an original and understood way.

October 1: Comes the time when you realize that words travel slower than light, that you are speaking your big thoughts to an echo and most of the time even *you* are not listening. Far into the night the talk goes on, but not into the ears for you can tell these same people the same news again and again—they will still be surprised, they will still not listen. Then the words of *your* elders strike you decades later, find you listening to a long dead voice because this day something happened in your life in which those long dead words were wrapped.

October 2: The kind of quick anesthetic effect of the words "Did I tell you the one about . . . ?"—the freezing arrangement of the face into an expression of interest, the attempt to disguise the glazing of the eye—then the name or words in the middle of the story that arouse one, the scrambled effort to guess what went before. But one cannot ask "Begin again" after one has laughed properly, interjected amused "Imagine that! . . . No! . . . That's wonderful."

October 4: Out Margaret's window—the lady on the floor doing her Elizabeth Arden or Success School exercises: two more inches off the bottom and the town is hers. The blimp dawdling over the river like a hawk waiting for its supper. Queen Mary wafting down the river. . . .

October 14: The reason friends in late middle age appear inadequate is that one expects them to give back one's youth—everything one once had with them—and one charges them with the lack that is in oneself, for even if they could give, your container is now a sieve and can hold no gifts for long.

October 29: Paris. Remarkable how a group of Europeans has masses of hair; is this due to wine or to excessive use of colognes and hair oils? And no showerbaths? Just as I was contemplating this discovery with self-satisfaction the suspicion struck me that the excessively pompadoured gray man next to me was wearing a toupee—in fact, such an obvious one that you simply refused to believe it. Do all Europeans then, I asked myself, wear toupees fearlessly?

November 2: The 4000 franc *couvert* at the Lido includes places and champagne and show. Alors, alors. The French women—beauties—have smaller waists—high busts—large hips and upper thighs and slender lower legs. C. thought couple at next table cold typical Northern type because they did not speak to each other, never smiled, never sipped champagne, looked impassively at show—but this looked familiar to me. Under table, more explicit operations.

November 3: Paris. I am fascinated by idea of changing Brooklyn Widow play to Paris, then back to Brooklyn.

A play about Paris noises.

November 6: Drink and reading tastes change with geography as if the place required some kind of balance—different for each person. Usually in a very beautiful, complete, complacent country, one is impelled to deep philosophic and intellectual thought—also true (but always thwarted) in social place like Hollywood. In Paris, cognac is indicated—because you must live *up* to Paris, rise above the basic gloom it inspires. Pernod is not for Paris, so cognac. Coffee impossible so chocolate really invigorates. Feel tired mostly—air may be debilitating but walking incessantly and unrelaxed self may also be responsible. Secretly sunk by *New Yorker* not buying story. No idea where else to go.

November 8: Took trip to see exhibition recommended by *Tribune*. Fascinated by the home of grandeur that was and no wonder these are the inherent French ambitions (for women)—to *have* rather than to be. Since women of France have gotten neither power nor comforts except through nimble use of their bodies no wonder France is the *mal de mer* of prostitution.

A very old Balzacian gentleman (I almost detected a snuff gesture) seemed more nostalgic for the old grandeur of this than for the objects inside and stood in the garden court contemplating it—those were the days—and then a very old chauffeur opened the door of a very old limousine and he got in.

The exhibition (first showing of priceless masterpieces for centuries in Paris private mansions) showed that private collectors have poor taste and buy the artist's worst works—something to match the curtains, a drawing of a book for the library, glorified beatifications of the lady of the house—no more "art" than Elizabeth Arden even though it is Raeburn or Rembrandt.

November 12: You can live very cheaply in Paris but it's no pleasure.

November 16: French frown on Pernod but actually it is their wines that kill. The most-moralizing people in the world drink quarts of wine—the way country people kill themselves eating pies and cakes, healthy because they raise it and they save money. After a couple of quarts, *one* Pernod and what a cluck-cluck goes on.

November 17: In Henry Miller's own language, I feel about his *Tropics* that reading him is like observing somebody belch—now *he* feels better but it doesn't do *you* any good.

November 27: Went to Balzac exhibition at Biblioteque Nationale. Papers, letters, bills for his books, etc., but moved by the tired peace of his death portrait, which looked oddly like Jack Lawson.

December 15: The people who sit around Harlem nightclubs in Paris and think how exploited they are (the entertainers who are so good). The Boy Existentialists wear beards, sort of like Young Pioneers, sit and yak.

The "missing" of New York is its essence.

[*Undated*] "The Last Time I Hope I See Paris"
I do not like the word alors
I do not want it anymore
This and "Madame!"
And those oui-ouis
I fear I am
Trés *hard to please*
Oh give me nevermore alors
Or alors *Madame will make war.*

1951

January 25: Returned on *S. S. DeGrasse.*

February 4: Story of couple breaking up—house, children, etc. divided but the rights to Bleeck's still a sizzling quarrel. Begin with cocktail hour. It's his place but he can't go because she's sure to be there. Who went there first? She is there with the man who first took *him* there. Who has first rights?

February 6: A novel of chance. People brush by each other—miss something by a second.

February 12: It is vital that this place—the Pavilion, where people wait for some solution—is actually set in 1947, when people waited. The war was over, but nothing was settled. This is a novel of the desperation and ruthlessness of peace.

February 26: I think Jerry should be less grand. More jolly-rowdy tastes with talent for wasting talents. Elsie wants to make match—decides Jerry's mistake has been not entertaining. She's got the most marvelous midget!

People waiting for inheritances—cautious of tiny incomes—writing postcards to ancient relatives so they would get left a handkerchief.

No Communist ever does anything for anyone but himself.

March 18: Jojo home. Very much improved.

March 26: Jojo went back to Gladwyne—his best period so far. The progress of his illness is the same but in-between he does mature in understanding, consideration. Hope he can continue up back there. If possible should have house for month—typewriter, piano, further Italian lessons. Garden or lawn for lawn-mowing.

March 30: The couple who befriend Sloan. They do not mind his alcoholism (though this is their bleat) but his choice of company for drinking and the places he goes.

X. always got to the best places after the best people had left; he got the deserted wives of the great men, the discarded lover of the famous ballerina, the well-known producer or publisher after they were bankrupt—the fallen snobs who had been left (as they had left their own stepping-ladders behind them) and now clung gratefully to a kindness.

April 5: Old theater talk showed that no one remembers Great Plays in production—they remember charming actresses, glamorous phonies, the "Staircase Waltz," the trip to the theater, etc. For me, the trip of my aunt, what I did while waiting, her and Lulu in new clothes, off to Cleveland.

April 18: Do light story. Paris. Get letters to Joe for material. Plot—Paris-mad father gives daughter and son-in-law honeymoon in Paris.

April 21: Coby—commenting on his foppish wardrobe: dozens of shirts in his shirt closet, dozens of suits either at his tailor's or in his wardrobe and in his shoe closet you can't even see the shoes for the trees.

April 23: One's dearest and oldest and faithfullest friends are the ones most astonished that the world finds any good in you. They want not to believe in you—but to generously disguise their doubts of you in order to prove their own high qualities. They are prepared to fight to the death for your honor against a jeering mob but they are utterly disarmed if their special heroic role is reduced to that of minor bit player in a cheering mob.

April 29: The way the ambitious young men—eventually well-married and on their way—turn on the equally ambitious lady, wife of the great man, who inveighed them into her bed in their weakest moment (why should *he* have everything?). Now that their lusts are dimmer and their ambition paramount, they are angry and desperate to see the enemy they empowered by cuckolding him, who can revenge himself on them where it really hurts. For this major wrong they hate the early bride, they wish to woo the man now but they know he will never forgive and he is too clever and too conceited to let them off easily.

May 8: Palm Beach diet (steak and unsweetened prunes each day) loses me six pounds, though I did it as a Gowanus Canal diet—hamburger and prunes. I will lose another ten pounds this lunch. Always toughest job is getting under a round sum. Once you're under you go down but one pound over and you go up. So plan to be under 150 by Saturday.

Low days, of a Parisian hopelessness, but now a glimmer. Breathing does it. And most important is departure of friends. Those who demand comfort and consolation are no more dangerous to clear work-thinking than those who offer consolation and comfort to practice their loyalty on—as on a handball court, keeping themselves fit and worn out for sleep.

May 9: I think I will aim at clearing up novel for straight reading along by June 1. This will be a long novel—covering more vagaries than any others—probably 410 pages. Do not hesitate to tell all about people, though main line must proceed straight with people crossing it, if not logically converging there. Sometimes the encounter is after one is dead—as one meets and understands and loves suddenly someone of long ago when one comes to the same spot in life.

May 16: Read Edith Wharton's *The Reef* and struggling with *Wings of the Dove* by James, simultaneously. Curiously alike, but she is so superior in this. Odd, her reputation for "moralizing novels" when it was her *age* which read its own moralizing into her. Not one word could be called moralizing—no villains, no heroes in the noble sense. Villainy is done by a group of characters behaving in the only way they, in all honesty, feel they can decently behave. They intend no harm—they are sympathetic to the lesser person wronged even if it is they who are wronging her; they intelligently perceive her side. Under the decorous dance, evil is done on all sides to Sophy Viner.

I must write to Sophy Viner, I woke up thinking. I must tell her—tell her what? She never existed. What a precise miracle of illusion Edith Wharton created—never showing Sophy's room, giving her only one dress, one cloak, describing her only as fresh-faced—but she is *real*.

May 19: Jojo went back. Still on amazingly high level. Hated to have him go as it's such a pleasure to find him improving.

June 23: Spent week on dream story—two scrub-ladies. Not sure whether money desperation or novelistic frenzy.

June 24: Last week I wrote (in ink) one simple story I dreamed up—17 pages—with the thirsty amateur pleasure of childhood days when you write endlessly and happily stories to your own momentary reading taste. My own momentary taste being practically lower than the funnies, this clips along with no merit other than author escape—escape to waste valuable writing time, to escape pressure of novel's September 1 deadline, *Bazaar* article horrors, etc.

June 26: Occasionally a thirst for Paris comes over me. It is like the thirst for ocean water that a shipwrecked man on a raft feels for the water he knows will not slake his thirst; long after he is rescued the perverse thirst for thirstiness comes over him. The limitless cool beauty of the city, the rest for a while of no new impressions since the doors of language are closed. For the artist, there is the nostalgia for nostalgia, for unfullfilment, for all the spurs to ambition and all the challenges to accomplish.

What French dread more than anything else is to draw a breath with no words in it.

July 11: Mabel's birthday.
  Gave short stories to Rosalind* for Houghton Mifflin consideration. My feeling is that I need the confidence of a book coming out to make the novel good.
  Novel began in January, 1950—and it seems to me steadily worked on but actually only a little done.

---

*Rosalind Baker Wilson, Edmund Wilson's daughter and an editor at Houghton Mifflin.

July 12: Esther and Margaret berate me for having "no sense of adventure" by not liking foreign travel. My answer is that there was no place on earth I wouldn't go if I lived anyplace but New York—and if I was not engaged in work I love I wouldn't even want to stay in New York.

July 14: This novel—which set out to be richly New York—is centering too much on a trick artist group, and this is not what I meant. I want the cafe to be a place where people come to remind themselves that once one could dream of doing something for oneself, for the world.

July 29: Incredible that after working steadily on this novel, with very few sidetracks except wretched and futile attempts at money (*Bazaar,* etc.) and seeming to go along nicely—suddenly, on accounting, I have gotten no further than 12 pages or so and this is due to talking to blank wall.

August 3: Women growing old—many traces of age. The fact is, many middle-aged ladies who look twenty years younger than their age show it. A stranger—marveling at the clear, smooth skin, unlined throat—is shocked at the age revealed by her thinking. There are things, like a bald head, that can't be helped but can at least be hidden. The end of sex finds women resenting older men, who are invariably childish, demanding, selfish and catty. Men as they age seem to go home to Mama, after leaving her on her own for 30 years. Suddenly their men friends are unsatisfactory; they want Mama's cookies and warming pan. This is just the time Mama finds the company of her own sex most rewarding. Don't be sorry for elderly ladies on sprees—they're usually having the time of their life without having to do what the Man says.

September 18: Yesterday almost ready for suicide with constant churning and desiccation of novel and drying it with each revision until the life seems squeezed out, each new day's labor seems to draw more blood instead of resuscitating it. This began in *My Home Is Far Away* when I was burning myself fishing live coals from what should have been a dead bonfire. By the time I had seared my soul, dressing my old wounds in new bandages—unrelieved, unilluminating, yet disguised—I had done myself the favor of taking the joy out of writing. Since then, all has been uphill with emotions spent on live situations and an increasing need to substitute ferocity of word thrust for feeling. By this time simple feeling in my writing has ended up in simple pain for me. Monday I was determined to hurdle this terrible barrier and from 10 A.M. to 10 at night, I took Dexedrine—dear little Maxitons—and for sheer fatigue, sherry, until I had magicked or bludgeoned Ellenora out of hiding. As for my desire for life as in *Creevy Papers* there is none of it—less indeed than any other work. But now it marches, I believe. Whether I can endure another desert I doubt.

September 24: Writers' lives worse in older age as family reaches out and grabs them. Finally, long neglected wife, or husband, or whoever, is obliged to be trained to be an intellectual to take place of distant or dead mental equals, and this self-carbon is not satisfactory, no matter how hard the poor mate tries, so more of the mate's carbon comes off on the writer than vice versa.

September 27: There are different kinds of writers. Story-writers, like Maugham, stand aside and present the object to the reader—a brand new story untouched by human hands. It is yours, yours alone, a gift with no strings attached, the reader's book. But then there are people like Koestler—his books are his—you are conscious every minute of the searching creative person of the author. This is *his* story; he has seen this, he has known it; this is his wisdom, his reasoning—and this living quality gives fire and truth to his story. You feel elated and privileged to be permitted in this great mind's company.

October 1: Tears of self-pity left her shaking and spent; one trembling hand reached out for the sleeping pill.

October 4: Marie spoke today of lady she works for who got hurt and is going to get a sediment.

October 7: How a person changes someone. Ellenora now does everything *opposite* to what she thinks Rick would like (to show her freedom). A casual person changes you more than someone you see all the time. Like you can describe a strange city—where you only spent 24 hours in a high emotional key, carved into your bones—more clearly than the place you have lived.

October 11: Virginia,* my half-sister, died—a delicate, sweet little thing bearing full brunt of my stepmother's nerve-wracking, nervous devotion. I do not even know her married name.

October 12: Curious and maddening that this novel—which I plunged into with the absolutely overwhelming intention of making more alive and living than life itself—gets deader and drier than death and seems more a paper life than anything I ever did.

October 13: Beerbohm's *Enoch Soames* startled me with its domino room in Cafe Royale—so like my beginning of *Wicked Pavilion*. Also West's *Day of the Locust.*

October 16: Koestler and Mark B.—the young man so anxious to meet the celebrity. Great man very kind to young man who later explains "I told that old bastard what was the matter with his writing. He just doesn't know what time it is."

October 18: He was cross at being asked about the Twenties. Very well, he was alive then but the Twenties had been *his* twenties.

October 22: At this time we have Kefauver investigations tracking down gamblers who must confess and be sentenced. At same time they are out on bail and nothing is done about them. Also we investigate Internal Revenue men who are accused of obviously taking bribes as their banks show $25,000 and more instead of a proper $3500. Here they make alibi of having merely won this by gambling at racetrack—lotteries—bridge, etc., and this, if proved, will clear them.

Again everyone stirred up because Josephine Baker gets poor service at Stork Club.†

October 24: What about "middle class"? It annoyed the Orphen family that he wrote about the simple, peasant pleasures of his simple family when they had to keep clear of the Country Club at that time.

---

* Virginia McLaughlin, born about 1912, was the daughter of Roy Powell and the hated Sabra Powell.

† African-American entertainer Josephine Baker went public with her belief that she had suffered racial discrimination at Sherman Billingsley's famously elitist Stork Club.

October 25: You must remember that you don't know what people find in your work so there's no sense in trying to repeat it. You can only *do*, in the way that seems best to you. Like not knowing really why people like or dislike you—do they like your brains? No, it is your cooking and perhaps your apartment. Is it your conversation? No, it is the fact that occasionally you let others talk. So—for reassurance in finding some of your work so bad—remember, you don't know.

October 26: Never forget geography. New York is heroine. Make the city live, so that reader walking about town thinks—here is the Fifth Avenue Hotel, where so and so came.

October 28: In Ricky's, we put our coats on a seat and the handsome colored waiter immediately put a napkin over them. "The old Pullman blood coming out," I said and then—as it sounded "discriminatory"—I added, to show it was a joke: "Glad to be off the old Santa Fe Chief?" "You can say that again," said the waiter. "Were you on that?" Margaret said to him, and it seems he had been for years and hated it—the boring scenery, no daylight, getting on and off at midnight, so his off-hours were no fun.

I had trouble explaining to Margaret I was only guessing. My jokes turn out to be extrasensory-perceptive. This is a curious but common basis in humor—the plucking out of the air something from the other's mind—something he vaguely wishes said or something he strongly wishes *not* said. Something telepathic indeed.

November 13: It is very heartbreaking to find one drawing so far away from definite goals. In this last *Pavilion* book I was determined that a reality of gossip could be achieved but my increased writing ability stands in the way of this fresh impact. How can one unlearn writing and relearn direct communication?

November 30: The case of Evelyn Scott.* Living in England. Friends are asked to send clothes, etc.—and she writes gratefully: "The blue dress is fine in spite of not being my color and as soon as I have cash I will get some silk to touch it up; the yellow is fine for wearing under my coat for marketing, etc."

---

* Scott and her husband John Metcalfe had fallen upon hard times in London.

December 4: Recalling the 20 pages of scrub-lady story—which I transcribed from dream. Went at night to Joe's office to ladies room where a pair of high-heeled red shoes and nylons were left. Looked around for scrub-women and sure enough saw a gay, middle-aged one and also a young one—both like my story.

December 7: To Latouche's, 136 East 37th Street, to hear his new "Golden Apple" done with Jerome Moross. A very thrilling experience. Extraordinary young man.

December 8: Dreamed of Aunt Bessie and Uncle Will supposed to come on trip to Europe—somehow Mabel involved here. (In fact my dream-life with my grandmother, Mabel and other dead people is more real—and much longer, God knows—than my actual life with them.)*

December 13: I cannot see why Shaw was called a hermit, a snob, etc., when he—out of almost the whole world, being childless and single-minded—was merely a self-preserver, wasting no time on the ordinary day, idle questions, etc. His wife was a buffer for him but herself not social. In order for a genius to be a genius, he must have a selfless slave between him and the world so that he may select what tidbits he chooses from it and not have his brains swallowed up in chaff. For women this protection is impossible.

December 15: Bunny in town. We dined at Princeton Club. He had been going over E. Millay's old letters and writing a memoir about her—his wife Elena typing all this by day and listening to same by night. (Just as Dos' wife† types by day all his love story of former marriage and then takes care of house by night.) "I think Elena is getting rather sick of it," Bunny said with an embarrassed smile.

December 16: Boy drearily playing tennis. "I have to do this because my father couldn't afford to when he was my age."

Taxi driver lost wife—"Married 26 years and in all those years I never had to raise my voice to her once and she was never short a dime."

---

*Powell based her tiny memoir, "What Are You Doing In My Dreams?" on her "nights with the dead."

†Dos Passos had married Elizabeth Holdridge in 1949.

December 27: In Dos' book, Bunny and Margaret keep identifying characters and exclaiming over Dos' outrageousness in writing about his friends. But the amazing thing is the way these friends select a most unsavory character and say: "That is you and I don't think it was fair of Dos to describe you this way—changing your background from Sweden to South Boston, having you a man instead of a woman, and a Civil War general instead of a World War III pacifist—it is most unfair." What they recognize as most inevitably you is the selfishness, gross taste, ignorance, unpopularity and, indeed, ugliness. Whose picture of you is this—Dos' or your dear friends'?

[*Undated*]
> "Troupial Bird"*—written 1950. Ober.
> *New American Mercury*
> *Harper's*
> *Harper's Bazaar*
> *New Yorker*
> Withdrawn March 1951.
> Sent to: *Today's Woman*
> April 12—*Mademoiselle*

---

*Became "The Roof"—this story was not published until it appeared in the anthology, *Sunday, Monday and Always*.

1952

[*Undated*] The following short stories could be used in another volume:
    "Enter Two Girls Laughing" (*Harper's Bazaar*)
    "The Survivors"
    "House Afire"
    "Green Bananas"
    "The Run-Through"
    "The Olive Twig"
    "The Devils-Grip"
    "Gypsies in Town"
    "Laughing Water"
    "Dynamite in the Office" (*Coronet?*)
    "The Winkenkoop"
    "Young Arnold By Night"
    "Slow Burn"
    "Florida Limited"
    "Slave Bracelet" (?)
    "Sample Size"
    "Everything is a Wife"
    "Now He Tells Me"

January 3: The way Bobby [Morrison], in new long pants and suit I bought him because it would help make him a happier and therefore better boy, now sits on porch in new clothes because I wouldn't want him to get them dirty emptying ashes.

January 18: The blind way people who have had blind success—[George S.] Kaufman, for instance, and some politicians—acquire a "sure" touch through their arrogant assumption that they have a special touch, never crediting luck, support or coincidental circumstances. Kaufman's plays always showed a contempt for public—"They" always love this, etc. The fact is, these people never knew what made their success. Not the tired vain egotism and arrogance but a spark of belief they once had—the challenge of insecurity.

January 20: To Maison Gaby (West 68th) for dinner. The Peter Blumes and Cowleys. Malcolm said I never ended my novels properly; they simply stopped. This could be true. The fault, I'm sure, is not in the end but in the structure earlier in the book, which should be so built to indicate the plausibility of the ending.

January 21: Starting aminophyllen for high blood pressure.

The way world insists woman is primarily woman—housekeeper, mama, cookie-cooker. Male doctors, lawyers, writers, artists continue to wear their robes even in swimming and are not asked to do a full day as father, husband, host, handyman. But women in these fields have merely arrested momentarily the trivial and human demands piling up outside their office door waiting to pounce on them the minute they emerge. It is not a feat for them to do their daily professional job and then rustle up a family meal complete with quarrels, demands, etc. This is expected, as are the duties of hostess, confidante, family sofa, etc. The life work to which she is dedicated is regarded as a selfish hobby of hers (supposing it *does* support them all, her real duty is Us, Us, Us—our bellyaches, etc.). Women have never been more enslaved—by their own fictions about how they handle their sick-life, how politely silent they are about their work. A novel could be written like *Uncle Tom's Cabin.*

January 27: This entire week has been doldrums. An almost paralyzing sleepiness that makes me sleepy from sleep. I think only that sunshine would cure this. All my married life has been search for sunlight. Wheeling the baby around town, I chose restaurants to point out later to Joe—daylight, but I always loved the forever-night of cellar restaurants and never took seriously my absolute thirst and need for sun and ocean air.

February 7: Referring to his new job, Joe said some men are born to be sales managers. You know their father and mother said to themselves— now let's stop fooling around, this time we're going to make a sales manager. Out he comes—full grown, large, bluff, close-knit, no extra fat, clean, almost baby-faced, loud laugh.

February 19: Key West. Surf and Sand Club.

Barker on cruise tells of calamities befalling men of millions. Preston built $250,000 house as a surprise to wife, brought her to it and she hated it and refused to spend one night in it so he put it up for sale. Another one (Deering) died five years after completed; heirs have to keep it open, champagne and food stocked every season-opening for his return from death to place he loved. 29 guards to keep out public. After one day open to public for benefit, they carved initials and hoodlummed the place so heirs refuse all visitors. Possible story here of young woman casually wandering around, accosted by old lady (or ghost). Heirs cannot give away property as city and state need the $60,000 yearly taxes too much.

Next is Colonel Green's place (Hetty Green's son) who was embittered by mother refusing him doctor (too expensive) when he was eleven and went out to resell newspapers. Amputated leg and when he inherited $187 million he devoted his life to spending it—50 ocean-going yachts for guests, 50 homes over America. Another man had millions, when he liked a show he bought it in New York and brought it down to his home for six weeks. Peggy Hopkins met Joyce there.

February 20: The pretty girl at a party who knew me well because her mother had told her so many stories about our girlhood together. Of how her mother broke with our mutual friend, Mary Lena, because latter insisted she distribute Communist pamphlets! (This in 1918 or 1919!) Of the good times the three of us had. Mother's name Virginia; wracking my brain I recall Mary Lena's confidences about her various girlfriends— some of whom I met—but recall no Virginia. Reminded me of little Cynthia Chapman who said, round-eyed: "Mother has told me of when you two were in the Navy"—(true)—"nursing" (wrong)—"and used to rush out on the battlefield and have soldiers die in your arms."

Flabbergasted at this rearrangement of our past in Naval offices in New York City but unwilling to call her mama a liar, I said cautiously, "They didn't exactly *die,* Cynthia."

March 3: The bar where bartender pleads: "Let's have no language here. I try to keep a nice place. I don't allow any language."

Having brioche for tea, I thought, Good God!—all France would be aghast. Brioche is for breakfast; no matter how you loved them or how hungry you were, you never have them at any other time.

March 16: In the huge, baronial new home of Katherine Cornell people meet. The guests make friends with each other—if you are a friend of Katherine Cornell then you must be worth my conversation—yet they make no move to talk to her, as if she was merely the fire by which human beings warmed themselves convivially. If she presumed to crash their group, they would look at her haughtily and say—"We are friends of Katherine Cornell and you are not."

March 17: At the Murphys' I am finally captured, though in all these friendships which are not friendships but being trapped, the conquest is a poor one. They envelop and ingest one: that is why they prefer one of a couple to both. They slowly batter down the selected victim until with its last spark of life it gets away or (as it is then of no use to them) they kick it out.

I have stopped trying to ward off the drinks and especially the wine for lunch as it is useless. Also (though they are the first to speak of people's weight), they browbeat you into the puddings, etc., which you do not want and should not have. In this dead-end the guest cannot escape. One sees how Honoria* was glad to get a continent away, for there is no meeting-ground—complete subjugation. They have no interest in the friend's happiness or lovelife; they are interested in his behavior and conduct in trivial matters. You must not open windows no matter how stifling it is in your room; you must have *these* pillows, no matter how you say you use hard pillows. At first you disobey but finally they get you; you lie awake waiting for day and air but then, too, you must not dress and get out. You must put on dressing gown and have brioche and coffee.

As a retired homo (I suspect), Gerald's pleasure is in bullying and reducing female vanity. Dictating every minute of the guest's day, the wine, the food, the walk (84 steps back and forth on porch is as good as a mile).

---

*Honoria Murphy Donnelly, Gerald and Sara Murphy's daughter.

Finally the guest gets schizophrenic. A curious evil. Their "gracious living" is only the contours.

March 21: Movie, "Room for One More," with Cary Grant and Betsy Drake, so certain in producer's eye that they offer refund to anyone not liking it. It offers explanation of how Soviet prisoners or starving citizens with grim haunted lives can go to their movies and relax happily before picture of plenty and joyous progress, seeing no irony or lack of reality in contrasting what they *know* and *are* with what is idealized before them. In America, children and adults leave their institutions or homes where they have just been squabbling or shut out or nagged and sit beamishly before these balmy pictures of a happy papa and mama pleased to let in all stray dogs, cats, children—at the same time exchanging sexy, coy remarks with each other. They see no irony in comparing these rosy fairy tales— "Cheaper By The Dozen," "The Best Years of Our Lives," and others— with the daily style of their own family.

March 23: The Child Dictatorship. Visiting parents must use language and ideas suitable for children. Couples visit each other and guests must play with children as babysitters. No contact with adult minds because censor is present. Revolt possible.

March 25: The way it surprised me that people of means and position accepted you wholly when you were in their house yet away you could not be sure at all of their opinion of you. In their dining room you were the equal of anyone there, entitled to full appreciation. I knew this could not be honest and it bothered me. These veils of politeness!

March 26: Capote's play "Grass Harp." Moments of beauty and glamorous theater but second act pompous and inflated. Talk sounded like pale echoes of Saroyan. Group Theatre enunciated by Collins, Ruth Nelson etc., a la Chekhov out of Lee Strasberg and Second Avenue. Words of unimportance given strange, "translated-by-the-Rabbi," importance.

Opening night fraught with hidden sex, due to high-octane of participants—Cecil Beaton, Bobby Lewis, Capote, Virgil Thomson, producer Saint Subber (who, according to Gertrude Flynn, is "six feet above ground" and has a colored fairy chum from Paris). Actually the play—

except for a "fastidy" about normal sex—has no fancy homosexuality in itself, though Carson McCullers' *Member of Wedding* as it came to stage did have.

April 2: Coby taken to hospital for stomach operation. Duodenal ulcer with perforation of walls to peritoneum.

May 1: Niles [Spencer] died. Cannot bear to think about this.

May 16: Was Niles' death the strange unforeseen? The strange dove-tail-ing—since I am writing about the death of an artist?

May 22: Spoke at Queens College.

Early success in sense of large following means writer knows who his audience is—what they expect and like from him. So he selects as he writes —either he disagrees and writes against this public or it is what he was only hitherto vaguely aware of wishing to say and now can say it better.

May 23: I am exhausted by another night with the dead. As a matter of fact I have spent more time with the dead than with the quick, for as soon as I pop off to sleep there is my grandmother (dead since 1922) waiting or my father (1926) or my mother (1903) or my grandfather (1902) waiting with a picnic basket and I'm off for a shore dinner with the stiffs.

These are pleasant, never depressing or ghoulish affairs, and I would not mind except I always wake up exhausted for they never do anything I want to do, such as lying down for a nap by the roadside. No, we must go on and on, catch the bus or the train, unhitch the sleigh or the surrey and get there before noon or before something or other. I am rushed along the way they used to grab my arm as if it were a squab wing, and tear across streets, up and down stairs. These dreams are never dramatic or plot dreams (which would help me out in my work) but are usually outings and exclusively family except when some death in the newspapers the day before brings in a stranger such as Niles Spencer, Julie Garfield,* or sometimes my own son, always four years old.†

---

* Actor Julius Garfinkle, better known by his professional name, John Garfield, was called "Julie" by friends.

†For whatever it is worth, Jojo was four in the year that Powell published *Whither,* her first novel.

Sometimes my father appears but not often and when he does, the Shermans, my mother's family, always pick on him and I dread having him show up. It strikes me as a joke for I was a non-family person and—except for a flying reunion every five or ten years and a fear that someday I might have to leave my dear New York and be set down in an ocean of fourth and fifth cousins all bossing me and each other—I was glad to escape. But have I? I have spent more time with them than the living have.

My older sister had been appearing in these dreams long before she died and, as in childhood, was invariably mystifying me by her savoir-faire—how did she know we were going to Pilgrim Lake this time? How did she know we had to stand on this corner to get the trolley? We were strolling through picnicland one night and just as we got to the bandstand she stopped and started rouging her face. I was secretly shocked, as always, by any daring gesture and as we went on—there were never any people in the dream except dead or living ones as babies—I finally said, disapprovingly, "Mabel, it doesn't look nice for you to use so much rouge. It isn't natural for a dead person."*

May 25: Uncertain about Jed Harris proposition to do a play with him (I fancy I'm to do it and he's to "collaborate" or heckle) but he is stimulating and I need that. Surprising how little of my novel is done—hardly 75 pages—yet it seems to me I have worked on it endlessly. The best part was in Paris, oddly enough.

May 26: The wave of parties for Alec Waugh—going, coming, leaving, arriving. People use this as an excuse for annual coming out—hooking on to all his international connections.

May 27: The way Mr. G. M. Skiles† struggled to the telephone as he died to call Auntie May.

June 3: Incredibly barren head. No excuse for it except Fear of Finishing. I shall do my next novel in longhand—perhaps finish this one like that as I have also a fatigue at typing.

---

*This would be developed into "What Are You Doing In My Dreams?", Powell's autobiographical sketch.

†G. M. Skiles, a Shelby businessman, was close to O. M. Steinbrueck and helped support Powell during her years at Lake Erie College.

June 13: Kay Brush funeral. Brain tumor. Thought I was in wrong funeral—looking around for the tall beautiful young men she liked around her. Here were respectable bald men and elderly ladies. Were they the beauties now grown up or were the beauties simply elsewhere?

June 24: Sunday, Monday and Always appeared. No reviews as yet and advance sale only 1500. However a daily sheet called *Celebrity Service* sent me its folder describing hotels and steamer plans of various theater and movie big shots and listed me as Celebrity of the Day, with review of book. Next day a fur company wrote me urging me to wear any of their minks, sables, etc., at no charge on my T.V. shows or social occasions, merely crediting the firm. Then advance news of reviews came—all good, in fact so incredibly good that my knees shook.

June 29: Extraordinary good reviews of *Sunday*—nice letter from Paul Brooks at Houghton Mifflin; *Atlantic Monthly* writes asking for story. Most flattering, the publisher attention and the reviewers' reactions astound me because these stories always seemed good and yet from the 12 years of offering them to agents, Scribners and all, I got the idea they were never to be mentioned. I was right in believing they would help my prestige and reputation and sales (I hope). I expect England to take *Locusts* and these now; also, I expect reprint sales.

June 30: Spurt of working intelligence due to encouragement.

July 12: Auntie May, Jack, Rita came for lunch.*

July 26: Malcolm Cowley review in New York *Evening Post* is sample of Old Friend T.T.B.F. (Trying to be Fair). In other words, the kind male—not at all secure in his own fame—viewing with not too mixed feelings a female friend receiving high praise and *not* from him. He wishes book were not so good so he could praise it wholeheartedly without inner uneasiness—he would like to stand up for it against a world of detractors and for this he had girded up his ballpoint. But his defense is not required and he is bewildered, unprepared for any other role.

---

*Rita Sherman, Powell's cousin, who was now living with her brother Jack and Orpha May Steinbrueck.

July 28: Splendid review from Orville Prescott in daily *New York Times*.

September 4: Advice usually doesn't have any meaning until after the deed, when you can check with the experience and see that the advice was excellent whether you followed it or not.

You and your enemy can see eye to eye—but one eye at a time, at different times. The earth revolves around the sun and people revolve around each other, sometimes seeing each other fully and sometimes in eclipse, partial or total.

September 28: The intensely political woman—"We Intellectuals"—although her legal friends and intellectuals treat her like a fondly regarded idiot child—yes, yes, throwing "how right you are!" etc., to her as you would quiet a noisy puppy with tidbits to keep him from interrupting your preoccupations.

September 29: The way the complacent Marxist refers to anyone he can't convert or convince as a "very mixed-up little man"—though he is barely 5' 6" himself.

September 30: The business of the novel is to create life.

October 2: The rich boy who was pathologically stingy—would not pay anyone else's fare, even. Spent three or four years at psychoanalyst's at cost of several thousands. Finally brought candy or whiskey to hostess, who appreciated it since it was not just a $4 but a $1000 one. Basically the improvement was not so tremendous, for the giver had not been analyzed beyond giving the gift. As a result he did not budge from the place till he had personally consumed the entire gift and the extras provided by the hostess.

October 6: Today illustrated the virtue and value of a week of absolutely no thought. I found myself whisking my novel in order—for without my exterior brain, the interior worked the fireless cooker. I realized that Rick must be warm, generous, kind—in fact the very special kind of American that can be nothing but American, the kind that no foreigner understands because he is genuinely democratic.

October 7: This should be a *War and Peace* of New York in mid-century.

October 14: Parties for Gertrude Flynn who is going to Paris—two years almost to the day after I did. Curiously sad in a way—as if she was going to bring back the happy times with her daughter (since dead) or change her luck.

October 16: The way the noblest of motives and emotions destroys and corrupts—for this pure love I will kill; to keep from being bought by this evil I will surrender to a dozen other evils.

October 18: Tell Bobby Lewis: play based on Modern House—"Ideal Home," satire on all modernity: pressure cooker blows up, dishwasher noises, furnace noises.

October 26: In the Frick Museum the decadent cherubs in the Boucher panels—all engaged in adult occupations, with darkly disappointed eyes and swollen noses. The oversupply of Gainsboroughs, Reynolds, etc.—ladies vaguely similar—long and lean with faintly pink long noses, lean rubbery necks, spineless backs, long, boneless hands, arms almost always reaching down to knees, velvets, satins and brocades touchable and provable, personalities tastefully veiled in textures.

In a David portrait of a young man textures well done but seeming to be barely controlling the heady virility of the young man. Thigh muscles and calf in puttees are straining to be in action, the dark eyes are held for a moment but the next second you feel he will spot a flying bird, a deer, a girl, an enemy—and the healthy glowing hand will gladly seize the rifle. This sense of a frame briefly imprisoning life is what a good portrait should be and I should be able to do that in words.

October 28: Lunch—Volunteers for Stevenson.

November 1: W. H. Allen Co., England, wishes to publish *Locusts,* also *Sunday, Monday and Always* and *Wicked Pavilion.* This is all due to Bunny Wilson's praise of my work.

November 2: I have no more gratitude than my benefactors have toward *their* benefactors. Someone gives me money their ancestors gave them;

I have no more reason for abject gratitude than they have and many more excuses and justifications. At least I *work*.

November 3: She always picked up her first martini with a self-righteous air of—I *deserve* this, God damn it, after the day I've probably put in.

Ethel regarded her first drink politely, allowing it to simmer before her for several minutes, as if it was merely a formality like a service plate to be taken away untouched when something she really wished would be served. However, just as the other ladies were ordering a second round she suddenly dashed off her potion in one gulp and by dinner time was quite as tight as anyone else.

On the other hand Joe drinks as if it was a medicine ordered by the doctor and was likely to say with a look of pious inquiry: "Order dinner now? But my dear chap, I have not had my cocktail"—as if it was a digitalis potion. In the course of martinis, if food was served he ate it with his eyes shut, munching away even while he snored, but at least he was sitting, not lounging in his soup like his friend.

November 29: In "Yow"—has friend, Bill (or Mac), grocery cat, expense account.

Describe meeting with Mac—very hungry. Mac says how about having a quick one (mouse)?

December 1: Sleeping all morning and typing afternoons seems to be helpful.

Wonder why I can't bring out paperback of short stories?

December 2: The Fifth Avenue bus in traffic jam took long and it was amazing how conditioned people are now so that no one bawled out the driver or anything. Pouring rain. At 12th Street, a man got out and driver said, "Well, looks like I lose a trip today." The man said, "You said it," and the driver said, "I don't care. It's my last day here, anyway. After 25 years." Nobody said anything or paid any mind. I wanted to say to him, "What are your plans? And why have you quit? Or were you fired? Are you glad?"

December 12: What I want to do especially in this novel is a James device (or attempt) in *The Ambassadors*—have the reader get acquainted with the characters in a particularly New York cafe way, knowing them in their public exhibition of themselves (not as one knows, or what one knows of, them in their homes or offices). They are mostly on show, and so we do not really see what they wish to conceal and it is impolite of us to pry.

With the characters' encounters comes the Place, the Geography. These are people accustomed to fronts wherever they are, for they are alone and dare not relax in family tempers, etc. Yet they must develop and grow—and though we are not won by Dalzell or Jerry or even Ellenora at first, they unfold and grow for us, as acquaintances we meet in crowds, and are sure we would like, come close to us when by accident we are caught alone.

December 14: People call you up till finally they stop and then you call them. Same with invitations.

1953

January 7: Finished dinner murder—called it "Dinner on the Rocks" and sent to Carl [Brandt] who finds it awfully funny and says he is "shooting the moon" on it.

January 8: Cat story—Uncle Tom prefers horses as pets to humans. A pet horse—poor dear wouldn't go anyplace without him.

January 9: Book about the Southern girl who comes to New York and then her mother comes to visit her. This is a blonde chic beauty, an obviously available beauty who makes a practice of collapsing under alcohol the way Civil War belles had vapors. Even her face collapses and she clings moistly and fragrantly to everyone. You have to keep undoing her soft arms and moist cheeks and lips—as if she were a too affectionate spaniel.

January 10: Annapurna, book of Maurice Herzog's mountain ascent and worship, reminded me of first awe and ecstasy of Nature I ever experienced—the plane view across the Caribbean to Haiti. The look down at the transparent blue waters to the bottom of the ocean and little submarine variations of waters and hills giving different colors and geometric designs as mathematical as if measured by a formal abstractionist, as brilliant in color and form as if God had hung from Heaven by his heels to paint this.

January 15: Stories to do:
> The Pathetic Fallacy
> The Restaurant, old pals.

The story of the man who always kept his old girl friends—each year a new one that he told about deep love someplace else.

January 17: Instead of going straight to the club party Mr. and Mrs. Corey dropped by to wait with the Temples for their sitter to come. This meant a few preliminary highballs to pass the time so that by the time Elly Lou arrived Mrs. Temple had passed out the way she always did after two drinks and couldn't go anyplace anyway. Little Susie, of course, age five, was wide awake in that sly, precocious way she had.

January 26: In night, thought of story—not light enough for fun—of woman having nightmare of bickering voices, just as she used to cry as child hearing her mother nag all the time. So she preferred her father. Easy nature and, in early marriage to Pat, easy-going but now—after seven years—she hears herself and thinks: Good heavens, I'm turning into a shrew myself. Looks contritely at bed: Pat—curly, rosy, innocent— how *could* she? Yet she knows she is beyond cure. When he wakes up and grins "Where's my tie?" she's all ready to shout "If you put it where you should, you wouldn't be asking!" Hates the kind of woman she is becoming. Her father and mother were separated—mother contented and girl never quite forgave her for not having been this way before with Dad.

Goes to her with problem—how did she cure herself? Didn't. If they hadn't separated she would have worn herself out nagging both of them to grave. Some men must have shrews to be the man they think themselves to be. Dad never did so well in new marriage—young, pliable girl, no opposition, so he himself became nag. Girl thought it was ulcers. Nonsense—he made himself an ulcer to blame his bad nature on. Some men think of themselves as men's men—they'd feel sissy to admit fondness for wife. They want to be selfish, spend all their salary on themselves, stay out as they please, go where they like and consider nobody else—but above all they want to be liked and popular. If wife is sweet, they are called names, so they goad her into shrewishness and no one blames them for their selfishness.

January 23: An article about odd inventions and former conveniences. The St. Louis Special out of Newark after Civil War. 24 hours. Found it could be done and never did it again.

February 2: The innate fear and cliché opinion of another race. Dr. Wing —very Babbitty Chinaman, never touches chow mein, likes good sauer-kraut at Lüchow's, golf, evening clothes. Shoots rats in cellar with pal.

February 4: Feel that much is being done by dreams now—as if the other D. P. is now working with me to get done all the things once started. In night I wake up and realize work is being done by my night self.

February 17: I feel that there is a sudden rush of utterly undeserved luck and attention weaving toward me and I must be braced not to be bowled over. Also, I know that my dead are all pitching together with me to hurry my work so I can join them. They arrange my ideas, give me stories, fill me with a long-ago mind, and I seem to be availing myself of their help.

March 4: Rejection letters make me feel that life is too short for patience. It seems funny that for years I wanted my short stories published in a book in order to bolster my name and sell more to magazines. Result— book appears, reviews superlative, from then on unable to sell any stories at all. For two cents I'd try selling them under another name.

March 8: The reason Van Wyck Brooks is a treat instead of a "treatment" (as the cigarette ads say) is that he wishes to share everything he finds— opening up millions of doors and boxes for others to select and enjoy. In so many others—E. Wilson, etc.—it is a performance. As reader, you have no say: you are Told and nobody but a fool (and snob) can be told. Curiously enough, there is never any meat for me in Bunny's works except in his satirical poems and studies. I feel that he has laid out the subject and while it is a grand funeral, done with style and majesty, I have no desire to attend, for perhaps I liked the subject, only alive.

March 21: The Evelyn Scott-John Metcalfe return was curiously exhausting and revealing. She represents the Disease of Literature at its peak— the disease of Writing for the Writer's Sake, not even for Art's Sake. Like a soft gentle deadly octopus, her destructiveness is more brutally, utterly insensitive than any sadist's. She searches for the poetic phrase to describe the blood she is drawing.

March 24: Lazard, young Haitian painter, came in with lovely fresh paintings—tempera, oil, etc. Margaret came in, exhausted by hours with excellent but wearing old writers Evelyn Scott and John Metcalfe who feel the world still owes them a living and are full of personal complaints and wrongs and demands and whimpers, so the dignity, courteous unselfishness but confidence of young Lazard (as well as the freshness of his work) made her buy three of his works for $45.

March 25: What about Latouche and other unique figures in this book? Deporting himself like a celebrity and actually being treated as one—not really his fault he has so little time to write, everyone surrounds him, strangers sit at his table.

The way certain girls are asked for their striking clothes and everyone annoyed and insulted when they show up in ordinary dress.

March 26: The couple that has so much in common they have nothing to talk about.

March 29: What novels have I liked best—
   Sister Carrie—Dreiser
   Dodsworth—Lewis
   Sentimental Education—Flaubert
   Satyricon—Petronius
   Daniel Deronda—Eliot (partly)
   Dead Souls—Gogol
   Lost Illusions—Balzac
   Distinguished Provincial—Balzac
   Our Mutual Friend—Dickens
   David Copperfield—Dickens
   Jenny—Undset

April 19: Did difficult key chapter—"Play Back"—and see ahead. Remember: quickest way to get money is finish novel and make contract for new one, two of which I have partly done.

April 23: Endow a prize at Lake Erie for Best Fiction—short story, novella or poem which non-academically shows ability to outside world.

April 29: Invited for dinner. I thought it a good chance to do Jerry Hickey a favor—all publishers there and he might get a job. He accepted and afterwards I thought—Good God, I'm doing him no turn if I show up with this 28-year-old beauty and Thyra Winslow is there with her trim baby fags. It classes him as fairy, going out with old bag right away.

May 1: Finished the Bellevue scene and curiously enough feel this is major, since it entered into original scheme for novel, which was to show the medieval evil of the time and place and the way something evil happening unfairly to you makes you feel and act guilty. But this experience is tremendous because only this way do you *understand*—and from then you know mercy and pity for the falsely accused, the unfairly punished, just as you understand the marvel of others' good fortune in *not* being subjected to such misfortunes.

May 6: Power of pen? [Joseph] McCarthy on books. Nobody hates Americans or gets the "wrong" idea of Americans because of any novels but because of Americans they see—the American colony, arrogant, selfish fourth-raters who could not rate in any American town.

May 7: The vagaries of *forte* women (Esther, Margaret, myself) in middle years—not the still-hoping middle years but the at-last-I-give-up middle years.

May 10: [Tommy] Wanning says there is something about his stomach that makes him sick.

May 11: The thing I fear in this novel is that while I had no intention of showing the "pathos" of artists and minor happy people ruined by the age and taxes, I do not want people to be able to say the characters were so trivial that the villains were doing good to persecute them.

May 13: Winchell makes me even madder than McCarthy because he megaphones him. A clue to a way of needling him was in the denials by Bette Davis that she had cancer. A few plugs in other columns hinting at incurable disease and what a pity—what gossip columnist-broadcaster bravely carrying on losing fight against dread disease? Kind of germ warfare.

May 14: The last four weeks have been most productive of any—novel getting on to wind-up. Due to seeing Solley, I guess, and new people, Dexedrine, sunshine. New dress?

May 15: Everyone claiming to be best friend of Marius [in *The Wicked Pavilion*], as everyone claims Dylan Thomas.

May 21: I cannot figure out why this novel is so fiendishly fluid except that the times, the points of view, all change so fast. Moreover my work seems so uphill—my career—nothing seems to grow. No extra rights or ordinary to-be-expected dividends. No stories sell. No sudden royalties. It is fantastic how I have to start at the bottom every day.

My next novel must be placed so that it is not affected by political climate changes.

May 31: Incredible that any novel should be so hard—each morning dreading it. Do I fear finishing it? Is that it—fear that it is not the masterpiece I planned? Do I fear the usual applause and meaningless praise with no sales or support or even the customary decencies of reward? I thought last month it was moving along. Daily financial and personal frustrations bring home how futile my work is—even when done it accomplishes nothing, proves nothing and terrifies me.

June 4: More depressed last week or two over novel and inadequacy. No reassurance coming from outside, but read my old play, "Walking Down Broadway," and astonished at how good it is. Expert, touching, simple, and true. No reason it could not be done. No reason I could not do play next—a simple, basic one like this. Maybe "Brooklyn Widow" could be simplified, too. Reading this early work—1931—is the nicest thing that's happened to me in ages—for I had an hour or so of believing I was good, that I did have something.

June 8: Reprint of Books for Writers—Creative and Critical.
  Gauthier—Preface to *Mlle. de Maupin* (on censorship)
  Robert Henri—*The Art Spirit*
  Marinetti—*Manifesto*
  Maugham—*The Summing Up*

June 12: Hope to be able to write play next. I deserve some *pleasure* writing. Play—maybe light and simple, one of my short story ideas. Like the one beginning with return of wife. Husband taken by surprise though he has been begging forgiveness.

June 30: Try paperback collection of stories: "The Gravy Girls," "Ladies in Pink" or "Long Dress," "Dinner on the Rocks," "Remember Sweet Alice," "Old Folks At Home," "Mermaid in Punchbowl," "Pathetic Fallacy," "Laughing Water," "Now Is The Time," "Green Bananas."

July 6: There is really one city for everyone just as there is one major love. New York is my city because I have an investment I can always draw on—a bottomless investment of 21 years (I count the day I was born) of building up an *idea* of New York—so no matter what happens here I have the rock of my dreams of it that nothing can destroy.

August 18: Cloisters with Jojo. Also visited Little Church Around The Corner—exquisite and tiny like Sainte Chapelle in Paris. Getting on subway, Jojo said in loud, weary voice: "Mother did you buy tokens to pay your fare or did you try to chisel your way with play money?" Everyone looked at me—I sounded very guilty saying I had bought tokens. "I didn't see you buying any token," he said severely.

August 19: My three artists are too stereotyped and alike—cardboard naifs and majestic and pompous.

August 20: Good God how this novel hangs—with all the domestic encroachments to which I have had to surrender in the last few years, till each page begins with a market list and each day begins with Nothings of daily trivia.

August 24: Thinking—if money should happen, I might buy working farm. Cottage to farmer free for working it and teaching Jojo who can work and own it.

Working over novel—well, I believe. Would like to finish it by day. Lafayette is down.*

---

*Powell's beloved Hotel Lafayette had been demolished to make way for an apartment house.

September 5: Return of what seemed broken rib—but went away.

Really, my publishers! What with Houghton Mifflin letting me down, then the English company Allen publishes *My Home Is Far Away* instead of *Locusts* and result—zero. No reviews, no word, no nothing. My great accomplishment this summer seems to be my painting and art works which are joyous to do and, good or bad, fill me with glee.

September 9: Still cannot find any notices of the English publication.

September 11: Joe's contact with old life always gets him on an emotional drunk like his old days. This was his great love—his happiness—the Boys, the Office, the perpetual club with home and family like a church where one goes (when there are no opportunities for temptation) to dwell on past sins, confess and maybe buy $10 worth of lettuce and caviar and pickles as penance—then storm out to bar enraged that such good providership is not appreciated. A disease, male friendship—more disturbing than sex, really.

September 19: Here was a group from Israel. They talked of America, an America not many Americans know—Johnny Ray regarded as the idol of every home, teenage petting in cars, etc.—explaining that this could not happen in Europe. Why not? I said—in 50 years, perhaps? It couldn't have happened here either 100 years ago, for very simple reasons. Each member of the family didn't own a car, there were no radios to popularize songs, a few traveling minstrels with very few songs. The difference is not a matter of geography but of time.

Always an argument with L. who thinks there is a genuine Cape Cod still lurking behind the new one—a place where they use simple good warming pans, can their own fruit, wear bustles and really good clothes.

September 23: Did story of beauty parlor with Dwight.

October 19: Wife of actor (or playwright) who is so much more important and happy with him away so she can tell all his stories, theater gossip, and inside stuff. When he's around, she has no personality, looks embarrassed and unhappy and a little resentful—he is stealing her stuff. Isn't it enough he *lives* it—has the applause, the name? Doesn't he owe her *something*?

Thinking of Josie Herbst, Max Gorelik, Jack Lawson, etc. More people turn to Communism because they have not been able to become the capitalists they want to be under Capitalism. As I recall, all these people in earlier days were completely opportunistic, wanting money and able to butter up anybody for it, but their failure to get into big dough right off turned them Communist through bitterness. When no money comes that way, they deviate or blab.

October 20: C.*—the completely student-literary man. No pleasure unless he'd read about it in an accredited place; no beauty or taste unless it first had a printed O.K. No discovery on his own nor did he respect original discovery in others. It must be okayed in a printed source first to unlock his palate, eye or ear. I doubt if he would have approved sex or food unless literary men of note had given it the printed okay.

October 21: Men whose days are full to all appearances, yet mentally and spiritually they retired decades ago—perhaps upon college graduation. They establish no contact with whoever they see but immediately replace or mask the present with the past. A camera with no film.

October 31: Furiously and insanely working over novel but so tired I dread sleep for fear I won't be able to wake up and get to work as I hardly sleep and then wake myself with parched eyes to go over book at 6 or 7 A.M. I never get anywhere no matter how many hours I spend. Another terrible year of fruitless work finally turned aimless. Simply remarkable bad luck—perhaps my just return but let us have some of the luxurious injustice other writers enjoy.

November 2: When publishers ask how many copies something sold—the equivalent of "How much did you make?" and a figure they can discover gracefully without the direct question—I feel like saying "How much salary do you make? For if you make less than $100 a week (as I suspect) it shows you obviously are not a good enough editor for me, in spite of my superficially favorable impression of you." If cards are going to be on the table, let's have both hands out, then.

---

* Powell's abbreviation; it seems unlikely she means Coby Gilman.

November 10: Poor Dylan Thomas died today at St. Vincent's of cerebral trouble—the only writer whose words burst into life through the "literature barrier," to be so alive and be able to make all his thoughts and images live more than life he must have been the child of death—that border of revelation on the edge of death.

November 12: "American Gothic," Victor Wolfson play in Round. Pleasant technically, substance watered O'Neill. Old whaling fairies off to New Bedford, as they whooped, etc.

November 22: Republicans act as if America had no future and no hopes.

November 28: Birthday present to myself of fixing up *Pavilion*.

Reading young Charles Flood's novel*—superior to but something like young Marquand. Marquand with his throwbacks has a lot to answer for—the shaping of a young person through his father's life.

I don't think anyone could understand me better by giving my poppy or mommy's life story. I never hatched from a regular egg, anyway, but from an aluminum decoy or darning egg, something for the needle. And these young long-novelists. First Papa's college days, then *his* papa's school, then his son's. I really don't want to go back to school. I worked my way through college once and I don't like to keep being sent back.

Actually, an awful lot of oatmeal. While champagne, fine wines, martinis and best Scotch abound, the final feeling is a surfeit of oatmeal.

In these young three-generation novels, there is an occasional shock of reading a schoolboy's diary—"Went to Laurie's coming out. Tubby made Black Velvets. Sick in Grand Central men's room." Each carefully detailed day in which nothing happens, produced as if it meant something. "He retched and was sick" always indicates that the sensitive fellow was only reacting emotionally to the wrongs of the world, not at all due to drinking hard liquor on top of all that fudge.

November 30: Dinner at Monroe Stearns'. Dos, Margaret, Coby. Terrific work on novel last few days—up early and working in my bedroom. Reviewed Simone de Beauvoir's book *America by Day* also.

---

*Flood's *Love Is A Bridge* was published by Houghton Mifflin in 1953.

December 1: "Yow" book. Tom the delicatessen cat on strike around Department of Health which forbade cats in delicatessens. Picketing cats.

December 3: Turned in novel to Houghton Mifflin. 294 pages. Last chapter not complete. Did most important work very fluently in last four weeks—about 50 or 60 pages.

December 9: Babysitter. Walk to Project. Afraid of them.

1954

[*Undated*] Mabel and Grandma Sherman's recipe for cough syrup.

2 oz. sweet Balsam or Life Everlasting

1 oz. horehound

2 lbs. white sugar

4 oz. honey

Stewed one hour with plenty of water.

Strain. Add brandy when cold and bottle.

January 1: Revisions on novel sent to Boston but more to be done.

January 3: Go away and do "Yow" story.

January 4: Simply incredible the waste of last three novels—millions of rewrites, new versions. I must make a thorough investigation of causes for this. Very little waste in *Time to be Born*—perhaps longer period of gestation. Perhaps handwritten jobs better. Next one will do handwritten.

January 17: There are people who would be disliked, even boycotted, if they lived an ordinary community life in town or city. But if they keep traveling, always saying good-bye, they are treasured and loved. Their short periods in one place are like an actor's moment on the stage—they can keep to their star hero role that long at least. If circumstance forces them to stay longer they are reduced to being the testy, selfish, monomaniacal hams they really are and wives, friends, husbands all desert them. Off they must go to distant shores to renew their lease on their hero shell—become again the far-away idol of legend.

January 21: If some magazines are "the slicks," are the rag-paper quarterlies "the swamps," "the woolies" or "the dusties"?

January 22: The domestic carnage of my life—fatigue and wearing down of hopes when no audience is around, the isolated life I am obliged to live, partly financial but also social shyness and the awkwardness of asking guests when Joe hates everyone and either gets plastered or makes a production of simple, friendly calls. Now I have manuscript back for revision and I realize I could revise forever but my frayed brain isn't doing what is needed for I've forced it and played it long after the original inspiration and joy had been beaten to death by boredom and isolated domesticity—Louise and Joe, Joe and Louise, and my own boring self.

January 25: Hemingway and wife lost in Africa plane crash near Murchison Falls. I thought of his bravery and bold facing of danger in which he always comes out okay but somebody else gets hurt. By Monday they were found and his sales had another jolt upward.

I have a hunch that Hemingway has muffed his death just as Marius does in my novel—the great to-do and raving praises always given the dead. But perhaps his real death will be unmarked, unnoticed. I tried once again to read *Farewell to Arms* and it seems as clumsily written as ever to me—wooden, like Walter Scott, difficult reading, pidgin English.

A Wasted Life is not a life of folly and excesses but a waste of patience, when *impatience* would have solved waste of goodness on wrong people, waste of brains, waste of time.

January 26: I regard this as my lucky day for I found my Rolls Royce again and suddenly wrote a perfectly brilliant, easy and necessary chapter (Jerry and Tessie). In collating this novel, I wanted a fan-like picture—closed, opened slightly to hint at more, then wide with each section a complete picture, yet all fitting rhythmically together.

February 3: Last night Charles Ingle came in with a friend, Kenneth Shepperach. Charles is the young writer whose novel *Waters of the End* I reviewed so extravagantly for the *Post*. Full of misprints as it was, the fulsome favorableness of it filled the *Post* with joy—evidence that to be respected and admired as critic you must always praise. I feel demoted 30 years back to earliest book-reviewing days when people discuss these reviews as if they never heard of anything else I did. Very odd.

However, Ingle telephoned and there was some talk (polite and uncertain on both our sides—me not knowing whether he wished to call but feeling I ought to ask; him equally uncertain) and then he came in with a friend. I felt compelled to spend precious dough on rye and beer but neither at first wanted any. Ingle, very Byronic or Greek-idol looking, said he had not been eating for eight days because he was allergic to food—saltines, nuts, beer, etc.

Shepperach, a thin, pale, book-keeper looking young man with protuberant pale blue eyes, well-mannered, quiet. It was all very stuffy.

S: I wish you would try to make Chuck eat.

Me: Shall I make some tea?

Charles: Yes, with milk.

S: I am looking for an apartment in the Village.

Charles: He's been fired from his job in Philly so he's here looking for one.

S: Not fired—*released*.

Charles: He's been living with a Swarthmore girl I was engaged to once.

S: Wait now, don't say I was *living* with her.

Charles: All right, living with her and her husband. That's worse.

S: No, I rather like him. He's bright but he covers it up with verbosity. Lenore is really awful, though—soap-opera, chocolates, never out of the nightgown, always telling me awful things about Charles.

Charles: She says I'm paranoiac.

S: She does say so. Charles, do eat. Miss Powell, do make him eat.

Me: Will you have some more tea? Or sherry, Mr. Shepperach?

Charles: He doesn't drink.

S: I'm excited because today I got a wonderful job at CBS. I'm a recording engineer. A terrific salary.

Charles: I don't eat because I felt terrible until I stopped eating.

S: But now you feel terrible again so he should start eating, don't you think?

(*Now they were trying to be nice to Fagan who was spitting and snarling at both of them. There was talk of Lippincotts, Gore Vidal, more tangles with cat, polite pauses, they wondering how to go, me wondering when they would, asking if they'd like more tea, sherry, rye? Finally, Charles had a slug of rye. Mr. S had nothing but cold tea.*)

Charles: Let's let Miss Powell in on the secret. Ken can't drink because he's full of heroin.

Me: (politely) Do you have it as a drink or in shots?

S: By syringe. As a matter of fact I only have it two or three times a month just for kicks.

Charles: I have my first heroin yet to take.

Me: (yawning) You mean alcohol confuses the kicks?

S: Oh yes indeed.

Me: I knew someone in the recording department at CBS, when Lloyd Frankenberg did his "Pleasure Dome" there.* Do you know Lloyd, Charles?

Charles: (politely) Yes. I've met him and Loren MacIver at Cummings'. I must show Ken the Village. Then we meet the English publisher of Frederic Prokosch's. I could take you to Louis' on the Square but it might be boring if you can't drink. I guess you should come up to Gore's with me.

(They start to leave but Charles has tousled Fagan who in turn has clawed his face and hair, drawing blood which I mop with whiskey.)

S: You're a real person, Miss Powell. If I get a job in New York I sincerely trust I will see you again.

We all bow politely, Charles blotting the blood on his cheek. I thought of Malcolm Lowry—the last time I saw someone I felt was a genius and how a ring of fire or blood is around these people—moving like angels, leaving blood and strange nightmare terrors for everyone else and feeding on it themselves. Whoever loves them or tries to save them burned or destroyed by their gentle, precious flame—a flame that burns everyone else when they do not use it themselves for it is atom fire and it is never wasted. If those who are granted this free light do not employ it then it sears and ravages everyone else. I think Mischa has it, too.

All during this outing young Shepperach was daintily cleaning his nails.

February 3: In last nine days, front pages have honored two writers. Hemingway crashed, reported dead, found again. Then, at the opposite extreme, Max Bodenheim murdered in a Third Avenue rooming house,

---

*Frankenberg had produced a celebrated early LP called "Pleasure Dome," featuring poets reading their own work.

all proving that violent deaths are the only thing that can give writers now any immortality. What a pair—one who never missed a bet, knew the right people, dropped the wrong ones as he went along, played it rich and social and for publicity. The other played the dunghill and his dunghills got lower and lower. Both quarreled with all old friends. Max killed with *The Sea Around Us* on his chest—a sea that engulfed him. I think his wife in drunken fit stabbed him and he was mad enough to stab back and the pal was so outraged he got gun and killed Max.*

Went to Metropolitan Museum yesterday to Columbia University show of American painting. Of old ones, Whistler's magic paintings seemed most original and exciting. Saul Steinberg's scroll "The Parade" wonderful.

On bus the two women (scarves over heads) in deep talk: "So I just took time out and sat down and analyzed the situation and after I'd analyzed it for a while the whole thing fell apart just like a jig-saw puzzle."

February 5: Virginia Woolf's diary. People keep diaries because they don't enjoy exposing themselves in conversation and furthermore they trust no one to understand. As soon as a writer finds a group that does understand him he stops writing and starts hamming. In diaries, revealing the innermost soul, the entries stop when anything interesting happens or whenever the writer is happy. Diaries tell nothing—chips from a heroic statue.

February 6: Margaret has wondrous ways of needling and so has Tommy Wanning—both so petty as to be funny and surprising. You think you're having a gay time and next day they call up and say unctuously, "Sorry I was so dull and absent-minded yesterday but I guess you were feeling pretty dull yourself."

February 8: I want last chapter again to have ecstasy of New York. The truth is not what the beloved failed to do—the hurt, the wound, the betrayal—but the lovely gift he intended to give, the faithfulness he would have wished to give, the nobility he would have liked to show.

February 10: Remember in Marcia book—sense of her feeling she had a message or a duty or a valuable package.

---

*Powell clearly dated this entry incorrectly: Bodenheim was murdered on February 7. A man named Harold Weinberg confessed to both killings and was declared insane.

February 12: To Dorothy and Malcolm Browne's extraordinary party. Charles Ingle there with his heroin-eating pal, Shepperach.

February 14: Reading Virginia Woolf's diary. Almost too much—a curious reaction as in reading Henry Miller. So self-conscious, intense, exhausting, pecking away at her heart, brain, soul.

February 18: Ridiculous not to hear anything from Houghton Mifflin.

Very like the time Farrar & Rinehart kept a manuscript five weeks without a word, then John wrote "Better put aside—not necessarily destroy." It was *Turn, Magic Wheel*—very likely my best, simplest, most original book.

I will send Houghton Mifflin a questionnaire: Has anyone read the book? Have people disliked it? I am working on plans for this year and would like to know.

February 19: Frightfully overdrawn at bank and yet I thought I was only two or three over. Must make plans beside desperation ones. I want to finish Marcia but cannot do except in calm and no worry.

February 22: Reading Virginia Woolf's diary edited by husband. After a while, marriage becomes a mutual blackmail or Trust—I forgive what you did 25 years ago and you overlook what I did 18 years ago. You spent the rent money on your poker game; I spent it on garden utensils. If Virginia Woolf's greatest love was V. Sackville-West, then husband Leonard is blind, merely exacting a book of essays for his publishing company in exchange for her pleasure in *Orlando*.

February 24: Russia Luca and her new love Bill Hughes come in. A very nice fellow—too Republican and conventional, she says. I think I have never met any radical or even liberal man who treated his women gracefully, lovingly or fairly. I think they sometimes deliberately take up a radical stand (like the Church) to excuse their plan to be selfish and thoroughly inconsiderate.

March 1: Another career girl with her Ph.D. boyfriend. Girls at lunch (buyer, decorator and writer) have argument on Ph.D. theses of their boys.

Books they don't have to read (Harry's reading it). One girl disgruntled because she has to do her own reading—her boy is just real estate man. Double standard?

Divorce. Friends afterward. Got acquainted because during marriage only finances mattered.

March 11: Latouche's "Golden Apple" opened at Phoenix—thoroughly fresh and delightful. At end, saw him by stairs in middle of cheers. He was weeping. "They've ruined my second act—they've ruined it—spoiled everything! Come downstairs and have champagne!" Down was a vast Sardi's. Gore Vidal—Luciferian-looking young man who called a couple of times. Very gifted, brilliant, and fixed in facility as I am.

March 12: Locusts published in England.

March 15: In return to hometown story write it straight, with man planning his return like a crime.

March 16: Found brief reviews in daily Manchester *Guardian*—very bad, but exactly my own opinion of my work right now so it didn't matter. Decided that all my good reviews had not sold books so maybe bad reviews would do it.

March 17: Lunch with Gore Vidal. He has more character, manliness, power, manners and general good breeding, intelligence than other young men—and capacity to work, in spite of perfect capacity for climbing as the others have and customary social charm and ambition. Latter has driven him to do too much and without direction.

March 29: Finished proof of *Wicked Pavilion* and whereas going over the earlier section alarmed me for I had revised, rewritten and woodened it up, so that it seemed heavy, labored, unreal and uninteresting, the last section retrieves it by being true and light-touched.

March 31: Went to opening of circus and saw mostly TV and Hollywood celebrities throwing themselves around like the local high school bunch showing off.

April 11: Joe and I go to Gladwyne for Jojo and I attend his services where he spoke fluently to a polite dozen or more patients.

Very good week at home—calm, better than ever—until rain on Saturday. He liked "Heidi" but felt oncoming nerves. Party—in cackle and clatter he tells me "I envy you your being such an excellent conversationalist, Mother. I am proud of you. I wish I could." Then, when I reassured him, he said "No, but I can't do it so easily and with poise the way you can. I admire you for the way you compliment my friends for me, too. You always do." It was so clear and normal that I was shocked and moved to tears, especially since the "conversation" was of a particularly silly, cliché type.

April 27: About Our Contributors (for a little magazine)

Stella Negs, author of *Flies On Paper,* is the sister of the editor.

Arthur Pugh, author of our novella, is the son of Mrs. R. Pugh, who pays the magazine's rent.

Astrid Bean is the editor's latest girlfriend.

Vortex Lieber is the nephew of the Foundation Secretary expected to give the magazine a large grant so it can come out twice a month instead of twice a year.

May 9: Read Gore Vidal's *Messiah.* More impressed by the writer than the book, which was engaging enough, but the trouble with being a clear, sharply cut, extraordinary individual with a rich articulate gift is that no characters can equal the author himself, whose muscular skill directs most complicated interplay of plots, guides contrapuntal themes with suave, veiled power and a doom-like rhythm that compels and lulls. A genuine novelist—power at the wheel, a rich, regal, original mind with unlimited treasures and the serene generosity of one who knows he will come into more and more. Something of Disraeli—a high, patrician, Solomon-like judgment and philosophic power, with wit, poetry and music. Not to be fit in any fashion, but will outlive them all, like the great ones.

May 10: Have feeling new novel is about to strike.

May 11: What I would like to do with money I am about to make is:

a) Buy small house in Gladwyne for Jojo where he may entertain old friends.

b) Set up college scholarship with attached job in Shelby High School.

Make will leaving royalties of one book each to niece Dawnie, Jack Sherman, Isabel,* young Harry,† Bobby Morrison, Coby.

May 14: Louise had stroke and I took her in a dolly to St. Vincent's Hospital. $16 a day.

May 15: To Newark to Minsky's Burlesque with Joe on Reginald Marsh recommendation.

May 23: Went to Staten Island. A tall, distinguished looking white-haired lady moved down the walk, lightly leaning on a slender cane—a living reminder that Staten Island had its old wealthy aristocrats just as its broken old mansions proclaimed. There had been several slight showers and suddenly there was a rainbow in the sky—something I haven't seen for decades, if indeed rainbows ever grow in New York. A warm, lovely little island with all those hills overlooking the Bay and New York. I thought of trying to rent a house for a week or two—Joe and Jojo for lawn work.

June 3: LeClercq's party—very splendid in an old LeClercq way. In corner was gray-haired lady looking like Edith revived. Startled by what seemed a reconciliation I went over and lo, it was his great love of 20 years ago, Martha, who had put the riveting crack in his marriage—the beautiful girl who contrasted with Edith. At 45, she looks like Edith did at 45, sweetly genteeled umlaut lips, prissy pronunciation (did she learn this from Edith?)—only warmer, softer on closer inspection, affectionate and shrewder.

Coby loud, drunk and spilling. "Everything is just the same," said Martha. Everyone a little hard of hearing, showing pictures of their grandchildren. ("Do be nice to Prof. L, darling—talk to him." "I've done all I could. I asked him to get us a drink, I asked him if he'd gone to Williams, I even showed him pictures of my grandchild—what else can I do?")

June 6: Louise still in hospital but improving. *Times* (Harvey Breit) says I am talented novelist preposterously underestimated.

---

* Isabel Hofmayr, Joseph Gousha's sister.
† Harry Gousha, Jr., J. G.'s nephew.

June 18: Went to Shelby. Switched from roomette on Southwestern Limited at Cleveland to train full of Stanley Home Products ladies (and one man) who had been traveling on private car to some eastern resort conference or jamboree. All seemed married and from southern Ohio or Kentucky, taking their jobs hard and enjoying them, exchanging Babbitty talks about which jamboree did the most for them—obviously not interested in anything except what their salaries could buy.

Aunt May looked lovely but grieved when people (Jack or I) talked of Paris or London or book or anything that was removed from family, and interrupted determinedly to point out a canary, robin, or bluebird or tell again how and which new babies had clung to her. Jealous of any interest her family took in anything or anyone she sometimes launched out bitterly against these intruders. Everyone had planned a treat of visiting Louis Bromfield's farm on Sunday and was stunned and bewildered that I didn't want to accept this honor.

Phyllis arrived and the talk of old geneologies (purchased for $2) went on. We went to graveyards and visited old and sick, visited Effie in lone drab Cardington. Back with Phyllis to Canton and her Uncle Kent—intelligent, lecherous old gent and endless chatter of family, strangers, family's woes of long ago and above all the hysteria over antiques—acquisition of, history of, etc. TV going and people telling their stories louder than it—visiting each other, nursing their babies to TV, glancing at it, then resuming conversation of antiques, friends ("They say she's crazy and awfully dirty on account of her boxers all over the house—*you'd* like her, Dawnie, she goes to museums and acts in plays").

Phyllis never got over thrill of trip to Bromfield's farm and sitting next to him (she talked of me and found it amazing and flattering that he'd heard of me—*certainly,* he said) and how lovely so-and-so was to her, how important they were and it dawned on me she was fearless in claiming a New York writing sister as social lever but regarded it as a credit to herself, not to me. I had a feeling of being a ghost, not present at all, and very deflated because I could not possibly be on the level with the Sister of hers who wrote in New York. Quite reduced. Went to Myrtle Taylor's at Phyllis's insistence where, like Auntie May, Phyllis took over and told of her family, antiques and became Mabel herself. Finally, afraid I would blast out or burst into tears, I begged to go to Cleveland. Everybody would *take* me—no trains out.

June 26: The unsatisfactory reunions—first the disappointment of people being different (not worse) than your imagined idealization of them—then the completeness of their life without you, so you try to push in some niche like trying to push through a crowd to see the great man on parade. Your memory is of being alone with them, a rapport, and the new picture bothers you until you adjust to it.

July 7: Walked over Brooklyn Bridge. Jojo is really very constructive and helpful—making beds, sweeping, etc., and allowing me to do my own work, which I can do better with him alone than I ever could with Louise. Adversity has its advantages.

July 15: Proves really true that creative freelance working at home more blocked and more basically damaged by maid in home than by having to do the work. During Jojo's visit I am doing more housework and outings than ever but less frittered and ragged by daily nerve tensions and inner rages—like having a house guest who never leaves.

Plan to finish Eva story, also "Yow" story over weekend, maybe. Use different name.

July 29: Took Jojo to Bellevue.

August 10: Jojo to Manhattan State Hospital. Ward's Island.*

September 12: Winchell broadcast this was Book-of-the-Week, a "must," etc. Front page in *Tribune*.

September 18: The rides to Ward's Island—the bus at 125th Street, five cents—which sweeps suddenly over the bridge. At one point where all other traffic continues to Queens, our magic bus takes off into space, swooping down as if into thin air, into the lunar world of lunacy. The people on the bus are bound suddenly by their one destination—they talk to each other, tell each other how long they have been coming here. "We've had some of the finest talent in the world here."

September 24: Sold about $900 this week.

---

*From this point, Jojo lived only in hospitals, with brief visits outside.

October 1: Cape Cod with Margaret and Josie.

October 8: Writing a novel is like building a bird's nest—and the bird is a magpie.

October 17: Jojo's leave up. Best Seller list in *Times.*

October 24: No further push of book—not on best-seller list—no ad. I do not seem at ease mentally as best-seller type but on other hand would like *something* to move by itself in my life without having to begin at the bottom of everything every day.

The worry over Jojo and inability to help gnaws at my mind like a disease so that I have been unable to function for months. I believe this is primarily due to my loss of independence some years ago and my inability to regain it. Now I want to do so many things that they all block each other and whatever I *do* do stops under anything less than supernatural pushing. Even the diet and pills; after seven days of loss, started right back up to 160. I have promised "Marcia" for May and will tackle it but would like something in-between—rewards for work.

October 26: Write Chase review, Trollope review.

Very low. Trying to recover mind and at same time triumph over Jojo situation. Believe that sudden wad of money could be spent on summer place with winter heat, perhaps in Jersey or Staten Island near ocean or Sound preferably. Possible place—say, near Hightstown, N. J., near Princeton. Hire couple or teacher for Jojo.

October 29: All week messing with Stamford Womens' Club Book Lunch speech. Sick to stomach and exhausted, finally made it. Curious life there —autographed 10 or 15 books largely due to its description as "naughty but not *too* naughty." Anya Seton a big, handsome, *forte* woman. Like Taylor Caldwell, these best selling-women novelists have a Big Industry quality—as if they were accustomed to make people jump, publishers, editors, etc. Whether this comes from already privileged backgrounds (Marcia Davenport, Anya, etc.) or is acquired after first big movie sale I don't know, but they create a respectful and awed air about them like president of Chase National or General Motors. More like great industrial representatives than the Great themselves, like Churchill or Einstein, who tend to be human.

November 1: Story of man (bachelor) whose only asset is an apartment upkeep and rent-free. Not a cent. Belongs to his ex-wife or mother or someone in army. Advertises it in weekly as for rent for afternoon parties. Maid furnished. Gets idea from other man who acts as bartender after 5:30 at parties—$15 minimum or $5 an hour.

November 3: Notes for talk—people like different books at different times in their lives. It seems odd that such difficult ponderous writers as Walter Scott, Dumas, Victor Hugo are so often pets of our youth when later in life they seem almost over our heads. It must be that, at 12 or 13, our heads need filling—there are few experiences and knowledge to furnish resistance, so the story has a wide screen. The young reader has no experiences of his own to debate the story; he accepts it wholly, is gullible, it blooms in his mind completely. Trollope is certainly a writer for adults.

November 15: Must start coming up to roof for reflection and work on Marcia.

November 17: Lunch at Upper Montclair Womens' Club and talk afterward. These women's clubs are curious and I find myself sympathetic to them because they are for women as women, instead of Mothers, Educators, etc.

November 25: Jojo came home. Looks well and mature. I do not accept this Ward's Island business still—not for anyone. The lostness of having no treasure chest of one's own, no place for private letters, a handkerchief, etc., so without any security at all. Smokes. When I asked him if doctor okayed it he said, "Mother, it's the only pleasure I have." He astonishes me by referring fondly to Bellevue. A night nurse there appealed to him. He confessed that at Ward's, he repeated so often that he wanted to have this lady as a friend that another patient yelled "Why don't you have her for a wife and then you could f—— her?" This amused and shocked Jojo.

December 5: To Ward's to see Jojo. A man, shabbily wrapped, crossing grounds, talking to himself loudly: "A stew—very well, but when I'm stewed I try to conduct myself with the greatest of gaiety—but some I know could be perfumed from head to toe and still they stink—"

Jojo has terrible cold but attendants say due to smoking 40–50 cigarettes which they deliberately give him. "Mother, I'm afraid if I stay here I'll lose my sanity."

December 10: Up early. Decided to do dream book again. No reason why not complete Manhattan fairy tale—fast.

December 16: Received $647.01 from Houghton Mifflin. Sales up to September 30—5,130, which means around $500 or so due in June.

December 25: To 29 West Ninth Street for party. Pollocks and various TV figments but apartment itself the only pleasure. Dull people have fine places—green gold lamé bath for Siamese pets, wine cellars, fountain in garden, etc.

December 30: A year of practically no writing. Louise's stroke with constant worry and visiting. Jojo home and visiting and care at Bellevue and Ward's. Synopsis of Marcia. Two short stories with no luck—starts at others. General social recovery and final domestic recovery—at least cleaned up somewhat via vacuum. End of year, am buried in cooking, isolated home life and slumbering indignation which may burst into writing again.

December 31: Invited to Frank MacGregor's but too sleepy to go.

1955

January 1: Pleasant cocktail party restored frazzled nerves. Frances Keene and Adrienne Foulke, the Stearns, the Frankenbergs.

The reason we read with delight so many ponderous books in our youth was that we led very boring lives. Now the book heroes' lives are much more boring than most of ours.

Esther and others felt very deprived because on sailing and fishing trips Hemingway talked out the story he was writing and then—plagiarist!—used the same expressions that they had enjoyed in the written work.

January 14: Picked up Jojo. He was weak and languid after measles, and without any interest except tying everything with Deesie*—her sickness and somehow unable to connect anything except why wasn't she there? Answers repeated again and again exhausting me and beating down hope in a new way, this being not hysterics but apathy. Sleeping any moment, heavy, stupefied sleep. Perhaps the thorazine does it. No concentration and dulling of appetites—I believe a kind of surrender to defeat. No hope, though he did say he felt better at Ward's than at Gladwyne and he repeated his pleasure in being at home. I would like the luxury of paying Gladwyne, of paying all bills.

January 15: Bought fur coat and won $46 on horse Moondog. The way the new blood goes into the firm (Monroe, etc.) but instead of invigorating it merely is changed into old blood. The oldsters want new blood to sour and corrupt, not to let it sway them.

---

* Jojo's pet name for Louise, Powell's housekeeper.

January 19: I must make the Marcia part, while separate, still cling in roots to first book. This is one where the baby fingers are gently being torn away—the growing person tries to reach toward adult life but inside the baby cries for consolation.

January 21: Out to Snedens with Gerald. Talked of people whose youth vanished overnight—Valentino's, for instance, an old man, yet not 27, a mass of varicose veins, all the result of early overwork, etc. Sugar Ray, prizefighter in glittering prime of youth only four years ago, now *Times* says no coordination, washed up, an old man, slow. Scott Fitzgerald with rubbers and slow tread, helped across street, only 34 years old. Gerald told of Scott's desire for nobility—an English nanny for daughter, so little girl of five saying "Don't be a silly ass." At 4 or 5 A.M., child clinging wide-eyed to Nanny while Scott and Zelda being carried in unconscious drunk by chauffeur and gardener.

February 7: Wicked Pavilion published in England. Decided on original approach to this novel—fictional once again instead of phony and queasy fact. But what it must have is not the old-home-folks familiarity but the strangeness of Egypt, the Orient. No excuse for redoing an old background unless magic of strangeness is brought to it.

February 8: Incredible block on Marcia novel due as before to problem of hidden fact or truthful fiction. Hate idea of beginning it all over but this absolute block to writing is killing me. My will power and obstinacy will not let me abandon it again as I have—once to do *Locusts,* then to do *Wicked Pavilion*—oh many times I've locked with it, paralyzed by it and with it.

February 9: Starting the nurse story as rebellion against novel. Perhaps if I unload enough of my blocked contemporary short stories I will be happier to relax into old Ohio novel. That is my prescription for myself now.

Thought of Ernest Boyd, a real Appreciator of Women—all types: whores, servants, social, old, young. Saw him very clearly.

February 15: Wanning said all of our generation seemed to have been radical in youth. Not true. I was Girl Republican, conventional (being born Republican is like being Catholic; you don't need to give it a thought). My early aim was writing—not the Great Novel or Poem but anything. Since it was important that anything you did must be self-producing, I daresay my aim was to write and sell stories to *Saturday Evening Post*. Failing, I found other, deeper levels in self—failing these, drilled deeper, like looking for oil or water.

February 16: Some people seem to "never grow up"—they do not take personal or emotional responsibilities. The fact is they are in reverse—they were forced to be adults as children, to understand and be part of extremely adult problems—financial, professional, amorous, domestic, psychological—and they cannot get to a certain other plane without some period (the equivalent of an ideal childhood) of security, love, money, being cared for and cherished. Many of us continue seeking this childhood of which we were deprived and will not surrender until we have had our share.

February 27: Jojo home. To Perth Amboy at last to see Louise—calm, obviously pleased to have people at her beck and call instead of vice versa. I saw all the angry worry I had about her not necessary. She was better off than ever, her family more comfortable than us, for Negroes don't have to pay taxes. They enjoy rights and also get feudal privileges.

March 3: Went to "Shoestring Review"—very funny, exquisite styles of comic acting, some of the fresh funniness of the old college show but none of the politics or messages that young humor bogged down in for years. Taking its place is expert training in voice, comic style and dancing. Chita Rivera, etc. Since the wonderful advance in costume and scenic design has been masking so many poor shows—and, in a way, making up for the stale bread in the glittering cellophane—this refreshed me.

March 19: Peter Martin belongs to a special class—frequently San Francisco—that is a mosaic of so many qualities that one day's impression of him is never repeated. As if a heritage of a dozen ancestors' frustrations, rebellious and wild egos locked horns here permitting frustration to block frustration so that there is no action. He is the Fascinating Uncle type—rolling cigarettes, able to talk on all subjects, sleeping late, knocking up the help and brothers' wives if possible, delighting the children.

April 4: To Yaddo. So exhausted (as always when knowing end is almost in sight) trying to finish Eudora Welty review and pack. Train and 100 lbs. of papers, etc. at 9:15. Very slow train but after two hours resigned to it. Worst possible beginning but on arriving find all benign and beautiful.

April 6: Yaddo. 11:50 A.M. Started new novel.*

April 9: Yaddo. Mrs. Ames told funny story of Horace Gregory's little girl. All other children telling what their fathers did and she was noticeably silent, jumping rope, till finally there was no getting around it being her turn and she said "My father's a poet but I don't care."

Have feeling that this is the most constructive period—decided country life is indicated. Merging of our several lives and quiet may allow for my many stories to advance to print.

April 19: I was thinking of Pete Martin's room, which seems answer to living—a room with shared bath in rooming house (he is on 12th Street) and regular house in country. There must a kind of luxury in living within your means.

April 23: The trouble with good advice is the only one who knows how good it is is the person giving it.

A pleasure of last half-century of life is the surprise in discovering how much you know, how much you've retained and in new situation how much you have to draw upon—but you're the only person who knows it.

April 24: Party at John Faulk's. They are going to resign from CBS and go to Waco and Austin, Texas. Jimmy Savo was there with wife—they are dolls. Savo has no idea of civilized ordinary human intercourse but is all Performer. He speaks special material, gags, jokes (never good but he is a disarming child and you laugh all the more). When that fails he does his songs in low voice for you.

April 25: I want this new novel to shine like moonlight—the quality must be a kind of pearly radiance behind which the hidden Evil from which Christine is fleeing becomes only a fairy-tale, never told. There should be

---
* *A Cage For Lovers.*

a gossamer charm masking the truth and fears, for the bondages are gossamer, so easily broken really in the long run.

April 29: Jojo home—good as gold though twice in "sheets" during week.

I think P.* is a Stripper. The pleasant, civilized quality of being eagerly receptive to everyone but what he gets is the right to strip everyone of themselves—their secrets, their confusions, their sins—as if to fit himself out leaving them a mere bag of bones. He must *try on* everybody in his search for himself and while the game is enormously stimulating for a while it is deathly exhausting for everyone.

May 1: Joe and I walked downtown crisscross the Square and MacDougal and West Houston toward Battery, crossing or turning whenever we saw sunlight or a curious building.

May 3: How wonderful if I could whiz through this novel without my usual torture—regain the joy of writing and getting out the dozens of stories I have piled up during the dusty years.

June 3: Impressed with the effortless mediocrity of View from Marquand's Head. Soap opera dialogue; a classy, high-grade plot laid out in all its meager splendor. Holds the reader paralyzed. Like walking on ocean bottom, being pushed back for every step forward. You can doze off and come back in. TV writing, weighted with commercials.

June 4: Jojo in fine shape. Made his breakfast and said "I had grapefruit and Cheerios and then a sort of an omelet. I didn't know I was making it but I put the egg in without any grease and stirred it and it came out an omelet, sort of."

June 15: Christine's voyage alone. Everywhere she has been carried along by older people—sisters, mother, Miss Lesley—fiercely longing for independence, wholly inadequate for it. We think we are what makes our perambulators move.

June 29: To Boonville to Bunny's. Talcottville.

---

* Probably Peter Martin.

July 2: Returned to New York. Utica to N.Y. Missourian. $14.

July 5: To page 60 on Christine novel. Marcia was much better book but for sheer limbering up I need this one. So far I do not feel anything distinguished or gay about it, certainly nothing funny, but I did want to pacify a public that seems to regard wit—especially if it sounds original or spontaneous—as immoral.

July 11: Out with the Stiffs again, but enlarging my group. No family at all. Annetta Hart somehow in it at first—as stand-in for Mabel. Then a red-velvet-hung lecture hall (changed from a parlor car) and there was Niles, very fresh-scrubbed and pink-cheeked, Joe, Harry Lissfelt, Reginald Marsh (dimly) and a faded matinee type, a cross between Barnaby and Bill Abbott (news of whose death had just come).

We were having an animated, interesting formal "conversation" in which Niles told some of his old anecdotes very well. Suddenly I wanted to whisper to somebody—Joe, I think—"Do you realize everybody here is dead but us?"—but then realized I would have to speak loudly as Joe is rather deaf and the news might hurt feelings.

In the intermission I went off to hunt a ladies' room (eventually this desire woke me) and ran into Joe who had gone out for something and come back carrying a large cabinet photograph. Who is it? I asked, and looked at a sort of elderly, dowager lady's picture with pince-nez. He placed this tenderly on wall near him and I realize it was a sentimental gesture about a former kindred soul now dead.

July 18: Pete and his beautiful California girl, Jacqueline Miller.*

July 27: On roof at 7 A.M. For some time, I have been enjoying early morning writing—the precious creative link between sleep and fiction without the increasingly unbeatable destructive interruption of the domestic voice. I do as much before 9 A.M. as I used to do struggling all day. Longhand is a help too.

Want to get peculiar atmosphere of a kind of zombie life—these Americans walking around against foreign sets, talking America, thinking

---

*Later Jacqueline Miller Rice; she would become Powell's executor.

America, preserving America, afraid vaguely to go home because in the back of their minds they know there is no America.

August 6: News that Gold Medal Books wanted *Angels on Toast*. Fantastic interview with the mad Dr. Rosen, the one who keeps people mad.*

October 10: In a familiar tension of weary desperation like the re-writing merry-go-round of Norman Geddes option days, or TV rewrite days, or *Bazaar* and *Mademoiselle* rewrite days, or musical comedy work—all on the seemingly all-set business of cutting and rearranging *Angels on Toast* for reprint. Okay at first but never any finality—always just one more attempt to "sex" it up, which at first I thought I could do in a legitimate, true, original way fitting the book, but obviously they must have it in the cliché way.

October 13: Turned in *Angels*—revved up and in some ways improved and depersonalized. Two days with no drinks leaves me in calm, pessimistic state of my adolescence. Nevertheless wish it was feasible to not drink for a while—sleep and work and plan.

October 15: In cat "Yow" book—he eats breakfast with each member of the family.

October 23: Jojo's visit this weekend very successful due to Bobby's visit on Friday night. "Am I welcome at your house?" he said to Bobby tentatively. "Listen, Joe," Bobby said. "You're welcome anywhere I am, my home, my ship, anyplace I am. Anyplace you're not welcome, the two of us walks out together."

October 26: Determined to get novel over hump. Take Paris part with more ease. Get to new chapter by Friday. Have typed up to page 50 but need looser approach. Wonder about going away for four days—say, small hotel upstate where I could be in some atmosphere. Peekskill? Hudson?

November 20: Dinner with Bunny at Brass Rail. 35th wedding anniversary. Jojo fine—alert.

---

* A reference to one of Jojo's physicians on Ward's Island.

November 22: The odd moment when the infatuated parents or sponsors find that the Young Man or Young Woman so excitingly promising for years is now (let's face it) 36 years old, and all your hopes and help and time have been poured in a sieve, which has made him nothing more than a better sieve.

November 25: Hemorrhaging of nose while Jojo home, but he proved to rise wonderfully to the responsibility of looking after me.*

December 8: Dr. Solley. Anemia 60 percent, whatever that means. Must collect energy to move someplace where I can return to writing. Joe assumes my place is drudge and his is in restaurants—two bucks for home, twenty bucks for his belly per day. No sense in maintaining house at my life's blood. Consider moving. During sickness realize I cannot be so utterly dependent (and consequently completely ignored). Must regain independence and right to write.

December 15: Novel about a man like Dick Halliday or Rita Hayworth's husband, etc., who really *makes* somebody after the person has had enough bad luck to know they need brains as manager. The guy knows he cannot help a real genius, only make himself a ridiculous pest (as Olivia de Haviland's husband). An original talent would rebel and be perverse at such handling and butt its head. But if his subject has intelligence and willingness, he can, with his superior mind, create a semblance of greatness by making an Industry out of her.

December 24: On Christmas Eve—a usual family, nerve-wracking business trying to sustain calm. I keep Jojo's wonderful poise in the face of neurotic drunken nagging, needling and almost determined destructive attacks. We went to carols and saw a lone, comfortably dressed young man who looked like Jack Sherman. Why alone on Christmas Eve? From some small town, too polite and shy to pick up new friends in the university or the theological seminary and in a daring nostalgic mood finding some human Christmas warmth in the group of sentimental old Villagers under Washington Square Christmas tree. Told Jack about his double

---

*Severe nosebleeds would plague Powell for the rest of her life; on several occasions she was forced to seek emergency treatment.

when he telephoned that eve. "That was no double, that was *me,*" he said. A few nights later started to see the young man come in Cedar and speak to artist Franz Kline. Was an artist, said Kline, named Bob DeNiro.

1956

January 6: Read Mary McCarthy's piece—another beginning of novel in *New World Writing*. These last two starts are invigorating—like a brisk whiff of the stable on a clear wintry day. She has her two manners—her lace-curtain Irish, almost unbelievably genteel lady scholar torn between desire to be Blue Stocking without losing her Ladyship; and then her shanty Irish where she relaxes, whamming away at her characters like a Queen of the Roller Derby, groin-kicking, shin-knifing, belly-butting, flailing away with skates and all arms at her characters and jumping on them with a hoarse whoop of glee when they are felled.

Elizabeth Taylor (English) is an agreeable, readable writer—a faint, pleasant smell of bouillon is the feast she serves and the reader, like a hungry tea guest, stays on, lulled by this promise and finally starved, dismayed but ready for the next story like a beggar deciding perhaps the smell of cooking must come from next door. Katherine Anne Porter has the same pallor—all are far-off echoes of Katherine Mansfield out of Virginia Woolf—but neither able to make perfume out of water in a perfume bottle. They have a poetic pace to their paragraphs but the shadows conceal holes, not poetry.

January 11: Excellent start for year on work. Gave Rosalind 90 pages of novel. Play shaping up I really believe.

January 14: The way when someone is dangerously hurt or sick some busybody or overly romantic friend calls in an ex-wife or husband or sweetheart (preferred by the busybody), convinced that victim has been nobly carrying a secret torch. Embarrassment for one or other as victim convalesces. The visitor—perhaps by this time alone, conceited, love-hungry or vengeful—pays for hospital, etc., and poor victim is under dire human obligations.

January 17: Heard from Rosalind re: Christine. Very enthusiastic.
 Frightfully dull couple (Pete says). Seemed wonderful at the party but when we had them in for evening, they were so stupid. Talked all during the TV program, made boring cracks about Berle.

February 5: Bobby Lewis party (161 East 80th Street) in his new house with handsome "houseman." Terry Helburn, Cheryl, Lillian Hellman, Maurice Evans, Hermione Gingold and staircase.
 Later John Hultberg at Cedar, complaining of critics—also, that a painting on your wall exposed your weakness and everyone had a right to comment.

February 6: It wasn't that he was loyal; it was only that he'd never been in a good enough position to drop his old friends.

February 11: Title for Christine—something like "Bridesmaid"—or "Lady in Waiting" or "Wedding Dress" or "Shadow of Love."

February 14: Did *The Acceptance World* (Anthony Powell) review for *Saturday Review.*

February 25: Jojo rather doped up, unresponsive, wanting more pills and cigarettes.

March 1: Week of absolute futile rage over *Saturday Review* butchery and distortion of review of Anthony Powell's book.

March 2: What surprises me still is the number of unknown writers who make fine livings out of writing. $10,000 advance—advertising—12,000 first printings. Staggers me.

March 6: Must collect all "Yow" data. A story to be read aloud and sounds and acting dialogue are part of it. A complete cat-world with humans as pets.

March 7: Read a novel, *A Room in Paris,** which was extremely profitable for it showed the French Left Bank cliché my novel had fallen into. This is so far a mere shell of a book and shell of a character. Better to continue it as a shell, then intensify, rather than try to warm up the outside with irrelevant bricks.

March 8: The Secret of my Failure: Just thought why I don't sell stories to popular magazines. All have subtitles—"Last time Gary saw Cindy she was a gawky child; now she was a beautiful woman . . ." I can't help writing "Last time Fatso saw Myrt she was a desirable woman; now she was an old bag . . ."

March 11: I have been denying for years any basis in *A Time To Be Born* for the general idea that it is Clare Luce. I swear it is based on five or six girls, some known personally and some by talk, and often I changed the facts to avoid libel with resulting character a real person evidently and libelously Luce-ian. I insist it was a composite (or compost) but then I find a memo from 1939—"Why not do novel on Clare Luce?" Who can I believe—me or myself?

March 12: Dreamed of Louise mixed in with Grandma on Main Street. She has postcards from wealthy old employer named Wallace who says she should come to their fine estate at Montauk. A large Christmas card shows snowy crags and cliffs in gray shadows and barracks on steep roads at Montauk. How can she get around there? Oh, very easily, she says—they can carry her.

March 17: Thought of doing TV of "Big Night." Wonderful snow yesterday and today. Up at 6 on roof hoping to get something done.

March 19: A great many people are propelled to success in certain fields through no inclination or even satisfaction in their work. Why? They look the part. A big, impressive, clean-cut man asks nothing but comfort, neighbors for cards or fishing, good steak—and yet his appearance and bearing pushes him to big executive post. In bad times he sinks comfortably back to night watchman or some cushy menial job—he hasn't

---

*A book by Peggy Mann, published by Doubleday.

"cracked up," he has merely bedded down without the sails that formerly hoisted him. Same with easy-going beauty—pushed to stage fame by looks but really only likes a good time—Saturday dance, bowling, good-looking usher or bus boy. Old age without glamour but with neighborliness and back on cozy level—she is more rewarded than if sustained fame had removed her from this world.

March 23: In Rickey's. Out window, ladies carry their great bags of groceries home as if it was the Infant Jesus—very reverently—and push their husbands along as if they were a bag from the Supermarket. Faces press against pane as passersby study the menu intently, peer inside as if to see strange orgies, while Montemora, proprietor, says fretfully "Don't just read about it—come in and see it."

Thought of title—"The Ways of Love"—so old that it's doubtless been used many times.

March 24: More blizzard so did not go see Jojo. Thought to use day concentrating on novel but have to keep getting Joe's breakfast, lacing him in truss for his back, and needling about raising money for back income tax. I told him of new royalties from England due and this only makes him think I should (or *do*) have more.

April 1: Easter Sunday. Jojo went back after Friday and Saturday looking hollow-eyed and gaunt and unhappy, though in many ways he has progressed—he sings at parties, helps Miss Murtagh, wins prizes, and next minute tears up clothes because "staying there seems an eternity."

March was a tough month and I am near wrecked by it—in a state of scrambled brains but still a sodden determination to save myself and my work under these hopeless onslaughts.

I still feel the need to open Christine—or else *dramatize* her. Fortunately there is no wit or humor in this story so it may be successful. Waugh, Huxley, Thurber—none were really able to make a decent living until they lost their sense of humor and practically their ability to feel. I hope for a happy turnabout myself.

April 11: Do Stiff story. Have risen at 6:30 every day—hot shower—straightening out novel.

April 15: Dreamed funny dreams and realized why I always laugh at my own jokes—because I don't make them. A character at the bottom of the well makes them and when they come out it's as surprising to me as to anyone.

I dreamed Jojo was writing a poem to Louise and wondered if he could rhyme watches with grasses and I said, no, either to rhyme masses with grasses or mustaches with watches. Then (we were as usual in a country house) he had allowed a cat to get out and I was worried it was lost. But the desk clerk (suddenly appearing) said he didn't think the cat was lost but went of his own accord as he called every morning for his mail.

May 4: Wasted week but at least I didn't try.

Coby pondered future and I reassured him he might make some rich woman a very poor husband. He thought he had the equipment for it, he said—a black tie. Supposing she insists on white tie? I said and he said "Oh, that's quite all right. This one used to be white."

May 16: A character like Honeycutt—determined to have (whether she wants it or not) whatever and whoever anyone else has—a book, a goat, a shop, a child, a dog—but since she has no inner self except this quite meaningless avarice nothing restores her for more than a moment.

May 20: Bon voyage party for Bobby Lewis. Promised him play when he gets back in July.

May 25: Jojo home. Longs for the day he can come out but says bravely "I am doing the very best I can so I can live on the outside. But if I do have to spend my whole life at Ward's I will try to make the best of it."

May 28: Coby said he was thinking something over in his mind. "That's where I do most of my thinking," he said, "instead of in the privacy of my room."

June 9: Jojo in very good shape. Went to Perth Amboy to see Louise. At end of visit he muttered aside to me like an irritated husband, "Too bad I didn't get a chance to talk to her. You did all the talking."

June 10: Bunny telephoned from Boston and I had dinner with him at Brass Rail. Excited and full of Dead Sea Scrolls—talk of intrigues among scholars.

We were discussing the Ph.D. thesis and how really you don't know your dear old friends at all. You pick out the part of them you need for yourself at that moment; in fact, you find a cozy vacuum in them that is not them and you fill it with yourself. Later, possibly as executor of their estate, you read their journals and letters and realize you never knew them. Bunny said in case of Scott Fitzgerald and others—when they are being themselves you brush it aside as momentary foolishness obscuring the Real, but decades later you realize what you thought was the foolishness was *them*.

June 13: Hopelessness of explaining a person to someone who knows the Legend. Young Mr. L. who is doing thesis on Dos: Why He Turned Conservative. He always was. I tried to explain that Communist rallies were always advertising him when he wasn't even present, that he never led meetings, had a horror of organizations, etc. At end of interview young man says—"Then it was *after* Sacco-Vanzetti that he gave up leading Communist rallies?"

June 15: Publication date of reprint* and as special prize I had first thorough night's sleep I'd had in years.

July 4: Bryan Robertson telephoned at 8:45. Lunch and afternoon. A delightful man—art dealer here from London on national tour of artists, collections and galleries. He telephoned from having admired my novels.

July 8: Dinner with Bryan Robertson at Rickey's. He finds me a combination of the Queen Mother and Mae West, God forbid. He is probably the most charming, honest young fellow I ever met—even on second meeting.

July 9: Had Pete, Jackie, Franz Kline, Loren MacIver, Lloyd Frankenberg and Monroe Stearns in to meet Bryan. Later they all went over to

---

Angels On Toast, substantially rewritten, had been published in a Fawcett paperback as *A Man's Affair.*

Cedar Tavern and I hope the customary brawl did not occur to foul up his New York good time.

July 13: Coby said losing memory was a terrible handicap for a name-dropper. For somebody who only remembers faces it's very awkward.

July 14: Terribly amusing letter from Bryan Robertson from 4 Louisberg Square (Rosalind's address)—particularly preposterous since I had wired Rosalind about him and told him to go see her and, without further warning, there he is in her apartment house. He accused me of being sentimental about young people (perhaps as true as my being bored by old people in bunches, all the faults of age multiplied by the large cast), and to remember they were harder and tougher.

My seeming sentimentality is based largely on the empty exhaustion I feel in a party of older people—being nice to someone because they are through, have failed, are poor—all requiring a kind of painful dry pity, because there is nothing you can do about it. You can't bring back their dead or give them fame or love or whatever the hell they want.

With young people, you can't make their loves be true or pass out wedding rings if that's their passion. (I can further say that at any time I have successfully played Cupid or Kewpie I've had my head bashed in later by the indignant beneficiaries.) But with some young people, you *can* give them an address to get a job or some money or a walk-on part or a hearing—and this is exhilarating and alive.

July 18: Rosalind said Bryan's remarks about my sentimentality were about my novels—that the young were always going hand in hand into the sunset. This of course is superficially true and my major handicap—though it is not so much the Young as the Straight Character. I have simply never been interested in the conventional straight person and so—knowing I need them like a cake needs flour in order to house the raisins—I use a sort of ready-cooked base, prefabricated. This is no more than Dickens or Thackeray or Balzac did. As for sentimentality about the young—yes, it is ignorance. I never knew when I was young what it was to be young. I only knew what it was to be me—and that didn't seem to be young but intimations of immortality.

July 19: People are slow diseases—they turn bad slowly which makes their loved ones able to bear it.

To Murphy's at Snedens, thankful for wondrous, black, hushed sleep, away from domestic yakkity-yak slavery. Wonder how I could ever get any work done without divorce. So much value in me absolutely murdered by hostile, deliberate, domestic "bliss."

July 27: Never give a guest Dexedrine after sundown.

August 6: Peter Martin has wonderful theory that everybody assembles a cast of characters about the time he is seven or eight, and all his life he fits people into this cast.

August 7: Latouche died!—in Calais, Vermont. Luckily his opera "Baby Doe" had been a great peak last month in Central City, a peak he might not pass. Incredible that this dynamo should unwind and I think I can guess how. Talentless but shrewd users pursued him always—he was *driven:* harnesses and bridles and wagons were always being rushed up to him to use this endless gold. I have seen him so harried by the users he burst into tears. Contracts, advances, deals, love offers were all around—trying to get him in a corner room, lock him up and get out the gold when he wanted only to talk all day and all night. He never could sleep—lights on all night—so there were sleeping pills and for the grim collaborators demanding the real work, he must have Benzedrine, Miltown tranquilizers, Nembutal, dex. I'm sure this was a desperate, hysterical escape from Lillian Hellman and others waiting for his output to finish up "Candide." Like George Gershwin—a natural gusher that grim syndicates tried to harness for the stock exchange. Ending up now an incorrigibly sweet, indestructible little ghost.

August 9: Coming in on the L.I.R.R. from Locust Valley, I thought again of how familiar and sweet bare, battered old Long Island was, with its weeds and marshes and rocking boats. The railroad has changed. The midnight train to New York had a few actors and actresses—an actress making carefully up for TV midnight show, green on forehead. Actors from Jones Beach show-boat.

August 10: Reading a lot of French women novels—Sagan, de Beauvoir, etc. Their popularity must be a desire on our public's part to hear of love. In our magazines and much fiction—dictated completely by the Republican party and Madison Avenue—marriage is based on breeding children, free labor, dividing up the family fortune, buying produce advertised, real estate, electrical devices, etc. Hero and heroine are married because the institution must be preserved.

Here is old-fashioned *amour* for *amour's* sake—children are in the background. In fact, the hell with the children, let them get their own patron. Love, love, love.

August 20: LeClercq called from Grosvenor where he was with Balanchine and Tanaquil and his new bride. Tanny, the ballerina, is thin, plain, pallid—unattractive in any other field, but when she gets up, she is very tall, full-hipped, and moves with great distinction, pivoting, as if each major muscle was synchronizing in a reach toward beauty.

August 23: A motto: Do it tomorrow; you've made enough mistakes today.

August 25: An election speech: "Progress will be made through the insidious lubricant of mass media."

September 6: Carol called that U.S. Steel-Theatre Guild deal for television—"You Should Have Brought Your Mink"—was set. Somewhat baffled by her figures.

September 17: If experience taught us anything it would be not to talk about it.

September 26: Turned in to Carol 53 page TV script of "Mink." I considered it very good and also a miracle as I don't know where it came from.

September 27: Carol said script "superb" with brilliant dialogue but wondered if she dared give it to Jamieson at Guild as it was very "tough"—tragic. No hope. I said it was a comedy and did *so* have hope. "What hope?" she said. "Well, she got out of the place," I said.

October 22: Turned in "final" script of "Mink." Good, I thought.

October 24: Saw William Moorwood at CBS—don't know why. He was mildly interested in "Grand March" as vehicle for Eve Arden. Decided if I am to take such long chances I would do better to do straight play.

October 25: Taylor Caldwell phoned to regulate my life.

November 8: Incredible how desolating my work has been—the frenzied pulling together of novel in July; the exhausted drive when I hoped to finish it in Boston and merely cut out and tightened; the frenzied blind plunge into TV; the complete assurance as so many times before that this was *set*—and the wicked way *chance* betrayed all my work and strength. Now word comes (after unable to work at anything till I heard re: TV) must take chance once again, without any support, my only energy being the dreary kind derived from getting at least a "reprieve" from domestic chores and worries.

November 9: Up at 5:30. This must be the answer. The big loose unkempt unfinished apartment and its chores, as well as my family ones, make me feel like a still good racehorse who is supposed to win races after finishing the plowing and trucking.

December 8: A musical skit with people singing their real thoughts. Guest's song: "Why Did I Accept Your Invitation?"

December 11: The social climbing struggle of a Midwest type to get in the Village crowd and the cruel brush-offs. A reverse social-climbing job. The heartache, the snubs, the trying to show-off to bourgeois friends that she knows these "Characters."

December 13: It seems incredible that another dreadful unrewarding year is almost over and still I drudge and write and try to hope enough to get me over the smallest hurdles with no results at all. Even the reviews I labor over—either they don't get printed on time after I crucify myself for deadlines or the checks—small as they are—are delayed for no reason except they're for me.

December 24: Went to Ann Honeycutt's party. Big error as I should have guessed the great reservoir of jealousy and hostility she has for me, based on her desire for a position in the world but unbeatable passion for the exterior rewards, which then seem hollow to her. Since so many of her friends loom up attacking me out of blue sky, I assume she has given them material. No one is more bitter than a well-kept dame (except dames who have not succeeded in being kept) because she daren't let go of the man, much as her vanity wants her to, because she would have nothing else—and this she knows.

So first Wolcott Gibbs—in a kind of LeClercq, feeble drunkenness—decided to aim at me, telling me I'm a kind of Katherine Brush (which he meant as insult but I admire K. enough not to find this so, and moreover was not displeased at being considered that successful). Then he said "Do you know who my grandfather is? President of Columbia. Where do you come from, Dawn Powell?" or "Where do you say you come from? How old are you anyway, Dawn Powell?" I said "Oh, I must be around there somewhere." Finally his cracks were so nasty [entry breaks off]

1957

January 5: Jojo moved for treatment. *Post* had editorial letters re: my *Organization Man* review.

January 8: Saw Solley who gave me alpha niacin for three days then a thyroid daily prescription for gland swelling.

January 12: Jojo for past week in surgical ward. When I called he did not know me for almost a minute—whether blanked out by surprise or too many disappointments I don't know.

January 14: Throat improved. Today for first time in weeks, *feel* like work whether I do or not.

Marie said sagely—young girls were stupid to lay around with men having two, three babies. "Like I tells 'em," she said, "if they won't marry you for one baby they ain't gonna do it for two."

January 19: Visited Jojo and found him calm, plump, poised, chuckling. Off tranquilizers for a week and not sick—it may be they are cause of stomach trouble. He was happy, too.

January 22: Pete Martin and Jackie "splitting," with usual soap opera. He thinks sincerely of himself as an "intellectual" and believes others regard him as such, though no one thinks of him except as a bright amusing character whose only ambition is to out-shout everyone else in a bar.

What is it he wants? Something like Honeycutt wants—a stuffing for the shell. A "California Writer"—a kind of Okie. His sights are very

365

low—a review, a bookstore—impossible to connect with his high critical talk. A "California Writer" is a West Coast drifter who uses all his imagination and talent on posing as writer. A radical sympathizing with the Working Man—he sympathizes because the Working Man has to work instead of being a radical and lying in bed Sympathizing.

January 29: Lloyd and "Lloren"* in for steak and reading his radio program on air. WNYC. Nice refreshing evening.

February 1: Started on wine.

The turning on radio—4:30. Big Joe and Long John re: the kindly intentions of the flying-saucer people. According to a Hightstown, N.J. expert who had seen flying saucers, they say they have a real brotherly interest in our civilization and wish it well, will not do anything hostile to us till we are further along and in a position to threaten them. Next night Big Joe and Choo Choo (wife) were guests doing their best to take over Long John's MC'ing. Talk of alcoholism, Big Joe's old foe, an allergy. Just a taste of rumcake—a real allergy. Choo Choo kept butting in, idolizing wife really fixing him: sometimes this allergy hit him so hard he didn't show up at his job for days, boy did he have an allergy.

February 2: In the last two weeks have progressed more in novel than anytime since July in Boston. Wish for two or three full days—say Monday to Thursday in concentrated hotel—upper Broadway, Cold Spring Harbor. Clear up Christine's desire to do—design and make her own clothes, invent dishes, be free and independent.

February 3: The way the confidence about a bad time in the past (after years of a love or friendship) binds two people again. I couldn't leave him—not after he told me about what happened when he was 12, 14, 16. Later—much later—perhaps there is little you remember except that subsequent acute tenderness of his long-ago desolation, which is now part of you.

February 4: Dinner with Bunny Wilson.

"She seemed brilliant to him because she said back to him all the things he had tossed off without remembering."

---

*Lloyd Frankenberg and Loren MacIver.

February 19: Guggenheim opening. Marcel Duchamp's "Nude Descending Staircase" (once called "Explosion in a Shingle Mill") seems better than 35 years ago. The meanings—as in the case of all great art—are now blooming. Whatever the lack appeared to be was in the viewer, not in the work.

February 25: Johnny K., now his daughters are grown, left alone with wife—cute, little small-town girl type frozen into middle age. He dines out ("work") almost every night because if he goes home (commuting to Rye) the minute he gets in house she calls out "Dinner's on the table," to prevent him having cocktails. On other hand she probably boasts to others that she has never kept his dinner waiting.

March 3: May go back to "Marcia" next.

March 4: If autobiography—horrible idea—begin with "Out with the Stiffs."*

March 12: Finished and submitted novel *Cage for Lovers*. Up every morning at 6 or earlier and sustained drive for past few days.

March 14: Rosalind enthusiastic over novel.

April 17: The violent scene is wrong (as Houghton Mifflin says it is)—blunt and unsupported by emotional reactions. These days of trying to revise this major scene—I feel I hate the book. It is pallid, fictional, and feeble. It needs more power than shock for its major scene. Wish I could do it and get it once more *out*.

April 23: Sent final revisions back. Desperately broke and Joe in fierce state. Cannot see how I can get out of prison of sarcasm, lack of belief, no help and constant denigration, except by earning money. Rosalind suggests more work on Marcia, but even $1000 advance would make small dent.

April 27: Thought of Jacqueline's curious strength—taking an incredible and humiliating beating from Pete, seemingly forever oblivious and

---

*Powell's grim working title for "What Are You Doing In My Dreams?"

obsessed and ever-forgiving. Then suddenly it's all over and she springs back. I am reminded of my first talk with Pete about her, his usual ego saying "I don't want to hurt her" which always means he does. I said, somewhat drily "You don't need to worry. That girl will roll with the punches." Then I thought I was wrong—now I see I was more than right. In her curious, unmalicious, unevil but deep, strong, Teutonic way, she can roll down everybody else in a most curious blind, Olympian, unplanned revenge, for she steals their life from under them.

Pete was a bar type—a bar intellectual, meaning a Talker, an Expert on any department. She complained of this life but insisted on living it with him—trying to show it was feasible and even respectable with her cooking, shopping, hostmanship, etc. and imitating his ideas and sayings. By herself she is smart enough really but she doesn't want to be. Then came the big blow and she struck. She was going abroad! Not only had she driven him to go to Washington since she had taken over his life and friends and interests (he had stolen these himself, too) but she had set her sights higher than his. She would be the foreign expert. She takes over Italy (Italy was his only he hadn't claimed it yet; wasn't his father Italian?). So there is nothing left for him but to find someplace and something of his own. He will probably appear in New York again, married to someone, to show his strength and her failure.

May 3: "Goody Goody"
> *So you met someone who set you back on your heels?*
> *Goody Goody.*
> *So you met someone and now you know how it feels?*
> *Goody Goody.*
> *And you gave her your heart too*
> *Just as I gave mine to you*
> *And you broke it in little pieces*
> *So you met someone who's singing the blues all night?*
> *Goody Goody*
> *And you think that love's a barrel of dynamite?*
> *Goody Goody*
> *Hooray and hallelujah*
> *You had it coming to you*

[much of entry illegible]

May 12: Hectic day. Found Jojo pleased with new move to Main—though the ward was vast and fuller of mixed types. He had started work (folding sheets) in laundry 8–3:30 daily. Said "I wish you'd see my diary. I have a lot of new memories since I moved."

May 21: Thought of wonderful title for new book—"The Characters." They use masks completely. Background—X is a writer who doesn't write anymore—made big wad on novel or play once, went to Hollywood. Every time he is about to do new book new checks come in so he gets hold of Marsh who quits job and they go places. Horses. Havana.

Cover all the characters instead of just one. They steer away from each other as people, never ask for loans, regard each other as always on stage, at same time each other's audience. In moments of real trouble, this is a vast comfort, as in the last analysis Renee finds out, as does Grace. Marsh can't play anymore. Begins sometime after WWII. Find models for all four, particularly Renee.

May 23: Hassoldt's party for "Merde Cheval"—man who listed himself in phone book as that (real name Babbs) because he was tired of name. Turned out he *was* rather a *merde* with very nice wife.

May 26: Nothing but sleep and brain-washing, though not much rest from it. Am trying not to plunge into novel in this worn state, though idea is all set. Rather like setting out for known defeat—trying to swim the channel after running the 5-mile.

May 28: Jojo moved to disturbed ward. Last time he was home he was back to yipping and fluttering hands and talking about carols—and I feared something coming up. He says "because I didn't hear about plans," though I had written him. Must put it out of mind to get things done.

Jacqueline writes from Italy she has visited Blumes—great party, etc. She knows more to make full use of contacts, timing, etc., dismiss them when used to the hilt. Anyone else would be terrified at seeing name in paper but this spurs them on. Honeycutt the same—they have more use of these contacts than the insiders but they are still un-nourished, unfilled, dissatisfied because basically they know they are *nada*. They have missed the one thing—having *done*—as well as having missed love, for they have wanted what other people want without wanting it. They are perpetual visitors, never insiders.

June 1: Jojo home yesterday. He and I wandered downtown—Fraunces Tavern, ferry to Staten Island—and in general he was delighted. "There is nothing better than a ferry ride in the morning." Sun-tanned and deeply and gravely interested in everything he saw.

June 2: In Sheridan Theater, Joe went to Men's Room and as it had been relocated I wandered and decided on Ladies' Room. Started upstairs behind stout man with kind of swollen liverish or kidney-swollen back, climbing wearily and cautiously. It was Joe and startled me more than anything.

June 3: Grace (like Ginny or Pauline*) recoils from open emotion or frank absorption in any intellectual or artistic subject, as if it was ill-bred. Perhaps so, but with Ginny absorption in stock market or races was okay. It was the *mind* that was as obscene as sex.

June 4: Post-dated check for $75 out. Very ominous. Don't know whether to lay low or to get high. Would be at end of rope if could afford rope. Let's say am at end of thread.

June 5: In-for-a-penny-Powell, waiting for bailiffs re: postdated checks, decided the "Mink" TV was fine—in fact well worth being made into play—and took it to Ann Meyerson, 101 Park, to have copies made to give Bobby Lewis, Harold Freedman.

June 10: Carol telephoned there was a chance of *McCall's* taking my novel serial rights. She wanted to know contract and whether Houghton Mifflin would postpone publication.

June 14: Called Carol re: *McCall's*. She said "Darling, we haven't heard but as I said there isn't a chance in a million!" Gave up translating female agent.

---

*The Pfeiffer sisters; Pauline had been married to Ernest Hemingway.

June 15: At the Spanish stocking man on East 125th Street, waiting for the Ward's Island bus and encounter with so completely delightful ironic Spanish wit. I asked for two pairs of hose, then decided on three. He said "There are four pairs here." I said "No, only three. In summer I won't wear stockings." He shrugged. "You don't go to church, you don't have to say you don't believe in God." I said, startled at the customary ploy of Spanish wit. "Does God care that I don't wear stockings?" Another shrug. "God's not in the hosiery business," adding, pleased, "a lot of those old firms have gone out of business." I said "What's He doing now—on the road selling?" "No," he said, more pleased. "I think He's buying." It was such a brief delightful breath of casual Spanish interchange that it made my day.

July 4: Thought of how radiant and lovely Jackie was—then how suddenly after Pete moved in and she could never find him—how ratfaced and snaggletoothed she looked—incredible that she had been beautiful. Then becomes so again. Then she had been up all night and dropped in and while others drank her head fell back on sofa and she slept—the face biscuit dough, slack jaw, eyes not quite shut, a charmless sleep. Also, when she wolves a sandwich—a peasant greed and sort of pious righteousness, as if "Food is Good For You. The Body Must Survive. I have a Right to this sandwich."

July 9: People and restaurants change. Last night went with Margaret and Herbert Solow to Charles Restaurant—one I occasionally went to 25 and 30 years ago without caring much for it except that it was impersonal. I took for granted I knew it as one knew people 30 years ago, without realizing skins are shed or different backgrounds light up new facts. So here was a charming luxurious place.

July 12: Bad week. No news of Jojo—run-around from doctors when I do get them. Walls everywhere—Jojo, work, money—everything but Cedar Tavern by day, which is charming.

July 27: Jojo back in Ward Eight at Main and his beloved laundry job and very cheerful.

July 29: Breakfast at drugstore—Andy Summers, the shape note Folk-ways lad holding forth. Seems he made new album for Folkways. Told of shape note singers in West Virginia—how a wooden church was a sounding board and choir of 40 sounded like 150. They called themselves the Fa-Sol-La Singers (do-re-mi). Told of ministers being the educated musicians who appointed different ladies to get on their horses and go up in hills, find new tunes and rush back while still in their heads and he'd put it in shape notes so all could sing it. In those days nobody thought whether they were singers or not—they just *sang*. Now everyone is educated to think you shouldn't sing unless you are trained.

August 5: A summer of nothing—chiefly struggle to keep up Jojo's standard and morale in spite of Disturbed Ward. Cedar for solitary lunch and crossword puzzles and roof as sole relief. Mental fatigue, depression, and tired look at future. Another year of promises—almosts—falling through by no fault except chance, a circumstance that makes me fear to start new work, though I have much to do.

August 7: Hungover, but after Scotch and orange juice, began novel at 2:30 and flew up to page five with great glee. How wonderful if New York could be bottled while it still bubbles—fast and furious and true.

August 11: Slept and regained original confidence in *Cage for Lovers*. This is almost a clinical record of a moneyed woman jealous of those without it. She is generous, not to "help," but to remind them that money (herself) is the greatest. She has never known love, laughter, friendship, adventure, achievement, or ambition—and it puzzles her and incites fierce jealousy that so many people are happy with these, and regard money as only a means. Almost involuntarily she must pull up their confidence—make them bow and recognize money, show them they cannot have it without her generosity, teach them to be unsatisfied (properly) with their own independence of it—to suspect they can never have that moneyed life, and to be as forever discontented without it as she is with it. A private revolution, which Christine dimly suspects and escapes just in time to keep her own self.

August 12: Another futile week—isolated, deflated and woodenly sunk. More defensive of *Cage,* however, and still convinced that it is a delicate, skillful dissection of Inherited Money Complacency. Like a dope addict, Miss Lesley wants to see others depend on it so she can constantly see its superiority to all human qualities or contentments proved. Take away the really limitless rewards of human qualities and emotions and make these fortunate people depend, like herself, on the solid, steady assurance of stocks and bonds—then let them try to get those and see who is boss.

August 14: One reason women (and some men) writers are kept back is that they spend their brains and heart on writing but their fighting ability they must use for others—to protect, advance, heal, feed, support. Whereas the complete egotist not only writes but fights every minute for his writing and his own professional advancement, losing no tears or blood on family or friends or even difficult lover.

August 15: The way Latouche and I always knocked ourselves out to entertain morons. The more useless and blah they were, the harder we worked for their amusement—as if they were such a waste that only by converting these ciphers into something (in fact nothing more than audience) could they be endured.

August 17: Splendid outing with Jojo in new linen suit (from Jack) on sightseeing boat around Manhattan. "I enjoyed seeing Ward's from the outside," he said as we sailed up East River.

Read Turgenev's *Smoke*—again, having not the faintest memory of it from my college infatuation with Turgenev. In this, his extraordinary "subversive" feelings about Russians—the oafish and determined illiteracy of the peasants, the brutality, foppishness and superficiality of the military, the passion for fads—"smoke"—one national passion is constantly replacing an opposite one, everything is unoriginal, rootless, all arts are based on East or West robbing, a faint knack assures a man he is a "genius," all are serfs still, ready to acknowledge as leader any man who claims to be a leader. No civilization, he cries, no lovers.

August 20: Wanning and I were discussing people who embarrass you by saying they only have four cents or something, leaving you to offer them *your* three cents or feel like a bastard. He said he liked the direct touch for a loan better. I said I didn't. I like them beating around the bush, as I can then beat them right back around the bush and no direct refusals. When a young man told me he hadn't had but two meals in two weeks, that he was in fact starving (a remark Wanning deplored as a whimpering bid for a loan) I had a choice of embarrassing myself by confessing I also had no money—a secret I saw no reason to share—or saying to him, "You tell me you're starving. You may trust me not to violate your confidence."

August 21: Some people have several lives (Auntie May); others die the first time and continue dying to their death. If they get through the death of youth—that is, the period when they admit the death of youth (anywhere from 30 to 50) and become the next person, middle-aged, they usually can go on till they are willing to relinquish middle age (60 to 70) when they begin to really enjoy life, the fruits of their experience, and are eager afresh for things about them.

August 23: Jojo home—splendid shape. Joe stayed sarcastic and plastered and almost obscenely drunk steadily. I must find some out to protect Jojo and myself and work.

August 25: The exterior design of superficial banter in novel must permit shades and depths, otherwise, it is trivial and will bore me. I like the seemingly simple exterior pattern, as in *Angels on Toast,* but with unlimited depths. Am considering MacDowell for September.

August 27: Up early and refreshed due to merely being out of my house for a few hours with something besides domestic prison, even though it was nothing new or lively, just not chained. Result—as usually happens after a few hours of comparative release from the trap—I found the wonderful aunt character to give body and depth to Renee.

September 5: Persecuted by creditors—postdated checks gone wrong, etc. Cannot answer phone. However today have sense of hope. Very peculiar in my life: I discovered so young to save myself disappointment not to expect so I am not surprised at the most ordinary of simple rights being denied. The day of my excursion ticket the train is taken off; usually I take it so for granted I don't look hard enough. The letter with check. I dread opening thinking it is a bill. However I am equal to sensational peaks of arrogant expectations too.

September 8: Jojo and I to Battery Park. Jojo splendid, convulsed with glee over my telephone troubles. Very talkative about sanitarium, life and drugs.

Wondering as I often do whether to make mad dash for the second Marcia book. After all, 80 or more pages is something. Wish for financial and domestic ease to adjust life.

September 16: I heard disk jockey say "And here come the Coe Sisters— talent we haven't heard from them in far too often."

September 18: Word "intellectual" means sometimes only the colloquial "mental."

September 20: Ginny in town. Lunch with Monroe [Stearns] and Pete and Ginny. Monroe told me he'd read galleys of my new book and thought it was most disappointing. Nothing like me. I was dashed at first till I realized this was what I expected—that the small group of fans who liked the familiar in me—what was like me personally to like or dislike—would be discomfited and thrown off. I was looking for a new audience—a story audience, after which I could restore my own self bit by bit to the novel. However I was sufficiently startled to decide on Marcia, for *Cage* and the new one were started and rushed through before the people were ripe or known to me and I had to grow to know them.

September 25: What a writer must do is use all facets of his imagination. Sometimes a book is so successful and so much loved by its public that the writer is imprisoned. Anything else he writes, people cry out: no, no, we want Little Eva again, we want the March family, like *Little Women*. The author is pleased at first—his work is made easy, he's rocking on the front porch the rest of his life. But he can't get away. When he tries to write of another side of life, his public says "We hate it—it isn't what you promised us." His publisher becomes a tyrant ("We've got a gimmick here, let's stick to it"), but a writer has to think, grow, use more of himself.

Usually after a novel I see a glaring fault growing on me that I must run from. I keep trying to make a conventional sympathetic character but they elude me because I find the reverence for the conventional almost criminal in life. A man wants a split-level house because everybody has one; maybe he's in a wheelchair and a split-level makes life inconvenient for him but he has so little pride or faith in his own choice that he must have other people's. Fear is what I despise—I despise it because I know it. I have to know it's to be despised unless it is the legitimate fear of injustice or disease. What I finally discover is that there are varieties of conventional people—some are convenient masks for conducting a thoroughly individual life—so I am appeased. In any case, it is an author's pleasure to experiment or run the risk of being wrecked. Scott Fitzgerald.

October 15: Book appeared (*Cage*) with no ad or review. If I had not been blessed with flu I would have been devastated. But Elliot Hess's long compliments—so obviously sincere—over the "professionalism" of the book had made me feel I had accomplished what I set out to do and anything else was merely extra. As for money or praise, they are already too late, for the catastrophes and disappointments have already occurred.

October 16: Wonderful letter from Bunny re: *Cage*. "Masterly performance . . . French-type purity of style and sense of classical form," etc.

October 17: In novel writing would say memory most vital—not mere recall of episodes but a classifying memory, memory like FBI. A girl saying good-bye to older man who is glad to go—amusing bit but when did something happen like that before—on a boat? Yes, as a child—and then too you were curious because you would have thought the older man would be the sad one, girl being so beautiful and young. No. Then another similar episode, the old woman and the young man. Again, the older woman eager to be off. Something clicks—yes, the strain and boredom of living with a younger generation, the racy joys of contemporary companionship.

November 1: Lies:
Thoreau didn't give up life in city; he had a country playhouse, a do-it-yourself.
Mrs. Trollope didn't attack America—she loved it and wrote truly about it.
Lucrezia Borgia didn't poison anybody.

Courtesans of kings weren't trollops. They were office wives, receptionists.

The North had as many slaves as the South and no later than 20 years ago—in Oberlin, Ohio, city of freedom—I was told not to go in a Negro shop or in the colored restaurant section.

November 29: Anne Baxter, actress and star of "Square Root of Wonderful," phoned to ask about stage and movie rights to *Cage For Lovers*. Referred her to Harold Freedman at Brandts. According to Carol this may mean nothing more than option at $2000 or so. Recalling how she bollixed "Mink" sale by not getting outright price and resisted sending it to *McCall's,* which almost bought it, one wonders but can't do anything.

December 1: Bobby Lewis's wonderful party for Lena Horne with Peggy Fears, Marlene Dietrich, Gloria Vanderbilt, Truman Capote, Tennessee Williams, George Lloyd, Billy Rose, Joyce Matthews, etc.

December 7: "Square Root of Wonderful" to see Anne Baxter performance. She looks exactly as one imagines Christine. Play rather insulting—not a play but a collection of characters, all from the Southern Trash school.

December 11: To "Look Homeward, Angel" play. Melodramatic but fine acting and a reconstruction of the wild, violent life Wolfe had in him. Hugh Griffith as father, Frances Hyland (would be ideal as Christine).

In view of the shocking disappointment of *Cage For Lovers* (whole presentation was faulty and apologetic) I have been most discouraged about tackling new one. Tried to get some indication for months on whether there was enough interest to go on with Marcia, but can't get anything out of Houghton Mifflin. Now am inclined to go back to it—at least a fat investment is already there, and there is life.

December 24: Jojo, after the most astonishing weekend at home, concentrating on 38 Christmas cards and work—then had disappointment at party at Ward's so was in M5 (disturbed) and no permit for Christmas. Saw him and really was shattered by the monstrous madmen there this time—(Madmen never smile—except in crime, I suppose)—really murderous looking. He had cut his wrists. So a grim Christmas all around, as the year itself has been. The years get worse; work is almost taboo because of memories of past failures.

December 25: Must find apartment as Joe is being retired and no salary after January.

December 27: Looking for apartments around Perry Street—very peaceful. Decided we wanted a "walk-out" apartment—someplace where one or other could at least go out (not too possible in most residential sections). Village is only place for this.

Wish I could have some genuine editorial guidance. I could have had with Max or Wheelock and perhaps could with the older ones at Houghton Mifflin but somewhat short-circuited by Rosalind's and my peculiar relationship—half-personal and step-personal—as well as age barrier and her lack of authority. Should I go back to the Marcia or on with the New York, which is really not ripe, whereas the other is too ripe. Wish I could slam through a good 50 pages or more fast on Marcia.

December 28: The Cedar. The twins. The girls who are easy to live with because they are used to the selfishness of artists and because they (although bemused by the public esteem in which this oddball is held) think they're not much and no reason why they shouldn't work in a garage, drive a taxi. In fact they dread the big windfalls, the fame—when so many are fooled into thinking this ordinary guy *is* something, an idea that leaves *them* in the cold, so they try to keep the wings clipped. In a way they are more deadly than the over-proud, over-ambitious, over-driving.

December 30: Ending of tired year of hoping and waiting and nothing. Could use someone else's power for a change as my own seems debilitated and my afraid reason keeps preventing further steps toward disappointment.

1958

January 1: Unexpected visit of Mary Grand and Monroe Stearns. We had Jack Sherman's ham and Scotch. Joe beginning "retirement."

January 2: Joe in alcoholic hostile frenzy. Very alarming.

January 4: Jojo pale, gaunt, unsmiling, cold—in M-5. Must work to get him out.

Hope to spend this week anti-domestically. Do the dead life story, then the writing article. Collect stories and edit for contract.

Do piece on "Live on $500 a Year."

January 6: Been trying to clear up the Ohio story, a rather strange memoir. Will try *New Yorker* with it, then *Atlantic,* perhaps *Harper's*. Must collect and reassemble all unsold short stories—also the published ones.

Jojo moved to M-2—semi-disturbed.

January 10: Paul Brooks came in. We vaguely conferred—me skipping off definite promise to Do As Told and he skipping off promise, too.

January 11: One reason for literary situation is that writers do one of two things—either write or make a name for themselves. Making a reputation takes all their time, so they have none left to write. The names of authors appearing regularly on best-seller lists are seldom known; their faces and private lives and habits are unknown because they write steadily. The Big Names have to be in the right places, do the right things, know the right people—everybody wants their autograph and nobody, as they know, cares whether they write or not. They had that hit play once, they wrote that sensitive long poem once, they wrote the novel of the moment—after that, they crouch on these decoy laurels, being the Campus Name, the Resort Name, the Social or Cafe Name—when is there time to write?

The so-called avant-garde are the would-be academics, long-to-be-stuffed-shirts. They blow and blow—not enough generations of wind behind them, just enough to blow own tiny candle but not enough to stuff a shirt.

Discussed expense of brilliant conversationalist who always gets check in the cafes, as admirers sit and listen—actually paying for his audience.

January 17: Jackie runs through her "phases" (which are really other people's lives) like books, but somehow people (who never really want her in there, are wary but not sufficiently protected to resist) don't want their lives after she has put them on. Without even being possessive, she has enveloped them completely. So she moves on and on, clean-cut, tidy, dewy-faced, in a gutter of her own making, torn lives of puzzled people swirling around her.

January 22: Dr. Wing. Extraction with tooth falling apart. "I am very grateful for this honor," said the dear man, his Chinese bland kind face very serious. "I haven't had a real workout in years. Things have gotten too easy—I can't make my students learn certain things because there is a new drug or machine or tool that takes care of all that. Things have gotten too easy." We were both dripping with perspiration. I felt somewhat the same—real physical pain was a catharsis after the daily nagging mental aches and burdens.

January 27: Cut finger. Dwight called. Went to PEN for James Jones, saw [Maurice] Dolbier and William Cole (Knopf). Cedar Tavern. Pete Martin said Coby had come up while he was drinking, laid a stern hand on shoulder and said "You're going over the hill fast, lad, but don't worry— I'm behind you every step of the way."

February 4: Spencer Vanderbilt and daughter Nancy—hearing him audition his musical. "Do not be afraid of the H-bomb, dear; it cannot destroy our love; You'll be my cinder, Ella; I'll be your burning coal."

February 19: The way some writers choose their subjects as stars select plays—not because they are good or new or say something they wish said but because they can star in them. No subject matter or minor background will obscure their spotlight. Can I be Literary in this, they say, or must I carry a burden of communicating something, teaching, telling, entertaining. No, no, they say, all I want is to stand up and be uninterrupted.

February 27: Have been lucky enough to be able to clear up "Marcia"—which is much too rich a lode to deflect any further. By getting up at 6 or so could possibly get 150 pages done for showing, get $1000 advance and finish—my perpetual fantasy, though God knows after 15 years simmering the actual writing ought to go fast.

March 3: Pete says he and Franz Kline compared notes. Nobody can ever change the twins, nobody can teach them, because they can't learn, they already know. Pete likes this unchangingness.

March 12: Getting along with "Marcia." Buoyed up by Priestley* and English reviews. Did notes on a Cedar novel where I could use myself instead of being driven into hiding.

March 15: Dreams of unexpected high tide—neither pleasant nor unpleasant but so sudden only reaction was panic of unpreparedness.

March 16: Curious consciousness of strange dooms. Margaret (apropos of some casual remark) said Albert, her first husband, refused to take naps on train because he was too proud, he said, to be taken at a disadvantage, caught with his mouth open or snoring by strangers. End: he was found by strangers on a train with his head off!!!—having been thrown off as train rounded curve.

March 19: On receiving Priestley encouragement reverted to Cedar idea and started Cedar novel—*The Golden Spur*.

March 29: This novel, *The Golden Spur*—minor hero thread like Dennis Orphen in *Turn, Magic Wheel*—a young man who comes to New York to

---

*The novelist J. B. Priestley was a great admirer of Powell's; he contributed a blurb for *A Cage For Lovers* and wrote an appreciative letter to *The Village Voice* after her death.

find his father. He has resisted the man he thought was his father, a conventional stuffy man. On father's death, mother tells him he is illegitimate. She has told him stories of Greenwich Village for years—Sam Schwartz's, Romany Marie's, Three Steps Down, etc.* She had a lover—a well-known man, gay artist, sees himself at once that way.

I regard *Cage For Lovers* as a vacation from myself—a sabbatical from which I return to self, renewed.

March 30: The English reviews of *Cage* were more helpful than any editing or criticizing. Everything said indicated how wrongly advised I'd been by Houghton Mifflin. The Paris part (as here) was the part most praised and regretted more not done there. When I recall I was headed for extensive background and then Rosalind said "The general feeling at Houghton Mifflin was hoping this wouldn't turn into another Paris Left Bank sort of book"—a warning so gently given that I rushed to cut out all the Paris plans for the old host, Paris party, etc. Also the flashback was criticized, however well done (I dislike it myself) and the general character of Christine as unimportant. This has made a deep impression on me—reminding me of a deep fault of mine. I frequently choose a hero or heroine I do not like myself purely as a personal exercise in trying to understand that kind of person. I never end up liking them any better. The minor surroundings are always better and more interesting. Dennis Orphen in *Wheel* I liked, but the fact is I like raffish characters and might as well make them heroes. Also these reviews and my experience in solid novel writing teach me at this time to specialize in my specialty—Bohemia, raffish people, and satire.

No flashbacks! People can reminisce, but openly—no stops and gos.

April 4: Started the 1,250 page James Jones book [*Some Came Running*] and drawn in. Then skipped 1000 pages and realized it was a sell—piddling people, being real wasn't enough and an under-aftertaste of plain bushwa. No aspirations except bed for any of them.

April 5: Radiating from *Spur* must be tangles with the other kind of life—PTA, den mother, children, etc. The visiting Englishman collecting data—but nothing jibes; reports from different ones on opposite poles of life, food, etc.

* All popular Village speakeasies or restaurants of the 1920s.

1958

April 30: Did about 10,000 words since March 19 on *The Golden Spur*.

May 3: Jojo still in M-11—disturbed. Beginning to get depressed. Of another patient—"He bites noses," Jojo said. "Herbert won't bite Joe's nose," he reassured me. "He only bites big noses."

May 4: In the *Spur*. Here in this quarter is a treasure, a fountain of youth and hope—love, too. The sheen the arts have for others, the glow shed by a dedicated person.

May 5: Reading Peter DeVries' *Mackerel Plaza*—funny but extraordinarily trivial farce, same grade as "Auntie Mame" or the contemporary farces that pass for wit. Finished it and baffled that it should be a best-seller—is it because of the bad-little-boyness of it? the wash-your-mouth-out-with-soap, people-are-cardboard farce? Curious that similar books have been flops and this one—much worse and less intelligent—should succeed.

May 6: Still running along on *Spur*—read parts to Joe and Margaret and profited greatly by idea of audience. Found myself instinctively skipping first chapter. Margaret said "Oh what terrible people—so unhappy and so depressing" which shocked me as I thought they were gay. It made me realize, however, that there must be more variety and more real appeal. My fault is in vivid reporting of flaws and taking the virtues for granted. If I insist on preferring raffish types I should at least justify myself by reporting their good points, too—generosities.

May 25: One importance of living in the Village for a writer is that it keeps him more fluid generally—more *au courant* with the life around him. For a historical novelist it might not be good—constant struggle between contemporary life and a set dead pattern.

May 29: I am working on this book in a somewhat different way. I am doing the sketches and scenes before blocking out the complete mural—as an artist does. In fact I may use these in a new way—not tightly chaining them but allowing a distant perspective of a whole design, made up of minor complete scenes—no actual linking as the real ones are generally more dramatic.

May 31: No such thing as present sight. Hindsight and foresight.

June 5: Went to Sag Harbor with Joe and Katherine Spencer. Breakfast next morning at Alec Brook's then drive back through towns—Henry Perkins Hotel at Riverhead. Saw Cedar Beach—our early shack completely vanquished by briars, trees and weeds.

June 9: I should do a piece on the drinks I give my characters—changes.

June 29: Ran into Dorothy Farrell in Rotunda under West Side Highway in Riverside Park at 78th. Dorothy, still with her first husband (James*) restored to her after about 15 years with Hortense Alden and French wife and now it's sweetheart-honey-dearest and seeming contentment for both. He told about his connection with Dreiser as literary executor. Dorothy says "Yes, this is the day *Sister Carrie* goes into public domain."

On bus coming down conversation behind me in tired old man and woman voices.

He: "He shouldn't have been standing there with nothing on. He could have picked up a bathrobe."

She: "Finding him that way! They could put him out of the church!"

He: "And she could have hid behind the door when they opened it. He don't care for her anyway. Hit her on head with a bottle."

She: "Hit her on head with a bottle."

He: "He could have had the shower running, said she'd come to see him unexpected asking his advice about her job. She's only 19."

She: "Only 19! She could have been asking his advice."

He: "He fixed up everything to get her her divorce, going to make a model out of her. Can't see why he fell for that old Western Union gag— 'open up the door.'"

She: "They didn't need to have opened up the door and let 'em be found with no clothes. They could put him out of the church."

He: "Soon as they say Western Union, he opens door and they all troop in and find em . . ."

When I left I looked back and saw it was a very respectable pair of colored people. The combination of church and complete wary sophistication and acceptance of sin should have told me.

---

*The author and essayist James T. Farrell.

July 7: Reading over *Wicked Pavilion* and *Locusts,* I think *Locusts* is better. *Wicked Pavilion* has superior patches but was written and rewritten and revised so much it lost juice. Gave Carol carbon of *Spur* to read. She said it was fascinating—"acid"—but too many characters right off. This is true. I may still lop off the first ship chapter as it is not good enough to justify its position.*

It is clear to me that the Marcia book is much richer and finer and juicier but I do need more encouragement than Houghton Mifflin ever gave me on it.

July 17: What a day! Discovered Jojo still in Disturbed. Carol Brandt called to say Paul Brooks returned manuscript, feeling no enthusiasm, so must find new publisher. She suggests Viking.

July 18: Letter from *Nation* re: review of Anthony Powell books.

July 21: Found some reviews—by [Orville] Prescott of *Time to be Born* and another of *My Home Is Far Away* by [Harvey] Breit and both hit on my chief fault: fine scenes, dialogue, people, but the chief story is thin, weak, or trivial if indeed present at all. This *Golden Spur* has practically no main idea whatever and none can be pinned on, certainly. It might be wise to give it the straight farcical idea of the guest—beginning with Jonathan as stuffy, oppressed, in bondage to father. Do it as a complete comedy.

July 22: Decided to stop planning and working feverishly which has never got me or anybody anyplace but just start waiting and expecting. Carol called that Covici at Viking knew and liked my work—remembered *Angels on Toast* especially and Marshall Best there was only one who never read me. Said Malcolm Cowley's opinion was I had always done two things—the sentimental and the satirical, that the satirical was one they should like. Would I send some books, also royalty statement? These I did. At same time note arrived from Malcolm saying he'd tried to reach me re: "exciting news re: change of publishers."

Dr. Lionel Casson on "Trojan Women," Euripides, re: the "Disposal of Helen." Here was the woman for whom the Greeks had been fighting outside the walls of Troy for ten years. Now they'd won, they'd got her

---

* Powell in fact deleted this chapter.

back, what the hell should they do with her? Okay, give her back to Menelaus and let him decide—kill her or take her back to Argos. Menelaus says, okay, I'll take her back to Argos and let her be executed. Helen! The woman for whom all the youth of Troy and Greece had been killed! So, says Euripides, what is victory? Just one more death.

July 29: Cocktails with Malcolm who represents Viking (where Carol wants me and where I would love to be but Houghton Mifflin company handling of my last book made me think I would be lucky to get printed by the Greenwich *Villager* at my own expense). At once felt fine about novel because Malcolm knows the subject.

Houghton Mifflin like airplane hostesses—smiling, attentive to little courtesies, impersonal and soothing, but when the plane crashes and you have a fit and your seat mate pulls a knife on you their expression never changes. They are still calmly "intoning" (Leonard Lyons' favorite word) —"Fasten your seat belts, please."

July 30: Tomato appeared on roof vine! Potted in shallow pan at that. Also, in the evening an enormous butterfly flew in the window, which I caught. Most beautiful creature, six inch wings almost of delicate pink verging on beige with a sky blue stripe. Cocktails with Malcolm Cowley re: novel at Harvard Club and Algonquin yesterday.

July 31: After working all week furiously on new first chapter I read the original boat one and realized it set the tone the best. Went over all and sent Malcolm 53 pages. I want the background to be the hero like a river, with the many characters popping into view as people do in this neighborhood, all with one motive—fame.

August 6: Joe beginning to come out of binge. Carol called that Viking will take manuscript—$1000 on signing contract, $1000 on finishing.

August 7: Anniversary of Latouche death (1956). Letter from Malcolm regarding manuscript with more constructive editorial help than I've had for years.

August 9: Jojo in 9-B. Better ward. Waiting for bus coming back a trim, soignée, fierce-eyed, perhaps Russian woman. Her son was in 5-B. Studied medicine, handsome, been there ten years. She said all the doctors were alike. She had beat up Dr. Kush with her purse. Stood him up on chair and said "You think I'm a cuckoo clock, not human? You want to play with me like I'm a cuckoo clock?" He called for help, police. They came. "Lock her up! Lock her up!" "Oh, no, I say, you can't lock me up. I'm not a cuckoo clock. I call the newspapers, I call the newspapers!"

August 10: This book must not only be the living Village of today—*without* the Bodenheims, etc.—but the reality of Quest For Pure Art and Pure Essence of Beauty, corny as it sounds, rather than quest for kicks.

August 12: To Loren and Lloyd's. Tim Seldes going to Europe. He told of Elena Wilson's Uncle Walther Mumm of Mumm's Champagne. Now gone batty with high living and in rest-home. I saw Elena the day she was arranging to get him from New York to Hyannis Hospital. A wine big shot came in, hand kissing and said he had been visiting old friend Mumm but wouldn't again, as he was too nasty and had said to everyone "He's all right but knows nothing about wine." No—Walther wasn't really "off" but he *shouldn't* have marched into the St. Regis bar and given the bartender a caning. (Perhaps for putting 7-Up into his Pimm's Cup?) Tim said at new hospital nurse said to Elena on one visit: "Your uncle has lost all contact with reality—he thinks he's one of the champagne Mumms." Another time a nurse shook her head and said: "Too bad. Your uncle is no better. Only yesterday he threw his tray across the room and shouted—'Decent people don't dine at four-thirty!'"

August 17: What about "Golden Spur" play? It can be a gay farce.

August 22: Jojo's birthday. Still in Disturbed after breaking windows again but we went on grounds.

August 23: Sherman, Connecticut. Malcolm Cowley's birthday party. Van Wyck and Gladys Brooks, the Peter Blumes, Russell Cowles, etc. Norman Mailer (in Bridgewater) wants to move as all that green makes him sick.

August 29: For marriage: never quarrel over money unless you're the one that's got it.

September 4: As late as 19th century a writer didn't decide to write, he *was* one. You can see in the old times not so much the skill or technique but the superior quality of mind, since it is more than mechanical. The most facile story by de Maupassant, Sarah Orne Jewett, throws off a glow of wisdom, human observation. Pressure cooking and electric logs make the same color but the glow does not come through.

September 5: "Yow"—old cat losing memory, stand at door scratching ear wondering if this was the way he went to jump up on a nice bed or was this where there was a broad windowsill with sunshine waiting to warm his back? Had he had breakfast? Or was it time for lunch? Did the queer feeling in his belly mean he hadn't eaten or had eaten too much or should he just throw up? If it was to throw up he must be sure to go in the living room, do it on a Persian rug so no one would notice.

This is a Forsyte saga.

September 17: Did over the Anthony Powell review for *The Nation*. Did it so many times and then over again that I wonder about it.

Wonder if I am not making *Spur* too realistic and losing the comic yeast. The quality of Jonathan is not clear yet.

September 27: Around June Mary Grand had party and Bill DeKooning, artist and father of Twin Joan's baby, arrived with plump, juicy, gypsy-type girl who, I thought, looked pregnant. It struck me that since he had told me he never loved Joan but loved the baby and was therefore tied in some ways by her nagging reproaches—that he was fighting bastard-mothers with bastard-mothers. When I whispered this, I was laughingly told the girl was merely wearing the new sack dress. However, someone just told me Bill had knocked up a girl who was soon to have baby, so I was really right.

October 9: I am utterly baffled by the time I spend on writing and the naive sense of getting on with the novel when actually there is only a snail's pace and an increasing sense of panic.

October 19: In Washington Square usual Sunday crowd around the fountain from whence came piercing sugar-sweet street-type male voice in popular songs. I went over and saw the center of attention—"Go on, Danny, let me hear 'One More Time' again," a young kid yelled, but instead Danny grinned and started in on some Seventeen-lyrics, came out mere words: "Never seen such a queen, I believe give me steam, seventeen, etc." Danny was black, about 35–45, in a white sort of silky suit with black velvet lapels, a black long-looped string tie, a leather-looking rain hat sort of lid. It was getting cold and dark—a chilly seven o'clock and he was singing as long as he could.

On subway from 125th Street, East Side—a little pigtailed colored girl, about 11 or 12, in slacks, started beating small bongo drum with hands, stopping to hold an aching cheek sometimes while bigger boy beat larger bongo. An eight-year-old lively little negro did hip-ups down the aisle, shimmied and turned somersaults. Suddenly girl stopped, passed a very dirty Coke paper cup around for contributions and all three, tired and bored-looking, vanished, perhaps getting off to board next train.

*October 31:** Put in King Arthur Express Storage—$97.50. Carton box with red blotter and blanket; set of *transition, Secession,* 1st Hemingway *To Have and Have Not,* Juvenal, Greek anthology. Box of books marked A or special. First editions of Dos Passos, *Manhattan Transfer,* most autographed, Hemingway *For Whom The Bell Tolls.* Extra storage fee $30 a month.

One hall desk, oak.
Doll heads in carton and dolls. Secretary desk.
Three straight chairs.
One large dirty rug.
Three small dirty rugs.

Moved to Hotel Irving—26 Gramercy Park, Apt. 59. Put Fagan (cat) at Dr. Asedo's, 113 Lex. $45–$47.50 a week or $150 a month.

November 1: The "roads of destiny"—an O. Henry short story in which one hero is shown what happens if he takes three roads. All end up the same. In life and entertainment (fiction, literature, propaganda, art, stage) the same two roads are equally different but ending the same.

---

*Powell and her husband were evicted—literally put out on the sidewalk—from 35 East 9th Street in late October for non-payment of rent.

The "Ways of Life" that you are taught are for another way of life—almost directly hostile to your own success, saving for rainy days—means that you are saving for somebody else's rainy day. We didn't have money, TV, or cars and some thought that we were poor but we were rich because we had our books. Books. So you have to get a bigger, more expansive apartment for them—you have to buy bookshelves, you have to pay someone to clean them—when you move you have to pay for cartons and $12 for packers and movers and $30 a month for storage until [entry breaks off]

November 6: Finally did review of Charles Norman's *The Magic-Maker* re: E. E. Cummings. Dinner at his house, 47 Perry. Saw Social Security, Miss Pohl, in room 400 at 42 Broadway and discovered Jojo eligible for $58.50 a month.

November 7: Paid Ellinger Warehouse on Hudson Street $127.50.

November 10: Charles Norman publication party in our old address 46–50 West Ninth Street. Malcolm and Muriel Cowley offered us their house for three months at Sherman, Conn.

November 12: Someone—perhaps Malcolm—said my characters were fine but interest sags when plot comes in. Sags for me, too, so why don't I evade it in *Spur?* No reason for realistic details except in characters. Be elliptical—a suggestion of Jonathan's determination.

November 13: Felt return of some pieces of brain. Charles Norman and Coby came in. I had experience with Bankers Trust.

November 18: Looked at grandiose seedy apartments. Decided to move from Irving.

November 19: Gore Vidal's party for Kenneth Tynan, new *New Yorker* drama editor. Zachary Scott and Ruth Ford, Moss Hart, etc. Gore said he had lectured at Harvard on me as America's only satirist.

November 21: Moved to Madison Square Hotel—room 1043. $42 a week. See river at each end of window (bay).

November 22: Fagan returned with fine new manners and noises.

November 23: Bobby's party for the Kenneth Tynans. Judy Holliday, Lillian Hellman, Strasbergs, Noël Coward, Hermione Gingold, Jack Benny, Leo Lerman, etc.

December 5: Repeal party (25 years) at Harrison Smith's with same people I'd "prohibited" with 25 years ago. Vincent Sheean, Edith Haggard, Elizabeth Bowen also there.

December 10: Cocktails with Bryan R. here. Dinner at Cedar. Decided Village is my creative oxygen. Buy house down there—let out basement to super and janitor and other floors to others to have income on honorable property.

In apartment hotel life—the lightness of no impedimenta has effect of making one more inward-turning. Ailments are more urgent and alarming because of absence of the million background ailments—a cough is TB; a nosebleed or headache submerged in the bills, cooking, cleaning and clatter of apartment house life becomes a major matter.

December 15: Men—retirement—should ensure themselves friends who are not just business. They live someplace else. The embarrassment of feeling stuck with their family—old pals are old pals only when in same company. Luncheon and cocktail friends and neighbors—neighbors are better because there is same basic feeling here—the shared love of home and shared living problems. Shared financial problems do not make friendships.

December 25: Bobby Lewis. The Tynans. Gore. William Inge.

December 29: Having watched the indefatigable industry with which the New York Life skyscraper has been painting angels, Christmas trees on its windows ever since Thanksgiving, now equally industriously rubbing them out.

December 30: To Loren and Lloyd's again for party for Rosalyn Tureck, the Bach pianist, who told of her friend the Padrone of Venezia, St. Mark's—

such a nice man. Later on a train traveling across Texas sees familiar picture in paper—he is the new Pope. The Savos there. Mrs. Savo on Zen and also saying to take something small and make a whole world of it—that is genius. (Because I was finding the all-day suckers were jewels through candlelight.) Gilbert Seldes on the perils to a writer of Dead Air.

This is a strange neighborhood. Nature on a bleak section of East 26th Street. The excitement at 9 A.M. of watching city come awake, people go to work.

1959

January 3: Saw Jojo and three mothers—all saying new building made patients better. Jojo stood by cigarette machine, after I'd given him Kools, and said "I'd like to get some for my friend." Why? "So he won't keep bumming mine." He introduced me to a colored man, a fellow patient named Burgess, who was a minister. He had a handsome mother and two exquisite and well-dressed little girls.

January 7: Did review—Soviet short stories.

January 20: Irish toast—may no mouse ever leave your cupboard with a tear in its eye.

January 21: Frances Keene re: critical book for St. Martins Press.
　　Post reviews.
　　Harper's Bazaar—Younger Generation.
　　Nation—*Groupthink,* Mary McCarthy, Anthony Powell.
　　Possible essay on Max Perkins as editor.
　　PM—Lowry
Comprise 15 *Post* reviews, 3 *Nation,* 1 *New York Times,* 1 *Partisan Review,* 2 or 3 *Tomorrows,* 1 *Harper's Bazaar* article, 1 *Mademoiselle,* 1 *Flair,* 2 or 3 *PM,* 5 *Promenades,* 3 *Esquire* short stories—"The Survivors," "Down on the Rocks," "Pathetic Fallacy."

January 27: Madison Square Hotel. This place makes me sick to my stomach—I mean really. I throw up if I eat out and then I throw up if I stay in all day. The halls reek of old people—the elevator and lobby smell of brown envelopes (Unemployment and Social Security checks), perfumed disinfectants, sanitized mold; the walls shake down powdered dust of ages and the trucks pound through the streets. The Socially Secure hobble and limp and waddle and creep through the Stanford White lobby and fall into place on the sofas or in their own wheelchairs in the lobby where they watch everybody in and out.

February 2: This novel is done in a way like an explosion. A whole world appears—not in orderly sequence but all around with Jonathan in the middle—a spectator in a Theater in the Round. He—like other adventurers—expects to ride over the city. Instead, it overwhelms him. He is a focal point—like a magnet drawing large objects and events to him as center.

February 6: My theory of senility—it is a state of confusion, finally congealed, induced by changing faces in familiar backgrounds or (less often) familiar faces in changing backgrounds.

February 15: Slept all day and very good brain nourishment. Eddie Mayer last night. All I ever knew of him was the 15 years or more he spent in Hollywood as a $3500 a week screenwriter. All he talks about is his own idea of his past, which was when he worked on the New York *Call*, probably two or three years in his early 20s. I have noticed this about Hollywood people, dyed in the gold as Eddie: their lives stop the day they get there.

February 16: Dinner at Sardi's East with Gerald and Sara and Mr. Cornish, their estate manager. He is a smooth, rather secret-looking young man; Irish-looking like George O'Neil but more firm; single; lives at the Harvard Club, reflective and genuinely literary in angles.

About the Harvard Club—the men who live there. The younger ones drinking moodily at bar, marriages on the rocks. Somewhat older, the more serious drinkers, glad of a refuge from overwhelming family, glance occasionally at the old ones, the admitted defeated ones—deserted, deserting and defeating, frankly and wholeheartedly and systematically Scotching themselves into the grave.

February 17: No money this week. I think of the difficulty of avoiding Louise's overdue salary, Marie's $10.60 due on Mondays, hotel and hardship of that, too. But I am completely sure of a financial triumph and will not be affected.

March 16: One reason I dislike the studied academosis of people like Mary McCarthy—people who have shown they have a good punch—is the rareness of good punchers nowadays, and the hordes of academic nosepickers.

In some of her early work a fine, sweaty Irish style was exhibited, then the lace curtain Irish came out as the social climbing possibilities of success were studied and though the pig was still in the parlor, they referred to his snout as Grecian and would no longer let him sniff and rout out his own roots, but spoon fed him through a straw.

March 19: Joe's seeming shingles were allergy and cured by Edlich's prescription at Brevoort Pharmacist—West 8th. $18.60!

March 28: Why are people so critical of those who like X for his money or his fame? Those nearest and dearest to him (by love or blood) prize his money and fame more than any stranger ever could. If Mrs. X was insolvent, her devoted children, instead of preserving an admiring, amused, idolatrous attitude would be the first to say *"Now* mother, off we go to the nice nursing home!"

April 1: This dear charming novel—one thing it must have is rich joy, which I have, but for some reason never write about.

April 11: Letter re: dramatization of *Wicked Pavilion.*

April 13: Jackie said in park one kid being clobbered by a bigger one shouted: "You stop that—my mommy can lick your mommy!"

April 25: Saw Jojo—very gaunt and bad cold. Imperative to get him away from there. Moved to Margaret's—using her apartment to finish up section of *Spur.*

May 17: Looked at apartments around Village. On Greenwich Avenue an old lady stopped me and said "Excuse me but don't I know you—?" We exchanged names—she was Katherine Anthony (granddaughter of Susan) and we had met at Malcolm's and elsewhere. She asked what I was doing in the neighborhood and I said I was looking for an apartment. She said "Take mine" and I said "I will." Next day she phoned and I went to 23 Bank Street. It was beyond belief perfect—beautiful, four rooms—so I paid $250 down and we go June 15.

May 20: National Academy rituals. Saw Djuna Barnes, Allen Churchill, Glenway Wescott, Truman Capote and other old friends.

The funny thing about this place: like all organizations, it has always been run by second-rate or no-rate people who have had to be careful not to reward superior artists lest they themselves be squeezed out. They reward Djuna, Parker, etc., late in life when they think they are de-fanged safely and pose no threat.

May 21: A piece by Elizabeth Janeway, an industrious, go-getting little writer, who says she writes without ever keeping a notebook. She believes evidently in her omnipotence and genius—sit down at typewriter and make up. She also does not intend to enlarge her field by noting people, places or ideas alien to her experience or present knowledge; she does not expect to be interested in anything she is not already interested in. When I hear someone talking about bridge building in Chinotka or politics in St. Thomas, I like to jot down their speech, rhythm and exact beat, as a musician jots down native chords and airs, pure compositional scholarship research. E. J. is a form of phony. A "phony" is always supposed to be a flighty, usually flashy, and genial person without solid background but there are stodgy, humorless phonies by the million, whose lack of wit is taken as evidence of depth.

May 22: Saw Mary Grand*—who thinks of everyone in relation to how much they have. She has exact sums. Who is that? you say. "Don't you know? He has $300,000 inherited." What does that woman do? "Don't you know? She inherited two hundred thousand dollars." These sums simmered through my head.

---

*Powell sometimes referred to Mary Grand as "Mary One-Thousand Dollars."

May 30: Jojo improved greatly these last weekends.

June 6: Long period of merely waiting—waiting to get into new apartment of K. Anthony's; waiting to hear from Malcolm, also from Frances Keene—and general low, detached from hope and contact with the living.

June 9: Saw Malcolm re: *Spur*—cocktails at Longchamps 60th. He was equivocal, obviously dubious. Said I was starting anew with each chapter—which is true, but I think everybody starts anew with each new person.

June 15: Margaret's car, Jacqueline driver, Tommy Wanning toting, and miraculously we move into this heaven at 23 Bank Street. This blissful place suddenly allows Joe a peaceful privacy—me, too—and we realize we have been wretched without knowing it, completely stateless and homeless and roofless.

I don't know why we should object to being sales-pressured and mass-persuaded when we are such self-persuaders and can con ourselves into any feeling that assures us convenient excuses for our plan of life. If it is necessary to excuse our immoralities, we sell ourselves the idea our mates are monsters, or our parents were. If we wish to continue abject love, we con ourselves into seeing these objects of devotion as angels.

June 16: This K. Anthony is an amazing woman—powerful in a quiet, efficient way, understanding. The aging female who has (regardless of love affairs) maintained an independence of family and male-tending, grows into a super-man, understanding of all errors, with a masterly ability to direct lives. There is no finer power than misdirected maternalism; instead of small pig-headed power-wishers misdirected into maternity, a Mass Mama who combines male authority with feminine understanding.

June 17: Early morning heaven on Bank Street. Nick, the 65-year-old handsome Italian, very quietly moving garbage around in the street, then bursting into song (an aria).

June 18: Ran into Max Gorelik's sister on street, whose husband is ill—bad heart, longing for company. I went with her to 31 West 12th, where he talked, though obviously very weak. An old-time honorable lawyer—philosophic and wise. Talked of corruptibility. I said all "sportsman" words are tickets to cheating. "Play ball" means forget honor and personal ideals, don't notice my cheating and I won't notice yours. Be "on the team" means you are advertising your purchasability.

June 20: Jojo came in and was at his best and maturest, revealing a depth of observation that showed his reactions had been far more mature than his behavior. The house delighted him—17th century, he thought, then decided it was same period as Margaret's Brooklyn house. Looked out back window on the charming back garden and observed "Typical Village." Said it was "tranquil" and that he'd like to spend Saturday night here to wake up on a Sunday.

In looking over Malcolm's comments on *Spur* and recalling his dubiousness at conference, I sense negative reaction. With deep, sentimental nostalgia for his old Village days, he is disappointed that my Village is not what he imagined and he is cross about it.

We have about 60 cents between us and *Post* check doesn't come.

June 25: Curious day. Frances Keene called re: possible publishers for short books. Monroe called (having lunched with Carol) and offered to buy Viking contract with "good" advance besides. This turned out to be $500, hardly enough to interest me in double-crossing anyone. I said $1000 and he agreed, reserving 10 percent for share of movie rights. However, I was disturbed over implications that Carol had okayed the offer and on later discussion with her gave it up.

June 28: Listened to re-run TV of "Open End"—the David Susskind panel—with Dorothy Parker, Truman Capote, and Norman Mailer pontificating on writing. Parker and Capote completely traditional and conservative, but all sounding like three armchair mountain climbers at the foot of Olympus, trying to describe the view from the summit. A good word for the Titans, a pat for the Classics, a shy admission that there are only 15 really good writers in the United States (who are the other 12?). Mailer had a beard but Parker and Capote had hoarier ones and they sat scratching each others' beards and presenting each other with their favorite tics with almost human dignity.

Writers are usually embarrassed when other writers start to "sing." Their profession's prestige is at stake and the blabbermouths are likely to have the whole wretched truth beat out of them—that they are an ignorant, hysterically egotistical, shamelessly toadying, envious lot who would do almost anything in the world—even write a novel—to avoid an honest day's work or escape a human responsibility. Any writer tempted to open his trap in public lets the news out.

July 9: Going through old books at Margaret's (my own) I realize I should reread my own novels as it shows my faults and repetitions in clear relief. Obviously revision in many cases has dried out the guts, especially when I have never hesitated to tackle such revision whether I feel inspired or have an angle or not.

Wish to God I could clarify this present work—clouded and blocked and desperate as it is with the axe hanging over it and me and us for all these last few years.

July 10: Tension of never knowing when any money is coming in—of the terrifying importance of getting novel in shape. Two months to go. What then?

Last night I decided I should not be influenced by Malcolm too much since it does not come from within. He dislikes my Ohio stuff; however I believe I should retain that Ohio chapter.

July 22: What I miss is that old sense of insecurity that comes from wondering if the $1000 a month salary will stop. Now that it has, I can't afford that sense of insecurity—so I miss the whip.

July 24: Margaret told me funny thing. Her brother Lutie, age 70, is conventional, rich, selfish, so she keeps her offbeat pals at a distance. She was taking a shower, however and did not hear the maid admit guests. When she came out she found her beatnik problem-grandson, David, and an equally odd lad with one earring, greasy hair and beatnik clothes talking to Lutie, who was dropping in unexpectedly from a business call. David, always demanding a spotlight, read a few dozen of his new poems. Then he and pal decided to take showers. To Margaret's surprise her somewhat mystified brother Lutie pulled some old doggerel from his pocket—evidently written years ago for family delight and always carried around

—and read it to her. What amused her was that his own verse was so much more juvenile than the young man's, and his jealousy even more juvenile.

July 28: Very poor pay, but worker bound by Fringe Benefits—Free Burial, Free Dentist, Pension after 50 years, minuscule bonuses—so there he is with fringe benefits but the basic bald spot all the balder for the fringe.

August 2: Money from Margaret saves all.*

August 6: The Wings Of The Dove—elegant story of James feathered by Meade Roberts for a fine TV show, best I ever saw. Impressed as always by the perennial power of the "companion" story—Jane Austen, Edith Wharton, James—the drama of the person who has a foot in each world and cannot really belong in either. *The Reef* would be good—beginning with the raffish party. Honesty in snobbery. *Cage For Lovers* could make play and say more what I intended.

August 9: Bunny phoned from Boonville and we went to dinner and movies. Later Margaret laughingly said she had gone on movie spree and was so dazed by double features that she thought she saw Bunny and me there (which we were).

He talked about his book *Apology to the Indians*. The house up at Boonville now being filled constantly with Indians from the Six Nations (Iroquois). These Indians, led by Chief Mad Bear, have been cheated by the U.S. of property on St. Lawrence and Bunny is their only spokesman. He says people are shocked by Indians going to college, living regular life, then coming back to tribal customs which he says is right—preserve them, translate them into modern terms. They use women for planting and agriculture, not through laziness but because they are fertile—traditional.

August 19: One reason I like the Norman Mailer book *Deer Park,* when I didn't before, is what has happened to me since I first tackled it. Nothing like anything in this story but the change is in me—complete nihilism and hard bottom—so although there is no click of comparable experiences, there is the click of identical conclusions.

---

* A trust fund from Margaret De Silver allowed the Goushas their first financial security in years.

1959

September 1: Lunch with Monroe and Stuart Michener (20-year-old prize winner of Crowell Collegiate Contest) at L'Aiglon. Bright, alert lad—a wizard as youth because he knew Classic Comics by heart at age of 10.

September 3: Cocktails and evening with George Davis' nephew, Pete Davis. This was like walking into my novel, for this bright, dedicated young man was here to collect memories and news of his near-famous uncle George. Since George's life was uninhibited, there was not much to be told to give his real nature to relatives. I was moved by young man's utter worship and defense of George—knew his book by heart, had studied all his letters. That night, as we drank gin and ate hamburgers, a George was recreated of such magnificence and genius that it is a wonder he could ever have stayed dead.

September 14: Moved from 23 Bank to Margaret's at 130 West 12th Street.

September 16: Auntie May died.

September 22: Heard Auntie May had left me $1000.

September 29: The Coney Island Sunday crowd around Washington Square—gimcrack earrings, art, everyone folding up at night to go back to North Bergen or even Newark. Two cheap, hard, pretty girls in black beat slacks rushing along; guys with them paying no mind. Girls carrying on fight. One walking ahead. Other shouts "I tell you I'm sick—I don't feel good—I'm sick." The other one pushes on. "Okay, you're sick. Eat a hamburger."

In the elevator, now that it's full of these sweet-faced pretty young student nurses for St. Vincent's, one says to other: "So I felt terribly when I found out he was writing to this other girl. I realized I'd have to break it off but I felt terrible. Of course he was younger than I."

"How much younger?"

"Two years."

"You're nineteen. He was seventeen. Gee, that's quite a difference."

"It wouldn't have been when we got older. But anyway now that it's over I'm glad because now I feel free to correspond with the other man. He's older—nineteen."

October 24: Eddie Mayer and Joe and Jacques LeClercq who spent 30 or 40 years of their lives in certain work but in old age talk of their "past" as the life they lived *before* they entered their careers. Joe never mentions anything since 1930—Eddie and Jacques the same. As if they had been absent from their own lives.

October 26: Dark clever girl on *Paris Review* told of her love life. Engaged in Mexico to lovely Italian because they had such fun skin diving. Then when they surfaced she found he was a real fish—couldn't talk. Only the silent love under water.

October 28: To John's Restaurant and "Once Upon a Mattress." Dos' "USA" opened. Very disappointed not to get first night tickets but it was sold-out.

November 29: To Russia and Bill Hughes for triple birthday with charming young Neill, age five, who said "I *feel* like ten" rather wearily. Babies all over. Morgan, age two, a sad, charming clown who puts peoples hats and gloves on. Wears anything.

Talk of doing child's book on monsters. Unafraid of all monsters but scared of daisies—bugs—little girls. Morgan laughs.

After the polenta and birthday cake I went into the bedroom where a dim night light showed up an earnest little boy in bed drawing, Neill. "Do you know what time it is," he said. "Ten," I said. "No, it is ten minutes *after* ten," he said gravely, still absorbed in drawing.

I started out and he called softly "Dawn!" I went over to him and he pulled my head down and said with great awe "Dawn, I draw so good! I draw *so good!* You see that switch over there?" I did and turned it on and he said "See, I have drawn it with the two screws on it and the place to turn it on and I'm going to draw all around that open place there." He was awed and blissful about this great gift he found in himself—a moment that happens only once or twice in an artist's life.

Russia scolded people for "kicking Charles Van Doren when he was down." But I explained to her that was the only time you could kick them—God (in his great wisdom) didn't make our legs long enough to kick them when they were up.

December 22: 5 A.M. nasal hemorrhage. Cold ice on nose and nape—not as torrential as one of a few years ago. Perforated septum.

December 30: Knowledge that Joe won't eat unless I put it before him or else he will spend $3 or $4 somewhere for same thing plus drinks. Can't think of how to handle this. Can't even think how to handle social life and new observations necessary to my work. Impossible to move out of concrete burial in the familiar and the dead.

December 31: Wish I could get a play in shape—the only really powerful way of blasting out of this trap. Maybe if I disguised *Golden Spur* as a play.

Haven't had any drinks since 21st. Still traces of blood and seepage and deep cough—need for sleep, falling into two hours deep stupor in day and ready for more at 8:30 or 9.

At Loren and Lloyd's for New Year's Eve with Gertrude Flynn. Gertrude told of her cat Dennis who was at a Motel for Cats in Hollywood ($1.25 per day) where each cat had his own patio and his special menu pasted on the door (Dennis was beef liver with cottage cheese for dessert). The owner introduced him to another boy cat his age first day to play with; later on he'd meet the Bigger Boys. One bully, he admitted— George Cukor's or some big director's cat who occasionally threw his weight around. Director's Cat against Actors' Cats.

1960

January 1: Note in Author's Guild Bulletin that novelette prize (contemporary theme) leading to motion picture adaptation. Highroad Productions (Harcourt Brace Collins). $2500 outright, year's option—$18,500 if used. Closing date, March 31, 1960.

January 4: Went to Reg Marsh's opening. Felicia* looking lovely, wistful, gentle, with a kind of pure strength, seeming to lean when she is really very strongly pushing.

Margaret said wistfully she "wished she'd been taught to read fast." She doesn't have time anymore, she said. I tried to say when you were interested you read fast but this did not penetrate. (Penetration gets more and more difficult with her.)

Thought of curious idea for story. Brother and sister or husband and wife (no, too obvious) or else friends who know each other intimately. One loves Paris and often there (or Haiti or any other place). The other, just a week or so later, unexpectedly finds himself there (he has been recipient of others' tales of life, gaiety, etc.) and suddenly hunts the other and sees him—his own brother or sister or pal—beatniked up (it could be Greenwich Village), either fairy or bum-looking—or possibly the opposite, very social. There is no comprehensible deception here, nothing to be gained so far as he sees, so he is stunned. Here is a stranger. Recalls—he did hint at some things but since there was no background picture, it didn't register. Now he feels so baffled he follows the stranger into further strange places where the other is part of a group. His own brother or sister.

---

*Marsh's widow.

January 5: I am tired of placating the rich—telling them they are clever, perspicacious and beautiful. (If I was rich, I would be tired of assuaging the poor.) But the rich need so much free analysis and free attention from the poor, though they pay rich doctors millions for the same.

January 9: Amazed to read *Sun Also Rises* and *Moon and Sixpence*—so-called classics of their time, the one thin and feeble, lacking in human depth, mean-spirited. The surprising thing is Maugham's clumsiness and aridity, for he usually has suave mastery of all materials. Here he fumbled them, finishing, then flogging, the dead horse.

On the other hand, a Henry James novel, *The Reverberator,* reveals more genius, depth, color and understanding than either of those other boys. James' work nearly always stirs the writing imagination. Some object to "involved writing," "obtuseness"—but none of this is irrelevant. He is like a sculptor in wood, chopping his own trees, hacking and sawing to get to the exact core of his design, examining each branch and bit of sap for its effect on the inner meat. He is after his story for truth's sake, not yours. He is not a tailor, whipping up a pretty costume for your delight. Authors have been stealing his plots for years, not because they are inventions (which always wear out with me) but because they are imperishable human truths. That is why he is caviar for the wise and old and experienced—nothing false.

January 10: Lunch with Bunny and Elena and the Kenneth Tynans at Plaza. K. told funny story of the London "literary molls" quarreling over their seniority. "Why I had Peter Quennell when you were in boarding school." "Never mind—you don't know who I had in boarding school." Champagne cocktails—I've had only two or three drinks since December 22 but I had three of these and some delicious 1957 Moselle with the chicken à la reine.

Later at apartment, had Gertrude Flynn, Frankenburgs, Marie Miles, Wharton Galantine and Harold Leeds. Marie told stories of Frederick Loewe (composer of "My Fair Lady") who took her with him to shop for a Vlaminck or a Kokoschka. At different galleries he likes to be known but doesn't like to announce himself so he takes her along to do it. He sees Vlamincks and Kokoschkas for $40,000, $50,000 and $60,000 and, back in office, he beats his head with hand exclaiming "$40,000—$50,000—for Vlaminck and Kokoschka—and they're *dead*. It's crazy!"

January 11: PEN. Maurice Dolbier, Whit and Hallie Burnett, Victor Wolfson. Victor grieving over Scar in his life—was for seven years lover of Sonia Brown, 45-year-old sculptress. Later married and had children. Now says he doesn't like wife or children, loves only Sonia, going to Paris and go back to her. Told of early days when he and Sonia and Aline Bernstein and Wolfe were a foursome. Wanted advice. I said if he'd run out of plots in Hollywood and was reduced to his own life as only plot left, then stay in Hollywood where he could sell it.

January 14: Editors nowadays, so influenced by the effect on genius of Max Perkins. Editors (Howells, say—or Ford or Pound) were effective groomers of talent once, 50 or 75 years ago, when they edited magazines and were purchasers, not mere patrons or empty encouragers. They bought and paid for the artist's work, enabled him to live with decency and dignity, raise his mind above the horrors of where each meal, each baby's blanket, each schoolbook, each pencil, was coming from.

As magazines began to pay less (due to advertising which encouraged more advertising) and writers were squeezed out, the empty-handed editors began—receptionists who took authors to lunch or cocktails. Their special talent was in knowing restaurants and how to get in and out of them without breaking all the dishes. The game was to find some tiny palatable talent in the writer—not writing, please, but fishing, skin diving, turkey-farming, hula-hooping, name-dropping—anything. Usually the "editor" reads nothing and prides self on it, has no voice in firm's policy, can promise but is not qualified or permitted to deliver.

Heads (who are called "heads" because they make their decision by tossing coins and heads always wins) are off visiting titled authors on their ranches or yachts—movie stars who may appear—or lecturing to various clubs on amusing gaffes made by the new buffoon (taking place of dumb Swede, Dutchman or Irishman)—the author. Apropos of this the dumb author is always asking where is his money, where is his book, where is his display, where is his product? (An interest in his produce, which in a publisher of course shows he's on the ball—a real Simon and Schuster—but in an author means he's an egotistical slob.)

Nor does the editor contribute anything. He is seldom sophisticated, rarely knows any language but a sort of sophomore English, does not recognize any allusions so therefore is unable to perform the simple service of correcting spelling, repetitions, contradictions in descriptions or names —in fact, such a thing as "editing" is beyond his powers.

In English novel (American also) more than any others, there is a traditional difference between that which people know and that which they agree to admit they know; that which they see and that which they speak of; that which they feel to be part of life and that which they allow to enter into literature. There is a great difference, in short, between what they talk of in conversation and what they talk of "in print."

January 15: Sometimes, when I think about certain novels of mine, the really clear memories are of the parts I cut out, as in the Marcia book (i.e. the Norwalk episode), the St. George's Hotel and Bleeck's episodes beginning *Wicked Pavilion* and the French party in *Cage For Lovers* which I cut out in the Boston Ritz, because I was trying to find out from Rosalind what Houghton Mifflin liked—or, failing that, what they *didn't* like—in the manuscript. All I got was a vague report that they hoped it wasn't going to be a Left Bank novel, so I cut everything out, as much as I could, and was set back a year or two. I should have known that no one had read it really.

January 16: Why does a rather upper grade looking girl choose to sell stockings at Klein's instead of at Saks or Lord and Taylor? First because she does not value herself particularly or is phlegmatically bluntly honest—it's a service job and at Klein's you're better or as good as the customers whereas at Lord and Taylor's you must remember (or be fired) that you are the humble slave of royalty (the credit customers). Also, the other clerks would more likely be snobs, not wanting to associate with other clerks, so you'd be lonesome. At Klein's, the managers' sales talk remind them that the customers must be kept in their place—they're a bunch of kleps, crooks and riffraff and the clerk has the dignity of being their policeman.

Peg, chambermaid at the Madison Square Hotel, does not smoke or drink—makes her sick—is very shy and gentle, disapproves of restaurants, rude classes, etc. One day she spoke of feeling sorry for people with sudden money because they didn't know how to enjoy life. Curious, I asked her what she would do with sudden wealth and her face lit up. I'd go right to Las Vegas, she said happily. I'd gamble, I'd play that wheel you hear about, I'd play the horses. I'd bet on everything. I wouldn't care if I lost. It's the gambling I love.

January 19: Dinner at Malcolm and Muriel's—18 East 84th. Told Malcolm Kenneth Tynan's story of the English ladies spatting over who was the senior literary moll and we talked of here, where ladies do not fight over literary men (unless successful). He said it was a greater triumph in England for a woman to get a man away from a man. In order to do so, he said, she had to look as much like a horse as possible, since the English first love was a horse.

January 29: She had a soft spot in her head for him.

February 11: Took apartment at 43 Fifth Avenue.*

March 1: Stuff from Ellinger's Warehouse arrived at 43 Fifth Avenue and seemed wonderful but exhausting after long nostalgia.

March 2: Blizzard.

March 3: To John's Restaurant and then to "Little Mary Sunshine" at theater. Audience wonderful-looking—survival of fittest—having braved the storm.

March 7: Arrived Yaddo. $14.35. Very keen bright girls. Hannah Green (Cincinnati, Wellesley, taught at Stanford); also Adele Wiseman, Winnipeg, worked in Rome, London, Paris. Broody Dane, Thomas Anderson and Chou Wen-Chung, Chinese composer. Hannah—like Eugene Comstock—warm, large, lazy, doggy-body, warm, juicy fruity voice, rich juicy blue eyes, clouding and brimming and laughing—edible blue eyes. Luscious. Eyes give impression of beauty—which may or may not be there.

Adele—tiny, gallant, trim, chickadee-strong, vivacious but perceptive to a painful (to her) degree—seeing, sensing, close to clairvoyant. Pati Hill arrives. All three girls are familiar Americans in Paris or Rome—skiers, swimmers, ping-pongers, free-wheeling, friendly. If poor, their manners, accomplishments and dress are casually aristocratic and rich. Looking for adventure, love, the new pioneers—not beatnik types but

---

*This was the first lease Powell and Joe had had for more than a year.

more adaptable, socially savvy. Pati—high style Paris model *maigre,* chic, boarding school voice, wide ugly face trained to photograph, the delicate lady manner that draws service from everyone. One automatically brings her the things she has failed to notice—so station wagon drives all around on her errands (as it would for K. A. Porter or Parker or Peggy Bacon or Jean Stafford). Everyone awards and services and appeases these ladies whereas Hannah and Adele and I charge around, expecting and wanting to do things for ourselves.

The table of little magazines—pure poison, a kind of moored raft in space that has nothing to do with life, any more than *Ladies Home Journal* or *McCall's* have. Stories all concern marijuana (gage or pot), dope, heroin, sickness.

March 15: M. A.—for many years a stately marble female in the great graveyard of stately marble women; powerful, yet always open to wily predatory artists. They are suspicious of well-behaved, normal people writing novels though they are relieved to have them in the background. But for their geniuses they want a "show"—hysterics, alcoholism, temper, jail, the genius bit. So M. A. feasts on this with youth and later successes. Now, rightfully proud of never having bent or crumpled before human destruction, she speaks of past crises—of crying or "close to tears" after decreeing the death of a pet, the destruction of the dairy, the dismissal of a servant, the sending to State of servant's dim child. But the *capacity* for these strong cold gestures is her heart—the "close to tears" is her mind— the reversal of ordinary arrangements (soft heart, etc.). She has hard heart, soft head.

March 24: The near-triumph catastrophes to humans are worse than failures. John Herrmann, whose *The Salesman* won Scribners prize, then they split it with Wolfe because Wolfe owed Scribners advance money and they could deduct it.

March 31: I learned early that best way to be alone with your own thoughts is to be funny. Laughter is a curtain behind which you can live your own life and think as you please—a sort of sound barrier.

April 3: Wen-Chung Chou. (Wen Tsung Tzao). *Book of the Dead* (Tibetan). 49 days after death, priest instructs the dead. Colored light of himself—

sees plateau he selects. New religion believes you can become a Buddha instantly. (Bodi—enlightened soul.)

April 4: The way an out of town New Yorker gets in frenzy of homesickness and excitement over what is happening—the Israeli revue, the Blue Angel comedians, the tape-recording concert—but if he were there he'd be having hamburgers at home or, at best, drinking in a low bar with dull cronies.

April 5: Polly* told of Yaddo young man—painter who had job here, not enough to go and not enough to stay. He had been in an orphanage in west and lived with adopted parents he never liked, always dreamed of finding real parents. Turned queer. Suddenly his dogged quest wins—finds father and brother living in Oregon. Goes out to see them. Satisfied. Doesn't like them. Freed, he takes money and goes to Europe—Denmark, marries girl and has children and sells murals, very happy. Importance of settling the birth definitely.

April 9: Polly told about drawing woman at Cambridge who studies Holy Family—Joseph, Mary and children in carpenter's shop. Woman says "I thought in that family there was only the one boy."

At picture of Leda and the swan, she says "I wonder what that duck is up to."

April 17: Wen-Chung tells of MacDowell when girl naked (pronounced like "slaked") appears on balcony and frightens young man. "Whatsa matter, haven't you ever seen a naked girl before?"—then jumped into room. Polly describes couple caught "in sex" on floor. Their alibi: they were listening to Beethoven. Wen-Chung chuckles; this must have been "Erotica" instead of "Eroica." Later I tell of seeing enormous robin as big as crow. Polly suggests it is a pregnant female robin. Wen-Chung (still chuckling) thinks it must have been a MacDowell robin.

Wen-Chung tells of Huntington Hartford application—so detailed he doesn't answer it, then decides a private corporation has better right than an institution so he carefully answers everything. When it comes to sample of handwriting, he says "It gives me great pleasure to present you with a

*Polly Hanson, for years the chief assistant to Elizabeth Ames.

sample of my handwriting." In next space he says "As I am Chinese-born for your further information it gives me great pleasure to present you with my handwriting in Chinese." So in Chinese, he wrote a Chinese proverb "When you see a flag waving it is not a flag that is waving, it is not a wind blowing the flag, it is the motion of your own heart." A sly Chinese implication that all you can see by handwriting is a mirror of yourself.

He gathered, since he received an almost immediate acceptance, that Huntington Hartford had a Chinese interpreter there. But now Wen-Chung wasn't going. "It gives me great sorrow, etc., etc.," in his pure, delicate Mandarin.

April 24: Saratoga Hospital. [John] Cheever and Lore Groszman* took me. Room 202. Horrible.

April 26: The Lyle Saxon of Saratoga—Frank Sullivan.

April 29: She felt as if she was always carrying around a bull fiddle that no one asked her to play.

April 30: Drove down to New York with Jacqueline in Margaret's car.

May 4: Joe to hospital. Hemorrhages. Police arrived and Columbus Hospital† ambulance but wonderful cop shifted him to St. Vincent's.

May 10: Orville Prescott (also others): "No, I think it's very bright, but certain personal digs absolutely inexcusable. For instance that reference to X—what, you missed it?—well, you know his weakness for V—that's his own business, after all. And so for this remark—oh, you hadn't heard he was that way? Well, here's what he said about X.... Now *that,* I contend, is beyond apology! And that dig at his very good old friend—nobody remembers about that old jail business, so why should he dig it up? Oh, you never knew? I thought everyone did. Anyway, here's the dirty low-down crack he made about it in his book—All right, you can laugh. I did myself. It is funny, brutally funny, but why bring up that old scandal? It is odd you never knew about it. It happened this way—"

*Lore Groszman would later become well known as the writer Lore Segal; Powell was suffering from one of her severe nosebleeds.
†Probably Roosevelt Hospital on Ninth Avenue.

May 21: Better prognosis for Joe.

May 23: Party of Kenneth Tynan's at Forum of 12 Caesars. Decided to brush off hospital obsessions with attending—as when I have stayed home to sleep phone rings all the time with demands for information about Joe.

Stella: Her precise features are really chiseled now and chiseled by a dozen plastic surgeons so that not one fold of fat drips carelessly over the photogenic silhouette. There is, to this old actress, no greater sin than fat. Silence or immobility, for instance, is fat air and must be whittled off into chatter, gestures are vices stuffed with silvery laughter. There are worse betrayers than fat, however; there are Thin Eyes—the Thin Eyes of Old Actresses, the Artless Blue now diluted with years of venom, so that under the heavy clownish maquillage-white, aqua-purple lines, the faded mossy pebbles stir in a lemon jelly and a flash of flame darts out when the vanity is hurt—a kind word about a rival, a disagreement with or (worse yet) a polite indifference to her constant performance and pronunciamentos.

This is a relentless sword of a face, and its sharp blade goes through her whole body. The thin, steel-sprung body is an extension of the eyes, beak and fang. She must be the pivot and it enrages her that old friends should know this so well, and she is too clever not to sense their chivalry in pulling people into her ring. Do sit with us—Stay with Stella—as if there would be a vacancy around her if she did not stand by. She can barely mask her hatred of her protectors, but since she must always be On Stage, the Star, she flings out long black-gloved arms right and left—pinioning an arm on her left, a knee on her right like the velvet robe of the maitre d', forbidding both their escape and then their entrance into her conversation.

June 13: Received honorary doctorate from Lake Erie. Drove back with Jack—dined with Eleanor Farnham at Stouffers and drove around Cleveland waterfront.

June 29: Jack Grant was in public relations but got the axe (he said) so now is in demolition business.

July 2: Dinner at Bruce Barton's with Ann.

July 5: John Lardner's death. Never a fully alive man but an enjoyer of life, a connoisseur of lives. There was an added zest to other people's lives, a consolation in their woes, absolutely confident that John (like Dos) saw all, understood all, did not need to be told, did not want to discuss. Whatever happened to him himself did not seem to be real—he was almost oblivious to it, inured, completely armored, feeling his own feelings only after he translated them into prose to be read critically, clipped of pathos and sentimentality.

July 6: Monroe and Honeycutt—too ambitious to struggle upward. They want to light on their goals from a helicopter. So they are glad to take jobs that pay well and above all give them authority over those who are higher up in the fields they admire. They are willing to suffer all the trivial trials and other mortifications of an office job in order to hold reins and crack whips over the artists or successes they do admire, quite satisfied to know their power is not in themselves, that without their chance position they have no importance. Their awareness of their personal charm and intelligence does not blind them to its minor negotiability by itself.

July 8: C. P. Snow, Marquand, say things we all know. It's better for old men than for young men to discover the old platitudes are true. Just as there is something a little crazy about an old writer (say, in his 60s) being wildly revolutionary—a little cranky and plain eccentric, twisted rather than young, a little chilling. Like a face-lifting job on an old woman's body, it arrests the attention but does not charm.

July 11: Joe off X-ray therapy but improving. Spirits low.

July 13: Dinner at Robert Payne's who has Hassoldt's apartment. Beautiful new young girl—he likes them shy, gentle, pliant and delicate. Patricia Ellsworth, who is at Junior Encyclopedia. Patricia said Mrs. Howard Chandler Christy is in Des Artistes restaurant every night getting drunk.*

July 19: Turned in 270 pages to Malcolm. I do not think he will like them as he has read sections before and it will be hard to fit past opinions onto

---

*Mrs. Christy, who would have been quite elderly at this point, was said to have been the female model for the beautiful, idealized young nudes in tame erotic play that are the subject of H. C. Christy's murals in the Cafe Des Artistes.

revisions and changes. Promised to have book ended by August 9—three weeks—in desperation.

July 22: After paralyzing effect of turning in so few pages, got started yesterday on proper light tone, maybe by re-reading *Turn, Magic Wheel. Locusts, Wicked Pavilion* too plotty. Liked hero of *Magic Wheel* best for one thing—a half-sentimental, half no-good guy.

July 26: Louise died—Boston City Hospital.

July 30: Got up at 5:30. I plugged at novel. No encouragement, really. No interest, as before at Houghton Mifflin. Don't care if they turn it down completely.

July 31: Jojo in Violent again—11-A. Joe scheduled for operation Thursday.

Must call Ellinger's re: books, Marsh and Quintinilla paintings. Discovery that the only things I have are what I've given away. What I stored is not ours anymore but the books I gave Pete I still almost own or somebody does. What you give that you like to someone who likes it is yours forever.

August 5: Joe's operation. Pete's party.

August 6: Joe very shattered after operation.

August 7: Saw Jojo but they would not let him go out. Got down to hospital to see Joe who suffers from discomfort—no mouth feeding, crowded ward, confusion, heat, nurses vanished.

August 9: Malcolm phoned that novel okay—worried about end, he said. If editor knew how it would end, why write it?

Went to dinner at Mario's, then to "The Connection," which brought back memories of old Lawson plays, without the magic and excitement of revolution. These dopesters are feeble little squares who rise to some kind of belonging with dope and who know they couldn't belong anyplace else—even the human race. So play lacks dignity and bone, because no genius is being wasted, no blood is being lost. These are the people whose life is dope and getting it; there is no tragedy here anymore than there is in cats waiting for mice. That's their life and it's too bad when no mice show up.

Later Bryan and I to Dillons for jukebox of "Chicago" and "Mack the Knife."

August 10: Found Joe in woeful state—resigned and wretched in mess—no nurse—so I got one to clean him up. Hiccups and unable to handle his mouth feeding. Couldn't find doctor. Scared by his new fear of eating.

August 11: Joe better and barbered and in pain but optimistic.

August 15: Joe much worse. On critical list.

August 21: Up to Ward's with Coby to give Jojo some birthday preliminaries. Do not trust tomorrow.

Joe gasping and getting intravenous—surrounded by nurses, interns, and too weak to eat or move.

August 25: Joe counted improving after regarded as no hope. However, acts as if waked up after brain surgery—knows me but not how or why he got there. "Who are these Chinese?" (the nuns). New and more intense job of orienting and reassuring.

August 27: Jack Sherman back and called up.

Joe full of dreams and mix-ups, further confused by policemen who are guarding a colored prisoner just recovering.

August 30: Joe sitting up in chair. Mind clearing to face pain.

September 7: Cocktails and dinner with Murphys, Maeve Brennan and Charles Addams at St. Regis. Gerald ordered a rosé (Chateau de Selle), the only rosé that keeps its body—must be this year's. Head-waiter rushed up rye toast (Mr. M's "appetizer") and said he had waited on Murphy family for 40 years or more. Worshipped Esther Murphy and had learned his English standing behind her chair.

September 11: Joe's clearing of mental confusion.

September 15: In Henry James' *Reverberator,* a key quality of his is at its best—the ability to maintain his own author's mystification and curiosity about a character unwrapping a little more each time. Not in the standard novelist's way (with him knowing the whole secret but letting the reader in on it just a little at a time, then teasingly hiding the end again). No, the game is all fair and square—you learn just as he does. You are not "out there" and the author on stage but you are part author—watching people together with shared curiosity and surprise, instead of being treated like a child who must have his goodies rationed. In Dickens, particularly in *David Copperfield,* you are growing up with the hero, a fusion of author and hero which still allows the reader to share the unfolding with the author—a preferred position which flatters the reader's intelligence more than the Teacher-Preacher-Boss approach.

September 22: Joe improved mightily. Mind returns. Says he feels like Falstaff's awakening.

October 9: Jojo home for weekend—very good. Joe much better.

October 12: Margaret and Harry*—dinner at 68. Pete came in. Mary Grand said I had made scene at Gene's over bad food, and I said I was glad she could complain as I had so complained of her. Margaret quoted me as defending Mary (her defenders say worse things than her attackers) by saying she was really necessary to the group—she was the hole in the doughnut, which without the hole would be no doughnut. Harry said "Don't worry about anything Mary can say about you, Dawn—she can't top that."

Poor Harry—finds self incapable (according to wives) of giving love. With last wife it is not love she wants or gives but flattery. Also what a woman wants in a settled marriage is a kind of support that enables her to be herself and to get the most out of herself—sort of support Joe has in large part given me, assurance of my value.

November 1: Eleanor Farnham phoning at 7:30. Dinner. Cleaned apartment; new curtains up; very pleasant. We talked happily for about half an

---

*Harry De Silver, Margaret's son.

hour to the inventions we had made of each other in years' absence (and through our inventions of ourselves) finally came on the real people and totally unsympathetic. She burst out how she wanted to help me—no money but she could at least clean up my apartment, so it would be okay for Joe (I was shocked!). Said she could do it because she knew my room at college! "You can't let Joe come home to *that!*" she cried (as if he would be glad to come home to my carefully coastered maple apartment).

November 7: Jackie got maid to come clean and lifted great load off mind.

November 10: Joe had skin-grafting operation. In afternoon he was "floating on air" from anesthetic still and very gay. Said operation was "amusing." No longer could say something was "no skin off his ass."

November 12: I saw that movie "Gaslight"* the other night again. Every time I see it I think what is so ghoulish about this—it's the history of every marriage. Men and women have been quietly murdering each other for centuries with tender lack of understanding and believe me, lack of understanding can be more affectionate than understanding. The only way to get along in marriage is to surrender at once, don't have the bedtime Ovaltine he hands you laboratory tested, don't resist, just say Yes dear, of course I'm nuts but let's just keep it light while we're playing.

November 24: Wonderful Thanksgiving dinner at Elliot Hess and Jack Grant's. No Lonely Hearts affair—but gay. On these semi-religious holidays families usually have solitary friends in—ostensibly as kindness, but really as buffers between themselves.

November 28: Have been in back-to-wall hostile self-protection rage at all enemies as well as friends. Don't remember such long sustained state of fury. Being prevented from work or even thought by simple necessity for friends in this situation. Now determined to recover self-protection instead of this deadly burden of favors, pity and patronage.

December 10: Nosebleed. Off to St. Vincent's Emergency at 5 A.M. $5. Packed.

---

*"Gaslight" was based on the hit play by Patrick Hamilton, whose work has enjoyed a revival in the 1990s.

December 11: Nosebleed worse. Started at midnight. Got to hospital at 6. Packed.

December 20: At night had throat stricture while eating steak (always seems to happen) and not able to get rigid ball (hair ball?) down or up or out of windpipe. Water (hot) or Alka-Seltzer could not down but brought on suffocation or drowning strangling sensation with chest about to explode. Finally thought of bread and butter as in chicken bone and it eased way. Am told this is not a local throat thing but a heart attack. Heart very fast and frantic since.

December 24: At the stationery store (11th Street) a prim, pretty dark boy asked the clerk to look over Scripto inks. Then he asked for note paper. "You see I have to write a lot of thank you notes," he explained fussily. "Today I am a man."

"What? Your Bar Mitzvah was today?" exclaimed the clerk. "You must be rich. Let me have a loan, eh?"

"Depends on how much you want."

"Oh, about $2000," said the clerk.

The boy was flustered. "I guess maybe if it was around $500," he said and soon fled in confusion.

December 26: Dan Aaron and Jackie in. We talked of Edward Gorey's grim Gothic comedy and the real hunger for Sour (not Sick) Humor that used to be satisfied when we were children by Grimm's Fairy Tales— mean witches, etc.—and is a necessary salt to happiness.

[Undated] Max Beerbohm was once engaged to Constance Collier, who inspired *Zuleika Dobson*. She broke it on pretext Max "had carpet slippers in his soul."

1 9 6 1

January 1: Elliot Hess phoned at 10:40 A.M. to come over for champagne breakfast so I nipped over and we all had another bottle or two of champagne and gay talk, much in the old manner of Fiske, LeClercq, etc. of the '20s. Elliot talked of Janine Parmenter (direct descendent of Abraham Lincoln) and her various affairs with characters she gives names—Governor Earle of Pennsylvania ("The Toad"), Jacques Bouvier, Mrs. John Kennedy's father ("The Armchair"). As he had wanted to marry her, she could now be the President's Mother-in-Law, so her pals call her "La Belle Mere."

In some ways these people (I am one) cannot exist without the oxygen of laughter. That was why I couldn't breathe in Paris—fear of strange isolation and the financial panic that precludes all comedy.

This is the very group for the Talkers' or Players' novel—the pathos of wanting to go back to old nonsense, the only reality, the one backbone. They can stand all disasters if they can feel those old feathers at their feet. Like Dwight phoning me from hospital: "I'm sick and scared and I've got to have a laugh," he said. "They've punctured my arms, my back, they've done everything. Oh Dawn, I'm so scared. Nobody laughs. They've done everything to me!"

"You haven't had everything," I said rather desperately, "until you've been goosed by a bicycle pump"—and he laughed and laughed. "Oh thank God," he said. "I've had my laugh—oh thank God!" I had not seen him for several months or more and I never did see him again.

January 14: Joe yelled (during his cold when I tried to give him Empirin) "You're not going to give me something to quiet my nerves!!"

419

January 16: Moved in to office—799 Broadway or 80 East 11th Street, Room 640. Very nice. Forgot to have Frank bring big chair so am not as comfortable as could be yet. May find new bed at auction.

January 17: No one knows the tragedy of the mate—least of all the longer they've been exposed or dulled to it. One gets a glimpse but it is like a shockingly unflattering glimpse in a sudden mirror; the mind erases it as fast as possible. For many years, for instance, Joe has been in a job where no one called on him. He was paid, and memos passed through his hands, but he could read the papers in his office all morning. The only time he was "used" was at noon when his conversation set a tone for his group.

January 25: It isn't the tragedies or triumphs that dig into the soul, it's the embarrassments.

January 26: Dinner with E. L.—another one of the footloose *nadas* of Village. Analysis, children's schools, bottles, walk the dog, beat-ups, talentless.

In afternoon, I called house and Marionette* said, "A Mr. Hickey called. He wanted to have Miss Miller's phone number. I tole him—Mr. Hickey, I don't do that kind of work. I just tole him. I don't even know if Miss Powell even knows you, Mr. Hickey, I tole him."

This is the wonderful sort of whorehouse gentility that shows the uselessness of words. Drawing oneself up to one's full tiara and the napkin over the toothpick.

January 29: Saw Jojo who was almost miraculously wonderful—loving, thoughtful, patient, sweet and quick. His money hadn't come and he'd had to borrow to telephone. "I hate to borrow," he said. He added piously that he had given his last cent to church. I said I thought his money had run out on Thursday. "I still had a cent left," he said.

A man jostled and whispered to him in the store and he said "Mother this is Bernie Schwarz. He's the reason I get broke. I shouldn't give him money but he asks me. A week ago Tuesday I gave him a dime. Then Wednesday he asked me for fifty cents." He frowned severely. "I don't think he should *be* in a hospital like this!"

*Powell used a cleaning service called Maid Marion.

January 31: In Lane's—the wrapper and cashier in private conversation. "My sister says she won't go on a plane again. She says even if they get another free trip to Nassau or Bermuda like they do, she gets plane sick. It began when her husband started drinking a couple years back. She can't stand the smell of rye and ginger ale and that's what he drinks. Anyway, they got on the plane. He was half-loaded already and he had this flask of rye and ginger ale and he kept making her taste it too and she just can't stand it. Well sir, by the time they were half there my sister says she was ready to die she was so sick and she just told him she wouldn't ever take a plane again."

February 4: If there's one thing Kingsley Amis doesn't know about nature it's everything. A fresh selection of assorted campus tomcats sporting about among some excessively eager breeders. Amis is to be read with [C. P.] Snow—antidotes for overdoses of each other.

February 6: This will be the Month of the Novel. I propose to wipe out everything—duties, etc.—except *Spur.* When it is done will arrange other book.

February 15: Dinner with Bunny at Princeton Club and then to Edward Albee's "American Dream"—extraordinarily fresh. Bunny and I, determined to be less than our sleepy age, afterward knew we wanted a drink but were hardly able to sit up and stay awake. Our feet with one accord strolled into Liquor Store where we each selected pints of rye, strolled out into cab and tore to our separate beds where we could drop our clothes, put nipple on bottle and slurp the whole thing down at ease.

March 6: Organizing novel now in rather encouraging way.

March 7: The way people carefully make wills—this to that one, the ring to Bertha, the house to Sally, etc.—but at the death whoever is on the premises gets the stuff, continues in the house. The family bullies the lawyer who cannot enforce the will, so he doesn't hunt for the named heirs.

April 16: David De Silver—like all young, thinks everything was born the day he first saw it. Folk-singing in Washington Square: He asks earnestly why old conservatives of Village uphold it—it only began last year, didn't it?—and is incredulous when told it is 17 years old.

April 17: Jojo exuberant over starting work with Ground Crew picking up things.

April 18: Joe to St. Vincent's for radium.

April 19: Joe radioactive.

April 20: It takes hours to move two blocks in this neighborhood, stopping on corners for people. Regretfully I lag toward home and work but an old lady accosts me extending book of Gold Bond stamps—where do I redeem them? (I know that my Redeemer liveth.)

April 22: Hannah loaned Jackie her car and we picked up Jojo and Coby and drove to Nyack across Tappan Zee bridge and home. Jojo back at laundry. He said "I feel the need of something hot—some substantial refreshment."

April 23: Angered at the silly hostility to Louis Kronenberger's book.* It is the 50s anger at wit or humor. Pity is in bad taste as often as humor. Smug people feel their smugness shaken when they cannot pity someone—that the pitiable objects should joke or have fun among themselves is not proper. Be sad, damn you—they want to say when they see children of the poor having fun with some old boards and cans. It is the great pleasure of the poor, the crippled, the doomed—laughter when they can—and the Haves are furious because their laughter-means are so limited. Look, they say, what are you laughing at? *We* are the ones in the Mercedes with the Sarasota tan and our jet tickets to Rome and our lists of Hilton hotels and our latest TV sets and our legs we seldom use and our educations laid on our heads like Man Tan—what are you people in wheelchairs, in hovels, in institutions, in debt, in a beat-up old car or shack, how can you laugh? How can you do anything but wail and weep and beg? See how pitiful, how unlucky you are.

---

* Some critics thought Kronenberger's novel, *A Month of Sundays,* made insensitive fun of psychiatric patients.

So you aren't lucky—even if you aren't rich, maybe you love your tiny security of laughter so much you are smugger than the rich.

To Russia's for party for her mother Carminda Piccinini and friend Marie Zita who had been a girl friend of Carlo's. She had known the Vacircas and said Mr. Vacirca, a dignified Italian editor, had been a congressman in Italy. Later coming to America, he decided to import cheeses so he took orders and money but never delivered the cheeses so the Italians called him the Honorable Mr. Provalone. Later he did the same trick as a type-writer "importer." The two Italian ladies—60ish—had traveled by bus from San Francisco and were having a ball. Next they go to Washington, Miami, Biloxi.

Harry De Silver told of going to big party Saturday night and seeing several girls. He picked out one beauty and made a play for her. Got going with her and seemed getting ahead, finally said "By the way, what's your name? Mine is Harry De Silver." She said her name and then she said "Are you any relation to David De Silver? I used to go with him." "I'm his father," said Harry, completely dashed, and that ended that.

I am amused when I realize how shocked my Ohio visitors and family are—as they always have been when they visit me—and realize again how frightening it would be to live here by their standards. Good God, how awful, how *sad*—no TV, not even a Roto-Broil or an FM radio, and the old Emerson—$9, 15 years ago—has no *knobs* so she turns them with a knife! Anyone reduced to that must be on dire straits indeed! Never be-lieving that the first thing is anything but Machinery in Order.

May 4: Mt. Sinai Hospital. Ward 11, Bed 3, Fifth Floor.

May 13: Do not think I made hit with doctor who asked how I liked Mt. Sinai (a Jewish hospital) and how they were treating me. "Why, they're treating me like Jesus Christ," I said.

May 18: Got out of Mt. Sinai, on promise to come back for operation on June 6.

June 2: Did not go to Mt. Sinai but will wait till book is done. I do not remember crying much as child except as a private secret luxury of overwhelming *weltschmerz*. I was braced against hurts and pains but wallowed in black philosophic bogs of tears alone, especially in my teens. I do recall my surprise at tears popping out (as if I was an ordinary child, I thought—rather proud) when I opened my first jack-in-the-box on a Christmas tree and I cried for shame, really, that I had expected something nice and here was a joke.

June 4: The reason men hate travel is that for once they're out alone steadily with their wives against the world and at home they're out with the world against their wives.

June 18: Took off with Margaret for Philly to see Esther at Friends Hospital. Curious, almost mystical visit with Esther in a blank heaven.

June 23: Dinner with Bunny and Elena at 68, then to Polish movie "Ashes and Diamonds," then (too exhausted to protest) up to Algonquin where they met the nightclub performers Mike Nichols and Elaine May. They were comedians who in spare time loved scholarly diggings, discussed Polish underground, prison camp regimes, and a game of guessing a work from last or first lines. Exhausted at 1:30.

June 25: Dinner at Cowley's. Heard that Conrad Aiken at age of 7 or 8 came home to find parents dead—father had killed mother and self. He still loves Savannah, however, and can point out the police station where he ran for help.

Bunny told me Kenneth Tynan was a bastard, brought up by mother knowing he was illegitimate son of assistant secretary to an Oxford Don. When he got to Oxford and distinguished himself found he was son of the Don himself.

Malcolm told of Mrs. Ames of Yaddo being most selfish person in world. Accumulated millions. Only love was Leonard Ehrlich, author. Finally fastened her love on his niece Mary Ann. Was to be her sole heiress. In 1947 or 1948, Commie witch hunt. Mrs. Ames' secretary Mary Townsend with poet Robert Lowell and Elizabeth Hardwick gave spy data to F.B.I. (including news of Molotov Cocktails served at Yaddo), so Yaddo was closed for a year under shadow. Mrs. A. was shattered but returned for vengeance.

Unhappily, her betrayer, Mary Townsend, was rewarded by being married to Mr. Luther, a director, owner of 10,000 acre estate nearby! Had son. Doting on Mary Ann, Mrs. Ames finally got her to go to college at Skidmore (Saratoga) but Mary Ann avoided her. Mrs. A. is hurt. Turns out Mary Ann was engaged and having affair with son of old enemy Mary Townsend Luther. Problem. Ehrlichs, anxious for daughters inheritance, lock her up and after three weeks get her to write apology to Mrs. Ames, also break off romance.

July 11: Patricia Ellsworth and I agreed New York is only place you can shift your life and circle. In London, you go up or down in a change, and in other cities you cannot simply *move*—you hide, perhaps, or change personalities.

July 23: Dinner with Bunny at 68. Genet's "The Balcony." Great!

August 1: In book re: Dr. Sheppard case.* Trial by public opinion. Also pressure of election. Both judge and prosecutor must win votes. One wanted re-election, prosecutor wanted to be judge. Both are rewarded by obeying public demand for conviction. Jury mingled with committee in ten weeks of trial—everyone wanted to be home by Christmas.

August 8: Started X-ray at Women's Hospital.

August 12: Jojo down to house. No ill effects of X-ray but the daily trip—through Saturday and Sunday—leaves me almost intolerably exhausted.

August 14: Margaret's apartment. Rode up to hospital with shaky, desperately unsavory gentleman who informed me he had Parkinson's disease. Had it 15 years. However, he spoke with complete intelligence. Asked if I lived in Village and was eager to talk about those weird looking characters down there. Beatniks. Sure funny looking. As I was afraid to look at him, I exaggerated a defense of beatniks.

---

*The much-disputed case of Sam Sheppard, convicted of murdering his wife in a Cleveland suburb. The conviction was later overturned.

August 21:

> The crotch a lovesome spot is not
> A returned traveler said to me
> And when bewitched by sword or flea
> It makes the owner crotchety.

> The penis mightier than the sword but licker is quicker.

> I'd rather be right than you.

> There is no place like nowhere.

August 22: Hannah drove me up—got Jojo—brought down to home—I cooked pork chops, corn, etc. Hannah drove us back. Dinner at Ticino's. Jojo very ecstatic, me a wreck.

August 25: Longest Day of Life and longest week. Finally encouraged by sitting at Margaret's executive desk to call Dr. Wallace at St. Vincent's, who had me bring Joe over (he had bled greatly in A.M., as he had been doing for weeks). Got stuff out of M's—where my mind has been sprawling—bed at 9:30.

August 27: Cleaning house and exterminating after Joe in hospital. He is relaxed but I fear has cirrhosis as side pains him in liver section and I recall Hassoldt had bleeding, too. Wonderful movie, "The Joker" with Honeycutt and later for delicious dinner at Le Moal.

September 13: Came out with novel to beautiful East Hampton. Whole house to self and lunch and dinner with Murphys. Wish we had such a place for calm reflection.

September 14: Calvin Tomkins for dinner. Storm. Sara and G. told about Stuyvesant Fish having trouble with wild boar on his California cattle ranch. Organizing with other young blades a wild boar hunt. (With lances? Space suits?) Had approached Max Kriendler (21 Club) and Henri Soulé for boar steak orders. He suggested a Boar Burger—also the tapestry rights to the hunt for the Cloisters.

Next door to Margaret's beach house is a new-built house, two acres purchased for $12,000 13 years ago (from Sara) and sold same year for

$13,000. Held till last year and sold to septuagenarian with new wife for $37,000 (land only). A house—single story—was then designed with care. Wife—a former Carolina widow—wanted five fireplaces, each with different kind of marble. Three bedrooms, baths, study and maids room. Husband says she mustn't spend over $100,000. However it comes to $175,000. Colored maid is not allowed to sleep on same floor with Carolina mistress so basement room arranged.

Mistress then decides on divorce. (She is about 50.) Husband left alone with maid is old and desolate. He appears every day at Maidstone Club for lunch, where he has six martinis with his breakfast. As he is a member of the Club, no one comments on the odd fact that he wears long underwear which dangles below his knees under his Bermuda shorts and down his arms. Poor dear, said Sara, he needs someone to look after him. I asked Sara if no one spoke to the old man about his undress and she said calmly, "Oh, no—he's a member!"

September 27: Read much-touted Auberon Waugh book *Foxglove Saga,* which was curious, mechanized toy—vacuum-cleaning dregs of all English sophisticated wits, but without originality or charm. Decided author must be personally the most beautiful, charming engaging young man to be puffed as such a great, witty writer. Not unpleasant, but unflavored, callous and resolved to get it done.

September 29: Several days of absolutely rare sense of control, due to Coby's appreciation of novel and diagnostic suggestions.

September 30: Wonderful day—murderous hard work but results.

October 1: This has been best month so far—most work, most results, house-wise, novel-wise and mind-wise. Probably due in part to no reviewing, no apologies. Tuesday to Malcolm who, poor man, must produce *me* as his job. Possibly could finish it this very weekend.

October 28: Lunch with Margaret at Grosvenor. She said "Cast your bread upon the waters and it will come back for more." I commented on all the colored help—waiters, etc.—exchanging hot stock tips and she said that was ominous—big investors said (1929) there's always a crash when they let the plain people in. Joe said this due to small investors' absolute hysteria when they lose their $300 or $1000. Panic. But I thought due to slicing up of stock.

November 6: Lunched with Malcolm and gave him complete manuscript. He came back to apartment and read last section. Said he had suggestions on whole but fact is he doesn't seem to realize I have revised and changed since he first read it so sometimes what he says has been changed long since. This is first time I am not satisfied with general effect (except in *Cage* when again I had not the personal appreciation I had with previous editors Max and Jack Wheelock) so I'm not sure I'm on target. Assured I can leap through the hoops.

December 6: Party at Coby's. Helen L'Anglais said artists and creative people had cats—not as preference to dogs but because they themselves liked freedom (as dogs did) and could not wish to tie up an animal that longed to be free. Cats loved being nestled and boxed, however, so they were pleased to have someone near for nestling.

December 7: Saw big sign in small gallery on 10th (off 4th) with blown up quotes:
"Trite subjects, ludicrously colored, JUST TERRIBLE"
—John Canaday, *New York Times*

December 10: Mr. Blitzer of State Income Tax.

December 11: Called up Hannah, sure I knew her number. Kept getting "Good afternoon. Parents without Partners." Finally checked and found I was dialing CH3–3060 instead of 3070.

December 16: Since our rent goes up in March must not try Margaret with office, too. Will do the Scrubwoman story and "Yow"—neither one over 75 pages.
Revising and clarifying *Spur*. Malcolm felt Jonathan didn't have any sex life and should sleep with the girls. I saw his point and did over a scene showing they both used him more or less as a hamburger. Last night I had a strong reaction that this was no good. For Jonathan to be

living with two girls is really comic and true—for God knows it happens often. But to be sleeping with them makes him ordinary and unfunny and a cheap convenience.

December 26: Went to dinner party. Talk of MacFadden and Fawcett publications—men's outdoor mag writer mentioned as a "Big Cat Claws Man To Death" writer.

Japanese cook in, making sukiyaki—Mr. Tanaka—turns out he has a hot dog stand in Coney Island and does this stuff just for money to play horses next day. Everybody was in writing but strictly as a business. Hated writing. Only amateurs loved it, they said. All took jobs in publications, TV, ghosting, etc.

Talk of a ghost painter, a girl who couldn't make out with her own painting so is on payroll at $150 a week to a religious artist who was paid highly to do church murals. She designed them, he sold them as his; she executed them and he signed them.

1962

January 5: Days of so much blood washing, etc., that I come to office and fall into deep drenched sleep with fascinating dreams—very plotful due to rather drained conscious mind. Effort to re-enter novel knowing it's not right but knowing I have a dull knife to cut it with.

January 13: Curiosity is a rare gift, particularly when combined with acute observation, understanding or perception—not mere nosiness of the baffled ignorant who are only curious because it is different from their limited views. I am always surprised at how rare it is; I can be with an intelligent friend and overhear a curious conversation and the person with me has not heard or seen the episode—not because it is none of his business, but because the concerns of strangers do not concern him. He is not interested in life.

January 16: Jack Sherman wrote of Auntie May's way of looking her problems straight in the eye. But my belief is she solved them by looking straight past them so they never had a chance to scare her.

January 25: Took revised ending up to Viking.

January 26: Capote—the Southern Trash and crème de menthe school as against the old mint julep school.

January 29: The double vision of the past 50 years. Something happens that surprises and amuses you and as you tell it you have a sudden hunch that you have told this story before—about the same person, perhaps—in fact the same contretemps has happened before. When you catch yourself on it the *third* time round, it's time for curtains.

Matty Josephson called up and he hears half alarmingly well and half stone-deaf, enough to confuse you. I was self-conscious regarding his book,* having found it pretty pompous and so said nothing. He asked how I was, etc. and what I was doing. I said I'd finished my book and he said good. Then he asked me to lunch and said "Well, I hope the book doesn't look too rotten to you" and I, taken aback, said "No—I—oh you mean my book or your book?" He laughed understandingly and said "Well, Dawn, you really should write one, too—your memoirs should be pretty interesting." I double-took on that and then realized that he thought everything had to do with him—but also that this same conversation had happened before—oh, your book? No, I was talking about *my* book—either with LeClercq or Matty.

Matty's obsessive ego is a weapon, just as Margaret's sense of guilt and Hannah [Josephson's] "paranoia"—useful in getting them what they want. To analyze these "sicknesses" away is like cutting out tonsils which protect the system from worse infections. He is so vulnerable (like other monstrous vanities) that you don't want to see this balloon exploded to pathos and whimpering.

I do not understand why he tried so hard to explain why he wrote his memoirs to me—how "memoirs" were his idea, that he had "sponsored" Malcolm in Paris and books written on the period were all done from the point of view of the writers and so he felt that *he* had to straighten out these stories so that they would be correct. It was no use saying "you mean from *your* point of view" for he said "Exactly—get it *straight*." He said this was a "pipe of peace" lunch as he had decided to butter up old enemies with his book coming out! Then his worry emerged: Bunny Wilson had telegraphed a threat to sue him for the book. It was ridiculous. Bunny was an old drunk. Bunny wasn't a writer but a "character." He couldn't see why anyone would read *To The Finland Station* because he knew that material and Bunny also was no critic. Whatever I said he snatched at and twisted to support him, calling on his deafness, obtuseness, and general self-interestedness to bolster him.

He said he supposed Bunny was having a hard struggle; I said he was very successful. You mean he gets $1000 from *The New Yorker*. No, I said $10,000 or $15,000. Impossible, he said. I get top prices—around $3,000.

---

* *Life Among The Surrealists* had recently been published by Holt.

I assured him Bunny sold in other countries 100,000 copies. The Big Tycoon collapsed almost in tears at thought of Bunny making more money. He begged me to be mistaken; he was suddenly reduced to Poor Underprivileged Jew. Suddenly he was complaining of expenses, sending sons to college—what was $12,000 when he had all that research, etc.?

February 1: I think my next work should be under a new name, giving me freedom from the general curse that seems to go on everything I do.

February 8: Dr. Edlich—lovely, intelligent, kind doctor. Nice cops—ambulance—St. Vincent's. Poor Joe in pain and Hannah came with me. Nice entrance woman at St. Vincent's—Miss Carver who knew my books. Waited four hours. Jackie came. Monroe Stearns and Hannah and Jackie and I came back to apartment, went to Enrico's for dinner.

February 10: Joe critical. Fever. Monroe had stopped in hospital and given blood though I did not realize it was demanded.

February 14: Joe died at about 2:30. Monroe came down—also Hannah and Jackie.

February 15: I remember one of Joe's remarkable sayings, when he regretted needing care: "Every girl should know that in her wedding vows she is promising to look after a sick old man."

February 16: Lunch with Jackie and Pete at Longchamps in vague need for a restaurant lunch. Drove up and got Jojo for home. Coby came in, also Hannah and Tommy. Jojo answered queries about when this or that song came out, when revived, etc. When we get our own house, will have reference library for him.

February 18: Find that the "reality" often stands in the way of the Truth, that Joe's poor pained body in bed hid the real Joe—jaunty, etc.—and now he is freed.

February 19: Fatigued, numb, brainfagged yet must reassemble novel. Could not do another under such circumstances, completely against a tide, no support anywhere. Now I must get it ready so that I will be able to resist friends taking over my life and bossing me. A few nights' sleep and loneliness may do it. Must have it done by Monday.

February 22: Decided to replace editorial revisions. These are sensible but out of rhythm with sputter style of my own and I can't keep step with a partner who counts.

The business of literal editing is dangerous. For example:

1. "Who was that lady I seen you with last night?"
2. "That was no lady that was my wife."

Copy note—"Seen" change to "saw." Or if "seen" is kept, questioner is obviously coarse type and would not say "lady" but "broad."

1. "Who was that broad I seen you with last night?" Specify place here? Wouldn't he have encountered several females in a large city during one evening?
1. "Who was that lady (or broad) I saw (or seen) you with last night on the corner of 60th Street and Central Park West?"
2. "That lady was my wife"—or . . .

Must guard against the curious form death takes. The bereaved suddenly must *hate* someone as if that person was to be punished for still being alive. I find myself schizying around hating, loving, etc., to fill in the strange numbness. I do know I could not have gone on in my desperate duties much more, and for a year or two or more have often stopped in street with my bundles and wondered if I was about to drop dead.

Mad Magazine very funny this issue. I decided that the sheer ugliness of this magazine is very wise. A beautiful layout means art director is going to rule copy for beauty, not for wit. Any choice between a comic line and a harmonious picture goes to picture. The other preservation of comedy is in the low salaries of staff which keeps them bitter and irreverent.

Dinner at Hughes'—lovely, original couple with enchanting children. Morgan very sweet.

Old retired couples (left alone after years of family which acted as buffer between them) are each other's prisoners, as Joe was mine and I was his. Lovers become prisoners, eventually needing each other against the world, protecting each other, kind to each other through necessity.

The cage is too small but they must live in it and with it so after a while they control the quick word because such intimate necessity is close to murder.

February 23: Do article on "In Defense of Laughter." A "phony"—someone you hear laughing, using good grammar, good pronunciation, giving a lady his seat. It is permissible to take off your hat at funerals and in elevators. You do not laugh at the middle class. You laugh down or up. There is nothing funny. Van Wyck Brooks mentioned that a "light" novel was humorous but that there were more frivolous novels with humor. The shallow mind is usually a humorless one. Middle class is offended at laughter among the poor. Often the poor don't know they're poor any more than the middle class knows it is ignorant.

February 24: Do a series of slightly autobiographical essays on loyalty, gratitude. You are consciously grateful to certain people though you ought to be grateful to many you are not aware of.

Brought Jojo home. He was depressed and not sleeping.

February has usually been my best month but this year's Valentine of Joe's death switched me to some other track, I guess.

February 28: Bought red rose in honor of our first lunch at Claremont Inn.* Went to matinee of "Subways are for Sleeping."

March 1: Must make will. Carol Brandt managing my mix-up over the Viking snipping and sniping by going over to Covici.

Dr. Solley gave me medicine for blood-pressure. A genuine doctor, he knows more about a patient without even examining him than all those who turn you over to the staff of "Factual" data, when different facts turn up with every team.

March 2: I am constantly surprised that a writer (me) faces a human experience totally new to him yet (as I did) finds that he has written of it long before experiencing it, with deep comprehension—so deep that he can learn from his own fiction how to cope with the actual event.

---

*The Claremont Inn, just north of Grant's Tomb on Riverside Drive and the site of first date, had long since been demolished.

March 3: Came in after harrowing play "Ross," about Lawrence of Arabia (man tormented, John Mills, even looked a little like Joe) and lunch at Blue Ribbon (Joe's oldest, favorite restaurant). Sheer murder of up and down panting staircases of subways, ladies' lounges, etc. and long walks frozen stiff in sub-zero weather, to apartment, shaken up and ready to weep. No firm, mocking voice to say "Is that Miss Powell?" and phone ringing. Afraid I would burst into tears at importunate friends' demands for attention. I was detoured wonderfully by operator saying "London calling, Mr. Robertson" and there was Bryan asking me to come to England and stay with him as long as I wished; he was sending fare. I explained I couldn't possibly. My later life—complete exhaustion and tragedy and ferocious problems on one track and astonishing bouquets on the other simultaneous, with net results that the good things have little or no meaning except to dull the knives, which is good.

March 5: Pete stays with Nancy because he knows he is only of minor importance so doesn't need to feel harnessed. These girls choose a bar life they like and then shack up with any member—rotating regularly. There's not much difference in bar stools.

March 6: Begging Letter From Eager Academic To Authors Alive:
   Please don't write personal note on front page as I can't sell it. If you're bringing me a personal copy, don't write in it. Also, don't write letter full of your libelous cracks at friends so I have all the expense of clearing them before reaping rewards.

Andrew Turnbull, who thought Scott Fitzgerald was so much nicer and more affectionate than his friends because he wrote them such beautiful tender letters (in triplicate) with filed copies and often got no answers and friends wrote coarse, gossipy (Hemingway) stuff back and often did not even keep the Fitzgerald letters.

March 7: The people who in their arrogant heyday snubbed you, then fall on hard times, lose friends and claque and expect you to redeem them. *Now* I will listen to you, doll, they say—*now* I have time for you; don't go, don't go. . . .

March 8: Someone asked me about the long marriage to Joe—42 years—and I reflected that he was the only person in the world I found it always a kick to run into on the street.

As for his death, this is a curious thing to say but after 42 years of life together—much of it precarious and crushing—we have been through worse disasters together, and I'm sure Joe would feel the same way about me.

March 9: The books about novelists and their lives as influencing their books provides nice games for unimaginative writers who dote on this work. Actually what influences a story writer most is the kind of stories he first thrilled to—and he is likely to put his own characters through *Sara Crewe* (my favorite) or *Graustark* or *Alice Adams,* situations completely removed from his own life or experience.

March 15: Novel of blackmail. All human relationships—sibling, marriage—are payoffs. You keep your mouth shut about me and I will about you.

March 16: R. Burke—boy of our Cardington youth—not seen since we were 12, phones me up in New York about 1946 or 1947. I assume he has read about me in papers though he only talks about news of Phyllis and Mabel. He tells me he was always crazy about Phyllis though he dated Mabel when he could. At parting he said—Dawnie, you won't believe this but there's a real famous writer same name as yours, lives right in New York, too. I seen books by her. My wife's always thinking how funny it would be if you run into her. I said—yes, it would be funny.

March 18: In the long run the world respects and condones pure selfishness more than unselfishness (as self-interest can be proved and the lack of it not). Bunny, Dos, etc., are so completely selfish that they allow it in others.

March 26: Cocktails with Brendan Gill and girl at Algonquin. Fight with Bunny, who said Elena found Gerald dull. Also that Elena had disliked me at first but later liked me. I blew up like a hidden bomb to my own and Bunny's utter amazement, probably because I *had* liked her at first.

Also, I hate men quoting what their *wives* like or say. What right does a wife have to an opinion? So I blasted away at Elena as a social climber, her child a monster hated by all, etc.—all this wrong, because Mary McCarthy was the climber and I had heard nothing but good of daughter in last few years. Sudden silence in cab as I raged, then Bunny said "I wish you weren't so jealous of me, Dawn. It makes it very hard for you."

This was a wonderful switch, which I snatched at and said, "It's because you keep me on that little back street and never let me meet your set and you're always going back to your wife and I have never seen you except when you're in town selling—" "Yes, I know it's been hard on you, dear," he said. So we were saved from a real embarrassment and I let him off at the Algonquin and the taxi-driver must have been surprised when I gave the Fifth Avenue address (he must have expected Ninth Avenue).

Next day I was ashamed but hardly could call and apologize for murder. So I sent wire to him—"Darling, what happened to us? Was it my money or your music? Was it the Club? Where did we go wrong, dear? Aurore." Today a postcard from him says "Dear Aurore. Perhaps it might be as well for us not to see each other for awhile. The strain of our relationship is becoming difficult. I am leaving for Boston tomorrow. Mille baisers—Raoul." This is great genius and I can see why no wife, especially a bright one, can live with him. He will always be too clever for her.

I guess he never ran into my ferocious loyalty before. I am ferociously loyal to my few dogs, upper and lower, and will brook no slurs on them, except from me.

March 28: I dread the dictatorship of loneliness, the collaboration compelled because that's all there is. The mind and sometimes the heart have rejected someone, weighed him ever as a loss in every way—but the empty hour forgives this and once again your splendid wings are clipped, the proud neck choked.

March 31: Lovely day to end schitzy March. Decided taxes are great cultural benefit. Sent more people abroad (to save taxes) so they get out of their ignorant complacency.

April 3: Carol writes about novel—"witty, vivid and convincing."

April 15: 170 pounds.

April 22: Riverside Drive lovely and pink and melancholy as Youth for it represents my youth. Youth is nothing but sadness and frustration and longing by itself but it flies on a *dream* of glamour. Whatever glamour is present is flyblown with true love unrequited, wall-flowerism, poverty, wrong clothes, hunger, etc.

One reason I am still numb about Joe and only feel a dim relief that he doesn't have to go through another day's false hopes and wearisome preparations for a new life is that we both almost simultaneously gave up about three weeks before he died. He had been so determined and we had a sort of conspiracy against the Guest (cancer).

In the years of Madison, Irving hotels, Bank Street, etc.—ever since 35 East Ninth Street—when he has been home, we have gotten acquainted really. I know him and I realize there is no need to feel guilty if I go to any country, travel, or plays because if he were alive and well I wouldn't be able to get him to go anyway, for he really never wanted to *go* or *do*—he wanted to read, dream, and have the leisurely discussion, the voyeur life.

The few times I tried to drag him into my life, he was angry and displeased. It is always hard to understand this but having learned it, it makes it easier for me to do things I want (if I have energy or dough) without grieving how much he would enjoy it.

Weepy in house and imprisoned and paralyzed. Need air and sun.

April 27: Feeling much better. Up at 5:45 by mistaken glance at clock. Good. Finally seeing some headway in apartment—transfers to store closets, drawers, etc. Beautiful new white hat. Look better, too. Will arrange room definitely as office. Get work file for desk. Able to sew ribbon on suit, sew up hem buttons—the kind of therapy I haven't had time for in years.

April 28: Jackie is a girl who must have a broken heart. I think it comes from consciousness of her own beauty as an unfair advantage so she must handicap herself, being a warm, generous person. Pete was different—he was the TNT that exploded her life in new directions. However terrible that experience was, she won freedom from it. Then must find new chains, new heartbreak.

April 29: Feeling better every day, especially after yesterday and outing with dear Jojo. Couldn't find car keys so we taxied—foot of Riverside Park. Hannah waded in river and we found wild chives.

Went to "Never on Sunday" and realized that wherever there is a cheerful, laughing group, there is nothing funny, no wit. Everyone approves of this kind of animal happiness. I love that sunshine, ha ha. I drank so much wine I feel good, ha ha. You are so pretty I like you, ho ho. It's good to eat and swim and that is healthy, ho ho ha ha. The mind, ah, that is what brings evil. The Apple in Eden was the Professor with the Word, not a new Taste Sensation because that would have been okay. Only Wit is unhealthy, unhappy.

May 4: Never press on anyone a book you love but if someone loves a book of yours, give it. They won't like the one you press and you won't like the one they love as much as they do.

May 9: Saw movie of a familiar type, "Rome Adventure" and thought how completely logical it was that I should not have popular appeal since my mind gets the messages contrary to what other people get. The novels, plays, movies about the American (or British) girl who goes to Italy, Greece, China (usually Italy) and has or doesn't have a hot lover in the country. She is pure, sturdy, honest, straight American and is first beguiled by the Latin's curious, warm passion—but in the end (before her travel money gives out) she realizes he does not mean to divorce his wife and have her children and marry and support her, for he has loose morals (as all Latins have) but intends to stay true to his family, too. So, brokenhearted at disillusionment (and besides her money and vacation is over) she goes back to the decent chap—American boy who also has found that the French girl he was sleeping with slept with other men she was also not legally married to—and the two fine Americans go hand in hand to the Building and Loan Co.

Who is the Fine Heroine here? A light-minded American girl looking for kicks to combine with a life-long patsy—a bastard willing to give up his career, family, country, for a stupid, selfish alien who is prepared to give nothing but her over-priced body, which has copies coming over by the boatload.

May 12: Jackie and I picked up Jojo at Ward's and we came home. Mr. Moon (supervisor) said he had reproached Jojo for some bad behavior and Jojo said "Mr. Moon, you forget I've had a very bad shock." Jojo was good but has to be eyed for his match carelessness and fires when lighting cigarettes and stoves so I can't leave him alone.

May 13: Franz Kline died this night at New York Hospital.

May 14: In the last two years Jojo has seen more of New York, been on more expeditions than ever, thanks to Hannah's car and Margaret's loaning Jackie her car. I have ridden more than I ever did in my life. My conclusions are that as a means of toting—as I have to do with Jojo's clothes, etc.—an auto is fine but I believe my fatigue is worse.

There is a dullness that envelops people who have no desires whetted. They yearn for years—if I could only go or do or love—knowing only a miracle will accomplish this and it becomes jeweled, beautiful, a far-off star. But if all you do is press a button and it's yours (installment plan or charge account) there is the whole pleasure watered down to the perfectly possible. And if you elect driving around before you know your wish, you've been there before you desire it and are tired of it before you've wished and been denied. The real sense of accomplishment and fulfillment comes from conniving, wishing to get or go, but there is just a kind of dull satiation with no zing in a few hours of riding. Joe and Jojo and I had more excitement and knowledge on our walking and bus trips than any of these auto tours.

May 16: Thinking of modern education (such as Lake Erie) which is to instruct a person how to be unable to survive alone—exact opposite of original purpose. How to get along with the community; how to mask your differences and to whittle off your superior gifts to level down with the lowest; how to follow, not to lead; how to be helpless without material goods; how to run machinery; how to be a slave to your home and family; how to do without thinking and let your individual talent atrophy or die aborning. Reading, Latin, Greek, walking, etc.—these give the greatest joys to a person without money, alone, sick. The present education presupposes the person will never be old, sick, alone, poor or unpopular.

May 17: L.O.L. (Liberal Old Lady of Greenwich Village.)

May 21: Restful and now I know why I am so exhausted mostly. It is what I always knew about myself—I have to have eight or twelve hours without speaking to a soul. Privacy is my oxygen for brain and soul. All these auto rides with people mean you talk going and coming and see nothing, think nothing and come home drained of even nothing.

June 1: Up at New York Hospital—room 1719. Margaret—gasping and sucking in life like Joe—dying about 12. Beautiful East River view—serene and lovely as all settings for death, orphans, tragedy are, and why the turmoil of city is less scary.

June 2: I decided that my basic idea of novels is that there is one character, a giant A. who is peeled off like an artichoke into several characters—for each one is but a mood or possibility of the basic one, and a novelist lights up one strip of the artichoke. In *Spur,* as in others, each character represents the hero at another time—in another situation—under different circumstances. The fruit opens, seems several people, then closes into One.

June 3: Went to Coney Island on the subway with the Dos Passos and there on Stilwell Avenue saw Mr. Tanaka, the Sukiyaki king with six troupial birds, telling fortunes. Then the Aquarium was lovely—white whale, the walrus, Colonel Blimp.

June 4: The struggle to restore my private mind after these last months of being obliged by necessities of Joe's illness and Jojo's dependency to share my troubles and duties and have a "communal life" such as most families live—utterly prohibitive of creative. The oxygen I always needed for work—solitude for the first 20 hours of the day—is impossible. Phones ring and the trivia of yesterday and tomorrow's minor fiddle-faddle and tonight's dinner. I seem to have been marking time till suddenly I realize grass has grown over all my exits and I must clear them again if I'm to think anything. It began in Yaddo and the Family Life there and has now become intense for there seems no sane arrangement.

I think I must find some retreat—like I used to have Central Park or the Library.

All modern life seems a plot to keep you from thinking.

June 23: Jojo shows increasing mature reasoning power, broader understanding and self-philosophy. Earnestly combs hair and shaves self. Wonders why I don't "mourn." He wanted me to be sure and frame all the
snapshots of Daddy. He also reminded me that I had not gotten the
remains back from St. Michael's. He vetoed Harry's suggestion of Pittsburgh burial and said he and Daddy and I should have our remains
together—a regular, mature family idea that surprised me. Yesterday he
came up with a new one—he would like to have a motion picture made
of Daddy's whole life. He would also like records of Daddy's voice.

June 24: Dreamed at last of Joe—very vivid and shaking. I was in my bed
on the street next to the Wanamaker building and he came and sat on the
bed—saying it was more than he could stand, our separation. There were
tears in his eyes and I held his head and tried to console him but people
were passing by on the street, staring at us.

In the morning I was sick and shook up—the first chipping off of the
ice barricade I built up in his last few months when he was already gone.
"I'm no good to you or myself or anybody anymore," he cried out one day
in December. "I'm no help to you." I said he was—that I couldn't work
or live without him to turn to. It is true that things do not have much
meaning.

June 26: People who try to boss other people excuse themselves by saying
they are "perfectionists" (meaning they demand perfection of everybody
but themselves). They do not know the difference between a Perfectionist
and the Common Scold.

July 5: Reading Gladys Brooks' charming rearrangement of her life.*
(Should I call mine "A Rearrangement of Things Past"?)

I decided that Van Wyck—her husband at 62—had given her a life
and that's what a marriage is for, to give each other a life, true or false. He
gave her a magic lens for seeing herself and her past just as another man
might have given her a hair shirt to send her to a convent with remorse. I
saw that what enabled her to clothe the past with such perfumed clouds
of beauty was her absolute romantic notion of herself as a fairy princess.
Sometimes a parent bestows this but Gladys had the deep vanity and

---

*Boston and Return, a memoir published by Atheneum.

imagination to wallow in this conception of herself and saw herself only as a darling, good, innocent outline—only the facts were wrong. (Like Joe.)

July 8: Life and Art. (Novel specifically.) There are novelists and novelists and only a small proportion are concerned with life, just as in medicine not all doctors care about preserving life. There are pathologists in the novel as well as general practitioners.

I intend to mix my figures extravagantly because I believe in life and life is full of mixed figures. Some novelists want to find life so they can jump on its back, after they've brought their characters alive, and ride it—Saul Bellow, for instance, and many men. They hang on their live characters like a child—take me, too, they cry and so they get to bordellos, bullrings and the reader has to have the author between him and his live hero like an agent, always intruding with an explanation. Other novelists use atmosphere, background, as beaters hoping something alive will run him out of the bushes. Their story is the place—any life has to be pasted on. Other writers simply want the stage—they provide dummies as front heroes or heroines, stick them in the opera box and they, the writers, do all the performing—imitations, bird calls, acrobatics, magic, discourses showing their learning. If at any time a character starts breathing, the writer jumps on it and deadens it with anesthetic prose.

July 10: Have been walking around in my Past—running into people I don't remember but who were part of a whirling party life of '20s, '30s, and '40s. Max Wiley (I didn't know I knew him) said: "I remember the laugh years ago when you said you had to go over to Elizabeth Arden's to get wormed."

I think magazines exaggerating Togetherness joys drive suburban young to crime and dope. Dope destroys the ego so no need to work or accomplish to appease it.

July 29: Took Jojo back. Shocked by his calm remark: "Daddy has been dead now six months but it seems now as if I'd never had a father."

July 31: Reading Leicester Hemingway's story of Ernest*—much like Nathaniel Benchley and sister Marcelline to follow. Fact is, no first-rate

---

* *My Brother Ernest Hemingway,* published by World.

genius was ever a family man and no reason for family to think they understood him or knew him just because he was obliged to board with them for 18 or 20 years. They are proud, jealous and bewildered when the world finds a swan—didn't Sister get better grades in Geography? wasn't Ethel a prize debater? wasn't Phil a leading man in the high school play? Where did this swan get his genius?

August 2: Joe's birthday began with call from Carol saying Metro wanted to buy option on *Golden Spur* but options often queer big sales so she wasn't anxious unless I needed money. I said I did, so she sent down $100, showing considerable confidence. I celebrated birthday by receiving first bounced check from National Bank and going over to bounce another— as if I was Joe. Then to Longchamps alone for three Bloody Marys and a meditation on Joe's complete passion for restaurant eating—whether he had clothes or not.

August 3: Ward's Island fees adjusted as of June 1962 and Jojo must pay $200 a month.

August 6: Carol called early to say Freedman enthusiastic over book and wanted to hold up movie sale so as to make musical with Comden and Green. No copies available.

August 13: Will Success Spoil Dawn Powell? I don't see why not. I'm no better than anybody else, never said so.

September 27: In the final redo of *Golden Spur* I was acting just as I did in the case of *Turn, Magic Wheel.* Farrar & Rinehart was furious when— after they had paid me $250 a month for a year—I turned in a measly 44 pages, which they disliked and later, on finishing more, hated because I was in my new natural style. When they advised tearing it up (as John Farrar wrote) I was so enraged I slammed into completely myself at my most nonconforming and so found myself.

Same in *Spur* when I was so dimmed by doubting publisher, editors that I could not sustain my original explosion of life technique until literal-minded editing made me so mad I tore back into it, throwing out every suggestion that had been made and being more myself than ever.

What editors want is the Dead Body so they can have an autopsy. What I know and always strove for was to convey life—to have the novel about people *be* those people, have a breathing story, not language separate from communication. I want to *alert* the reader, not lull him. Sentences must explode and bloom.

October 5: Published *The Golden Spur.*

October 7: One reason women are always devoted to a drunkard (unless children pose problems) is that one major flaw conceals all other defects. Stinginess, extravagance, brutality, selfishness, rudeness, slovenliness— everything is blamed on drink. Often a woman finds a reformed drunk is a worse monster than any. Her maternalness and tenderness are called into play by the DTs—easier to cope with than a stubborn, mean, selfish sober man.

October 8: PEN Club—cocktails for Langston Hughes, Mortimer Hunt, and me. Reviews of *Spur* are more understanding and intelligent than usual. The spotting of Jonathan as classic, artful simpleton Candide is good, and Charles Poore's detection that Jonathan loves his ignorance more than women or art.* The general reaction so far is of a waiting audience parched for fun and irreverence and a mood to praise humor as a virtue instead of a forgivable vice. This must be a swing in the times, for these reviews mention the seriousness of the theme and purpose and seem grateful for entertainment dealing with real foibles, real people, credible situations, whereas most modern humor is completely removed from human beings and no catharsis of recognition of clues but complete escape.

October 9: I get more out of art and music reviews than out of literary talk.

October 25: In the New Realism or Pop Art I see the contours of "Summer Rose"—that is, it will be as real as the phone book.

October 26: General ambition is to see how much writing I can get done before my mind starts working.

---

*Poore had written about Powell and *Spur* for *The New York Times.*

November 1: Humor. Wit. In my case a form of panic or rage, essentially—or fatigue. Like poetry which occurs when the brain is asleep and the hidden treasury of memory, imaginings, undeveloped pictures is freed. In *Spur* sometimes the four hours of strain and drudgery were necessary for the brain to be conquered and the fancy to be released unchained—jet directed, its trajectory determined by the force of its imprisonment.

November 14: Phyllis sick.

November 21: The queries about the Village—why? There is concentrated here a population of strangers, almost half of whom are people you would have as friends. Less time is wasted.

November 23: Forms of fans. You write a book—it's your book. Someone reads it and is enthusiastic—it's his book. He tells you what's good about it. He isn't trying to flatter you; he's bragging. He's telling you that he knows what's good and he hints that a stupid oaf like you bumbled into writing it by accident and don't know what you've got.

November 27: In art review talk of creating art works by *objets trouvé* which is, I believe, my own philosophy. Just as, at Mt. Sinai beach, I loved making cupboards, tables, etc. out of driftwood, abandoned things and things that came naturally—a kind of pot luck creativity from farm-poor traditions of imagination rather than the How-To passion which requires new tools, etc. Same way I object to "research" on novel. Use what is going to waste in your memory, experiences you never sought.

December 1: The *objets trouvé* theory of my Ohio farm background. Do not hunt or scratch for new ideas—let them be turned up by natural rain or floods.

December 14: The only way to spend time or money profitably is to have little of it. All day to do nothing means not even letters get done or manicure. Time budgeted to chores, the free hour or two goes for something important.

December 15: "Summer Rose"—the pleasure of genius is for the spectators and hangers-on (as Esther Murphy). The happy lives are those hanging on to a star's coat-tail, not the hard-working star.

1963

January 5: Picked up Jojo at 11 A.M. and in evening Bobby Morrison and son Junior came in to his delight.

January 8: Only 3 pages into Claire scene and not at all sure but Lee Adams was delighted with possibilities for them. Have not worked with such eager enthusiastic cooperation since college days. Maybe this will work out. Usually the theater people are rigid with their set theories or bound by some former success and all I can do is follow. I am a very poor follower.

January 12: Indiana University asks me to conduct creative writing workshop, which is no interest to me but more and more I feel the pressure put on a doer like myself to do things that enhance the watcher's status. Academic friends or relatives can boast in their own circle of close contact with superior academic shot and get preferment themselves. The doer has to keep *doing*—seldom enjoys or appreciates the rewards, has vicarious pleasure in his audience's enjoyment. Similar to hard-working businessman getting material things that please his wife or children, though his own pleasures are difficult to indulge.

(In same way I hold out against the larger apartment I really need—for fear I will have no excuse for not welcoming visitors. Outside of time nuisance of moving I think that is it.)

The wives and mothers and neighbors enjoy the triumphs most and are free to brag—the victim or hero dare not. Sometimes he tells out loud of some victory only to make it real to himself—this emerges as bragging but is a form of doubt. It always amazed me that some people are prouder of knowing a celebrity's ex-wife or cousin than they would be if they were the person. Actually this is the voyeur pleasure—the peephole view that gives them the advantage over the star. Knowing them would put them in an inferior or sycophantic position.

No work done all week since conference Tuesday. Dull head. Last night Wanning, Coby, etc. and Monroe Stearns in. Monroe newly married but as both he and wife are 50 and like their own homes neither one gives up. Monroe stays on Riverside Drive and she stays in Snedens. I had thought this was a reckless sex venture. He spoke of his novels and writing and when I was puzzled it turned out "his" novels were *David Copperfield,* etc. either abridgements of classics or translations.

Saturday night. Disgusted with blockade finally invited Coby over at 6. Then had a Pernod and did new scene in about 40 minutes. Alice and young Phyllis phoned to report improvement in Phyllis. Alice's husband (divorced and remarried) beats on door every night at 10, according to Phyllis who calls him her "double Bourbon brother-in-law" as "double Bourbon" is all he ever says. He wants to move back in, get Alice a $90,000 job in another neighborhood where there's a better high school, as in five years they'll want one. Alice says he doesn't worry about them now—just when they'll be sophomores because that's the time he and Alice were happiest. Alice says why should she give up a boyfriend who dates her every night for a husband who's never home—so she doesn't want to remarry him.

Thought of Madison Square apartment—strikingly dismal in its halls but pleasant enough in rooms. We felt we were on cruise and went out together oftener than we ever had. I kept my notes and current writing *(Spur)* in paper bags around desk in bay. Leaning out could see East River at end of 26th and North River other. Surrounded by insurance company, great stone skyscrapers and at strange daybreak, the sun, muffled in soot, fog, neons, mottled the fringes of these hard cold gray buildings with salmon outlines, white chalky underlines, sharp yellow lines so definitely colored I was convinced they had been painted these curious clown colors in the night. Clown skyscrapers.

And then when I'd look out again they would have settled into their 9 o'clock gray. Below the street was a river of ugly Lerner busses in and out of their warehouse—but sudden splashes of banquet colors could be racks of cheap bright evening dresses being shoved onto trucks. On rainy mornings, the insurance workers under their rain-colored umbrellas looked like anemones or colored water lilies. My tenth-story window— huddled in clusters before their entrance gates below they seemed to be a pretty window-box garden and the taxi cabs fluttering along with black and gold so many honeybees. Inside the apartment, sometimes the sub-way below shook the walls so that a snow of fine sooty dirt filled the room—shaken out of some 60 or 70 years of New York dirty living. Next door banged all night with what turned out to be a couple engaged in prostitution—the man rounding up customers in near bars for his wife or gal, then coming back to see if it was over so he could go to bed. Joe and I shopping in Third Avenue dreary supermarkets, eating all meals (almost) in—more than we had in three years of housekeeping with maids and kitchen.

Viking tells me reviews picking up all over country, due to *New Yorker* Wilson piece probably. Also *Spur* is on final list of National Book Award. And Mrs. Vincent Astor loves book and wants me for cocktails. Why? Does she think we writers should band together?

January 17: Not so good, this scene of Claire's, though I thought so until I read it to the group. I got up at 7 and slaved, and perhaps slavery is no an-swer as it came out very talky.

January 20: Listened to FM program—probably WBAI—where some Midwest professor lectured on Mark Twain, explaining Huck Finn. As usual, the stupid academician was repeating what his own teacher had said about Twain and the general idea was that the lecturer and his teacher knew what Mark meant and what his problems were, but poor old Mark didn't.

January 24: Tea at Mrs. Vincent Astor's. 778 Park.

February 2: Got Jojo in Hannah's car and found him patient and in excel-lent shape. Bedded at 6:30, came out at 10 after Hannah left. "I thought Hannah looked very well," he said. Had aspirin and slept with Wanning's heat pad. Woke at 5 and apologized. "After all, mother, I went to bed at an ungodly early hour." I filled out a Contemporary Authors question-naire and he told me which year each of my books came out, which surprised me as I thought he rather resented and ignored my work as a rival interest. "Why do you have to answer these questions, mother? Is it for the Hall of Fame?" A very satisfying visit. When we went into the plush warm Fifth Avenue Hotel for papers he murmured rapturously to himself "I love being in a hotel."

February 5: Woke up in tears, crying because of terrifyingly real dream of Joe in one of his old tender protective moods. Shaken.

February 8: Up at 6:30 to get Act under control.* To Charles Strouse at 4—heard wonderful opening song, which dispelled dreary exposition. Read Cassie Bender and Dan scene, which delighted them.

February 12: After struggling and straining of the *Vogue* "Steak" article I realized it was ruining the energy that should go into musical or *Esquire* piece so I gave it up. Grimly coy. Hated to surrender. Then Carol decided I should not do *Esquire* piece for $750 because they only guaranteed $200 if not used. However, I wanted to go through with it as it has enough roots in back of my mind and I did want the market as the commercial option runs out in March I believe. Feel like a prize beef being sized for the big corporation cut.

February 13: There are reasons but no excuses.

February 15: Up at 5:30 and 6 every day and find a certain glow in freedom to get started before the World begins. Have done usually a day's work before noon. People's peaks vary. Am impressed always by the Planetary theory (my own). People—not the sun—revolve around each other, sometimes being in eclipse, sometimes in full blaze of sun, sometimes touching each other, then remote for eons. We are moved by magnetic forces beyond our control as if we were dolls; our reactions to each other are just that. Same way we are able to hook on to Infinite Power accidentally or in a particular point in orbit, of time or place. At certain times of life you are at peak power at midnight (if you only knew it), at dawn, at noon, at certain places, near water, near mountains, near factories (as I used to generate near factory towns). Right now, early mornings are for me but I must use these few remaining years to get my

*Powell was working on a musical comedy of *The Golden Spur*.

own mind free—not to have it harnessed at this late date to articles and popular magazines, as Twain, Lardner, etc., were harnessed and wasted so that they have a bulk of trash to show for their minds.

February 16: Visited Jojo at Ward's and we met many other patients. One girl, Virginia Parks, who missed Maryland and who wanted out and seemed all right. Would like to send her something. Jojo sent Ann a card; I suggest his ending with Italian phrase but he said "It isn't etiquette to sprinkle your English with foreign phrases."

February 17: Lunch at Captain's Table with Djuna Barnes. Very nice. Dismayed and paralyzed by my *Vogue* and *Esquire* pieces. Gave up *Vogue* one and now giving up *Esquire*. Very alarmed at my chickening and numb brain.

February 24: Matinee of "Asylum" by Arthur Kopit at Théâtre de Lys. Awful. A crass, sadistic, cretin nightmare presented as comedy. Beckett, Ionesco and others had a background of poetry, humanity and wisdom but through the cracks of their imitators' stucco structures we glimpse only the empty interiors. This is a humorless leap for comedy onto some old crippled blind horses. If you laughed over *The Snake Pit* and chuckled over Hiroshima you will have a ball over "Asylum."

February 26: The query—why did you write this or that?—is almost always answered in my case by a sense of historical duty to get a picture of a fleeting way of life. Probably began with my youthful joy in vignettes of ancient Rome or Greece, which made life real instead of re-embalming dead life. Usually the urge comes when the special scene is fading—the new one hasn't been formed yet but is waiting in the wings. Swan Songs are my specialty.

March 7: The artist or great man's two-headed bogey: the hope of being discovered and the fear of being found out.

March 8: Met curator of Egyptology at the Met Museum. Told of relief at museum of "Mona Lisa" leaving. Guards had been getting hysterical shunting visitors off to the Aristotle (didn't know difference). Said small six-year-old boy in line with his group kept overcoat buttoned up and his hands crossed over it patiently all during waiting. In front of "Mona" he opened up coat and there was his little puppy he wanted to share the thrill—then hastily closed coat again.

Girl said to me "Have I ever read any of your books?" I said "You look as if you had." She took this as insult—I assured her author-ego made it a compliment.

Was told yesterday I had not won the National Book Award. I felt some relief as I have no equipment for prize-winning—no small talk, no time for idle graciousness and required public show, no clothes either or desire for front. I realize I have no yen for any experience (even a triumph) that blocks observation, when I am the observed instead of the observer. Time is too short to miss so many sights. Also chloroforms, removes the weapons—de-fanging, claws cut, scorpion tail removed, leaves helpless fat cat with no defenses and maybe exposing not a sweet, harmless pet but a bad case of mange.

March 12: I thought of Margaret and how she once said—when lunching alone in an expensive place where only high-paid businessmen went—that she enjoyed this isolation for she could gloat that she was better than they, for her money was inherited, really *hers,* whereas they had to work for theirs. This turns out to be strangely true—the self-made man must always deprecate and apologize for his magic Midas touch—the heir has built-in smugness.

March 16: Jojo told me re: missing his father—"I think if he couldn't work he'd just as soon be sick and if he was going to be sick he might as well be dead." I said "Where did you get that philosophy?" He said "I thought of it."

Reading *Esquire* piece on Dos, I thought of my early experience with radicals. Railroad men in Ohio who were very intelligent but stingy and shrewd with other workers (Auntie May had boarding house). Radicals in Village. Everybody talked fascinatingly—made fun of me for naiveté. Republican. When I went off to vote they laughed. I thought, how strange. A Republican doesn't feel passionately about anything except duty to vote—so I went and voted straight ticket, no idea who the people were.

The others sat and had brilliant conversation about Debs and marvelous radicals. I could hardly wait to get back to the Prince Street restaurant and join this superior group.

April 5: Thinking of the Armory show—that the pioneering artist is a medicine man who operates on the eye, so that you can see more completely and wholly. When Duchamp's "Nude" came first it looked like a row of boards because people had cataracts. Now, due to labors of modern art for 50 years, it is marvelously a downstairs-going bare figure and we see the motion because our eyes have been educated by other artists.

April 6: Cut review in *Post* of Alice Toklas. Annoyed.

April 7: The Private Papers. The news of Oaf Giving Private Papers to Princeton. Realization that no one should write private letters. The receiver sells or gives them to University where thousands of strangers from campuses read what you confided about your lover, grudges, betrayals, etc.

April 8: Don Elder bitter about publishers' illiteracy. They are in Culture Racket—so they don't need to know anything. They know music: "We published Lenny Bernstein's book." Architecture: "We have Frank Lloyd Wright's book." They have credit cards, get good tables where they get authors drunk for $8 a lunch, explaining why they can't advance them $50.

Ted Peckham a blonde cherub in lavish first-floor mansion apartment he got by going to church where an old lady, 75, said she was going to be married and did he want her apartment? She'd had it 30 years and he must pretend to be relative. Vast place. Antiques. $167 a month!

April 11: People *want* to be used—they *want* to have their brains picked, like a cow wants to be milked. Old ladies like to be conned by polite beautiful young men, leave their fortune to them instead of their honest, nagging, belittling, boring children.

April 13: The more I see of couples who married their childhood sweethearts, the more I think they missed living—as if they carried their Veil forever and saw everything.

April 16: The rich need poor relations and poor friends more than the poor need the rich. The rich need poor old Cousin Betty to be glad of a home so she can be stuck on the farm looking after the balmy progeny or the dogs. They need wastrel gambling nephew for same reason—they need poor second cousins to send their old clothes to, or their mistakes in shopping, so they don't feel extravagant.

April 26: Carol called to say *Vogue* had bought "Lesson for Runaways" for $500—written at 35 East Ninth (1957).

May 2: Matinee of lovely musical "Little Me"—very marvelously contrived and organized. "I love you—as much as I am able—considering that I'm very rich—and you are very poor."

May 12: Jojo fine. We ran into an elderly man on 23rd Street and Jojo said Hello, Mr. H. We shook hands and Jojo said Mr. H. had been in a ward of his. He came to town weekends, but "I'm always glad to get back," he said with a scornful gesture. "This town's dead nowadays. Nothing doing. I'll take the Island any day."

"How long have you been on Ward's?" I asked. "40 years," he said. "I went over first for narcotics cure." So he'd been there since he was 30 and had free weekends but still felt New York was "dead." Like elevator man at 35 East Ninth, who toted me and my notebooks up and down the elevator to roof workroom day after day and finally said "Do you do this all the time—just go up there and write?" I said yes and he said "It must be especially monotonous work." He'd been running the elevator 30 years!

May 13: Very happy over wonderful recognition piece about Gerald's painting in *Art in America*. There is no thrill like having witnessed appreciation for something you know is fine—perhaps great—and it happens too seldom.

Interested in change of people. In '30s, Gerald and Sara disliked *Tender is the Night*—in fact, could see no resemblance to themselves beyond some physical aspects and relationship to other people. I saw difficulty writer had in making his story so close up to live models. I have no satisfaction in reporting exactly and journalistically the camera view—reality must be melted down and reshaped to appease the writer, often unsatisfying because he cannot approach the depth and fascination of the real people and must try and try to create stand-ins.

May 19: The importance of the oxygen of humor in dealing with sick, old, dying and retarded.

May 23: Extraordinary. *Saturday Evening Post* bought "The Elopers" for $1500 and both Brandts and I are more delighted than almost anything. The sale to *Vogue* and to *Post* of these two stories which were completely myself—what I wanted to say and what I felt must be told for people's good was almost a lifetime justification for doing what you *feel* instead of what the market seems to ask. Like sitting tight on old bonds until they are worth much more instead of following every passing breeze.

"The Elopers" was the final essence of four or five years of visiting Ward's with anguished eyes and ears and also many years of trying to do something about Devereux or Gladwyne but too bleeding to write it. The material must be there, but most of all the knowledge of your *message*— what should the reader be left with? In this case I finally decided on a most basic message to those who are burdened with fear and pain for their sons or daughters in State hospitals (which seem always the worst of such hospitals).

A. There is always a chance in a rotating staff of a State institution (rather than a private one) of a new drug, a sympathetic doctor or companion (also a chance of dangerous experiment which I must leave out as already a fear). There is hope, there is sympathy, etc.

B. People outside should be told how to help the ones there by visits, cards, etc.

C. The problem of What-Afterward? should be opened up.

D. Specifically and especially—glimpses of the brightness of Puerto Rican or Spanish Harlem.

The importance of faith and love for the patient. How wonderful that a mass medium like *SatEvePost* should be publishing this.

May 26: So and so is reported as many times a millionaire. I could qualify as many times a pauper. The ease with which I get pocket money now— more if I dared—frightens me with a kind of delayed fear, as if you were heroic in a sudden crisis unconsciously but afterwards got in a cold sweat of panic realizing the old danger you had so calmly ignored. So I think of a lifetime of wondering if there were enough pennies in my coat pocket to augment those in my purse and buy a subway fare home—and cannot equalize this with wondering if I have three tens in my pocket or three twenties. I was bolder in big deals then than I am now and more extravagant in little frantic $2 dresses.

August 8: In marriages—more selfishness and saying what *you* want. Otherwise each keeps giving the other what they think it wants and blocking their dearest wish, just because they don't say it. (Put this in play—"A to Z").

August 10: To Fellini's "8 and 1/2" movie. Technical pinpointing or album of cut-out high points in theater—a sort of sampler of every theatrical thrill hooked together, from the unexpected drop into soft shoe routine, sudden nostalgias etc.

September 7: For many years X had celebrated Lent by presenting himself to the old friends who were jealous of him so they could insult, etc., to their heart's contents. He made a list of their remarks. If he had a front page rave in *New York Times* they said "I see Raleigh, N.C. didn't even give you a notice."

September 10: Jack Sherman got in on *S.S. United States.* Looked great in French-tailored blue suit. Studied at the Jesuit Academy and Alliance Francaise. Young and buoyant for 50. Amazing young man—of courage and disguised indomitable will. A person (much like Rosalind Wilson) who had such responsibilities and adult demands for understanding in youth that he carries the yearning for a childhood through life—wearing young clothes, young excitements, disguising his sophistication and refusing his disillusionments. In their masquerade as wide-eyed youth, such people acquire a great deal more knowledge and human background than more openly cynical adults do—and this feeds into their work, giving Rosalind's writing a depth and compassion and brilliance.

September 17: First day of feeling like work on "Summer Rose."

September 18: Ann Corio's—Red Skelton there. Dinner at Beatrice (West 12th).

The advantage a writer with no children has is that other people's children tell him the truth about their lives, whereas they can't tell their parents anything or it will be used against them.

September 22: Scrabble in A.M. Then Jackie and Dan* drove us up to Ward's. Rental cost of car for two days about $20—cheaper than taxis and other entertainment and having them in charge lightened the whole weekend enormously for me.

I find the new social life here terribly wearing but nourishing, too, though I have done practically no work. I keep house because guests are usually expected but I must get back to early writing.

September 24: Gore Vidal at Algonquin with Claud Cockburn, John Dexter.

October 6: Went to Irwin Shaw's "In the French Manner," produced, written, etc., by him. Now believe the Fat Life has permanently disabled him creatively. He moved to Europe to keep from paying taxes but instead he has been paying out his blood and brains and getting Nothing pumped back in but labels—wines, names, references, dishes, cheeses. He knows no more of Europe than on a guided cruise ship; he knows the names, the faces; he could have stayed on a Bucks County farm and read *Vogue* and the *Bazaar* for that. As for technique—it is smooth and old and superficial, the content is like the contents of his elaborately labeled expensive luggage, a good haberdasher's standard equipment, extremely light and lacy.

The story is the same—American girl in Paris or Rome, with money from home for dilettante study of art or music, usual run of lovers, dolce vita, parties with Happenings. Runs out of lovers, money, finds truth in Solid Husband Back Home. These lovers are all playboys, not real, etc.— she has been *Robbed!* Big scene—you're all shallow, I must have depth. Now what is this American paper doll going to do with depth? She can wear it, she thinks, like you wear love or art, changing with the style. The author never seems to see that she is the Robber, an absolutely empty thing that needs refilling constantly.

---

* Jacqueline Miller had married the painter Daniel Rice.

October 28: Cocktails at Algonquin with Elaine Dundy. Charles Addams, Jim Garrity (*New Yorker*). Met Upton Sinclair.

October 31: Another Halloween—which has been curious always, moving usually. This one marks change in morale—suddenly feel like my writing self again.

I feel novels should be more functional than before, *viz.*—this new one, briefly guidebook, map, etc.

1964

January 4: Went up to get Jojo (out for first time but improved by getting out of house). Jojo in violent due to impatience but Mr. Moon allowed me to take him home. Restful for both of us—he doped up and sleepy, me weak. Quiet dinner and Scrabble. Early bed and good sleep.

January 9: Staggered out in rain and wind up to Dr. Solley's but felt better at having him check me even though I think he was sicker than I was. He sent me for chest X-ray—further rain but this seemed to be better for me than staying in this poisoned-air apartment.

January 10: Had to cash check for Jackie—bitter, savage wind—but, as yesterday, I stood it better than the dull steady poisoning of the apartment mildew. Bryan in town again.

January 11: Feeble again. Amazing. Solley said keep on with iron and antibiotics.

January 12: Determined to make it up to Motherwell's (174 E. 94th) for dinner for Bryan and finally did, wondering how, and again felt better for it. Delightful, lovable man, Henry Geldzahler of Met, there—also witty A. Liberman of *Vogue* and wife (head of hats at Saks'), Mark Rothko. Constant reminder that I must do a thousand things for mere daily living whereas here in a rich, servanted house nothing is demanded of me so myself can once again rise (only to be clobbered later by home).

Motherwell, once a blonde, poetic lad, now very successful artist (but railroaded nicely by papa being head of Wells Fargo) and he is about to get a big new Guggenheim prize—$10,000. Wife, Helen Frankenthaler —lean, Bennington young woman painter of thin talent (afraid to be bad; thinners worse than bold eager badness). I had told Bryan how much I like Rauschenberg—how he made light come from no place. Geldzahler said this was sheer Delacroix, *viz.*—color magic. Motherwell is near being an oaf. Helen opened old bottle of Mandarin.

February 6: Weight 164.

Came to St. Luke's Hospital. Anemia. In ward Stuyvesant 4 (4 beds) to wait private room. Fine food, good bed, etc., but my two bed mates had this layabout family hanging around gabbing and smoking from 11 A.M. to 10 P.M.—some drunk, all stupid and completely nosy blacks, peeking through my curtains and making naps and bathroom impossible as well as smelling up the place with smoke.

Charming, witty French doctor made special tests, gave me Venus Pressure test—a dehydration job to take off the stored liquids of this anemia. Seems fatigue and heart burden due to this store. As soon as test was done weight started down from 164 to 151. On 1200 calories a day diet also, very filling as well chosen—no salt and sugar but hot cereal and juice, toast, egg, coffee and milk at 8; chop, steamed potato, asparagus, salad with fake dressing and dietetic fruit noon; ditto at 5:30. Piece of bread also and fruit juice in-between or saltines. These meals are more than usual but the premature hour gives no chance for snacks or appetizers. If I can manage it will make pot of unsalted stew—lamb, potatoes, carrots, cucumbers, lettuce, tomato, onion.

February 15: Weight 151.

February 17: Left St. Luke's.

March 13: Writing novels—curiosity and the game of putting the puzzle together by studying clues and other evidence from other people—also from a sense of duty to fill in blanks in history, as some explorers feel a dedication to report on unknown places. I feel some completely accepted patterns of life are never reported—a fictionalized way of life is used for fiction as a special English (not what we use either in speech or daily life)

for writing. Also the Brief—when I feel completely against certain people, places and ways of life, my legal sense works on a defense and explanation of them—not for the world, but to convince myself. Sometimes
my defense is so good it sounds like a sentimental glorification, like a
criminal lawyer's plea for his murderer. Since you are the clever enemy
prosecutor, you see every flaw clearly and therefore know how to defend
it better than a loyal friend could.

March 24: In novel especially—lately used so much for a wastebasket or
sewer of a self-centered mind, with no sense of duty or the pleasure of
opening new paths to less privileged.

March 31: Finally got three pages almost on *Saturday Evening Post* story
by combining it with Latouche memoir. Now must do over "That Was
Broadway."

April 1: Up at 6:30 for work before maid comes. Usual straining and
schizo struggle, nausea and despair at all old stories written so many
times over 30 or even 40 years for changing editors and tastes all to no
avail but doggedly kept. Noted that the stories always had a basic original
and realistic point of departure and obviously this was what put the sale
off but which made me keep on with them—like saving the good soup
bone. Curiously enough I was as provident in my way as a Yankee miser
—saving ideas and passing bits of string (thoughts) for a sterile old age,
counting always on an attic country home where I would hatch out these
frozen eggs as I seem to be doing.

April 13: Started "Widow" story.*

April 14: Carol Brandt called to say Doubleday wanted decision. Said I
could have any publisher in New York. I personally would rather have
Pantheon—prestige and small—but Doubleday is bigger and richer
maybe.

May 24: Took 8:40 train to Ashtabula. $26 in regular coach—endless and
wearing and hot. To Mrs. Dean (Helen) Matthew, historic manse at 309

---
*Yet another version of "The Brooklyn Widow."

Mentor Avenue. Charming woman looking like Auntie May. Canopy bedroom, old photos, etc.

May 26: Speech at College Hall [Lake Erie College] and tea. Harold Fink, head of Fine Arts, played "Pavane for a Dead Princess" while I tried to figure what to say. Finally told seniors not to use minds in making decisions (save them for making excuses). Experience had told me women can't get down to their real work till the man thing is settled—not for material urge or status, just possession. Own a man, but learn a trade on the side. Beware of waiting—leap before you look. You learn by leaping; if you look first you never leap. Don't wait till wisdom sets in—wisdom is ruin. Someday these happy happy days will seem pretty miserable to you. Girls cheered and were delighted. Said later it was just what they wanted to hear and what they'd been saying.

May 27: Called Dawnie.* They came and drove me for dinner then to their place in Mentor. Believe Dawnie is nearest approach to vague natural artist.

June 17: Sudden rays of novel! Tried to fix up "Summer Rose," then read Renee one to Coby who was enthusiastic. Decided it was richer and juicier. Immediately had food appetite. How wonderful if I caught back to my life!

June 23: Continuing sleepiness—unable to pull mind up for Friday conference with Viking (Aaron Asher). Decided too restricted life. Went to "Home Movies" at Provincetown Playhouse because of Orson Bean and this was a shock treatment. A first performance of a Lawrence Ferlinghetti one-acter—"The Customs Officer With the Baggy Pants"—of unparalleled obscenity, lascivity and sheer boredom of a painful, dirty kind (even to orgasms, etc.)

July 3: New York *Herald Tribune* had interview.

July 7: 138 pounds. Decided to defer short pieces as not held together by major one.

---

*Dawn Jarvis, Mabel Powell Pocock's daughter, of whom Powell was particularly fond.

July 18: Dinner at Dardenelles with Robert Payne and Patricia Ellsworth —later to O'Henry's. Lunch with Jojo at China House—87th Street and Broadway. Cocktails at Longchamps with Dan and Jackie.

August 6: Lunch at Longchamps with [Morris] Philipson of Random House, who gave me his novel to read, then said why not come to Random House? I said okay. Meantime Ken McCormack called (Doubleday) for tea and Carol said to play it safe. Told her my terms.

August 12: Returned from Bunny's. Random House deal set $1000 on signing contract, $1000 more on first section, $1000 on completion, $1000 on publication! How grateful I am to Aaron Asher for not pushing my case at Viking.

August 24: Word that my blood count was down to 4.9—must go to hospital fast for transfusions, also intestinal something. Choice of St. Luke's or St. Vincent's Hospital. Knew I couldn't stand another hospital session.

August 25: Went to Dr. Solley's substitute, Dr. Ben Kightlinger, 943 Park Avenue, for confirmation and assurance after ferociously painful stomach all night in ferment as it has been for weeks. Found intestinal lump and recommended instant hospitalization but understood my problem of cottage and Jojo so said if I thought I could do it, go ahead—a week wouldn't matter.

August 26: Bad night decided me to cancel everything and get right to St. Luke's. Called him. He was insistent on ward as saving money—"writer" and "Christopher Street" must have alarmed him as to my finances. Had to go up to be interviewed as for welfare at 7, so Monroe came along. Very troublesome—receiving examination and waiting to see admission— finally said why not private room and he said "Where you going to get that kind of money?" In anybody else this would have been insulting but he is pure country boy and sympathetic—wanted to help. Finally agreed to my plea that I might be able to work in privacy—so got nice little room for same price as ward.

August 28: X-rays and barium of kidneys and elsewhere—very bad.

Almost gave up—continued with ice packs. In general however much, much better—no stomach ferment. Sleeping constantly.

August 29: Dr. Kightlinger came in with bad news—lump growing in ascending colon. Must come out. Scared. However we agreed to wait for Dr. Solley's return to choose surgeon, etc. Meantime I go home this noon—with some dread of the week's explanation to people and preparation of papers, etc.

September 19: Felt well due to pills from Solley. Got Jojo. Fine.

September 27: Slow stirring of creation—which usually has the wet logs of old, forgotten, trivial episodes as a kindling. These have been all too damn wet till lately.

October 19: Went with Monroe Stearns to Pierre to PEN. Leo Rosten, the Chutes, Alec Waugh, Jack Leggett.

October 21: A Paul Schreiber phoned about movie rights to *Golden Spur.*

October 22: Gerald Murphy's funeral at East Hampton. Perfect small Murphy party as Gerald himself might have arranged it.

October 28: Finally resorted to Ritalin and tried fixing up Marcia dress story.

October 29: Took dex and recovered first Marcia chapter. Hope it's as lucid as it should be—certainly seemed remarkably good per se.

November 4: Will:
>All rights to *Wicked Pavilion* to Isobel.
>*Locusts*—
>All rights to *Cage for Lovers* to Rosalind Wilson.
>Rights to *Golden Spur* equally divided between Jack Sherman and Harry Gousha, Jr.
>All Ohio novel rights to Phyllis in trust for her daughters.
>All rights to short stories [entry breaks off]

November 5: Went to opening of Calder at Guggenheim and amazed at grandeur and beauty of whole show. Surprised to concede this is probably greatest artistic genius of the century, comparable to Leonardo.

1 9 6 5

January 7: 130 pounds.

Dr. Solley found my anemia okay—12 instead of 4 or 6 so I stop nasty iron pills and hope for relief from stomach fizzing which may cheer my long suicidal blah blah paralysis of mind and body. Went to 79th Longchamps alone—very lousy. Have new passion—beer! Big relief to find 1964 diary in bookshelf—felt as if no use in anything if past is lost.

January 10: Found writing boards in hall—always a stimulation if anything could stimulate. Must begin morning work on novel this week or else face necessity for going to Yaddo or someplace if home proves increasingly impossible. Evidently I am unable to work except under insurmountable difficulties.

January 13: Went to see lawyer about lease case. Don't really rely on him for other things as he is so unsophisticated and agog over cultural matters. Said 43 Fifth Avenue would settle for $500* but I hesitated to give them anything so left it at that but must get general lawyer who understands royalties, etc.

Taxi driver on way down discoursed on his admiration for Thomas Wolfe, Eugene O'Neill—also liked *Candy,* etc., and felt drug addicts were cruelly treated. Very intelligent, as many drivers are.

Taking pyrroxia but having bellyaches anyway—it helps, however. Wish to God I could get in novel. Maybe "Summer Rose" is answer or else transferring Ren to third person will give more freedom.

---

*Powell had moved from 43 Fifth Avenue to 95 Christopher Street, while owing back rent.

January 23: Esquire asked me to do article on Staten Island—$750, with $250 guarantee.

February 14: Sad anniversary of Joe's death. Typical of that loving golden Leo lad to die on Valentine's Day.

February 18: Have done nine pages on play which at least I enjoy doing. Cannot really endure this paralysis of writing. Ideas continue but stagnant physically. No idea what will goad me.

February 21: Off to Staten Island with Jojo and Hannah.

February 27: One of the curious things about a change for the better in fortunes is the way you suddenly realize how poor you were before. There are too many other problems in being poor for you to be conscious of your underprivilegement at the time. Do the new poor realize suddenly how rich they once were?

February 28: Bobby came up and took Jojo to lunch at Howard Johnson, then Jackie drove them both up to Ward's while I did a fresh page on *Esquire* article. I think what unburdened me was Bobby and Jackie each relieving me of sole sense of responsibility which is hard to spring out from. Anniversary of Joe's and my first lunch, so I bought red roses for luck, which they brought me.

March 1: Finished article. Seven pages through two Ritalins and mailed Special Delivery. Greatest achievement in a year and cheered me. Piece pleasant and plausible. If they don't take it, probably someplace else will and will pay more.

March 2: God, what a relief to have finished some brain work. Very hard with constant diarrhea and no interest in nourishment.

March 11: Started tincture of opium for diarrhea. Works fine. Felt better after one dose than in months.

March 14: Jojo and I clashed. He was in a Gousha sarcastic dig mood, which is more mature, as he is getting to be.

March 15: Getting excited and clarified on novel. Would like to rush it—also do the lovely play and the "Summer Rose" one and the cat one. Think fix-up of back room would do it, or help anyway. Considering Yaddo for two weeks.

March 22: PEN party for Norman Mailer. I stay excited over novel but getting nowhere. Random House wants set date.

March 24: Stopped opium as sleeping too much and no good effects otherwise. Slept all day and night—dreamed of swimming which is always good.

March 25: Water dream produced bond check this A.M. for $5003.54 plus *Esquire* check for $675. Brandts' have reversion of rights from Houghton Mifflin on *Sunday, Monday and Always.*

March 27: To buffet at 277 West End Avenue. Nostalgia for old West End and Riverside Drive. Home at 1:30.

March 28: Felt as if had stroke—eyes not focusing, thick head. Went to "How To Murder Your Wife." Bobby went to see Jojo—great event and kind of him.

April 4: Interview with *Villager.*

April 8: Dinner with Monroe and underground movies at City Hall Cinema on Nassau Street. Kenneth Anger's "Scorpio Rising," "Fireworks," etc.—no imagination.

April 12: Newberry Collection opening at Museum of Modern Art with Irving Drutman. Fine dinner at Italian Pavilion.

April 15: Sleeping and doing nothing mostly—some nightmares about Joe and Jojo running away. Read Brooke Astor's charming novel *The Bluebird Is At Home.* No more strength to do anything. Jackie's to do Income Tax with John Larson.*

---

*Larson, a C.P.A. and friend of Jacqueline Rice, would write Powell's will.

April 16: Bought lovely red dress. I dabble in this funny play now that I told Philipson wouldn't have book ready.

May 9: Took Jojo back after restful weekend and stopped to see beautiful baby of Jackie's named Dawn Hilary so far. Most exquisite little yellow rose of a child, elegant features—wild Irish rose.
    Published review of Fred Allen letters in *Tribune*.

May 10: Feeling better for first time. Switched back to opium drops from Lomotil. What heaven to feel almost an appetite and almost *thinking*. Is it possible I can write again?

May 11: Wrote Carlos Baker re: Hemingway. Still improved stomach-wise.

May 13: I am really going to go straight into Church out of astonishment and gratitude for four days of ordinary appetite and no stomach. I had almost given up hope of ever feeling *alive* again and I cannot quite understand the miracle. Reduced and dried to 122 pounds and dulled mentally then tried Lomotil again—two pills, four times a day before meals, Compazine afterwards, Comsat at night. Very little change so switched back to opium—seven drops, three times a day (no Lomotil or Compazine but nightly Comsat) and this worked the miracle in part or else a new social interest in guests, new people, reading, etc. (Maybe Jackie's new baby brought change for everybody!)
    Philipson says I should do Hemingway memoir for a magazine but I feel presumptuous. This need not be really for I'm sure he would rather I write what little I know of him than his relatives. Could be based on Esther in a sentimental way who introduced so many things in my life.
    What I want to do is the old "That Was Broadway" piece—describing energetic farm women like Grandma, who got her excitements on remote farms from traveling, hucksters, cousins or distant relatives who wandered up the cow lane to stay and help hay or thrush. Grandma always welcomed these tiny little Jewish or Polish travelers and fed them and kept them overnight. "They won't be back next year—carrying those big trunks with that cough will kill them." Minnie was lady Armenian lace seller. Grandma never thought that maybe they had been snapped up by well-fixed widow farmer or else stayed in Akron or whatever city they collected their samples in. I remember the velvet painted cushions, the

leather-fringed Indian pillows for the Cozy Corner, the tatted table run-
ners, embroidery patterns for the home women to copy. So, after children
grew, farm ladies moved to town, let out rooms for $1 a week, raised the
loose children and orphans in the family, kept traveling men, actors, etc.,
who told stories of far places.

May 14: Pete and Madeleine and I at Longchamps then at his home for
dinner. Bleeding but painless.

May 15: Big day! Got on right (I hope) novel track for a page and this
must be it and how wonderful that would be to get up and write of
Madison Square Hotel and Aunt Osie and Tucker's Green.

May 18: Have been doing a page or page and a half a day and reverting,
or at least recalling, my original plan which was to have a small cast of
Players who deal completely in play talk—never touching reality, but
when reality touches them they curl up and crumble. No laughter equals
no life. In this work I see that I may find my own oxygen again which was
the Comic Breath—on stage always, for Death waits in the wings.

There are very few gay souls in life—few if any contemporaries. The
young are heavy and full of Causes.

May 19: To American Academy. Lewis Mumford gave jolt to occasion
and I realized I had gotten as chicken as the rest of America because what
he said—we had no more right in Vietnam than Russia had in Cuba—
was true but I did not think he should use his position to declaim this.
Later I saw the only way to accomplish anything is by "abusing" your
power.

May 24: Lunch with Philipson at Ambassador. He is very sympathetic,
brilliant young man but paranoic—finds insults and wounds so often that
I am alarmed for him. It might be the sheer exhaustion of being a writer
plus an editor. Saw the Rices later—Hilary Dawn charming.

Carlos Baker wrote for letter of Hemingway's but it is too scandalous for
public. Philipson insists I should offer my own memoirs to *Playboy* instead. Baker writes Hemingway's letter refers to Sara, Granny Rice and
me as his best friends. I feel like writing something about him as so many

detractors are around. There was the unappreciated fact that he spread excitement and glamour wherever he appeared. Dylan Thomas did, too, and Dreiser's Thursdays were glamorous and invitations sought after.

May 27: Went to see debut of Hilary Dawn. They came here and we drank on terrace.

June 3: Incredible fatigue again. Hoping zabaglione and vitamins will get me into novel or some work.

June 7: Page 19. Got into hotel. I always feel better once I get into these hotels—just as I used to feel from childhood on. Jojo loves hotels too.

Stay in this dreadful bowel state which Solley seems unable to check. I am afraid it is same as Joe's and Margaret's ailment but maybe tomorrow will cure me.

June 11: Saw the wonderful Dr. Solley who had an inspiration for my cure—treat it like dysentery or diarrhea, common type. A laxative but not a strong one (I would have erred here on my own) as the obstacle in the colon is obstructing food, preventing normal bowel movements, preventing appetite so no energy. I took wine glass of citrate of magnesia Friday afternoon—no effect; more on Saturday A.M. Lunch with Honey —ate only two Tom Collins and two iced teas—still no effect but dizziness and faintness. Threw up in afternoon—weak and hungry and ate beef sandwich for dinner. No drinks. Double opium drops to 10 three or four times before meals. Woke up Sunday, after everything worked, a new person. Brain going even.

Esquire had phoned enthusiasm over S.I. piece*—October issue. Art layout wonderful—six pages. Wants new contemporary piece. Raymond Walter at *Times* also wants piece. Decided to do piece on editors for *Times* but will ask first if *Esquire* wants it, which would make it more of a jaunty job—expense accounts, power over talent to take place of talent, new editors think it's grading papers. Actually the gift is to make the writer aware of his own power. Get a talented writer and boss him— some writers like this but no real artist does. We had conferences once a week and never mentioned work. Editor told anecdotes about great

---

* "Staten Island, I Love You," the last piece published during Powell's lifetime.

writers he had had; when we parted I could hardly wait to get back at novel because his confidences had made me feel I was the equal of these great ones and I belonged with them. Sometimes an editor had the gift but was being pressured by the sales or advertising department.

Once I was told by an editor that I had to have more consummated sex in my work—readers wanted it. I never felt novelists' function was to service the reader's ego, that the hero with whom he "identified" had to be younger, the girl more willing, the lovemaking more explicit. This push-button sex doesn't work except for undersexed readers. The old *Smart Set* and a number of magazines before the '30s went in for asterisks and this blank check on sex seemed to me sexier than a heavy garlicky breath in my ear (supposedly an erotic zone). Most exciting thing is the longing—a caveman pounce often paralyzes the responses in a female. Explicit sex can freeze—just because the author is ticklish at the nape of his neck doesn't mean every reader will throw an orgasm at the mere mention of nape.

June 22: Most important thing for novelist is curiosity and how curious that so many of them lack it. They seem self-absorbed, family-absorbed, success-absorbed, but the new social-climbing writer professes indifference to the couple across the aisle, the noise from the next apartment—as if a gentleman does not concern himself with things not his business.

I contend that a writer's business is minding other people's business. It is his oxygen and all the vices of the village gossip are the virtues of the writer. A strange car is in the driveway of Neighbor Jones; the Jones' children are home so must have been excused from school for some big reason; Mrs. Purdy, Mrs. Jones' sister, has put her house up for sale; a Western Union messenger went to the Jones' house at 3 P.M.; the Hi-Fi was on full tilt last night there with Gilbert and Sullivan operas (not likely if there was death); a trunk was delivered from the department store; a case of beer delivered from the grocers; Mr. Jones phoned Phil Bailey that he couldn't make the poker club this week. Well, something's going on, says the gossip. What is it? says the writer and both snoop for the story.

The new writers disdain human curiosity; they wish only to explore and describe their own psyches; they are too egotistical and snobbish to interest themselves in neighbors. The urge to write now is no longer the love of story-telling or even the love of applause for a neat turn or dramatic twist. It is the urge to show off, the author as hero is a big sex success and leaves them gasping. The book's drive is only the desire to strip the writer's remembered woes and wrongs and show his superiority to the reader—not to communicate with him or to entertain.

June 24: Last night decided to do "Summer Rose" story and feel really excited today at prospect. How wonderful if I had excitement of contemporary work to wake me up—how fantastic if I could whiz through in joy and fun.

June 28: Improved in general after citrate weekend. How wonderful if I could climb into "Summer Rose" and ride away on gay wheels everyday. Say five pages a day. Also must do the *Times* piece on editors. Maybe in pen can manage this.

July 3: Taxi strike. Took subway to get Jojo. To New Yorker theater to see "My Little Chickadee" and "Room Service." Jojo very delighted, then subway down. I am no longer short-winded and don't mind subways.

Somewhat better on four doses of ten drops opium but bad time later —sore stomach. Losing weight again—down to 115 pounds. Started on Jackie's yeast in lemonade and find it helpful amazingly. Startling how Joe, Margaret and I all end up in same digestive jam. How alone we all are—even Joe with me on hand. God—how wonderful if I could get energy back and control of digestion.

July 6: Feeling better due perhaps to no drink. Will try that for a while if this rise in energy is true. Hope to do *Times* essay, then short story, "Aunt Hannah from Pike's Peak."

July 11: Still in same state of bowels and taking about 30–40 drops of opium per day. Wonder if there is any hope at all for bowel or brain. Had Lloyd and Loren in for dinner Friday and Lloyd's neck is like my problem—nothing does any good.

Loren told lovely stories of visiting Cummings at his farm—of feeding the hummingbirds, filling the little glass vases on the pine trees, and of Cummings as a real farmer, born and bred. I must report this as an

Esquire job possibility for Lloyd. How heavenly if I could get to work my-self—either the *Times* job or the novel.

July 13: Had a feeling for novel Tuesday, after calling off the Ipswich trip with Jojo because of my stomach and sudden awareness of trying to carry luggage and find airport entrances alone, let alone with Jojo. Arrival just beginning of getting meals constantly. Realized I'm in no shape for this.

Decided to go back to Renee novel, as I checked on it and realized I want to *read* it and this is important—an incentive to see what happens as it will flow from my head, I trust.

July 17: Saw Solley on Thursday to see if any hope but he only switched me to pills instead of drops and Fleet's Phosphate instead of citrate and things were much worse if anything. Vitasorbin again but it is an encour-ager of diarrhea, it says on bottle, which God knows is all I need. Worse weakness and no appetite but I realize I must try to handle this myself, weak as I am.

July 18: Speculated that possibly Pernod was an irritant to bowels as I have had it all week and everything worse so decided to switch back to whiskey and milk as tipple as I seem to be averse to nourishment. In-testines seem irritated lately. Must try to Coué myself out of this as I am in same spot as Margaret and Joe—drying up, weak, no appetite. Will take liquid opium plus pills I guess. God how wonderful if I could get some writing done—if, for instance, I could knock off the cat book just for fun.

July 23: Lost more—down to 112 pounds and weaker with rusty stomach. Stopped the diarrhea Tuesday, thank God, but still no appetite or strength. Must try to get out of house. Did so on Wednesday and met new editor, Joe Fox at Random, a completely simpatico and secure person which is a good thing and I felt better at once. Hope to make best of this. Jojo com-ing home next week and we will tour New York and experiment with him going to barber alone, etc.

July 24: Picked up Jojo for a week's vacation at home. Bobby offered to come along so we went up and later went to Aldo's Sidewalk Cafe for a good dinner which I also ate.

July 27: Went up to Times Square to buy tickets for "My Fair Lady" at Criterion and then thought to pass the time till dinner by going to "What's New Pussycat?" at the Astor but it was so pointless and dull that we couldn't stick it out more than 20 minutes and went over to dear old Blue Ribbon for delicious supper of knockwurst, boiled potato and sauerkraut, then home to bed.

July 28: Go to drugstore almost every day for breakfast or lunch. Went up to movie of "My Fair Lady" which was really great and Jojo loved it. Also, he went out during show to men's room downstairs and found his way back to our seat all by himself—a tremendous feat. Then we went to Blue Ribbon again and had the same table and the same menu and he thought of old times there with his daddy. It was all very New York-y and choked me up more than anything as my buddies are all in a sodden rut and I have fallen into it, so I might as well be in Podunk. Am improving amazingly in energy and hope to beat the dysentery.

July 29: World's Fair at 5 P.M. with Bobby. Most exhausting but worth it to get it off Jojo's mind. Went to Pepsi-Cola show and to Schaffer's beer garden for dried sandwiches. Then a tractor ride around the Fair with fountains—getting lost mostly and finding no glamour as people wander around in sloppy clothes and sour faces as if they were already stung and gloomy. Subway home at 10, dead tired.

July 30: Jojo and I both done up from Fair but managed to take short bus ride and Coby came in for beer while Jojo had beans and franks, his favorite dish. I feel better all the time except for bowels but more energy from vitamin pills and Jojo getting me up and out in the world instead of me squatting here staring into space watching my dull friends drink and pass out with nothing new to tell or report. Jojo very sensible and takes charge of decisions in a very sensible way. "Instead of your going out alone to get bread and stuff and coming back to fix something, let's both go over to the drugstore and eat to save us the trouble."

July 31: Jojo wanted to go back yesterday—anxious for laundry and golf and church—but managed to wait till today so we got taxi back after drugstore lunch and then I got some dresses at Lane's and came home, expecting to fall asleep but found a week of Jojo had revived me so that I wasn't even tired. Have decided to go to Cape Cod to Jackie's on Monday. Hope the all-night woopy life won't be too much.

September 7: Came to St. Luke's—room 1529.

September 28: Bunny came in.

September 30: St. Luke's. Normal day fairly. Perhaps combo of opium and Colaco at night periods will organize this. Weight 105 again, though eating more. Will . . .

["Will" is the last word in Dawn Powell's diaries. She died in St. Luke's Hospital on November 14, 1965.]

BIOGRAPHICAL NOTES

Aaron, Daniel (1912–): critic and historian, probably best known for his book, *Writers on the Left;* a close friend to Edmund Wilson.

Abbott, George (1887–1994): author, actor, producer, director, and legendary "grand old man" of the American theater, he was still active after his 100th birthday; worked with Powell and Leonora Corbett on "Every Other Day" in the early 1940s.

Adams, Lee (1924–): American song lyricist, worked with Powell on a musical version of *The Golden Spur.*

Addams, Charles (1912–1988): American cartoonist and illustrator, celebrated for his visions of the macabre, and long associated with *The New Yorker.*

Adler, Stella (1901–1992): American actress, director, and drama teacher, associated with the Group Theatre and later with her own Stella Adler Conservatory of Acting; appeared as the lead in the Broadway production of Powell's "Big Night."

Aiken, Conrad (1889–1973): American writer, known for his poetry, his novel *Blue Voyage,* and his unusual and abstract autobiography, *Ushant: An Essay.*

Alfau, Felipe (1902–): Spanish-American author whose all-but-forgotten fantastical novel *Locos* (1936) was reprinted to acclaim in the late 1980s.

Ames, Elizabeth (1884–1977): the first executive director of the Yaddo artists' colony in Saratoga Springs, New York, where Powell spent parts of 1955 and 1960.

Anderson, Maxwell (1888–1959): American playwright and screen-writer whose plays presented historical events in a manner that reflected contemporary issues.

Andrews, Esther (c. 1890–1962): American editor, a close friend of Powell's from the early 1920s, spent much of her later life in Key West, Florida with her lover Canby Chambers.

Anger, Kenneth (1932–): experimental filmmaker and author of two volumes of *Hollywood Babylon,* engaging but inaccurate retellings of Southern California scandals.

Antheil, George (1900–1959): American composer, celebrated for his "Ballet Mechanique" and other modernist works. He entitled his autobiography *Bad Boy of Music.*

Anthony, Katherine Susan (1877–1965): American biographer and niece of Susan B. Anthony, sublet her apartment at 23 Bank Street to Powell and her husband in the summer of 1959.

Astor, Brooke (c.1910–   ): American philanthropist and novelist.

Bacon, Peggy (1895–1987): American poet, author, artist, and illustrator; drew several portraits of Powell and maintained a difficult friendship with her over many years.

Baker, Carlos (1909–1987): American author, educator, and biographer, interviewed Powell in 1965 for *Ernest Hemingway: A Life Story*.

Banning, Margaret Culkin (1891–1982): American novelist of the Midwest.

Barere, Simon (1896–1951): Russian-American pianist, remembered for his dazzling technique and his spectacular death in mid-concert at Carnegie Hall.

Barnes, Djuna (1892–1982): innovative American novelist, author of *Nightwood* and *Ryder,* lived in Greenwich Village for much of her life and was a long-time acquaintance of Powell's.

Barry, Griffin: Washington legal counsel with ties to the New York writing world.

Barton, Bruce (1886–1967): advertising executive and author; wrote the bestseller *The Man Nobody Knows.*

Basshe, Em Jo (1900–1939): Russian-American dramatist of radical views; one of the five founders of the New Playwrights Theater and author of "Earth," its first production.

Baxter, Anne (1923–1985): American actress of stage and screen.

Beaton, Cecil (1904–1980): English photographer, memoirist, and social figure.

Beebe, Lucius (1902–1966): American journalist, author, and professional dandy, associated with the New York *Herald Tribune* and later with the San Francisco *Chronicle.*

Behrman, S. N. (1893–1973): essayist, playwright, and biographer of Max Beerbohm and Joseph Duveen.

Bein, Albert (b. 1902): Romanian-American playwright, scenarist, and producer.

Bercovici, Konrad (1882–1961): prolific Romanian-American novelist, playwright, and essayist, wrote a lively and neglected study of Manhattan in the 1920s, *Around The World In New York.*

Bergner, Elizabeth (1900–1986): international star of the stage and screen, better known in Europe than in the United States.

Berlin, Isaiah (1909–   ): British political philosopher and essayist, Oxford don, known to Powell through Edmund Wilson.

Bernstein, Aline (1881–1955): wealthy, talented stage-designer and novelist who was for eight years the lover of Thomas Wolfe.

Bernstein, Leonard (1918–1990): American conductor, pianist, composer, and educator.

Billings, Henry (1901–1987): American artist and architect, a long-standing friend to Powell.

Bloch, Bertram: American playwright and a long-time friend of Powell's.

Blume, Peter (1906–1992): distinguished Russian-American painter, greatly admired by Powell and a faithful friend and correspondent for many years.

Bodenheim, Maxwell (1893–1954): American poet and novelist who came to seem a virtual embodiment of Greenwich Village. In later life, he was reduced to selling his poems in bars and on street corners.

Bogan, Louise (1897–1970): American poet, essayist, and poetry critic for *The New Yorker*. Powell cared little for her work or her person.

Boni, Charles (1894–1969): American publisher who helped found Boni and Liveright, an influential publishing house; Modern Library, their most lasting success, was later sold to Random House.

Bowen, Elizabeth (1899–1973): Anglo-Irish novelist whose *The Heat of the Day* (1949) has been widely admired and remains in print after almost 50 years.

Boyd, Ernest (1887–1946): Irish-American critic and raconteur.

Boyle, Kay (1903–1992): American poet, novelist, short story writer, and essayist.

Brandt, Carl (1888–1957): American literary agent; with wife Carol represented Powell for much of her life. Their firm, Brandt and Brandt, continues to this day.

Brandt, Carol (1904–1984): Powell's literary agent from the early 1930s, known as Carol Hill before her marriage to Carl Brandt.

Breit, Harvey (1913–1988): American writer and reviewer; long a book reporter for the *New York Times*.

Brennan, Maeve (1917–1993): Irish-born short story writer whose work regularly appeared in *The New Yorker*.

Bromberg, J. "Joe" Edward (1904–1951): American actor of stage and screen, associated with the Provincetown Players and the Group Theatre early in his career; appeared in original production of Powell's "Big Night."

Bromfield, Louis (1896–1956): popular American novelist from Mansfield, Ohio; briefly an elementary school classmate of Powell's.

Brook, Alexander (1898–1980): American artist known for his firm committment to realist and representational painting during an era of experimentalism; married for a time to Peggy Bacon.

Brooks, Paul (1909–   ): American editor and author, for 25 years editor-in-chief at Houghton Mifflin.

Brooks, Van Wyck (1886–1963): American literary critic and historian whose later books became popular bestsellers but whose legacy is to be found in his iconoclastic early works such as *America's Coming of Age* (1915). Married to Gladys Brooks.

Brophy, John (1899–1965): English novelist and journalist.

Broun, Heywood (1888–1939): American writer, best remembered for his journalism, his liberal views, and his enormous charm.

Brush, Katherine (1902–1952): highly successful American novelist, essayist, and short story writer; a long-time friend to Powell, who esteemed her wit and facility.

Burke, Cornelius G. (1900–1971): American poet and record critic, a friend of Powell's from the 1920s, later an editor of *High Fidelity* magazine.

Burnett, Whit (1899–1973): the founder and editor of *Story* magazine, who helped promote such writers as Truman Capote, J. D. Salinger, Joseph Heller, and William Saroyan.

Butler, Nicholas Murray (1862–1947): legendary long-time president of Columbia University.

Byington, Spring (1893–1971): American actress who appeared in many plays and films but attained her greatest celebrity with the television show "December Bride" in the 1950s. Starred in Powell's "Jig-Saw," produced by the Theatre Guild.

Cabell, James Branch (1879–1958): American novelist, extravagantly praised in the 1920s, now virtually unread. *Jurgen* (1919), considered highly shocking when it was published, became a bestseller.

Caldwell, Taylor (1900–1985): prolific and popular American novelist.

Cantwell, Robert (1908–1978): American author and editor, best remembered for his "proletarian novel," *The Land Of Plenty*.

Carlisle, Helen Grace (1897–1968): American novelist whose many works include *See How They Run, We Begin,* and *Merry, Merry Maidens.*

Carmer, Carl Lamson (1893–1976): novelist, editor, and anthologist who specialized in stories of his native upstate New York.

Carneal, Georgette: American novelist; published *The Frog Pond,* a first-person study of psychological disturbance, under the pseudonym Joyce MacIver in 1961.

Casson, Lionel: writer, lecturer, and professor of classical literature.

Cerf, Bennett (1898–1971): publisher, co-founder of Random House; later a celebrated raconteur, humorist, and radio and television personality.

Chambers, Canby (c. 1895–1958): an early friend of Powell's and the long-time companion of Esther Andrews; stricken with polio in the mid-1920s, after which the couple lived in Key West.

Chapman, Katherine (b. 1896): a friend of Powell's from her first days in New York when the two were working for the Naval Reserve at the end of World War I; later Katherine Busch, director of K. V. Busch Realty in Biloxi, Mississippi.

Cheyney, E. Ralph (1897–1941): American poet and lecturer, edited the *Independent Poetry Review 1925* which published Powell and her friends Charles Norman, Cornelia Wolfe, and Genevieve Taggard, among many others.

Chou, Wen-Chung (1923–   ): Chinese-American composer who became friends with Powell during her stay at Yaddo in 1960.

Claire, Ina (1895–1985): American actress best known for her performances in sophisticated comedies.

Clark, Barrett (1890–1953): American editor and drama critic. A lecture he presented at Lake Erie College during Powell's undergraduate years made a lasting impression on her; he later helped persuade the Group Theatre to stage "Big Night."

Clurman, Harold (1901–1980): path-breaking American director and producer who, with Cheryl Crawford and Lee Strasberg, founded the Group Theatre; also an author and critic and the editor of numerous drama anthologies.

Cockburn, Claud (1904–1981): leading left-wing English journalist and editor.

Cohen, Lester (1902–1963): bestselling novelist and screen-writer, known to Powell mainly through his early association with John Dos Passos.

Colby, Natalie Sedgwick (1875–1942): American novelist of manners.

Cole, William (1919–   ): prolific American poet, editor, and anthologist.

Connelly, Marc (1890–1980): American playwright, affiliated with the Algonquin Round Table and best remembered for "The Green Pastures."

Connolly, Walter (1887–1940): American character actor of stage and screen.

Cook, Phyllis Powell (1899–1985): Powell's younger sister, later wife of Morgan Cook, an architect and builder in Canton, Ohio, and the mother of Carol Warstler, Phyllis Poccia, and Alice Mollet. Phyllis was the dedicatee of *Dance Night* and the model for the adored baby "Florrie" in *My Home Is Far Away*.

Corbett, Leonora (1907–1960): English actress best known for her role as the ghost in Noël Coward's "Blithe Spirit." Powell worked with her in the early 1940s on a prospective staging of her play "Every Other Day," which came to naught.

Cornell, Katherine (1893–1974): distinguished American actress and a casual friend of Powell's.

Coué, Emile (1857–1926): French psychotherapist who emphasized self-help through auto-suggestion.

Coward, Noël (1899–1973): talented English songwriter, playwright, author, director, and actor.

Cowles, Russell (1887–1979): American painter.

Cowley, Malcolm (1898–1989): American critic and editor, later a memoirist. An acquaintance of Dawn Powell's for four decades, he was the principal editor on her last novel, *The Golden Spur*.

Crawford, Cheryl (1902–1986): American producer, director, and a co-founder of the Group Theatre; directed Powell's "Big Night" for the Group in 1933.

Cummings, Edward Estlin "e e cummings": (1894–1962): American poet and novelist who eschewed both punctuation and capitalization in his mature work. Although he was never one of Powell's close friends, the two knew one another for almost 40 years.

Davenport, Marcia (1903–   ): American novelist, biographer, and memoirist.

Davidson, Jo (1883–1952): celebrated sculptor who referred to himself as a "plastic historian" and cast busts of famous people from Helen Keller and Mahatma Gandhi to Woodrow Wilson and Franklin Delano Roosevelt.

Davis, George (1906–1957): American novelist and editor, worked with Powell at *Mademoiselle*, married to Lotte Lenya at the time of his death.

Davis, Hassoldt (1907–1959): American explorer and writer. A favorite drinking buddy of Powell's, his last book was entitled *Bonjour Hangover*.

Dehn, Adolph (1895–1968): American painter and lithographer whose work was imbued with gentle satire.

DeKooning, Willem (1904–   ): celebrated American artist, part of the abstract expressionist movement and a regular at the Cedar Tavern, which Powell also frequented.

Dell, Floyd (1887–1969): American novelist, playwright, and activist, best remembered for his autobiographical novel *The Moon-Calf* and his early, passionate advocacy of socialism and sexual freedom.

De Silver, Margaret (1890–1962): heiress, hostess, and supporter of liberal causes, perhaps Powell's closest woman friend, and the dedicatee of *The Golden Spur*. Widow of Albert De Silver, a founder of the American Civil Liberties Union; later lived with Carlo Tresca.

DeVries, Peter (1910–1993): American novelist and short story writer, sometimes compared to Cheever and Thurber; *The Mackerel Plaza* may be his best remembered work.

Dexter, John (1925–1990): British stage director, particularly renowned for creative productions of contemporary operas.

Divine, Father (1879–1965): originally George Baker, Jr., charismatic African-American religious cult leader who bilked millions from followers.

Dolbier, Maurice (1912–1993): novelist and book critic, long associated with the New York *Herald Tribune*.

Dos Passos, John (1896–1970): American novelist and essayist, whose politics over time shifted from radical left to staunch conservative; one of Powell's best friends from the 1920s until her death.

Douglas, Norman (1869–1952): British novelist and essayist, hailed for the philosophical comedy *South Wind* (1917).

Dreiser, Theodore (1894–1945): American novelist, poet, playwright, and would-be philosopher, he was not a close friend of Powell's, but they knew one another and socialized occasionally.

Drutman, Irving (1910–   ): American theater critic, editor, and memoirist.

Duke, Vernon (1903–1969): born Vladimir Dukelsky, Russian-American composer, songwriter, arranger, and idiosyncratic music critic.

Dundy, Elaine (1927–   ): American novelist and playwright, married to Kenneth Tynan for thirteen years.

DuPont, Irénée (1876–1963): one of three brothers who built a small Delaware manufacturing company into one of the most successful corporations in American history.

Duranty, Walter (1884–1957): British-American journalist, long the Moscow correspondent for the *New York Times,* now generally considered a shameless apologist for Stalin.

Eastman, Max (1883–1969): journalist, critic, novelist, and editor, closely identified with the first wave of Greenwich Village bohemia.

Emmerich, Franz (b. 1892): writer and editor of the short-lived magazine *The National American*; used the name "Frank Emerick" professionally.

Fadiman, Clifton (1904–   ): American lecturer and popular literary critic.

Faithfull, Starr (d. 1931): wealthy and attractive young Manhattan woman found drugged and drowned off Long Island in a much-publicized case.

Faragoh, Francis Edward (1895–1966): playwright and an early friend of Powell's, with whom she maintained contact through the early 1950s.

Farnham, Eleanor (1896–1995): a classmate of Powell's at Lake Erie College who later became a journalist—one of the first women to work on *The Plain Dealer*—and a successful publicity agent in Cleveland.

Farrar, John (1896–1974): editor and writer who, with Stanley Rinehart, founded Farrar and Rinehart in 1929, Powell's principal publisher for most of the 1930s. Later a co-founder of Farrar, Straus & Giroux.

Farrell, Dorothy: wife of author James T. Farrell (1904–1979).

Faulk, John Howard (1913–1990): American journalist and telecaster, blacklisted during McCarthy era, wrote a protest/autobiography titled *Fear On Trial.*

Fears, Peggy (1903–1994): Ziegfeld Follies showgirl, nightclub singer, and Broadway producer.

Feigay, Paul (1918–1983): producer of Broadway shows, television, ballet, and sports events.

Feld, Itzik (1897–1943): Polish-American Yiddish comedian and director.

Ferlinghetti, Lawrence (1919–   ): American poet, playwright, and, with Peter Martin, a founder of City Lights Books in San Francisco.

Fiene, Paul (1899–1949): German-born sculptor, long based in Woodstock, New York. Powell admired his work enormously.

Fiske, Dwight (1892–1959): successful nightclub entertainer, worked often with Powell, and dedicated his book of satirical skits, *Without Music,* to her. She, in turn, dedicated her 1939 novel, *Turn, Magic Wheel,* to Fiske.

Flagstad, Kirsten (1895–1962): Norwegian soprano, especially esteemed for her performances of the German repertory.

Fleming, Margaret (1803–1811): known as "Pet Marjorie," American child whose precocious diaries were published many years after her death.

Flood, Charles (1929–   ): prolific American novelist.

Flynn, Gertrude: American actress of stage and screen, appeared in the premiere of "Jig-Saw."

Foley, Martha (1897–1977): American writer, editor, and Columbia University professor, who founded *Story* magazine with her husband, Whit Burnett, and later edited innumerable anthologies of short stories.

Foulke, Adrienne (1915–1993): author and editor; for two decades copy chief at *The New Yorker*.

Frankenberg, Lloyd (1907–1975): American poet and translator, married to the artist Loren MacIver; a friend and Greenwich Village neighbor of Powell's.

Frankenthaler, Helen (1928–   ): American painter who fashioned her own style of abstract expressionism.

Freedman, Harold (1897–1966): associated with Brandt and Brandt, Powell's literary representatives for much of her life, handled dramatic rights for her plays.

Fuller, R. Buckminster (1895–1983): American architect, engineer, and social theorist, designed the "geodesic dome" and became an intellectual cult figure in the late 1960s and early 1970s.

Gangelin, Paul: film scenarist, active in Hollywood in the 1920s and 1930s.

Gannett, Lewis (1891–1966): American critic and editor, long the chief book reviewer for the New York *Herald Tribune*.

Geddes, Norman Bel (1893–1958): designer and producer of more than 200 theatrical events ranging from the Metropolitan Opera to Ringling Brothers Circus.

Geismar, Maxwell (1909–1979): populist American critic and essayist, best known for his book length attack, *Henry James and the Jacobites*.

Geldzahler, Henry (1935–1994): art curator, historian, and, for a time, Commissioner of Cultural Affairs for New York City.

Gibbs, Wolcott (1902–1958): *New Yorker* writer, best remembered for his parody of *Time* magazine.

Gieseking, Walter (1895–1956): German pianist known for his immaculate technique and elegant taste.

Gill, Brendan (1914–   ): novelist, journalist, and memoirist, long associated with *The New Yorker*.

Gilman, Coburn (1893–1967): Denver-born magazine editor who became a great love of Powell's and, in her last years, her closest companion.

Glasgow, Ellen (1874–1945): prolific and much admired (although not by Powell) American novelist of the South.

Glenn, Isa (b. 1888): American novelist and short story writer.

Goetel, Ferdinand (1890–1960): Polish author, missing during World War II and believed dead but reappeared; only a few of his works have been translated into English.

Gold, Michael (1894–1967): American novelist, playwright, and journalist, remembered for his novel *Jews Without Money* and his passionate Stalinism. Powell knew him in his early days with the Playwrights Theatre.

Gordon, Max (1903–1989): Lithuanian-American jazz promoter who founded, then operated, the Village Vanguard for fifty-four years. Opened the Blue Angel, a midtown club, in 1942.

Gorelik, Mordecai "Max" (1899–1990): visionary and influential stage designer, director, teacher, and author of *New Theaters For Old*.

Gorey, Edward (1925–   ): writer and illustrator known for his deft evocations of the macabre.

Gorky, Arshile (c. 1904–1948): distinguished Armenian-American artist and muralist whose work has continued to grow in both critical and popular esteem since his suicide.

Gorman, Jean: wife of journalist, critic, and first biographer of James Joyce, Herbert Gorman.

Gousha, Joseph (1890–1962): a Pittsburgh-born reporter and music critic who later became an advertising executive; Powell's husband from 1920 until his death. Brother of Harry Gousha.

Graham, Irvin: American composer and lyricist who worked with Powell on her "Taming of the Shrew" project.

Grand, Mary (1910–1977): a friend of independent means and fellow Greenwich Villager.

Gray, Albert Downing: childhood acquaintance of Powell's in Shelby, Ohio. Jack Sherman believes Gray was the son of a worker at the train station.

Green, Hannah (1926–   ): Ohio-born novelist, author of *The Dead of the House*; met Powell at Yaddo and was her devoted friend during the last years of her life.

Greenbaum, Edward S. (1890–1970): a leading lawyer and court reformer, a founder of the law firm Greenbaum, Wolff and Ernst. His wife, Dorothea ("Dotsie") (1893–1986) was a sculptor and graphic artist.

Gregory, Horace (1898–1982): American poet, editor, and biographer.

Gross, Ben (1892–1979): radio and television columnist for the New York *Daily News*.

Guinan, Texas (1884–1933): nightclub entertainer, hostess, and self-styled "Queen of the Speakeasies." Powell wrote several skits for Guinan with Dwight Fiske.

Guthrie, William Norman (1868–1944): Scottish-American clergyman, rector of St. Mark's-in-the-Bowery in the East Village for three decades.

Halliday, Richard (1905–1973): theatrical producer and professional manager of his wife, Mary Martin.

Hamilton, Cosmo (c. 1875–1942): English novelist, dramatist, and short story writer, best remembered for his many light romantic tales.

Hamilton, Patrick (1904–1962): English author of psychological thrillers, including the novel *Hangover Square* and the plays "Rope" and "Gaslight."

Harris, Jed (1900–1980): American theater producer who respected Powell and attempted on several occasions to involve her in one of his productions.

Harris, William Jr.: American theater director and producer.

Hartford, Huntington (1911–): American financier and arts patron.

Hatch, Eric (1901–1973): American novelist, short story writer, and scenarist, best known for "My Man Godfrey" which he later adapted into a classic film.

Hays, Arthur Garfield (1881–1954): American civil rights attorney and a founder of the American Civil Liberties Union.

Helburn, Teresa (1887–1959): playwright, director, and producer who was a leading force behind the Theatre Guild from its beginning; produced Powell's "Jig-Saw" in 1934.

Hellman, Lillian (1907–1984): American playwirght, later the author of the controversial memoirs *Scoundrel Time* and *Pentimento*.

Hemingway, Ernest (1899–1961): distinguished American author and a distant but admiring and affectionate friend to Powell. Hemingway would seem the model for Andrew Callingham in *Turn, Magic Wheel*.

Hemingway, John Hadley Nicanor "Bumby": (1923–): first son of Ernest Hemingway.

Hemingway, Pauline (1895–1951): second wife of Ernest Hemingway, and the sister of Virginia Pfeiffer.

Herbst, Josephine (1897–1969): American novelist whose trilogy (*Pity Is Not Enough, The Executioner Waits* and *Rope of Gold*) is considered by many the apogee of American "proletarian" fiction.

Herrmann, John (1900–1959): American novelist and husband of Josephine Herbst.

Herzog, Maurice (1919–): mountaineer, the first man to reach the summit of Himalayan peak Annapurna, the account of which is recorded in his book, *Annapurna*.

Hess, Myra (1890–1965): elegant and poetic English pianist, celebrated for her work in chamber music.

Hibben, Paxton (1880–1928): revisionist biographer of Henry Ward Beecher, William Jennings Bryan, and others; the lover of Powell's close friend Mary Lena Wilson.

Hill, Carol (see Brandt, Carol).

Hill, Pati (1921–): American fashion model, novelist, and, most recently, visual artist specializing in work created with photocopying machines.

Hiller, Lejaren (1880–1969): American photographer, father of the composer of the same name.

Hoke, Helen (1903–1990): pen name for Helen L. Hoke Watts, American educator, editor, journalist, novelist, and publisher.

Holden, Raymond (1894–1972): American poet and novelist; second husband of Louise Bogan.

Holman, Libby (1905–1971): American actress and torch singer, accused in 1931 of murdering her husband, tobacco heir Zachary Smith Reynolds; charges were later dropped.

Honeycutt, Ann (1902–1989): author and radio producer who worked with Powell on the "Music and Manners" series on WOR in the late 1930s; despite an uncomfortable working relationship, the two became good friends.

Hoult, Norah (1898–1984): Anglo-Irish novelist and short story writer.

Hughes, Russia Luca (1920–): American educator and for many years research assistant to Dr. Kenneth Clark. Mother of Neill Hughes (1954–), now an artist, and Morgan Hughes (1957–), a writer.

Hughes, William (1916–1995): American photographer and cinematographer. Husband of Russia Hughes; father of Morgan and Neill.

Hultberg, John Phillip (1922–): American artist, knew Powell through gatherings at the Cedar Tavern.

Ingle, Charles (b. 1926): American author, *The Waters of the End* was apparently his only novel.

Irwin, Inez Haynes (1873–1970): American author, suffragist, and feminist historian; first woman president of the Authors' League of America.

Jack, Peter Monro (1895–1943): Scotland-born literary critic whose classes at the New School were the model for Frederick Olliver's courses at the "League for Cultural Foundation" in *The Locusts Have No King*.

Jameson, Storm (1891–1986): English novelist, some of whose works were reprinted and reappraised in the 1980s.

Janeway, Elizabeth (1913–): American novelist and short story writer.

Jesse, F. "Friniwyd" Tennyson (c.1885–1958): British author of numerous novels, plays, and poems and a grand-niece of Alfred, Lord Tennyson.

Johnson, Hall (1888–1970): American composer, violinist, arranger, and choral conductor whose elegant transcriptions of spirituals are still sung.

Jolas, Eugene (1894–1952): American journalist and editor who founded the literary magazine *transition* and published much of James Joyce's "Work In Progress" (later *Finnegans Wake*). Husband of Maria Jolas, father of composer Betsy Jolas. The Jolas brothers were among Powell's closest friends.

Jolas, Jacques (1895–1957): brother of Eugene Jolas and a pianist of international reputation.

Jones, James (1921–1977): American author of lengthy war novels, best remembered for *From Here to Eternity*.

Josephson, Matthew (1899–1978): American critic and biographer. A long-time acquaintance of Powell's, he published the first posthumous re-evaluation of her work in 1973 (*Southern Review*).

Joyce, Peggy Hopkins (1893–1957): American actress, dancer, and showgirl.

Kaufman, George S. (1889–1981): American drama critic who went on to become one of the most successful playwrights of his time.

Kazan, Elia (1909–   ): Turkish-American director of stage and screen.

Keene, Frances (1913–   ): American author, translator, editor, and educator, a close friend to Powell in the 1950s and 1960s.

Keller, Greta (c. 1903–1977): Vienna-born actress and cabaret singer; active from the 1920s through the 1970s, she made hundreds of recordings.

Kiesler, Frederick (1890–1965): Austrian-American sculptor, architect, and stage designer, a neighbor of Powell's in Greenwich Village.

Kline, Franz (1910–1962): American painter, a leader in the abstract expressionist school, and a favorite drinking partner of Powell's at the Cedar Tavern.

Kober, Arthur (1900–1975): American playwright, scenarist, and humorist, associated with *The New Yorker*.

Koestler, Arthur (1905–1983): Hungarian-born writer, journalist, and scholar of enormously varied interests, best known for his political novel, *Darkness At Noon*.

Kopit, Arthur (1937–   ): American playwright, best known for "Oh Dad, Poor Dad, Mama's Hung You In The Closet and I'm Feelin' So Sad" and "Indians."

Kreisler, Fritz (1875–1962): Austrian-American composer and violinist of matchless charm.

Kronenberger, Louis (1904–1980): American author, critic, and anthologist, long associated with *Time* magazine.

Langner, Lawrence (1890–1962): playwright and a founder and director of the Theatre Guild, which produced Powell's "Jig-Saw" in 1934.

Lardner, John (1912–1960): sportswriter son of author Ring Lardner; his essays are collected in the volume *The World of John Lardner*.

Latouche, John (1917–1956): charismatic American poet and lyricist who wrote words for the Earl Robinson cantata "Ballad for Americans" and the libretto for Douglas Moore's opera "Ballad of Baby Doe." Latouche was one of Powell's favorite people.

Lawson, John Howard (1895–1977): radical American playwright, scenarist, and essayist, jailed in 1950 for Communist activities. Powell was deeply involved with Lawson during the late 1920s and early 1930s; she may well have been in love with him. Married to Sue Lawson.

Lazard, Lucner (1926–   ): Haitian painter, became a friend of Powell's during her vacation in Haiti.

LeBrun, Portia: a long-time friend of Powell's, the first wife of artist Rico LeBrun and later romantically involved with Alexander Brook.

LeClercq, Jacques (1898–1972): poet, writer (sometimes under the pen name of Paul Tanaquil), translator, and the father of Tanaquil LeClercq. He was one of Powell's closest friends for most of her life.

LeClercq, Tanaquil (1929–): New York City Ballet ballerina, daughter of Jacques LeClercq and fourth wife of George Balanchine, crippled at the height of her career.

Lee, Auriol (1880–1941): English theater actress and director, a close friend to Libby Holman, made a specialty of the plays of John van Druten. The narcolepsy described by Powell eventually led to her death in an automobile accident when she passed out at the wheel.

Lee, Louise (c.1890–1960): Powell's housekeeper for more than three decades; mother or guardian to Bobby Morrison, Joseph Gousha Jr.'s favorite playmate.

LeGallienne, Eva (1899–1991): London-born stage actress, director, and producer; later a memoirist and the biographer of Eleonora Duse.

Lehmann, Rosamond (1903–1990): distinguished English novelist who claimed to write her books in a "half-trance"; rediscovered and republished in the 1980s.

Lengel, William C. (1888–1965): American author and editor, associated with *The Smart Set* and later with Fawcett Publications, which brought out Powell's substantially revised *Angels On Toast* in 1956 under the title *A Man's Affair*.

Leonard, William Ellery (1876–1944): distinguished poet, essayist, teacher at the Univeristy of Wisconsin, and author of one of the strangest and most curiously affecting autobiographies in the literature, *The Locomotive God* (1927).

Lerman, Leo (1914–1994): American writer, editor, and raconteur, associated with Conde Nast for many years.

Levant, Oscar (1906–1972): American pianist, composer, radio and television host, and memoirist.

Lewis, Robert "Bobby" (1909–): actor, director, producer, and all-around theatrical guru who developed and nurtured numerous stars of stage and screen.

Liberman, Alexander (1912–): American artist and editor, associated with Conde Nast for more than fifty years.

Lissfelt, Harry (1889–1945): New York manager for the Corning Glass Works; a friend of Joseph Gousha's from their Pittsburgh childhood and one of the few people who were close to both partners in Powell's marriage.

Liveright, Horace (1886–1933): American publisher and producer, co-founder of Boni and Liveright; brought out early books by Hemingway, Eliot, Faulkner, Djuna Barnes, and Nathanael West.

Loeb, Harold (1891–1974): American novelist, editor, and memoirist; lampooned by Ernest Hemingway as Robert Cohn in *The Sun Also Rises*.

Loeb, Philip (1894–1955): American actor best known for his role in the early television show "The Goldbergs." Committed suicide after being blacklisted in the McCarthy era.

Loewe, Frederick (1901–1988): American composer of popular musicals, including "My Fair Lady."

Loos, Anita (1893–1981): American novelist, playwright, scenarist, and biographer, best remembered as the author of *Gentlemen Prefer Blondes*.

Lowry, Malcolm (1909–1957): English-born novelist best remembered for *Under The Volcano* (1947). An awed Powell reviewed *Volcano* and befriended its author; the two corresponded for a time.

Lowry, Marjorie Bonner (1905–1988): mystery novelist and wife of Malcolm Lowry.

Luce, Claire (1903–1989): American stage actress, made occasional ventures into film.

Luce, Clare Boothe Brokaw (1903–1987): American playwright, journalist, and congresswoman, wife of *Time* magazine founder Henry R. Luce; Powell made merciless sport of her in *A Time To Be Born*.

Lumet, Sidney (1924–   ): American director of stage, screen, and television who began his career as a child actor.

Lyons, Leonard (1906–1976): American journalist whose theater column, "The Lyons Den," was syndicated throughout the country.

MacIver, Loren (1909–   ): distinguished and original American artist, wife of Lloyd Frankenberg and a long-time friend of Powell's.

MacLeish, Archibald (1892–1982): American poet and writer, served as Librarian of Congress under Roosevelt.

Mailer, Norman (1923–   ): American novelist and journalist; Powell's opinion of his work fluctuated from moment to moment, book to book.

Maltz, Albert (1908–1985): radical American novelist and screenwriter, blacklisted in the 1950s, self-exiled to Mexico and forced to write scripts under pseudonyms.

Manone, Wingy (1900–1982): New Orleans-born trumpeter, singer, and bandleader who remained active through the 1970s.

Marlowe, Sylvia (1908–1981): harpsichordist, teacher, and bon vivant, married to the Russian painter Leonid Berman.

Marsh, Reginald (1898–1954): painter and illustrator celebrated for his views of life in Greenwich Village; painted the illustration for the dust jacket of Powell's *The Wicked Pavilion*. Married to Felicia Marsh.

Martin, Peter (1923–1988): American writer, editor, and bookshop owner; co-founder of *City Lights* magazine in San Francisco, later opened the City Lights Bookstore and the New Yorker Bookshop in Manhattan.

Marvin, Rumsey Walter (b. 1900): American businessman, one of John Dos Passos' best friends.

Matthiesen, F. O. (1902–1950): American literary historian and Harvard professor, remembered for his book *American Renaissance* and important studies of such divergent figures as Theodore Dreiser and T. S. Eliot.

Maxwell, Elsa (1883–1963): famous hostess, columnist, and memoirist who prided herself on never having had a home after 1907 except suites in luxury hotels.

May, Elaine (1932–   ): comedian and director, and part of the comedy team of Nichols and May.

Mayer, Edwin Justus (1896–1960): New York-born newspaperman who, despite only a grade school education, became a leading playwright and screenwriter. Frances Mayer was his first wife.

McBride, Mary Margaret (1899–1976): American broadcaster with large following, known for her homey style—an unexpected but genuine friend to Powell.

McCarthy, Mary (1912–1989): American novelist, essayist, and memoirist whose work Powell followed with unusual interest and decidedly mixed emotions; third wife of Edmund Wilson.

Metcalfe, John (1891–1965): English novelist, husband of Evelyn Scott, known for his stories of the macabre.

Miller, Charles: a distant cousin of Powell's on her mother's side and a successful businessman in Johnstown, Pennsylvania; he served as the model for Chris Bennett in *Story Of A Country Boy.*

Miller, Kathryn Bache (1896–1979): American philanthropist and socialite, wife of the theatrical producer Gilbert Miller.

Mizener, Arthur (1907–1988): author of *The Far Side of Paradise,* the first biography of F. Scott Fitzgerald, and other works.

Moneta, Cesare Antonio (1878–1948): chef and proprietor of Moneta's Restaurant on Mulberry Street, perhaps the most celebrated restaurant in Manhattan's "Little Italy" throughout the 1920s and 1930s and a Powell hangout.

Montana, Pietro (c. 1890–1978): painter and sculptor best known for his work on religious themes; later sculptor-in-residence at Fordham University.

Moross, Jerome (1913–1983): American composer of theater, film, and symphonic music; collaborated with Powell's friend John Latouche.

Morrison, Bobby: raised as the son of Powell's maid Louise and a favorite playmate of Jojo's.

Mosher, John (1892–1942): essayist, short story writer, and the first film critic for *The New Yorker.*

Motherwell, Robert (1915–1991): American painter, printmaker, and art professor, saw Powell fairly often in the early 1960s.

Mumford, Lewis (1895–1990): American cultural and architectural critic, author of *The City in History.*

Murphy, Esther (1898–1962): sister of Gerald Murphy, regarded as an expert on Madame de Maintenon and Edith Wharton but never published.

Murphy, Gerald (1888–1964) and Sara (1883–1975): wealthy couple who presided over a social circle that ranged from Southern France to the Hamptons and included F. Scott Fitzgerald (who dedicated *Tender is the Night* to them), Ernest Hemingway, John Dos Passos, and Dorothy Parker. Gerald Murphy was also an artist of distinction.

Nash, Ogden (1902–1971): American writer of humorous verse; also an occasional playwright.

Nathan, Robert (1894–1985): poet, scenarist, and highly successful American novelist.

Nazimova, Alla (1879–1945): Ukrainian-American actress of stage and screen; particularly renowned for her performances of Ibsen and Chekhov.

Newman, Robert: Broadway producer, conferred with Powell on staging "Big Night" before she signed with the Group Theatre.

Nichols, Mike (1931–   ): American director of stage and screen, first won acclaim as part of the comedy team Nichols and May, with Elaine May.

Niles, Blair (c.1887–1959): American novelist and travel writer.

Norman, Charles (1904–   ): American poet, biographer, and memoirist. A friend of Powell's from her first days in Greenwich Village, he provided a tender and acute reminiscence in his autobiography, *Poets and People*. Husband of Diana Norman (d. 1994), an artist who sketched Powell in the early 1960s.

Noyes, John Humphrey (1811–1886): idealist and founder of the Oneida Community in upstate New York, an early experiment in communal living.

Odets, Clifford (1906–1963): American playwright and the unquestioned "star" author of the Group Theatre.

O'Neil, George (1897–1940): poet, playwright, novelist, scenarist, and biographer of John Keats.

Ornitz, Samuel (1890–1957): American writer associated with the "proletarian" school of literature.

Parker, Dorothy (1893–1967): poet, short story writer, critic, and much publicized wit associated with the Algonquin Round Table. Powell didn't think much of Parker's work but enjoyed her company on occasion.

Parrott, Ursula (1902–1957): prolific American popular novelist.

Payne, Robert (1911–1983): English novelist and biographer who lived in the United States for a time and served as the director of PEN.

Pemberton, Brock (1885–1950): drama critic who became a leading Broadway producer from 1920 until his death.

Perelman, S. J. (1904–1979): American humorist, wrote sketches, stories, plays, and films.

Perkins, Maxwell E. (1884–1947): legendary American book editor who nurtured Ernest Hemingway, F. Scott Fitzgerald, and, especially, Thomas Wolfe. He was Powell's editor at Scribners; she dedicated *Angels On Toast* to him and named her cat after him.

Perry, Antoinette (1888–1946): American theatrical personality, actress, director, and chair of the American Theater Wing during World War II. Broadway's "Tony" awards are named for her.

Peters, Paul: radical playwright, co-author of "Stevedore," among other works.

Pfeiffer, Virginia (1902–1973): sister-in-law of Ernest Hemingway, long-time companion to Laura Archera Huxley.

Philipson, Morris (1926–   ): American novelist and editor; in later life Editor-in-Chief of The University of Chicago Press.

Pitts, Zasu (1898–1963): American actress, best remembered for her extraordinary performance in Erich von Stroheim's "Greed." She appeared in Stroheim's ill-fated film rendition of Powell's "Walking Down Broadway."

Pocock, Mabel Powell (1895–1949): Powell's older sister, later the wife of Edgar Pocock, a successful Cleveland businessman, and the mother of Dorothy Chapman, Keith Pocock, and Dawn Powell Jarvis. Mabel was the model for the character "Lena" in *My Home Is Far Away.*

Powell, Hattie Sherman (1872–1903): mother of Dawn Powell and sister of Orpha May Sherman Steinbrueck. She died at an early age, apparently from tuberculosis.

Powell, Mabel (see Pocock, Mabel Powell).

Powell, Phyllis (see Cook, Phyllis Powell).

Powell, Roy King (1868–1926): Powell's father, a traveling salesman for various companies.

Powell, Sabra Stern (c. 1875–1956): Powell's stepmother, married Roy Powell in 1907 and survived him by thirty years; mother of Dawn Powell's half-sister, Virginia McLaughlin. Powell hated her stepmother and savaged her as "Idah Hawkins" in *My Home Is Far Away.*

Prescott, Orville (1906–   ): American writer; daily book critic with the *New York Times* for many years.

Prokosch, Frederic (1908–   ): American novelist, poet, and translator.

Putnam, Phelps (1894–1948): poet and friend of Edmund Wilson, who contributed a forward to *The Collected Poems of Phelps Putnam*, published after Putnam's death.

Quintinilla, Luis (b. 1905): a Spanish artist who ran into political trouble during the Civil War and was brought to the United States with the help of Hemingway and Dos Passos. Powell owned at least one of his art works but it was lost after the 1958 eviction.

Raphaelson, Samson (1896–1983): successful American educator, playwright, screenwriter, and author.

Resnikoff, Mischa (1905–1971): Russian-American artist, loosely associated with the abstract expressionists.

Rice, Jacqueline Miller (c. 1930–   ): one of Powell's closest friends in the last decade of her life. Introduced to Powell by Peter Martin, she married the painter Daniel Rice, named her daughter Hilary Dawn, was present at Powell's deathbed, and served as her executor for almost 30 years.

Rinehart, Stanley (1897–1969): American publisher who founded the firm of Farrar and Rinehart in 1929; published all of Powell's books between *Dance Night* and *The Happy Island.*

Robertson, Bryan (1925–   ): English art historian and curator and a good friend to Powell in her last years.

Ruggles, Carl (1876–1971): American modernist composer and painter, completed less than two hours of finished music during his long life, yet the quality of that two hours has ensured Ruggles' continuing importance.

Saroyan, William (1908–1981): Armenian-American playwright, novelist, and short story writer.

Savo, Jimmy (1896–1960): entertainer and mime, popular vaudeville and nightclub star whose enthusiasts compared him to Chaplin. Powell was enormously fond of him.

Saxe, Albert: radical playwright and passionate advocate of "agit-prop"; a founder and early director of the Workers' Laboratory Theatre.

Scheff, Fritzi (1882–1953): operetta and musical comedy star, made occasional forays into opera; known for her eternal renditions of "Kiss Me Again."

Scott, Evelyn (1893–1963): American poet, novelist, and memoirist, whose books *The Narrow Room, Escapade, The Wave,* and *A Calendar of Sin* have recently attracted both passionate admirers and equally fervent detractors.

Segal, Lore Groszman (1926–   ): European-American author, essayist, and translator.

Seldes, Gilbert (1893–1970): American critic, playwright, translator, and novelist.

Seton, Anya (1904–1990): bestselling American novelist, daughter of naturalist and author Ernest Thompson Seton.

Shaw, Irwin (1913–1984): American author of stories, plays, and highly popular novels.

Sheean, Vincent (1899–1975): American novelist, essayist, and music critic.

Sherman, John F. "Jack": (1911–   ): Shelby, Ohio business executive and educator; Powell's favorite cousin, the dedicatee of *My Home Is Far Away,* and the guardian of Joseph Gousha, Jr. after Powell's death.

Siegel, William (1893–1966): Yiddish-American playwright and the author of more than 150 plays, most of which received their premieres on the Lower East Side of Manhattan.

Simonson, Lee (1888–1967): American scenic designer and a founding member of the Theatre Guild.

Sklar, George (1908–1988): American novelist and playwright, associated with the radical theater in his early days; later a novelist of manners.

Slesinger, Tess (1905–1945): American writer and scenarist whose sole novel, *The Unpossessed,* is considered perhaps the funniest send-up of parlor Leftism written between *The Apes of God* and *Radical Chic;* wrote a sharply negative review of *The Bride's House.*

Slocombe, George (1894–1963): English journalist and writer.

Smith, Harrison (1888–1971): American critic and editor who helped found three publishing houses and later served as the president of the *Saturday Review.*

Smith, Oliver (1918–1991): celebrated American stage designer and director who worked on numerous Broadway productions.

Smith, Stuff (1909–1967): innovative American bandleader and violinist, cited as an influence by Dizzy Gillespie, among others.

Smith, Thomas Robert "T. R." (1880–1942): American author, editor, and a champion of works by women writers.

Smith, Y. K.: writer, editor, horticulturalist, and older brother of Katy Smith Dos Passos. Married to Vieve Smith (d. 1971).

Sobel, Bernard (1887–1964): press agent and raconteur who wrote several nostalgic books about vaudeville, burlesque, and his days working for Florenz Ziegfeld and Earl Carroll.

Solley, Dr. Robert (d. 1986): Powell's principal physician in the final decades of her life.

Solow, Herbert (1903–1964): American journalist and editor, investigated the Stalinist charges against Leon Trotsky as part of John Dewey's team; husband of Sylvia Salmi, a photographer for whom Powell sat.

Soupault, Philippe (1897–1990): French surrealist poet, novelist, and journalist who became acquainted with Powell through his association with Matthew Josephson.

Speare, Dorothy (c. 1898–1951): novelist, playwright, scenarist, and professor of creative writing at Boston University.

Spencer, Claire (1899–   ): Scottish-American novelist and the wife of editor Harrison Smith.

Spencer, Niles (1893–1952): American artist associated with the "precisionist" school and one of Powell's best friends. Married to Betty Spencer.

Stead, Christina (1902–1983): Australian-American novelist whose *The Man Who Loved Children* is considered by many a neglected masterpiece.

Stearns, Harold (1891–1943): American critic and editor with a strong sociological bent.

Stearns, Monroe M. (1913–1987): teacher, writer, and editor. A close friend to Powell during her last years, he was at her bedside when she died.

Steinbrueck, Orpha May Sherman (1869–1959): a Shelby, Ohio businesswoman, sister of Powell's mother Hattie Sherman Powell, raised Powell and her sisters from adolescence.

Stewart, Donald Ogden (1894–1980): novelist, playwright, humorist, and screenwriter; later blacklisted for Communist activities.

Stout, Rex (1886–1975): American novelist, created the enormously successful Nero Wolfe detective stories.

Studin, Charles (1876–1950): lawyer, crusader for liberal causes, and early board member of the NAACP; famous for his salon-style parties in Greenwich Village.

Sullivan, Frank (1892–1976): American humorist and regular early contributor to *The New Yorker*. A friend of Powell's from her early days in the Village, he became reacquainted with her during her stays at Yaddo, near his home in Saratoga Springs.

Summers, Andrew Rowan (1912–1968): American musician and folk song collector, made many recordings for Folkways.

Susskind, David (1920–1987): American television, film, and theater producer whose program "Open End" was considered a highlight in the early days of public television.

Swanson, Harold Norling (1899–   ): the editor of *College Humor,* a popular quarterly in the 1920s and 1930s, where Powell frequently published.

Swinnerton, Frank (1884–1982): English novelist and critic.

Taggard, Genevieve (1894–1948): American poet, editor, and biographer. She was one of Powell's closest friends in the 1920s and early 1930s, after which time the two fell out.

Tate, Allen (1899–1979): American poet, critic, and novelist, associated with the "Southern Agrarian" literary movement.

Taylor, Elizabeth (1912–1975): English novelist, not to be confused with the American movie actress.

Thurber, James (1894–1961): American writer and artist whose contributions in both media to *The New Yorker* made him one of the most popular humorists of his time.

Tobey, Berkeley: associated with John Reed and the original *Masses,* the leading radical organ of its time.

Tomkins, Calvin (1925–   ): American author and art critic, associated with *The New Yorker* for many years.

Tresca, Carlo (c. 1875–1943): Italian-American revolutionary writer and a leader in the domestic anti-Fascist movement, lived with Powell's best woman friend, Margaret De Silver; murdered outside the office of his newspaper, *Il Martello.*

Trilling, Diana (1905–   ): American journalist, essayist, and literary critic, the wife of Lionel Trilling. Reviewed *A Time To Be Born* and *The Locusts Have No King* for *The Nation.*

Truex, Ernest (1890–1973): American stage, screen, and television actor, appeared in Powell's "Jig-Saw."

Tully, Jim (1888–1947): American "hobo-novelist," known for his hard-boiled and rather primitive narratives.

Tureck, Rosalyn (1914–   ): American pianist and harpsichordist, respected for her interpretations of J. S. Bach.

Turnbull, Andrew (1921–1970): American biographer of Thomas Wolfe and F. Scott Fitzgerald.

Tynan, Kenneth (1927–1980): English writer, playwright, and drama critic, affiliated with *The New Yorker* for several years.

Undset, Sigrid (1882–1949): Norweigian novelist, essayist, and biographer. Undset won the Nobel Prize for her medieval trilogy *Kristian Lavransdatter* but Powell especially admired her early, realistic novel *Jenny,* set in modern Rome and Oslo.

Van Doren, Carl (1885–1950): American critic and biographer, awarded the Pulitzer Prize for his 1938 life of Benjamin Franklin.

Vanderbilt, Gloria (1924–   ): American heiress, actress, and businesswoman; married to agent Pat Di Cicco when Powell first knew her.

Vidal, Gore (1925–   ): American author and essayist admired greatly by Powell; his 1987 essay on her novels, published in the *New York Review of Books*, was crucially important in the current revival of interest in her work.

Waddell, Helen (1889–1965): Irish translator and medievalist, known for her sensitive English renderings of Latin literature.

Walker, Stuart (1880–1941): American actor, director, producer, scenarist, and playwright, founded the Portmanteau Theater in 1915; visited Lake Erie College during Powell's student years.

Wallsten, Robert (1912–   ): American theater actor and writer.

Wanger, Walter (1894–1968): theater and film producer, married to actress Joan Bennett.

Wanning, Thomas: a wealthy young friend of Powell's in the 1950s and 1960s; nephew of Esther Andrews.

Watkins, Ann (1885–1967): Powell's literary agent during the late 1920s and early 1930s; her practice survives to this day as the Watkins-Loomis Agency.

Waugh, Alec (1898–1981): English novelist and brother of Evelyn Waugh; a casual friend of Powell's for many years.

Waugh, Auberon (1939–   ): novelist, columnist, and social critic; son of Evelyn Waugh.

Wells, Thomas Bucklin (1875–1944): American editor and publisher, associated with Harper and Brothers publishers and *Harper's* magazine; known familiarly as "Harper" Wells.

Wescott, Glenway (1901–1982): American novelist—like Powell, a small-town midwesterner gone cosmopolitan—remembered for *The Grandmothers, Goodbye, Wisconsin,* and the bestseller *Apartment in Athens.*

Wettling, George (1907–1968): American jazz drummer who worked with Artie Shaw, Paul Whiteman, Bunnie Berrigan, Billie Holliday, and Eddie Condon, among others.

Wheelock, John Hall (1886–1978): American poet and editor, associated with Scribners for almost half a century, where he eventually rose to editor-in-chief.

Widdemer, Margaret (c. 1885–1978): successful American poet, novelist, and short story writer, with many bestsellers to her name.

Wilson, Edmund (1895–1972): American critic, historian, and man-of-letters, probably the first important critic to take Powell's work seriously. The two enjoyed a long friendship, through occasional quarrels and misunderstandings.

Wilson, Rosalind Baker (1923–   ): oldest daughter of Edmund Wilson and an editor at Houghton Mifflin in Boston. Powell thought her a brilliant writer and liked her enormously, despite unhappiness over some of her dealings with Houghton Mifflin.

Wilson, Mary Lena: one of Powell's first friends in New York, romantically involved with the biographer Paxton Hibben. She disappears from Powell's life in the early 1930s.

Winchell, Walter (1897–1972): American gossip columnist and broadcaster, all but ubiquitous in American life from the 1920s through the 1950s.

Winslow, Thyra Samter (1893–1961): novelist and short story writer whose works, like Powell's, combined the Midwest with Manhattan.

Wiseman, Adele (1928–1993): Canadian novelist and writer, became acquainted with Powell during her 1960 stay at Yaddo.

Witherspoon, Cora (1890–1957): American actress, appeared in Powell's "Jig-Saw."

Wolf, Robert: American poet, novelist, and first husband of Genevieve Taggard.

Wolfe, Cornelia (1896–1983): Lake Erie College friend of Powell's, later a neighbor in Greenwich Village and later still associated with the Walt Disney Studios in California; Powell and Wolfe both published verse in the *Independent Poetry Anthology 1925*, edited by E. Ralph Cheyney.

Wolfe, Thomas (1900–1938): American writer who wrote massive and poetic autobiographical novels.

Wolfson, Victor (1910–1990): American playwright, novelist, stage director, producer, and educator.

Woodburn, John (1901–1952): American book critic and editor.

Wortman, Denys (1887–1958): American artist and cartoonist, known for his funny, poignant drawings for the New York *World* and later for the New York *World-Telegram and Sun*.

Young, Stark (1881–1963): American novelist and drama critic.

ACKNOWLEDGMENTS

Hundreds of people have contributed to this book—with facts, comments, suggestions, clarifications—and I apologize to those whose names have been inadvertently left out.

First and foremost, let me express my gratitude to John (Jack) F. Sherman, Dawn Powell's favorite cousin and the guardian of her son, Joseph Gousha, Jr. (Jojo), after her death. Jack has served as my guide throughout the assembly of this book. He is a great and good man; without him, the Powell estate would likely have remained in its long and curious legal limbo and these diaries might never have come to light.

My mother, Elizabeth Thaxton Page, indulged her son with a deeply appreciated loan that allowed the Powell papers to be brought to the Rare Book and Manuscript Library of Columbia University, some hundred yards from the hospital where Jojo was born and where Dawn Powell died.

Powell's family—especially Rita Sherman (my Ohio hostess during some of the most pleasant stays of my life), Carol and Dwaine Warstler, Dorothy and John Chapman, and Phyllis and Nicholas Poccia—has been unfailingly supportive and profoundly generous. Joseph Gousha, Jr. retains an extraordinary memory for people, places and dates; in 1993, at the suggestion of his devoted social worker, Michelle Borsack, he assembled a notebook called "Memories of my Mother" and it has proven invaluable to me on several occasions.

I am grateful to Peter Skolnik, legal representative of the Powell Estate, for his support and help on matters too numerous to mention. My friends Bruce Brubaker and Hilary Dyson were resourceful hunting names and dates in half a dozen New York libraries.

Honoria Donnelly, the daughter of Gerald and Sara Murphy, has been very kind to me, making copies of all of Powell's hundred-odd letters to her parents and researching family dates in an East Hampton cemetery. David Kanzeg of WCPN-FM in Cleveland has taken me through most of Ohio in search of Powelliana and we have had many valuable and intensive discussions of Powell's work.

I am also grateful to Antoinette Akers, Leonard Altman, David C. Barnett, Avis Berman, Carl Brandt, Alexander Brook, Jr., Margaret Carson, William Cole, John Gregory Connor, Hope Hale Davis, Anna Lou Kapell Dehavenon, the late Maurice Dolbier, Susan Elliott, Olive Ernst, Allan Evans, the late Eleanor Farnham, Johanna Fiedler, Michael Flynn, Sylviane Gold, Hannah Green, Margaret Geissman Gross, Halley Harrisburg, Carol and Patrick Hemingway, Jeffrey Herman, Neill Hughes,

Russia Hughes, Frances Keene, Dr. Ben Kightlinger, Allan Kozinn, Hildie Kraus, Bobby Lewis, Gloria Loomis, Loren MacIver, Sally Maier, David McDonald, Heather McGahee, Michael Miller, Donald Mineldi, Charles Norman and the late Diana Norman, Ellis B. Page, Dr. Richard Page, Morris Philipson, Robert Pound, Eva Resnikova, Daniel Rhodebeck, Dr. Morton Schwimmer, Michael Sexton, Gene Seymour, M. George Stevenson, Amei Wallach, Robert Wallsten, Andrews Wanning, Esther Wanning, Maggy Wendel, Rosalind Baker Wilson, Anne Yarowsky, and Michael Zubal.

Many thanks to the staff of the Columbia University Rare Book and Manuscript Library, particularly Jean Ashton and Bernard Crystal. Thanks to the research librarians at the lamented New York *Newsday,* especially Karen Van Rossem; to Barbara Emch, Amanda Byers, Carole Houk, and Christopher Bennett at Lake Erie College; to Morgan Cundiff and Charles Roberts at the Library of Congress; and to Jeanne Somers at the Kent State University Archives.

In Melanie Jackson I have found a literary agent who combines talent, tact, faith, and the highest standards. I am equally thankful for my ongoing association with Steerforth Press—particularly Michael Moore, my editor, but also Stacia Schaefer, Daniel Dellinger, and Angela Thor.

All love and gratitude to my wife Vanessa Weeks Page—who read every word of this manuscript not once but several times and caught many editorial infelicities—and to my sons William Dean, Robert Leonard, and John Sherman Page.

Finally, I should like to acknowledge my friend Kevin Cawley, with appreciation for an unbroken dialogue (on Powell and myriad other subjects, great and small) that has now lasted 30 years and has enriched me enormously in the process. Everyone should have such a pal.

INDEX

Miller, Philip, 107–8
Miller, Rosie, 107–8, 143, 276
Miles, Marie, 405
Mizener, Arthur, 287
Montana, Pietro, 84
Month of Sundays, A (Kronenberger), 422(n)
Moorwood, William, 363
Morency, Maurice, 270
Moross, Jerome, 252, 306
Morrison, Bobby, 15, 146, 308, 339, 351, 432, 448, 468, 469, 475
Morrow (publisher), 11
Mosher, John, 7, 8, 9, 11, 12, 108, 119
Motherwell, Robert, 460–61
Mumford, Lewis, 471
Murphy, Esther, 249, 447
Murphy, Gerald, xi, 142, 181, 200, 208, 210, 233, 240, 242, 249, 262, 263, 265, 270, 286, 287–88, 289, 311, 346, 361, 374, 415, 426, 436, 455, 465
Murphy, Sara, xi, 142, 181, 200, 210, 233, 240, 242, 262, 263, 270, 286, 287–88, 311, 361, 394, 415, 426, 427, 455, 471
Music and Manners (radio show), 165n
My Fair Lady (Loewe), 405, 476
My Home is Far Away (novel), 6, 104, 158n, 190n, 200, 211, 213, 214, 216, 218, 219–20, 222, 223(n), 226–28, 230–37(n), 239, 271, 273, 302, 327, 385, 465

Nash, Ogden, 71
Nation, The (magazine), 385, 388, 393
Nazimova, Alla, 67
New American Mercury (magazine), 307
Newman, Robert, 48
Nichols, Mike, 424
Nightwood (Barnes), 142
Niles, Blair, 31
1919 (Dos Passos), 45
Nirvana (Lawson), 8
Norman, Charles, 5, 390
Now He Tells Me (s. story), 308
Now is the Time (s. story), 326
Noyes, John Humphrey, 113
Number One (Dos Passos), 239
Nurse Book. See *Turn, Magic Wheel*

Oasis (McCarthy), 281
Odets, Clifford, 110, 111
Old Folks at Home (s. story), 326
Olive Twig, The (s. story), 308
O'Neil, George, 76, 329, 394
Ornitz, Samuel (Sam), 23
O Strange New War. See *Locusts Have No King, The*

Paramount (studio), 16, 86, 90, 93, 126, 140
Parker, Dorothy, 178, 200, 208, 209–10, 243, 398, 409
Parrott, Ursula, 20
Partisan Review (magazine), 393
Party, The (play). See also *Big Night.* 13, 14, 15, 30, 32, 34, 37, 42, 48
Pathetic Fallacy (s. story), 326, 393
Payne, Robert, 413, 464
Pemberton, Brock, 37, 70
Perelman, S. J., 212–13
Perkins, Maxwell E., 177, 223, 229, 233, 236, 238, 241, 259, 261, 264, 265, 378, 393, 405, 428
Perry, Antoinette, 37, 189
Peters, Paul, 235, 284
Pfeiffer, Virginia, xi, 127–28, 142, 149, 155, 157–58, 370(n), 375
Philipson, Morris, 464, 470, 471
Phillips, Sydney, 76
Piccinini, Carminda, 423
Pin to See the Peep Show, A (Jesse), 132
Pinwheel (Faragoh), 11
Pitts, Zasu, 235, 241
Playboy (magazine), 471
PM (magazine), 393
Pocock, Mabel (nee Powell), 7, 9, 41, 42, 103, 113, 205–6, 242, 246n, 282, 285, 286, 301, 306, 314, 331, 340, 350, 436
Poore, Charles, 445(n)
Powell, Hattie (nee Sherman), 313
Powell, Roy King, ix, 6, 7, 9, 30, 105, 127, 185–87, 221, 282, 304n, 313–14
Powell, Sabra Stern, 1, 185–87, 221, 304n
Prescott, Orville, 271, 316, 385, 411
Private Lives (Coward), 21, 62
Prokosch, Frederic, 133(n), 334

A NOTE ON THE BOOK

The text for this book was composed by Steerforth Press using a digital version of Granjon, a typeface designed by George W. Jones and first issued by Linotype in 1928. The book was printed on acid free papers and bound by Quebecor Printing~Book Press Inc. of North Brattleboro, Vermont.